Before I Forget

Before I Forget

Moments and experiences with Bill Graham who was an incredible entrepreneur and innovator of the music industry

Compiled by Rita Gentry

McCaa Books • Santa Rosa, CA

McCaa Books
684 Benicia Dr. #50
Santa Rosa, CA 95409

First published in 2022 by McCaa Books,
an imprint of McCaa Publications.

Library of Congress Control Number: 2022919975
ISBN 978-1-7378683-7-8

Printed in the United States of America
Set in Minion Pro

Book design by Waights Taylor Jr.
Front Cover by Stefan Gosiewski
Photos by Pat Johnson

www.mccaabooks.com

Special thanks to
Stefan Gosiewski for Cover Art

Pat Johnson for Cover photo of Bill Graham

Waights Taylor Jr. of McCaa Books for his guiding light

INTRODUCTION

I WAS BORN RITA GALE GENTRY on a Monday in March of 1947 at 11:30 a.m. at Saint Francis Hospital in San Francisco. My antique birth certificate states that my mother had a Caesarean section due to prolonged labor (over 48 hours) and I believe I was about two weeks late; so, thank God I was born an Aries, a fire sign. When I was born, my mother, Betty Gentry, was 22 years old. She was born and raised in San Francisco and was a dance teacher. My father, Jack Edward Gentry, was 25 years old and was born in Albuquerque, New Mexico; he was a floorman at a garage. My father was in the Navy when he met my mother at a USO dance in San Francisco. They stayed in touch through the war and were married when our country was at peace once again..

Up until high school, I lived on 10th Avenue in San Francisco. My parents then moved to Fremont, California and I didn't like it very much. Going from a city where I could jump on a bus and go just about anywhere to a place that had just been incorporated as a city-no buses and no driver's license-well, I had to do a lot of walking. As a young woman after high school, I eventually escaped and ended up back in my city by the bay, my San Francisco. Both of my brothers, Lee Gentry and Mark Gentry, were also born in San Francisco. Lee still lives in Fremont and Mark lives in Etna, California.

My life wasn't anything like what we saw on television (only black and white reception when I was growing up) with mom at home cooking with an apron on. Actually, that was my grandmother, Vivian, in whose house we lived in San Francisco, and for which I'm so thankful. Our home was kitty corner to the famous San Francisco original O'Shea's Bar. In my childhood, I could just go into with my dad. Got a whole other education hanging out with my dad in good old O'Shea's.

Learned a lot about pinball machines, shuffleboard and maraschino cherries. I will never again eat the latter, as I was able to go behind the bar to retrieve them myself, ate way too many at one time and made myself sick.

From the time I could walk, my mother and my Aunt Ardith taught me to dance. I learned tap, ballet, jazz, acrobatics, flamenco, Hawaiian, Tahitian; you name it, I did it. From the time I was born, music and dance were my life. I thank my mother in heaven for giving me the love of dance and music for without it, I would have ended up a completely different person. I danced it up until I was an adult and left home. Dancing was in my blood and with the convenience of a dance studio on the bottom floor of my house, it was natural for me. Instead of playing with friends or toys, I would go downstairs into the studio, put on music and dance.

Because of dance, I learned to roller skate at Skateland at the Beach, taking lessons and entering competitions. I would jump on the 38 Geary bus and ride to the end of the line at Playland at the Beach, then walk to Skateland. In this day and age, I surely would not let my grandchild do that at age 12 or 13. I'm sad to say San Francisco is not what it used to be, but that's what happens with time and too many people. During my childhood I thought the 450 Sutter Building was so tall and loved getting into the art deco elevator with an operator manning it. Days long gone.

My first real job was in a steno pool at American Telephone and Telegraph (AT&T) in San Francisco. I used a manual typewriter and had to use carbon paper to create copies of what I was typing (no copy machines). You could not make mistakes in your typing in this job, so I became an excellent typist. Little did I know that, in time, typing and Gregg shorthand (which I learned in high school) would become very beneficial for me in my future endeavors. After a few secretarial jobs, I decided I wanted to work in the entertainment industry.

The first music industry job I landed for myself was at Don Andersen Agency, which booked lounge acts in Reno, Lake Tahoe and the like. The office suite was located at 680 Beach Street in San Francisco. It was the hub of all the top record companies. At this job, I learned how to do artist contracts.

During that time, I shared a house with a married couple. The husband landed a job with Out of Town Tours, the Grateful Dead's booking agency located in San Rafael. The three of us moved to San Anselmo, and fortunately I got a job there too, doing artist contracts.

Out of Town Tours represented the Grateful Dead, Michael Bloomfield, the Band, Ramblin' Jack Elliott, Doug Sahm, Old & In the Way, Merle Saunders and the Sons of Champlin, to name a few, and my boss was Sam Cutler. When that came to an end, I was hired as personal assistant to New Riders of the Purple Sage.

The next band I worked for was the Sons of Champlin. After that, I worked for Commander Cody & His Lost Planet Airmen. Then, the job that would be the highlight of my life appeared in 1979 when I began to work at Bill Graham Presents; it would last for exactly 20 fabulous years.

My last full-time job before I retired was with Santana Management as Personal Assistant to Carlos Santana, and I give thanks to Carlos, Deborah Santana and Kitsaun King. As you can see, I have been very fortunate to work with so many fantastic artists.

My musical hero and guru will always be Mr. Bill Graham, and not a day goes by that I don't think of him.

After I retired, so many people would say to me, "Rita, you need to write a book." Well, that sounds good - and don't get me wrong, I've thought about it – but I want to keep my reputation intact, as well as protect the privacy of all those I've come into contact within the industry. But the gods work in mysterious ways.

One day I was on the phone with the great Lionel Bea of Bay Area Productions and Black Promoters Collective, and it came up in the conversation once again that I should write a book. At first, I thought maybe I could write it from the perspective of a woman in the industry, but this has been done a few times before. Don't ask me how we got there, but Lionel and I came up with the idea of collecting stories about Bill. Lionel and I both have the love Bill thing. Every time we talk there's always an incredible Bill story that comes up, so this seemed like that was the way for me to venture forward.

And so, it began in 2017. I started collecting Bill stories and now, here I am, with over 200 Bill/BGP stories from people in all walks of life. It is just so amazing to me to receive all the different experiences which I have compiled here. What people have remembered (sometimes differently than I remember it, LOL!) has been an incredible experience. The main gist of all this is just what an incredible human being Mr. Bill Graham, born Wolfgang Grajonca, was in our lives. From the bottom of my heart, I thank all of you who participated. You all took the time to sit down and write your story for me, and I so truly appreciate it. This book could not have happened without each and every one of you.

I'd like to extend particular thanks to the following people: The Ramirez family of Don Ramon's Restaurant, San Francisco; David Zouzounis and family of Ted's Market, San Francisco; Ken Friedman, photographer; Danny Scher, Dawn Holliday, Jan Simmons- Portman, Casey Jones Bastiaans, Colleen Kennedy, Ron Bergman, Steve Paine, Bonnie Simmons, Colleen Kennedy, Laura Fraenza, Bob Barsotti, and the Bill Graham Foundation, Michael Carabello, as well as my best friends, Nina Urban Bombardier, Ditka Reiner, Sheila Bridges,Tomi Liddell and Ruth Montellano Gentry.

A very special thank you to Ms. Sherill Conley for her many hours of love, devotion, and expertise. Without her, this book would never have made it to its final stages.

Though many of our friends are no longer with us, I'm giving a special heavenly shout out to the incredible Ms. Shelley Lazar for our comradery and great adventures together; Mr. James Battle, Jr., a great and kind man who always made me feel safe; Mr. Gary Orndorf, who left us way too soon.

And last, but always first, I'd like to dedicate this book to My two understanding and loving children:

Jake Gentry and Gina Turrini

You have both shown me support even though, at times, I'm sure you thought I was not the typical mom your friends had (funny how I followed in my mother's footsteps!) I do know that both of you sacrificed a lot of your growing-up years with all the comings and goings, and long hours away from you both (thank God for Daddy George).

Your love and understanding have always helped me endure any obstacle that was in my way. I am so proud of who you have both become as adults, and I love you both more than words can say or type!

That being said, if nothing else, this book is a snapshot of a unique time in music history. I am so thankful to have been a part of it and hope you enjoy these wonderful stories. Once again, thank you to all the people who made it possible for this book to come together…from the bottom of my heart and soul.

A

ALAN BAGSHAW

1970-1972: Student stagehand at Berkeley High School, many times working four shows a month for Bill.
1972-1974: Carpenter, electrician with FM(Fillmore) Productions and stagehand at Winterland.
1974: On tour with Bob Dylan, The Band, Crosby, Stills, Nash & Young, George Harrison.
1975-1982: Truck driver, roadie, tour manager with Santana.

I met Bill in 1970 while a student at Berkeley High School working on his concerts at the Berkeley Community Theater. I joined Bill's FM Productions after graduation, supporting shows at Winterland and various venues in California. In 1974, I toured with Bob Dylan & The Band, CSNY and George Harrison. From 1975-1972, I worked with Carlos Santana and the Santana Band.

A poignant story I remember from the '70s is Bill mentioning he was looking forward to the joy of walking around his office when he was old surrounded by his extended family.

ALAN BUDENZ

I started working for BGP in early 1979 (or maybe late 1978) as a volunteer doing security at the Warfield. I loved and it and quickly became a regular Bluecoat. I then branched out into doing ambience crew, front of stage barricade with my roommate Art Kimura, and doing carpentry jobs in the office and at Bill's house. I saw and heard so much incredible music being made and met so many different people from all walks of life.

It was wonderful!!! Eventually, some of these people became my patients - a true compliment. I miss the comradery of shows and of Bill Graham Presents.

Some of my favorite memories are of late-night conversations with Bill when I was moonlighting on a carpentry project in the BGP office. Sometimes he would come wandering by as he stretched his legs while working late in the office and just start talking - about shows, about projects, about salsa music, politics, art, whatever. Bill was tough, complicated, sometimes difficult, but he had a big heart. I respected and admired him and learned a lot from him and from our BGP family.

They were good times; his passing was a big loss. I continued working security at The Fillmore through 1999 (another big loss, Art Abuse!) and occasionally doing a gig at the Fillmore or for Dawn Holliday through the early 2000s. The scene, the work environment, and I changed. I miss it, but I couldn't keep doing it.

ALAN WOODS

I worked for Bill at the Fillmore West from 1970 and after it closed in 1971.

After my discharge from the Navy, I drove around the United States and Canada until running out of money in San Francisco. I took my last money and went to a show at The Fillmore West. I loved the experience and was completely taken with Bill – the Master Show Promoter.

I came back to the Fillmore West during the day and sat in front of the offices. When people asked me what I wanted, I told them, "I want to work here!" Again and again this happened until they closed the office and I had to leave. I slept in my hippie van and came back the next day and did it all over again. Finally, someone (Keeva Kristal, Bill's business manager) asked me what I wanted to do. My answer was, "I'll do ANYTHING you need done," and they hired me!

My first job was to count MONEY, to tag it and bag it and take it to the bank. I had never seen so much money.

Later on, I worked many jobs at the Fillmore such as bartender (no alcohol), security, stagehand, light show, and roadie. Bill became my mentor, teaching me how to produce shows. We all had a special devotion to Bill, who viewed us as his Fillmore Family.

One story of so many which showed Bill's toughness (he will always be the toughest man I ever knew) was on the top of the stairs at the Fillmore. People would enter the ballroom there and they were searched. All bottles were taken away from the patrons. When a gang of Hell's Angels tried to come in, Bill stood them down and would not let them in until he took their guns. He got their guns and let them in and then returned their guns to them upon their departure. Bill was so tough!

AMELIA DAVIS

The notorious Jim Marshall and the infamous Bill Graham were very similar in many ways. They both were mavericks in the world of music, Jim being the pioneer of music photography and Bill being the visionary of what would become music festivals. They very much respected each other, but had a love/hate relationship. Maybe that's because they were so similar in their work ethics or maybe because they were both Type A personalities. No matter what, Jim respected Bill for his commitment to making sure the musicians and the attendees had a safe, clean and joyous time at every event he put his name to.

Bill Graham and Jim Marshall are gone now, but they left the world an important piece of history to look back at and for future generations to enjoy.

Rita's Note: Amelia worked closely with the famous photographer, Mr. Jim Marshall, for many years and when Jim passed she became the executor of Jim's photography.

Through her love and dedication, she has allowed Jim's legacy to keep going and going.

AMY FINK

I'm not sure exactly when I started handling Bill's travel arrangements, but I'd guess it was in the late '70s when he was also working with Blue World Travel due to the fact that Herbie Herbert, Journey's manager, owned the travel agency. It's a long story how I ended up being his full-time travel agent and I think I will save that for the book I might write some day.

He was demanding and I always had to be on top of my game. When Rita or Jan would call and say, "Hold for Bill," my heart would race. Why? Because he'd come on and skip the pleasantries, although a warm and appreciative man, and just start shooting questions, orders, demands, etc. Pay attention for sure.

I spoke to him on the phone at least 200 times, yet he started every conversation with, "Hi Amy, this is Bill Graham," which always made me chuckle, hearing the full name instead of just Bill.

One of my favorite tales was a call he made to me late on December 23rd, probably about 1979 or '80. He simply said, "Hi, Amy, this is Bill Graham. Sorry to bother you at home, but I need my family here for Christmas. Would you please take care of it?"

This was pre-computers and internet, pre-cell phones, pre-ticket-less air travel and all the conveniences that now make planning travel so easy. I used to have to call each airline, sit on hold while listening to music, and get their schedules and prices along with the availability. I would then make a decision and call back the airline of choice and give an authorization form number over the phone that was similar to buying something with your credit card. That was the authorization to provide an airline ticket to someone in another location, paid in full.

His sister, Sonja, lived in Vienna; son David was in Philadelphia; sons Alex and Thomas were in Maui. I made many, many phone calls, secured the best flights, spoke to each person so they would know what their itinerary was and then provided an over-the-phone spread-sheet to Gary Orndorf, Bill's caretaker, who would be doing the airport pick-ups. Everything was booked and paid for. Everything was in place.

About 24 hours later, my phone rings. "Merry Christmas Amy. This is Bill Graham. I'm sitting at my dining room table with both of my sisters, all three of the boys and we are about to have dinner. I just want to thank you so much for everything you do for me." It puts a smile on my face just to tell the story.

He was a challenge, but a pleasure to do business with. Never a dull moment and never unappreciated.

ANDIE RICE

Very early on in my years working with Rock Med and before I ever met Bill, I remember working at a Grateful Dead show at Winterland around 1974 when a young woman was brought into Rock Medicine by the Blue Jackets (before their name was changed to Bluecoats). Apparently, she had come to San Francisco from Texas (if I remember right) for the Dead shows. She had parked her car in a garage in the vicinity of the venue and while walking to Winterland had been mugged. She was pretty shaken up, but physically okay.

While she was in Rock Med, Bill showed up. He was absolutely wonderful when he spoke with her. It was absolutely beautiful to see how he was able to calm her. In addition to that, he also sent his security guys out to look for the mugger(s) and offered to pay her way back to San Francisco to testify if the guy(s) ended up in court.

That was my introduction to Bill, and it made a deep impression on me. I always felt that I was so lucky to have seen that side of him and felt privileged to work with him over many years.

I also remember back in the early days of the Fillmore East (maybe 1971) that he made the theater available for local political groups on the Lower East Side (now known as the East Village) to hold meetings there.

I was one of the founders of the St. Marks Free Clinic in New York which was about a block from the theater and we were invited to all the shows gratis.

ANGELA FLAVIANI

I started at Bill Graham Presents in 1989 as a security guard at Staff Pro at BGP shows on and off until 1998, then back again from 2003 to 2004 working the ticket booth at the Warfield Theater and the Fillmore. I am now a product designer and developer with artisan leather handbags and accessories (maker and stylist for men's custom clothier).

My favorite Bill story: Ironically, most of my interaction with him was when I worked as a Staff Pro employee. I was often staged at the backstage door of the Oakland Coliseum, Berkeley Community Theater, Cow Palace, etc., so I had a lot more direct contact with Bill, as I saw him come and go. The one memory I have of Bill proved what a grandioso persona he was/had.

I was manning the backstage entrance (top of the ramp) at The Coliseum. I was standing with my back to the ramp looking out onto the parking lot with two barricades in front of me. Things were quiet and no one was around, but suddenly I felt this really heavy/strong feeling. No one was in sight, no sounds of anyone around. So, for whatever reason, I turned around to see if anyone was behind me… and there was Bill walking up the ramp in complete silence. I opened the barricade to let him out and we exchanged hellos/goodbyes, as we always did. Then I just stood there in a bit of a daze. It amazed me how strong and powerful someone's presence could be; you could FEEL Bill coming from the bottom of the ramp!

His presence was so strong!

ANN KRCIK

Rita's Note: These stories were dictated to me by Anne Scheer. Ann Krcik passed away on February 26, 2018.

In her day job, Ann Krcik represented people involved in extreme sports: rock climbers, mountain climbers, skiers, etc. She had no idea of how to put on an outdoor rock-climbing exhibition. She took the idea to Bill, who didn't particularly think it was a moneymaker, but because of his own history of producing somewhat odd events and his admiration for Ann, he decided to co-sponsor (with North Face) the first ever Pro Rock-Climbing Challenge at the Greek Theatre in Berkeley, California. Ann was nervous about it from the start, and to say that the event lost money would be an understatement. But Ann remembered that his only comment to her was, "Well, you tried. It may have turned out like shit, but at least you tried."

It was the Oakland Coliseum Arena and the show was Run-DMC and the Beastie Boys. The band's security guy wanted to meet all the front of stage people before the show to school them on what to expect from the crowd. When he noticed one security person was a woman, he went straight to Bill and told him she had to be reassigned because front of stage was "no place for a woman." Bill listened to the guy, walked away quietly away, then immediately asked Molly Frink to pull all the women working outside to the inside to work the aisles and especially front of stage. Molly assigned all the "Anns" (there were three of us) to supervise the inside to further confuse and confound their security guys.

Since these changes happened once the front door staff was reassigned after the show started (and it was dark), no one really noticed. It was very brutal front of house and in the aisles, but there were no big problems. After the show, the band's security guy told Bill it was the best security they had seen on their tour, especially front of stage, which he had to admit worked very well with all those women. It was nice to see Bill teach someone a lesson in gender equality.

ANNE SCHEER

Some short memories I have of Bill.

Both during and after each Grateful Dead show in Telluride, Colorado, Bill and several Bluecoats would walk through downtown and pick up garbage. He wanted to make sure we left the place as clean, if not cleaner, than before we were there. He always seemed to know that his shows came at a cost for neighbors.

Christmas/holiday parties, especially at the Warfield Theater in San Francisco, were great and consisted of food, entertainment, guests and drink. One of my fondest memories was Bill dancing with me, Sugar, Colleen, Rita, and Susie B. to the sounds of the Neville Brothers who were up on stage.

I had to work the Laguna Seca Dead shows. My husband at that time was working KMEL Summer Jam at Shoreline. During one of the set changes, Bill invited me to fly up to Shoreline with him so he could check in on the show there and I could visit Steve. It was very sweet and thoughtful, especially for someone who had so many other things to think about.

Bill (who hated to lose in sports) let my daughter Alison beat him in basketball at a party at his house. Of course, she was only 8 at the time, so I suppose his ego was still intact.

Ry Cooder was the one of the opening acts at the Dead in Laguna Seca, and Ry had inadvertently parked his giant 1950s big-finned car in the wrong place backstage. Bill wanted to know whose f*#*ing car it was. When he was told who the owner was, and remembering that I had named my son after Ry, Bill instructed me to go tell Ry to move his car or he was going to move it with a forklift. Ry was very gracious and just flipped the keys to me. So I got to drive the car and Bill got to see me very embarrassed.

A few longer ones.

During a U2 show at the Oakland Coliseum (outdoors), Bill saw me backstage and started yelling at me because he thought I was loafing while everyone else was working, because he heard we had lost the aisles and was on his way out to the front of house to "fix" the problem himself. What he didn't know was that we had just finished clearing all the aisles and everyone was back in their seats. I was coming backstage to get water for the front-of-stage guys. I was so surprised (and angry) that he was yelling at me that I yelled back at him that he should mind his own business because I had already taken care of my business. He followed me out to the house where everything was just fine. After the show, he came and found me and tried to apologize. He said he would bring me a present, some perfume from France. I said I didn't wear perfume. He said he would take me to France. It became a years long joke, me often asking when we were leaving.

Dead run at Oakland Auditorium (Henry J. Kaiser). The show was in progress. I was working the front doors. Bill came outside and saw that there were people camped in the park across the street, so he wanted us to clear them out. Unfortunately, most of the campers were in the show. So, he decided to give out a few "miracle tickets" instead, which created a stampede. While Dan Jacobsen and I, along with a few other Bluecoats tried to save Bill from his own generosity, he got into a screaming match with one Deadhead who called him several colorful names, including "Nazi." Big mistake. I'm not sure how we got Bill out of there without him killing that guy.

One of the Dead runs at Ventura County Fairgrounds - it was the last day of the run, and somehow Bill had gotten dosed backstage. He was starting to trip a little, and Peter and Bettike thought it would be best if he left ASAP in his plane. They picked me as one of the people to accompany him. No pun intended, but it was a long strange trip indeed. Lots of staring out the window and holding clammy hands. We got back to Novato around 2:00 a.m. and I realized I had no way to get back to the East Bay. I think I had to take a taxi. Bill never mentioned the trip – I often wonder if he just thought he was dreaming the whole thing.

Bill was big into sports. He would host baseball games down on the municipal field near Masada, then we'd all go up to his house for food and drinks later. This one game was against someone like Metallica or Eddy Money. Bill really didn't like to lose so he always handpicked the best athletes (always men) to be on his team.

But it was co-ed, so a few unlucky women had to play. We were behind. I got up and got a double. Bill stopped the game, and because he assumed I knew nothing about baseball, walked out to second base to let me know that if the next guy up hit the ball, I didn't have to run because first base was open. I thanked him for the clarification, but told him I really did know how to play baseball. He nodded, said okay, started to walk back to the dugout but then walked back to tell me about tagging up on a fly ball.

It was several days before a Dead run at the Greek. Bill called me at home to tell me he was "worried" about David, and wanted him to start working at shows. He thought security would be a good spot, but not inside the venue. So I said we could put him out in Kleeburger Field, across from the Greek, where we set up speakers so people without tickets could assemble and listen to the show (and therefore, keep them out of other places). David did a great job, but didn't come back the final day of the three-day run. When I saw him later inside the venue and asked why he didn't show up he explained that his dad said he didn't have to go back.

After many years of spending New Year's Eve with the Dead and, therefore, Bill, I once asked him what he would be doing if he didn't have to be pushed through a crowd of Deadheads at midnight. He said he'd probably just like to go to a nice quiet restaurant and eat lobster bisque. So, for the next several years, I made lobster bisque at home and brought it to the New Year's Eve show along with a lace tablecloth, china and silver and we had dinner together backstage in catering. It was always my favorite part of the NYE run.

I was working the Jerry Garcia Band shows at Squaw Valley. I was in the middle of a somewhat messy divorce so was a bit distracted in my work. Bill wanted to know if I wanted to take a walk, so I said sure. We sat on a bench with a beautiful view of the Sierras, and he said that Bettike had just filled him in on my troubles. He wanted to know how he could help - he offered monetary help, which I declined. He offered lawyers - which I also declined because I already had one. I explained there wasn't much anyone could do, it just had to work its course. Then he brightened up and said, "Well, I could have him killed - I know people who could do that!"

The Oakland Hills Fire had been all over the news, and as a fire-fighter, I had just gotten home after three days on the fire line. The phone rang, and it was Bill. He had been following the fire and just wanted to know how I was doing. We talked awhile, he asked a lot of questions about the fire and what it was like, and he reminded me that I could always come and work for him full-time because it would certainly be a lot safer than being a firefighter. We laughed, he said he was glad I was okay, then said goodbye, see you soon. That was October 24, 1991, and it turned out to be the last time I talked with Bill.

ARLENE OWSEICHIK

Eight years after the Summer of Love, I made my post-college migration to San Francisco. I lived in the Haight on Masonic Avenue. One of my first pilgrimages was to view the Airplane Mansion on Fulton Street. I had "followed the music" from the East Coast to the West.

At the time, I thought I would explore photography as a career. But, always practical, I found work in the printing industry, which led to a job at Ampersand Design, a graphics studio. It was the time before computers – featuring X-Acto blades, press- type, Rubylith and wax machines. I loved working with all these tools. I created advertisements, business cards, flyers, etc.

Ampersand was a happening place. The owners were lively guys with connections to the entertainment world, early Beach Blanket Babylon, for one. It was an "alternative" environment, a place I felt comfortable in.

One day in 1978, I answered the phone. It was Queenie Taylor on the line. Queenie was Advertising Director for Bill Graham Presents. My heart beat faster. To me, BGP was the coolest business in town.

Queenie was looking for someone to create ads and street posters. Prior to this, their ads were hand-lettered by Randy Tuten, one of the early poster artists. I grabbed on tightly to the opportunity, and, in time, BGP became my main account. My first assignment was to make an 11 x 17 street poster for the Commodores. I pasted up ads that ran in the San Francisco Chronicle's Sunday Pink Section, the go-to place to learn about what was happening in the Bay Area.

BGP was bursting at the seams at the time, which turned into more work for me. They were building Shoreline Amphitheatre in Mountain View, had ongoing shows at Winterland Arena in San Francisco, Henry J. Kaiser Convention Center in Oakland and Concord Pavilion in Concord. It became almost a full-time job to fulfill the graphics needs of the company.

By 1984, I knew I wanted to work for Bill Graham and BGP directly. I proposed to them that if they were to bring me in- house and set up a dark room with a stat camera, I'd be able to make the final copies of the ads that were delivered to the newspapers. They would save money and have the convenience of having me close at hand.

They sat on my proposal for months. The office at 201 11th Street was a rabbit warren of offices and, even though they all thought it was a good idea, they were not ready to reconfigure the space to make room for me.

In May of 1985, the Bill Graham offices were firebombed closely after Bill hosted a rally at Union Square to protest President Reagan's visit to the Bitburg Cemetery in Germany where Nazi SS officers were buried. Though the perpetrators of the fire were never found, it is believed it was a neo-Nazi response to the rally.

BGP was forced to move out of the 11th Street location. In August of that year, they moved to 260 Fifth Street with an art department included in the floor plan. My self-appointed job title was art director.

I went on to spend 19 years at the company. I adored Bill. For my first six years there, while he was still alive, I worked fairly closely with him. Fantastic projects abounded. For example, I was asked to design a paint job for his prop-jet.

Once the design was settled upon, I got to fly shotgun with Bill's pilot, Steve "Killer" Kahn, to Portland to deliver the plane to the paint shop. After discussing the design with the painter, it was lunch atop Mount Hood.

It happened to be the same day that Prince was playing with Sheila E at The Warfield Theatre, San Francisco. I remember racing to the airport in Portland for the flight home and thinking, could it get any better than this?

We opened Shoreline Amphitheatre in 1986 to much fanfare.

Each year, New Year's Eve was a company extravaganza with bands playing every venue. Foremost was the Grateful Dead show, culminating with Bill's entrance as Father Time. It was a favorite time for Bill. He said, for that one time annually, he knew what it felt like to be a performer, awash in the loving energy of the crowd. The feeling around the office was a constant all-hands-on-deck to keep up with all that was going on.

The building at 260 Fifth Street was shaped like a shoebox with a warehouse on the first floor and offices on the second. My office was halfway back adjacent a firewall. It was also where the freight elevator door was located. Bill parked his car, either the Mercedes or the Jag, downstairs and rode the freight elevator upstairs each day that he was in the office. I could hear the rumbling of the elevator inside the walls whenever he ascended. I loved that sound.

He was always in bustle mode. He had a rubber face that was always revealing emotion. He spoke with a loud voice and had a commanding presence. He held the attention of any room that he was in.

He was a great storyteller and always moved his body about for emphasis. He was funny and articulate. At company meetings he often spoke from the larger perspective of the company's place in our musical world. I always came away from those meetings feeling like I was exactly where I was meant to be. We were fighting the good fight.

Bill was no snob; he liked everyone equally. He could hang with Mick Jagger one day and the guys who worked security the next. He had a laser focus. When he studied something, a poster comp for example, he was riveted. I thought his comments were always based on elevating the art rather than simply from his ego.

He loved athletics, and he had to win. It was frightening to play on his team and disappoint, or to play on the opposite team and be the object of his wrath. Soon after Peter Barsotti purchased the Iron Door Saloon (from the Gold Rush era), in Groveland, California, the office took a weekend there. Bill and I were partners in a game of pool. I know little about pool, and it was a harrowing half hour to say the least. I do not remember the outcome. I would guess that we won.

He did not care much about the clothes he wore and would buy multiple copies of what he liked and would wear them until they were threadbare. That is, unless it was dress-up time. That man could rock a tuxedo!

One time for his birthday I presented him with a silly inflatable cake dubbed the official "BGP Party Cake." I had written slogans all over it – Happy Anniversary, Happy Birthday, It's A Girl! Even, You're Fired! He loved the cake and thereafter brought it to all of the office functions. (He was always railing about the expense behind our little parties, in a joking way, of course.)

When Bill Graham died in October of 1991, it was shocking, to say the least. The heart had been ripped from BGP. To the credit of everyone who was there, the shows went on, that night included. We pulled it together to host Laughter, Love and Music the next weekend in Golden Gate Park. It was a grand tribute to Bill, Steve Kahn and Melissa Gold, attended by 350,000 humbled patrons. Bill Graham had led a flock of youth into a new cultural era.

The company remained strong, even without Bill, and for years maintained its position as the premier concert promoter in Northern California.

Working at Bill Graham Presents set the course for my life, i.e., work ethic, political values and public assemblage on a grand scale. I always appreciated that Bill could simultaneously see the big picture of where we stood culturally and the smallest detail of what true hospitality meant. To me, he presented them to be equally important.

He was a mentor, an inspiration, and a thrilling person to be around day after day, the likes of which I surely will not know again.

Thank you again, Teacher.

ARNOLD PUSTILNIK

My very first time working for Bill was eventful. I was asked by the production manager to monitor one of the two entrances to backstage at the Berkeley Community Theater. I was sitting on the steps when said production manager walked up to me with a joint in his hand and offered me a toke. I assumed it was cool and gladly accepted.

As I was puffing, Bill walked out from the backstage area and looked at me and snarled, "What is that?" I readily admitted that it was a joint. He stared for a moment and said, "Put that out and don't ever let me see you do that again."

That could have been the end, but instead it was the beginning of a career that lasted for over 40 years…it was a blast!

B

BARBARA HORN

So, I'm not sure what year it was, and I believe it was a Jerry Garcia show at the Warfield Theater. The doors had not yet opened to the public when I got a call that Bill wanted to see me. As we know, that is not the call you want.

On my way to the main entrance I'm thinking to myself, what did I do? I arrived to find a woman sitting on the ground leaning up against the marble wall next to the ticket booth. Bill asked me is there anything that I could do for this aggressive and combative woman that the officers had in handcuffs. I approached her and told her I was there to save her ass from going to jail. She responded to me, "Fuck you!" and spit in my face. I reacted with an automatic response and slapped her.

I heard clapping and, turning around, saw Bill clapping with a smile on his face and others joined in. I felt like shit for doing that, but it was just a reaction.

After she was hauled off to jail, Bill approached me and said, "You did nothing wrong. You have the 30 second rule. You were in the fight or flight mode." I told him, "But I assaulted her in front of the officers." He promised me I wouldn't be arrested and if I was, he would bail me out, as he laughed while walking away to deal with other hippie dramas.

Rita's Note: Barbara Horn is also known as Nurse Babs. She has helped and served so many patrons at BGP shows for many years. I've seen her in action and she will definitely get her reward in heaven.

BARBARA LEWIT

Here are a few memories.

After the Grateful Dead concert in Telluride in 1987, thanks to Jan Simmons, we got to be guests at Bill's house for a dinner with the Grateful Dead. I'll never forget sitting outside at a long table with Bill sitting next to me with his arm around my chair and Jerry sitting directly across from me and everyone was laughing. Steve Parish was yelling at people and laughing, and everyone was enjoying themselves. It was so nice of Bill to include me, Lou, Maggie, Tom and Jan.

I got to work as a production assistant in the summer of 1987 and I remember working all week at Laguna Seca for Peter Barsotti, which was a really wonderful experience, except when the music started and I couldn't watch the band play.

I remember the joy of making Bill throw back his head and laugh or seeing his approval when I did something he liked.

I was lucky enough to go for a drive with Bill in his convertible in San Francisco one night. I can't remember the circumstances, and neither can Jan. When we pulled up to our destination, he parked in a red zone and when I expressed shock he said, "My time is too valuable to care about a parking ticket."

Bill seemed fascinated by the fact that I was so genuinely devoted to Grateful Dead music. Jan told me he watched me dance at a Frost Amphitheater concert and said, "She's really into it, isn't she?" One time we talked about the Grateful Dead and subsequently, I received in the mail a classical CD with a lovely note from him that read:

Dear Barbara,

You never know, you could become a Bach Head or a Verdi Head or a Handel Head and become a regular at Tosca's. Enjoy!

Bill came over to my house in Berkeley after a Grateful Dead concert at midnight or something and ended up staying up 'til the wee hours of the morning. So much fun to have him in my house (with everyone tripping and music playing loudly). He was one of us!

BARON WOLMAN

I never had a job "job" with Bill Graham, although I did shoot several of his legendary Day on the Green stadium concerts for him for which I was paid, although it was never about the money – I would have made pictures for free – but about the concerts themselves, the music, the bands, the backstage hospitality and the presence of Bill's unique energy that always assured things went well, both for the bands and for the audience.

Early on, around the time that Rolling Stone Magazine was started and I became its first chief photographer, Bill granted me and my cameras the gift of "all access" to all of his productions, no matter where or what the venue. It was a golden gift that allowed me – would allow any photographer – to do my best work, unhindered by closed doors, arbitrary rules and shouted "noes!" All access meant I could shoot anywhere and everywhere – backstage, on the stage, in front of the stage, over the stage; nothing was off limits. In a meaningful way that maybe even he didn't understand, Bill, therefore, helped my career enormously.

I remember one day in 1970 he phoned me and said he wanted some informal portraits of him and David, his son. The two of them came over to my house in the Haight-Ashbury, plopped themselves in a comfortable rocking chair where I photographed them, together and singly. Hanging around his neck – I assume it was always there – was a silver six-pointed Star of David, confirming to all he was Jewish and no doubt reminding him of his journeys from Germany to America. Perhaps because I was always somewhat intimidated by Bill and had difficulty relaxing in his presence, the resulting photos didn't please him, although they are very intimate and I've exhibited and published them often, and usually to considerable praise.

I'm a pilot and am always aware of the weather. I clearly recall that stormy evening in 1991. I was lying in bed in my Sonoma County home; both my plane and Bill's helicopter were hangared in Novato, California in Marin County, just south of where I lived. I thought to myself, perhaps with some prescience, "I sure hope nobody's out there flying right now." Sadly, there was; it was the night that Bill left this world forever, much too soon. I, for one – and I know I'm not alone – sorely miss the man.

BART JEFFERSON

I submitted my resume to FM Productions, the sound and lights division of Bill Graham Presents, on February 4, 1975.

I was hired for a monitor engineer position and was to "second engineer" for three shows before I could solo with an assistant. BGP was expanding at the time and was short on tech help. So, they let me solo after just one show! I was informed that if the monitors were to feed back three times I would be fired.

I started as stage monitor engineer on February 13th, with Electric Light Orchestra and Little Feat at Winterland. During Little Feat's first song, Bill Graham came and stood right next to me behind the monitor board at stage right. After a few songs went by with no problems Bill patted me on my back, spun on his heels and walked away. Good thing for soundchecks!

Working in the FM Productions shop during the week, among our other tech duties, I would be tasked with putting Bill's desk phone back together after he had thrown it against the wall to make a point! That's why Bill's desk phone was made up of all different colored parts from previous repairs.

Weekends were spent as monitor engineer for shows at Winterland, Day on the Green at the Oakland Coliseum, Berkeley Community Theatre, etc.

On the road for FM/BGP:

Stage monitor engineer for 1976 Santana tour.

Stage monitor engineer for 1976 Jefferson Starship tour.

BGP Road Manager and Front of House for Eddie Money and Ronnie Montrose in 1978 and 1979.

BENJAMIN WINTER

Mark Lewis was a good friend of mine in high school in Newark, California. He and I used to do art shows together: me jewelry and Mark made ceramics. He then moved to Oakland and, I guess, finished high school at Berkeley High. I assume there he met the Barsotti brothers, Anne Scheer, Anne Rockwell, Paul Miller, Erick Indvik - that whole crowd at Berkeley High and Merritt College. Eventually, Mark started working for BGP and quickly became head of security.

I started working with him and BGP around 1978. I moved to San Francisco in 1980 and shared a warehouse with Mark and Erick at Fifth and Folsom in San Francisco. The very first Bluecoat Awards Banquet was held at this warehouse - our home.

At one time, Mark Lewis and I were asked to make a life mask of Bill for an upcoming Grateful Dead run (15 shows) at the Warfield Theater. We had Bill lying down on a desk in the garage of the office. We had Vaseline on his face and protected his clothes and put straws in his nose to allow him to breathe. He seemed a little nervous and maybe vulnerable. He started talking about how he didn't own a lot of property because he was afraid of the pogroms (definition of pogrom: an organized massacre, especially of Jews) that had happened to the Jews over the centuries and that he had a deep unconscious fear that a pogrom would someday happen again and that Jewish properties, etc. would be taken away.

I thought, wow, what a great insight into a really self- assured powerful man. The plaster mask set up and we removed it. Later, when Mark did a positive of Bill's face for this huge butterfly that was displayed at the Warfield Theater in San Francisco, I was a bit disappointed as the face did not look a lot like Bill.

It took me a few days, but I finally realized that we should have had Bill sitting up when we made the cast of the mask. Bill's face had prominent jowls and when he was lying down, they pretty much flattened out making his face less wrinkly or jowly. Since then, when I've made life masks of friends, I've made sure that they are sitting upright.

Once I made an appointment with Bill to consult with him about a product that I had designed. I showed up a few minutes early and was sitting outside his office. He was on the phone and seemed to be very angry. He was speaking very loudly with that deep voice of his. He was saying that he didn't like what the guy had written and called him a few names and told him that he would not be let into any more shows. He slammed down the phone looked up at me and said very calmly, "Come in, Ben." It was so interesting to see him switch from so much anger to being very calm and welcoming - a great actor?

One of my favorite stories was about how hands-on Bill was even in the later years when he had so many assistants, vice presidents, etc.

I think we were at Hughes Stadium in Sacramento (Willie Nelson concert and the famous gun settlement story that I did not witness) and a bunch of us had gone up the night before and slept out in the back stage tents. I was sitting on the edge of some bleachers drinking coffee from catering. It was about 7:00 a.m. and I saw Bill and one of his sons (Alex, I think. Must have been 12 years old or even maybe younger). Bill had his ever-present clipboard with him and as he got up within hearing range I heard him say, "Not enough garbage cans," as he was writing on the clipboard. I almost choked on my coffee!

Here was a man who was already successful in this business at a relatively minor concert at a minor outdoor venue at seven in the morning and that was the level of detail that he was worrying about. He didn't even need to be at this concert. He had several managers there seeing to everything.

This is just one minor example of why he was so successful.

BENNY COLLINS

Rita's Note: On January 13, 2017 I sent an email to Benny asking him to please contribute a story about a Bill Graham experience for my book. He was one of the first people I contacted regarding my new book project. I just could not leave Benny out of my book, as we'd worked many hours and shows together. I loved him so much!

He wrote me back saying: "Yo Rita. Thanks for the greetings and sending the same back to you and your family as well and here's to a truly incredible 2017. Hugs & Kisses, Benny

Fourteen days later, January 27, 2017, Benny passed away. I was crushed and memories of our times together flowed through my head, not believing that my long-time friend would be gone forever.

I will always remember that raspy voice and the bigness of his stature and heart.

BERNADINE KIRBY FERGUSON

I worked in the production department staffing stagehands and later, security. My bosses were Peter and Bob Barsotti from 1985 to 1995. I also worked with Ron Bergman, Brian Auger, Steve Paine, Tom Howard and Rita Gentry.

My best Bill Graham story was when he asked Vicki Helms and me to deliver a case of Dom Perignon champagne to Peter Barsotti in Groveland, California, which was an approximately 120-mile drive. Peter's bar, the Iron Door Saloon, was closed so we tried to find his house, which took us hours (remember, this was before cellphones), but we finally found it. Then we had to park and walk across a creek to get to it.

Just a little request from Bill…

BERNARDO D. GONZALEZ III

I started high school in 1969. That should be enough said right there. I had just completed junior high school listening to The British Invasion with The Beatles, the Rolling Stones and everyone else from across the pond then leading into the mother of all music festivals, Woodstock.

When I saw that movie at the age of 14, I no longer wanted to be a baseball player; I wanted to do what I saw on the screen. The whole experience was mind blowing, but the footage of "Soul Sacrifice" by unknown Santana from San Francisco was what will stick in my mind from that day forward.

I could not wait to see the band when they came to Winterland. We asked my uncle, who had gone to high school with Carlos Santana at Mission High, to drive a group of my friends and me to the concert if we bought him a ticket.

Now I was living the dream, coming right smack dab in the middle of the whole music experience, right before my eyes. I can still hear Bill Graham announcing, "Ladies and gentlemen, Santana," and the band starting out the set with "Treat."

I would live at Winterland the next few years. I recently came across an old college calendar and I was at Winterland three out of four weeks of every month seeing anyone, but never missing a Santana concert, living through the changes in music and personnel all along the way.

Going through the concert process as part of the audience, you could only be in awe of the people who worked with Bill Graham and were around the music and musicians all the time and wonder what it would be like. Then one day during college I found out you could volunteer at The Warfield.

Sign me up! I started out by doing security where we were placed at the exit doors for the entire concert to make sure that no one came in or out during the duration of the show. I was a part of Bill Graham Presents if only as a volunteer. It was great because during my years in dental school money was minimal for concert-going so I was able to see shows that I would not normally be able to see; it worked out well for me at the time.

I would sign up for as many shows as I could fit into my schedule. Then one day I was approached by the head person in charge of security who asked me, "How would you like to get paid for this?" I replied, "You can get paid for this?" Well my first paid assignment was three days of the Grateful Dead at the Berkeley Greek Theatre. At that time, I was all about Santana and Journey. Really was not into the Dead. Listened to records and just didn't hear it.

Well, after three days of the Dead at the Greek, I was a Deadhead.

Like they say, you had to be there. Well, I was now also a full member of the Bill Graham Bluecoat security force.

Again, I signed up for as many shows as I could fit into my schedule and was now receiving a paycheck. I would work at Stanford Frost Amphitheater, the Cow Palace, numerous Day on the Green shows, the San Francisco Civic Center (now the Bill Graham Civic), as well as the Greek Theatre. Wherever I was needed, I was there. I wore the coat proudly and worked for many years.

Taking my position with pride, I would always do my job to the fullest, which brings me to my one face-to-face with Bill himself. One night while working a concert at the Berkeley Greek Theater, we would watch people running down the hill at the back of the venue who would then leap to the top of the fence and then drop down behind the row of porta-potties that were just in front of the fence at the top of the venue. We would stand near the people in line for the porta potties and watch the people running down the hill ready to make their move. Once they hit the ground we would tackle them then escort them out of the venue. No one was getting past us. High fives all around every time we caught one.

The next day at the following show, a group of us were summoned to wait because Bill wanted to talk to us. We could only imagine what for, but we figured it was for the great job we did capturing the fence jumpers. WRONG!!!

This is what we heard from the man: "Who do you guys think you are? Are you trying to get me sued?" I guess we were not to tackle people, but the capturing was okay. Lesson learned.

I saw a show on the Biography Channel on Bill Graham and it started with the statement, "If you were not yelled at by Bill Graham then you didn't know him." Well that was my badge of honor that I carry to this day.

Working at these shows gave me a chance to get an education by the seat of my pants watching all the preproduction and show production that goes on as we had to be present hours prior to the shows. I would watch many a band go through soundcheck getting ready for that night's performance.

From that, I carried my education into a life in the music business now with my own company, Dr. Rock & Latin Rock, Inc., as well as being able to manage Malo for 25 years.

The highlight of that career was opening for Santana at The Greek Theater, as well as the next day when Santana played on the streets of the Mission District. I was able to run into some of my supervisors from my Bluecoat days that were asking what I was doing on stage when I flashed them my backstage pass for the day. The looks on their faces were priceless. Days I will never forget.

BETH BROOKHOUSER

I arrived at Bill Graham Presents long after Bill had passed, but his presence and impact were still palpable. From the framed handwritten notes on the wall to the many stories of, "I was standing right here when Bill...." It was truly an "if these walls could talk" experience.

Bill lived on through all those who had known and worked with him, and their tireless work to ensure his name was still important and still meant something profound. And he lived on through my mentor and advocate, Rita, who taught me the importance of giving audiences that perfectly memorable experience, the art of laughter and kindness, and how to professionally deal with the not-so-kind and irrational calls we received from time to time.

I lucked into that place. I didn't truly know how blessed I was when I was hired for a three-day temp gig to answer phones and keep the office going while the rest of the team was in San Jose producing a Bob Dylan/Wallflowers show for Applied Materials. On Friday, my boss invited me down to see the show as a thank you for my work. At the show, he asked me to come back Monday to finish up a few things.

Those few days turned into three years of the best learning experience of my life, full of laughter, tears, blisters, stress, and perfecting the art of making flawlessly straight laminates with no bubbles or fogging, so everyone would have a perfect memento of a perfect night.

The hardest part about leaving all those years ago was giving up my keys to the Fillmore, a place that, because of Bill, was more than just a building, more than just a concert hall. Walking those stairs for any reason – a concert, to set up for a private event, or to give a quick tour - always makes your breath catch in your throat a bit, like you're walking into a spiritual place. You can feel the energy moving through your chest like a series of distant bass notes. I miss that family, that energy, that familiar smell of the Fillmore home.

I'm now the Director of Community Outreach at the SPCA for Monterey County and every day I use the wide variety of skills I learned at BGP to help animals. I traded rock stars for dogs, and I get bitten far less often.

To this day, I still think of Bill Graham whenever I walk through the SPCA and stoop to pick up a stray piece of trash that missed the bin. His belief that no one is above picking trash off the ground is embedded in my cells.

Although I never had the wonderful, life-changing (and somewhat frightening for a shy kid like me) chance to meet him, his impact will be with me forever in the small ways I can make this world a better place, for pets and people.

BILL CHAMPLIN

Musician and Bandleader: 1966 first gigs at the Fillmore for the Sons of Champlin; played the Fillmore West and Winterland up to 1976.

We were working at a Winterland date and Bill Graham was playing ping-pong backstage, as he was known to do. Our keys player, Geoff Palmer, had spent many hours playing ping-pong with great players when he was in the Army Band, so he was at the PX pretty regularly becoming a great player.

Back to San Francisco: Bill was pretty sure he could beat anyone and we almost got him to go double or nothing on best of three games with Geoff on our somewhat low fee for playing the Winterland date. At the last minute, Bill felt that he was being hustled and bailed on the bet. Geoff skunked Bill three times in a row after that. Bill would have ended up paying us double our fee, but he was smart enough to bail on the bet.

BILL GLASTRIS

I turned 21 years old working for Bill Graham Presents as an intern from Northwestern University in Chicago in the spring of 1981. I applied for the NU San Francisco internship program, certain that I wanted to work for my hero, Bill Graham, but also knowing that there no formal internship program at BGP and I would need to commit to moving to San Francisco for the academic quarter having not even interviewed for a job.

On Monday afternoon March 30, 1981, I met with Danny Scher who, after visiting with me, very kindly welcomed me aboard and let me know that he would have me rotate around the organization, including ultimately working in the main office, at the Old Waldorf with Queenie Taylor, on some upcoming shows at California Hall (Madness, Split Enz and U2) with a young guy named Ken Friedman, and helping Danny with a family show – Sesame Street Live. As I left the 201 11th Street office that day, news was breaking that President

Reagan, along with Jim Brady and a Secret Service agent had been shot in Washington.

It's one of those days I will never forget.

Bill was very busy working on the Rolling Stones tour at that time, but one day someone - it might have been Rita - told me that he was going to be speaking to some students at UC Berkeley the next day and I should go listen. I thought it was a great idea until I realized that I would not be allowed inside without a Cal Student I.D. So, I mustered up my courage and walked into Bill's office - probably sheepishly - and explained my situation. As I recall, he looked up from a busy desk, grabbed a piece of stationary and scribbled a note that would help me get in.

Great, I thought as I folded the note and placed it in the front pocket of my army surplus jacket. Naturally, I got sidelined at work the next day and was unable to get across the bay to see Bill speak.

Well, the weather got a bit warmer and the army surplus jacket hung in our crowded Russian Hill apartment. When I got back to Chicago a few months later I reached into the pocket and found the note. I think it was Bill's way of helping me get into the building that I wanted while I was working at BGP. I never used it, but it has hung on my office wall ever since.

Working at BGP was a tremendous, life-changing experience. Before I left, Danny offered me a real full-time job. I had one more year of college left and as much as I desperately wanted to say yes, I listened to the wise words of my mother and girlfriend who reminded me that I was on a more or less full financial scholarship at NU and that if I stopped now I may not be able to afford to finish my degree. I also told Danny that I wanted to go to business school and that I hoped someday to be able to do what he was doing. Both Nick Clainos and Danny Scher had advanced degrees and that seemed like the right path for me.

Two years later in 1983, I was Concerts Director at Northwestern, finishing my first year as an MBA student at Northwestern's Kellogg Graduate School of Management and starting what became my now 37-year career in the venture/capital/private equity industry in Chicago. I'm still investing with a few partners, but also spend a good deal of time as Chairman of Fabretto Children's Foundation based in Nicaragua (www.fabretto.org). I married my girlfriend from back then, and Carolyn and I have three wonderful grown daughters – one of whom attended USC and is managing a band of former USC classmates in Los Angeles called Moontower (shout out to Queenie). Since 2014, I have also owned a live music venue – The Wild Hare & Singing Armadillo Frog Sanctuary Ltd. in Chicago, also known as "Reggae Capital USA."

BILL WALLAGE

I was first introduced to Bill Graham Presents through friends Molly Frink and Steve Rigney. I had finished art school in 1978 and went traveling and stayed in Providence, Rhode Island for a few months. One of the things I did back there was work security at the Ocean State Theater for a promoter name Russo. The only show I remember was the Talking Heads and Pearl Harbor and the Explosions, who opened for them.

When I returned to the Bay Area, I was doing a little cabinetwork and Steve Rigney started being the head of security at the Old Waldorf after Bill bought the club from Jeffrey Pollack. I attended one show at the Old Waldorf - Joe Cocker - back when Jeffrey owned it. I remember seeing video equipment and having just gotten a BFA in Film/Video those images stayed with me when I decided to help Steve at the Old Waldorf. So, when Steve asked if I wanted to work some shows I thought that would be an opportunity to get close to the music video scene and also give me a little extra spending money. Well, after a few dozen shows I started working full-time and stopped the day work.

Shortly after this time, Steve was asked by Bill to go on the Rolling Stones Tour. I became the head of security at the Old Waldorf and later the Kabuki nightclub. I would see Bill Graham at the club (mostly when bigger acts appeared) but just saying hello and not much conversation.

The first time I had any real contact with Bill and BGP was when Ken Friedman (the booker for nightclub entertainment, not the photographer Ken Friedman) asked if they wanted to play the club team in half court basketball. A few of us would play at a court that Queenie

Taylor got for us at the Golden Gateway Complex. So that was where the games were set for and took place. Well, there was a change in the venue and I didn't get the message until late and I headed then to the right place, the BGP office where they had a hoop in the parking lot.

They had been playing awhile and the nightclub team was not doing very well, even though Ken was 6'4" and a really good player. We also had a couple of other solid players: Jimmy Uhl, the bar manager, Kurt Bridgman and me from security.

I think Ken's friend, Chris Seline, played on our team also (I think she played college basketball). Bill was intensely competitive and a very good player and he had Gregg Perloff and one of his stage managers, David McLean, if I remember correctly.

These guys never missed! How could they? Bill would have been all over them. I don't know if we ever won a game, but we looked cool in our Motörhead T-shirts. They had just played The Waldorf a few nights before.

BILLY COHEN

The Boy of Summer Who Stayed Name: Billy Cohen.
Short Job Description: Bill Graham Project.

Started working for Bill in May of 1990. Left to go back home to work for David Graham's company, Music Unlimited, in NYC in May of 1991. Returned in December of 1991.

When I started my junior year at Columbia in 1986, David Graham entered as a freshman. Within the first few days of that semester I was introduced to David and we became fast friends, brothers really. In fact, I'm his older brother in our fraternity. I'm the one who started calling him DG, which morphed to Deege.

I was something of a campus instigator of fun and hijinks at that time. Between being a ringleader at one of the campus's most spirited fraternities, Delta Phi, and being a songwriter and member of the psycho-electric Organic Boogie Rock band, dreamspeak, there was always something going on.

During that time, I spent many of my nights down at the Inner Circle on Jane and West Street in the West Village. Kenny Gwyn and the Board of Directors played there every night. They'd play for hours and cover huge swaths of the classic and psychedelic rock songbook. Kenny was a true guitar god and a fantastic singer and many Deadhead kids from Jersey and the Island and Westchester and all five boroughs were at the Circle most nights of the week, unless The Dead were on the East Coast.

I took it upon myself to bring David and bunch of freshmen down to the Circle to introduce them to one of the great joys of New York nightlife at the time. Bill had his apartment and office in New York. He came to town all the time for business and to be home in NYC and for deli. That was the night and the place I met Bill Graham.

To be honest, I didn't really know who Bill Graham was before I met David. I was a Deadhead and knew a little about the San Francisco scene, but wasn't really knowledgeable about it. Shortly after becoming a Deadhead, I had my own band and there was a lot of other music I was discovering and New York City was amazing, is amazing. I was a teenager at Columbia in Manhattan with a band. So, while I'd heard about the Fillmore and loved the Dead, I wasn't fixated on that past. I was making music now and other people were making music now! I was possessed by that.

Our band, dreamspeak, was born out of songwriting in the dorms and the blockade of Hamilton Hall, where we protested for the university to divest from South Africa to try to end apartheid. The Columbia protests helped ignite the college divestment movement that did help end apartheid.

Years later, Nelson Mandela would say in interviews that the college kids in America helped to free him. It was thrill and an honor to work on the Mandela event in Oakland when I worked for Bill.

Bill wanted to see what David was getting up to. So, he came down to The Inner Circle to check out the scene. It is funny. I've read accounts of that night. It was notable that Bill Graham had found his way to the Inner Circle and it has been conflated with the discovery of Blues Traveler. No, Bill came to check on his kid and make the hang. What he ended up doing was standing in the middle of the floor all night and talking with me. Bill, while being from Berlin, is a Russian Jew. He stood about my height and had hazel eyes about like mine. David's eyes are hazel too; so were my father's. So, there we were Bill and Billy, two New York Jews of Russian descent. We were very relatable to one another, and I wasn't starstruck; it was just natural.

I wasn't starstruck, but I had enough sense to be excited to meet an important person in the rock world and talk with him. I remember the night well. We were talking music, and about the power of music to create positive change. I was telling him about the scene. The kids of NYC were all about the scene. We were on it! We were it! The energy in New York in those days was exquisite.

At one point, Bill looked at me and said, "I haven't met anyone like you in ten years." At another point in the evening he said, "You have the mania." We were kindred spirits, it was clear right away. Then, when he had to leave he said, "Kid, welcome to my movie." That was it. From that point on, Bill and I had our thing.

We had some wonderful times in NYC. Bill relished having a son in college in New York. He loved David being old enough for them to really enjoy each other's company and share the love of music and sports. Bill got a big kick out of David's friends and included us in great adventures.

Bill had David meet me at the stage door to give me Bill's laminate to wear to come hang out at the Atlantic Record's 40th Anniversary Show in the Garden. Zeppelin played. We played ball in Central Park. Bill had Queenie Taylor book a mini-tour for dreamspeak in California, December 1986- January of 1987. We had Christmas at Masada with the Dead. Bill was not like our other friends' parents. I could call BGP and Bill always took my calls or called me back. It wasn't until some years later that I could understand what a rare honor it was to have that kind of access to Bill.

My band broke up in the very end of 1989. We played our last show at the 712 Club, which I booked up in Harlem at 712 West 125th Street, underneath the West Side Highway.

David was in San Francisco for winter break, hanging with Bill and enjoying the holidays with Bill and the Dead.

When David got back to school, he said, "Bill heard the band broke up. He's sorry to hear that. He wants you to call him."

So, I called Bill. Now, over the three and a half years that I had gotten to know Bill and David I had become very close with both of them. I would regularly implore Bill to come back and work in New York, making the case that if he would come back to New York with the way the scene was happening, I knew there could be magic. We'd be his troops.

He considered a few possible venues over those years, but always decided it wouldn't be worth the hassle. I spent a night with him and his girlfriend at the time, Rosie Hall, Jerry Hall's sister, checking out the Palladium on Union Square. It was Latin Night. The place was packed. There was giant band, maybe 20 pieces, on stage. We were up in the balcony and he says to me, "Look at the guiro player. It's all about him." Then, Bill mimed along with the guiro player, emanating machismo and delight, a huge grin on his face. I think he was both amused and genuinely respectful of the player's passion.

In late January or early February of 1990, I called Bill. He expressed his condolences for the death of dreamspeak. We talked about what I would do next. I was booking the 712 Club. He said, "Look, I'm not coming to New York. You come here and I'll show you how it is done."

I told my parents. They had lived in Tiburon from '84-'86, so were familiar with who Bill Graham was. Now, they thought, "Okay, this is a real job in the business." They were thrilled. My dream of my own band, they were never thrilled with. My father suggested that since Bill hired me and I had to move to San Francisco, I should see if Bill would pay for my move. He told me to call Bill and ask him for moving expenses, at least the plane ticket.

I called Bill. Bill exploded! He was sputtering mad; he couldn't believe the chutzpah of this kid who gets a dream job, now he's going to ask for a plane ticket. He let me have it pretty good, though, he spent equal time on the call venting about The Rolling Stones. I was afraid I'd lost the job. He let me know I still had the job, but I could get myself out to San Francisco. He kind of made it clear that part of the heat I was taking was because he was pissed about the Stones. I apologized and tried to end the call quickly.

Later that day, I was walking on Broadway and I ran into DG. He was with Tom Gruber, another one of our fraternity brothers. They were planning on signing Blues Traveler and forming Music Unlimited at the time. David said, "Hey, I talked to Bill. I heard he let you have it." He was smiling. By that time, I was hip enough to know that Bill's anger was a thing. Then, David said, "He's sorry." I appreciated that. Then, David said to me, "Bill's never sorry about letting someone have it."

God, I loved the Old Man and he was so good to me.

A little while after I moved out to San Francisco, Adam Schneider, another one of our frat brothers, arrived to work for the company too. Over the past three the summers, David's friends had come out to work, and then we'd go back to school. I was out the summer of '88. I'd graduated, but went back home in the fall to be with dreamspeak and the NYC scene. Because we worked in the summer and returned to NYC in the fall, David and his gang got the collective nickname The Boys of Summer. The women of BGP gave me an additional name all my own, Billy Buns. I did not bake. Long past the time when I get that kind of attention, it is fun to remember that the women of rock noticed me.

In the spring of 1990, The Boys of Summer were now not just coming for the summer. David, Tom Gruber and Schneider had all graduated. Adam and I had moved to San Francisco to work for Bill. David and Tom were starting Music Unlimited in NYC. They had signed Blues Traveler

to a management deal. There was a big meeting in the back of the office, a company meeting, for Bill to introduce all four of us to the troops.

We stood up at the front of the room with Bill. Of course, everyone knew David. Bill introduced the three of us to everyone, and let everyone know we were now making our way in the world of music. We were the next generation. We had arrived. The thing that has stuck with me from that meeting was that he called us The Four Horsemen. I have thought about it a lot over the years. I guess I am the Last Horseman. I am the Boy of Summer who stayed.

BILLY SAVAGE

I worked for Bill Graham Presents/Fillmore Fingers from 1987 to 1991. People might have known me as Brian back in those days.

Those were the final years of Bill's life and I am still grateful for the small glimpse behind the curtain.

I spent most of my time at Shoreline, but I did gigs at the Oakland Coliseum (Stones/Who, etc.), Henry J. Kaiser Auditorium (Keith Richards, The Dead, etc.) and others. I was living in San Francisco at the time and both my roommates, Slug and Adam, worked at BGP too. A lot of good people and a lot of good shows.

My story takes place at the end of the season in 1989. It was in October, but there were still a lot of shows on the BGP books at all the venues. The Stones were coming to Oakland in two weeks, which had everyone with an employee number fired up. On the evening of October 17th everyone in the Bay Area tuned in to watch The Bay Bridge World Series. The San Francisco Giants and the Oakland A's were about to start Game Three at Candlestick Park. Minutes before they took the field, the Loma Prieta Earthquake hit. It was big. In an instant, it killed a lot of people. Buildings collapsed. The 880 Freeway collapsed. A Bay Bridge section collapsed. There were fires. Hundreds of people were out on the streets, their homes destroyed. In the hours afterward, there wasn't much word coming out of Santa Cruz, 70 miles south and much closer to the epicenter.

I made a decision with my roommates to go to Santa Cruz immediately to check out our friends down there. The main artery to Santa Cruz, Highway 17, had been cut off. We went the back way along the coast. We were able to purchase a case of those silver emergency blankets and boxes of Top Ramen to give away.

Although Indian Summer was in full force, those blankets came in handy. It seemed everyone in Santa Cruz was too afraid to sleep inside their houses with all the aftershocks and who doesn't enjoy a cup of Top Ramen? We stayed there the 18th and 19th. Stevie Nicks was scheduled to perform on the 20th at Shoreline, but we figured it would be canceled.

News reports said there was still no power in large sections of San Francisco. The high school in the Marina District of San Francisco had been set up as an emergency shelter for all the people displaced in the north end of the city. People were sleeping on cots in the gym. There were food shortages. The 'quake had thrown everyone and everything in the Bay Area into disarray. That is to say, everyone except Bill. We got word on the 19th the show was on. Feeling good about our humanitarian efforts with our friends out on the coast, we went straight from Santa Cruz to Shoreline Amphitheatre and on the way, we got an idea.

During Stevie's soundcheck we went around to the food vendors and told them not to throw out all the hamburgers and hotdogs after the show. They had to dispose of them by law. We told them our plan was to take them to the Marina High School. We also told them we'd take the heat if there was trouble with the higher-ups. After the gig, we started hitting the various stations, filling them up into the van. We were getting tons of stuff: hamburgers, hot dogs, condiments in giant gallon jugs.

Our last stop was the backstage area.

We were able to get the van down there (a steep grade to backstage area) with no problems. I popped open the rear doors and was shuttling the stuff to my buddy inside the van. I swung around to grab some more and standing three feet from me was Bill. In the time I had worked for him I never stood this close. It was unnerving. He did not look happy. There were no pleasantries exchanged. "What the fuck are you guys doing?" My buddy cowered in the van as I fumbled for words. "Mr. Graham, there are a bunch of hungry people at the high school in the Marina District of San Francisco. We want to ta…." Before I could finish my sentence, his eyes softened. Maybe he knew. He folded his arms and shot the two of us a thoughtful look.

Without saying another word, he simply turned and walked away.

By the time we made it to the high school, it was nearly midnight. People were awake and hungry. Now they had food. We got to be heroes…thanks to Bill.

BLUECOAT MANUAL

Copied from the original manual by Mark Lewis, 1981 History.

Bill Graham staged his first concert on November 6, 1965. It was a benefit for the San Francisco Mime Troupe, of which Bill was the business manager. This concert featured the Jefferson Airplane, Lawrence Ferlinghetti and Allen Ginsberg, among others.

These early concerts launched Bill's career in concert production. His organization, Bill Graham Presents, now produces well over 200 shows each year. Though the number of concerts is increased yearly, Bill's trademarks have never been compromised: the best sound and lighting equipment, a friendly and comfortable atmosphere, and an overriding concern that audiences get their money's worth.

In the early days, Bill created and managed three famous rock emporiums: Fillmore East (1968-1971) in New York, Fillmore West (1968-1971) in San Francisco, and Winterland (San Francisco), which closed on New Years 1978.

This is where Bluecoats' history begins.

The Bluecoats originated as a replacement for a group of rent-a-cops who worked inside Winterland. Besides the rent-a-cops, there were five "Please People" who cleared the aisles and wore T-shirts that read "Please stay out of the aisles or we'll lose our permit."

In 1974, Jerry Pompili asked David Mayeri (one of the "Please People") to form a larger crew to work inside Winterland. He then designed blue windbreakers (hoping they'd be "too ugly for anyone to steal") with "Bill Graham Presents" on the back, so they could be easily recognized. Thus, the name "Bluecoats."

The original Bluecoat crew consisted of 12 men who were not the typical football player, large-size security. They were paid $12.50 per show!

The company has grown a great deal since then, as has the Bluecoat security crew. We now use between 10 and 50 (and sometimes up to 100) Bluecoats for a given concert, depending on the show and venue.

Philosophy

In order to be an effective Bluecoat, certain philosophies must be followed.

Our main concern as Bluecoats is to ensure the safety and pleasure of the public. In so doing, we maintain a working rapport with the audience. There are two main concerns which must be understood and followed:

The patron must come first; he has bought a ticket and is there to enjoy himself. Be polite and treat each patron AS YOUR EQUAL.

Because of the nature of this job, it is imperative that we back each other up.

We must always give assistance and support to each other.

ROBERT (BOB) BECK

Sadly, my time as a Shoreline stagehand and a member of Jane Sullivan's Fillmore Cleanup Crew was after Bill's time. I worked for BGP from 1994-1997.

One night after a Santana show we were cleaning the Fillmore. There had been a break-in a few weeks before, so the cops were keeping an eye on the place. We had the front door open to air out the front stairwell.

Well, we forgot it was open and at about 4:00 in the morning I'm standing on the steps leading down to the front door when I hear a gun cock behind me! I twirl around to see a San Francisco police officer with a gun drawn on me! I look at him. He looks at me and I say, "Welcome to The Fillmore officer. Want an apple?" He starts laughing and says he was concerned because the front door was open.

Strange days indeed.

BOB BARSOTTI

I started working for Bill when I was 16 years old and a student at Berkeley High, home to the Berkeley Community Theater. In 1973, after one semester at SF State, I quit school to work full time for Bill. I was the Winterland Arena assistant box office manager and I worked the front door; what a place to learn about people! By 1976, I became the general manager of Winterland. When we closed the place in 1978, I began looking around the Bay Area for new places to present shows. We found the Oakland Auditorium and the Warfield Theater, and we began working in places like Stockton, Fresno, Santa Cruz and Sacramento, in all the little civic auditoriums around Northern California.

The early 1980s found us beginning the Grateful Dead camping shows, and soon after that it was all I did for the next 15 years or so. In the end, I was producing festivals and special events with my brother,

Peter. In 1999, Live Nation told us we weren't needed any more as all we did were festivals and they didn't see any future in that. So, we did our last gig for BGP, the Millennium Celebration for the City of San Francisco, and retired in 2000.

I ended up working for Bill and BGP for 30 years and when I retired I was the longest employed person left.

My gold record story: One day I went into Bill's office for something and while I was waiting for him to finish a phone call I see a gold record leaning against his desk. I take a closer look at it and see it is for the Dylan-Dead live record, recorded while we were doing a string of shows with them up and down the west coast. When Bill finished his call I say to him, "I see you have my gold record here." He looks at me with a queer look and says, "What? That's my gold record." I look back and say, "If it was your record it would say presented to Bill Graham. It doesn't. It says presented to Bill Graham Presents. That's me!" He laughs and says, "Go ahead, take it." I finally had a gold record, and he had admitted to me that I was BGP! What a morning that was.

BOB CHRISTENSON

At Bill Graham Presents, I worked Bluecoat security from January of 1975 until April of 1990.

Bands would come and go into the San Francisco Bay Area to perform a show or two. Bill would challenge some of these bands to a friendly game of softball, basketball, or volleyball. Bill would set up the parameters for the game. Basically, the losing team would have to take the winning team out for a meal and drinks.

This story involves Bill challenging the Lynyrd Skynyrd band to a softball game in Marin County in the summer of 1976. Both teams recruited their best players. It was a well-played game. I think there were no errors. BGP came away with the victory. We won by only one run. Then we all headed to a nice white tablecloth restaurant, I believe in Corte Madera, California. I end up sitting next to Bob Barsotti. I study the menu and I notice they have lobster on the menu. I had never eaten lobster up to this point in my life. I turned to Bob and asked him if I could order lobster. His reply was, "Damn right you can!"

I started laughing.

What a day, playing sports with my co-workers and Bill Graham against Lynyrd Skynyrd, and them buying me lobster and a Heineken.

What a day and what a job!

BOB LEVY

In September 1977, Bill Graham joined Santana as they wrapped up their European tour with dates in Verona, Turin and Milan. The Red Brigades, an ultra-left Marxist-Leninist organization, responsible for, among other things, the 1978 kidnapping and assassination of former Prime Minister Aldo Moro, was attempting to broaden its base, and the political climate was tense.

We'd arrived the day before our show at the Arena Di Verona, and some of us went to see Chicago performing there that night. Police were scuffling with protesters as we drove up, and soon tear gas was wafting over the walls as we stood watching the show.

The next day as we set up, walking through passageways filled with summer opera sets, Bill led one-handed, one- legged touch football games on the stage of this magnificent venue. It was a beautiful sunny day and David Zard, the local promoter, had gone all out. Delicious food was plentiful all day, with an after-show candlelight dinner, served by tuxedoed waiters in a cave-like room built in 30 AD.

Arena Di Verona holds 30,000 people, 15,000 when setup for concerts. That night as the arena filled to capacity, the floor was curiously empty. As the first couple walked to their seats on the arena floor, the crowd erupted in boos, with a shower of cups and objects thrown down, as if to criticize those who would pay more for a seat. As the lights went down and the show began, crowds moved down from the sides to get closer to the stage. As armed guards rushed in to restore order, Bill, sensing disaster, moved to the front of the stage frantically waving and yelling, "Go back! Go back!" I watched as the guards looked up at Bill, stopped, turned and walked away. The next two nights, at Palazzetto dello Sport in Turin, and Velodromo Vigorelli in Milan, with protesters intent on making a statement, things would not go that well.

Turin was an indoor show, and we couldn't see or hear what was going on outside, but we knew protesters were rioting. In a book I paraphrase from by Claudio Giacchino, a concertgoer recalls, "We arrived to see a police car burning in the middle of the road, so parked a little further away. Approaching on foot we see overturned cars, police in riot gear coming from all sides; it was an inferno. At the time we were so used to these things they didn't frighten us at all, we just wanted to get there on time. Inside, the situation was more peaceful and the concert went smoothly, only a few brief protests immediately silenced." One protester recalled, "I was in the middle of the fight. We fought those thieves of the concert organizers. We shouted music belongs to everyone. It's not fair that multinational record companies speculate on the needs for youth music, and make us pay for tickets to the show."

The next day while setting up in Milan, Bill was in an animated discussion with protesters outside the locked gates. "You should let us all in for free," one said. At some point Bill replied, "What does your father do?" The protester responded, "My father is a baker." Bill replied, "Tell him we want free bread for everyone."

The stage was set to one end of the oval shaped infield; the venue was filled with people in the stands and on the field. Well into the set, what looked like tire bolts started pelting the stage. Bill and Ray Etzler walked to the front clapping and dancing as if to say, come on, it's cool, lets all have a good time. Suddenly, the crowd parted. In clear view, wearing red bandanas, some being beaten by those unsympathetic to their cause, were people throwing Molotov cocktails. One hit the stage-right PA stacks, others landed on and in front of the stage. Bill started yelling, "Everyone off the stage!" Steven "Killer" Kahn, blankets and fire extinguishers in hand, climbed the PA stacks and put that fire out. Other fires were stamped out before causing real damage. Amazingly, it seemed no one was hurt.

Stunned, people demanded the microphone to address the remaining crowd. Finally the signal was given, wires were pulled, the PA sounded as if it was failing and the evening came to an end.

Later, walking the field, I found un-thrown, a clear fluid bottle in a brown paper sack, thick fuses taped to its side. Stagehands who'd worked security in front of the stage were loading the trucks in half burned T-shirts. Ray Etzler recounts there was one more tour date in

Italy, but flights were booked out for Milan. The tour was over, and we were happy to be going home.

BOB WUY

In 1972, I started work at the Tower Records store in Berkeley, California. Soon after I started working there, a co-worker introduced me to an album called Drums of Passion by Babatunde Oluntunji, an African drum master. The record introduced America to African drumming and I fell in love with African drumming.

Fast forward to 1977. Bill Graham bought a house in Telluride, Colorado, and the first thing he wanted to do was bring the Grateful Dead to Telluride and started the process of fulfilling his dream. So the band is booked to play Telluride and I was lucky enough to get to go there to work. I get there to start to work and I find out that no other than Babatunde Olatunji is going to be the opening act. I'm like, can this really be happening? I was so very happy.

So, show day comes and I'm standing on stage right with Bill Graham, and Peter and Bettike Barsotti listening to Babatunde when Bill looks at me and says, "Bob Wuy, go tell Baba 10 more minutes." I walk onto the stage to tell Baba 10 more minutes. I thought that I had died and gone to heaven.

This is just one of my many incredible experiences that working for Bill Graham Presents brought to me and my life. I will be so forever grateful. A blessed life for sure.

BRIAN AUGER

The first time Bill spoke to me, I had been working shows in 1975-1976 as a Bluecoat and started that fall of 1975 working at Winterland, Cow Palace, Berkeley, Day on the Green, etc., as well. So, there I was at Winterland for The Last Waltz. The dancers and orchestra had finished the opening and the Bluecoats were asked to clear the "dance" floor of equipment, mostly monitors, and Bill is standing on a riser in front of the stage being handed equipment.

I start to drop a monitor onto the Winterland stage, not knowing that the old footlights were there and Bill looks over and says, "What the fuck are you doing?" Of course, I wilt, but that moment is followed by an incredible, historic evening and I now love the memory of it as well as cherish Bill's first words to me. Little did I know that it was the beginning of a beautiful, wondrous, amazing career and life.

Thank you, Bill!!!!

P.S. Also I remember Mick Brigden, Danny Scher or Peter Barsotti saying to someone, "Tonight, a magical evening with The Band. Tomorrow night, Ted Nugent"

BUTCH HENKE

Life-altering moments: I'm a Bay Area native and I grew up in South San Francisco. My dad was in the transportation business and had a contract looking after United Airlines crews at SFO. These were really short rides, and in between those trips, we would hustle airline passengers for limousine rides downtown out of the airport. I was a 22-year-old, wearing a tie and working long hours. It was the middle of the day.

A slightly older guy, maybe 40, breezes by me. I asked him if he needed a limo ride, but he kept walking; a few minutes later, he came back. "You really got a car, kid?" "Yes, sir, it's in the garage," I answered. He said, "Let's go!" He looked a little scruffy as he got into the backseat. As we left the airport he started asking me a lot of questions. I thought to myself, "Oh shit, he's a cop," hoping not to get to any trouble for hustling. He directed me to take him to his office. He asked me if I knew who he was. I said, "No, sir." Then he asked what kind of hobbies I had. "Girls and cars," I answered. He chuckled! "Do you like music?" was the next query. Of course, I said, "Yes." In those days, my taste ran fairly mainstream, Beatles and Beach Boys. "How long you been doing this?" He asked where I was from and it must have pleased him that I was local.

Looking back, this next moment changed my life forever.

He asked me for a business card, but I had none. He then asked if I had a pen and paper to write it down; I didn't. He ended up writing it himself. Then Bill said he produces concerts and asked if I would be interested in driving some of his clients and, of course, I said, "Yes." He said someone from his office would be calling.

A few weeks later, my dad called asking if I remembered driving someone named Bill Graham who does concerts. I said I drove a guy who mentioned he did concerts, but I couldn't remember his name.

The First Ride

They gave my dad a request for me to do a pickup at the Sausalito houseboats at 5:00 a.m. It turned out to be Dan Hicks and the Hot Licks. I drove them to the airport. Smooth and without a hitch. From that first ride, the reservations and bookings grew rapidly.

My early highlights of working for Bill included the Rolling Stones playing concerts at Winterland with Stevie Wonder in 1972. The Miyako Hotel was often used, and only a few blocks to Winterland. I remember Mick and Keith in the car together in those short runs. These one-on-one relationships blossom and now I've looked after The Stones for 50-plus years. Time really flies. We would often park the cars on Post Street and you could regularly see Bill walking the perimeter of the arena.

I remember going to the airport one time to pick up John Entwistle and a roadie. I didn't know who they were. As I was driving them to a guitar store in the city, I asked them the name of their band. He answered "Who." I asked, "Who?" He repeated his answer, "Who" again. Finally, at that moment we understood each other! I look back and laugh.

The '70s were like a baptism by fire of major music acts. The Who's 1973 Cow Palace show is infamous for being the night Keith Moon collapsed on stage, and the backstage chaos. They had him halfway into the ambulance when he came back to earth. Watching that unfold was wild.

A few years later, The Who came back to play some make-up shows at Winterland. Their antics continued. Keith Moon had gone out and about, and came back to the hotel with six naked girls in the back of the limo. He had thrown all their clothes out the window. I am sure there is also a waitress in North Beach that will never forget The Who spreading butter onto rolls of bread, and flinging them to the ceiling trying to get them to stick, or when they dumped a platter of spaghetti on her head for their finale.

The musicians would often ask me if I wanted to partake. "I need to stay straight to keep us all safe," has always been my motto.

I was entrusted to roll with many of the most creative people of the century. Beatles moments included taking John Lennon and Yoko from San Francisco to Big Sur and overnighting there and continuing on to Los Angeles. When hours on the road go by, you see people for the human beings and mortals that they are. Some are really nice. I remember the George Harrison Dark Horse tour in 1974.

Who can forget 1976 and Paul McCartney and Wings' two shows at the Cow Palace? So many of the shows there were big events and included David Bowie, Kiss, Ted Nugent, John Denver and the other acts that were touring in the 1970s.

Most of the time, I felt pretty safe. Security and safety were huge for Bill, and the local police were always part of the payroll. The concerts were getting bigger, the venues were getting huge, as the years went on 30,000 or more wasn't unusual.

The biggest worrisome and tense weekend was at the Oakland Coliseum Stadium for one of Bill's Days on the Green with Led Zeppelin for two days in July of 1977. Logistically, that event was challenging enough. A private charter jet was due to arrive at 1:00 a.m. or so the night before the show with the band, entourage and lots of luggage. It finally landed at 4:00 a.m.

Seven cars and a luggage truck standing by as the door opens and the tour manager emerges, a bloody mess tumbles off in what had been a bunch of drunken violence while in the air. I drove Robert Plant, himself very nice and cordial, and got them to the San Francisco Downtown Hilton. They had part of the tower of the hotel for themselves with a private entrance on Taylor Street.

That afternoon, July 23rd, is one that I will never forget. Everything was going fine. They were all in their backstage dressing room trailers. Bill was always into the extra touches to make the performers feel special. He had carved redwood signs made with their names attached to each trailer. John Bonham's young son, Jason, took the sign off dad's trailer.

Jim Matzorkis, one of Bill's security people, tells the youngster that he can have it after the next day's concert, but the misunderstanding snowballs. Led Zeppelin's own security guy gets involved; next thing you know Bill Graham gets thrown out of their area and they beat up Jim. Zep's manager, Peter Grant, was big and intimidating. He was the definition of an abrasive prick in those days.

After the first night's concert, the limos were lined up and, with a police escort, we returned to the hotel and were standing by. It was a late dismissal that night. There was chatter in the cars over whether they were going to leave town. Bill calls and a car ends up taking the band's attorney to meet and put together an emergency "truce" agreement. Sometime after that was done, the chauffeur later spoke about that attorney ending up in the emergency room for a possible heart attack; he had been sworn to secrecy.

Bill wants me to keep in touch on top to make sure they aren't going to bail. I knew that with 200 pieces of luggage it wouldn't be easy. The tension was thick but the second concert went off without any further incident. The moment the concert was over it was "straight to the cars" for their exit, but there sat Bill in all his glory on a forklift, surrounded by his Bluecoat security. Peter Grant saw a larger-than-life Bill Graham with the parting words, FUCK YOU, you asshole and a middle finger salute.

The next morning, the San Francisco Police Department and the Oakland Police Department were standing by at the private entrance to the hotel and took them to be booked at the Oakland jail for their mayhem. Eventually, we went to the Oakland jail and brought them back to the city; the band paid for all their limos.

Frampton Comes Alive was a big 1977 Day on the Green show, and this is the only time that Bill Graham got angry with me!! After the concert, Bill had arranged an after-party on a Hornblower Yacht. Peter Frampton and his lady, Penny, decided they wanted to go to the Miyako Hotel first. It turned out to be a longer stop than expected. Bill apparently was flipping out. I got an urgent message to call him. He immediately started screaming at me telling me to go to Peter's room and get him in the car.

Thankfully Peter arrived in the lobby. Once we got to the pier, Bill continued to yell at me (WTF were you doing?) I thought that was the end of my relationship with Bill and BGP, but it wasn't. A week later, I saw Bill at another show and first thing he did was give me a big hug and a big smile!!!

I remember getting an invitation to the BGP company picnic that was being held at the Wild Horse Ranch in Napa 1977. It was a big surprise. Bill arranged a limo (from another company!) to drive me and my date to the picnic. It was a thank you for those recent turbulent and eventful services.

Nobody Gets in for Free

In 1985, Madonna was doing the Like a Virgin Tour at The San Francisco Civic Auditorium. While standing with Bill, and Peter and Bob Barsotti (and a couple of other drivers) in the underground garage, we noticed the big roll-up door being hoisted up by hand and about 15-20 young guys running in to gatecrash. We all ran to stop them and I grabbed two guys in headlocks. They took me to the ground. Luckily, our Bluecoat security guys showed up to assist. When Bill saw me after the scuffle he said, "Jesus, Butch get up to Rock Med." I asked why. He said, "Look at your knees!" Yikes, I was bloody mess; my suit pants were ripped at the knees and my knees were a bloody mess. Later that night, Bill came to me and said to go buy a couple of suits on him for my hazardous duty.

The Organization had International Respect; I was Always Proud. I was referred by BGP to the Vatican's management handling Pope John Paul's II stop in San Francisco. My dear friend, Mike, and I made sure that the Popemobile had smooth roads.

The first time I ever saw Bill get into a brawl is memorable. Bette Midler's manager at the time was Aaron Russo. They were doing rehearsals at Bimbo's 365 Club and an argument between Bill and Aaron broke out. Aaron hit Bill on the shoulder and the next thing you know they are rolling around on the ground with staff people trying to do the pull apart. Within an hour or so, two the two had made up and were hugging each other. It was probably an argument over the expense split.

Year after year, venue after venue, I've been proud to be around Bill and BGP wherever the auditorium, concert hall, arena, or stadium is located.

October 25, 1991 is a date I will never forget. I received a call from the production department at Concord Pavilion asking how soon I could get there to pick up Bill and drive him home. I told them I could rush and be there in about an hour to 90 minutes. They talked to Bill and said never mind, that he would take the helicopter. The next call I got was at 3:00 a.m. from Jerry Pompili informing me of the crash and they would need me to handle some family pickups.

Bill was a perfectionist, every detail precise, time wise, with the best people that he could find; not much got past Bill. Different moods, heavy negotiations, happy times, no matter how exhausted, I never saw him fall asleep! Not even in the back of one of my limos.

He would never miss a beat, always saying, "Hey Butch, how's it going?" Everything's fine or so far so good was my usual reply, that he would acknowledge with a nod or smile.

There are so many more stories and adventures that have taken place in my 50-plus year relationship with BGP/Live Nation. I'm continually being told I should write a book. A while back I estimated at one time that I drove and handled over 250-plus bands performing in the Bay Area and nationally.

I miss him a lot. He made so many monumental changes and developments to the concert industry. I don't believe he would have ever sold his company. He was starting to travel and enjoy life a little with the sisters, but it was still his baby.

I have so many things to be thankful for in my relationship with Bill and BGP and made so many long-term friends with BGP and the music industry. The one thing that stands out is how loyal and cherished these friendships and relationships endure. It's rare these days.

C

CARLOS SANTANA

If anyone ever makes a movie about Bill Graham - and someone should - it would have to be called "Bigger Than Life," because that's exactly how he was. I saw him at the very beginning in San Francisco, just when he was starting, and I watched him become a legend around the world. He could do anything and would do everything. He was a promoter and event producer. He managed bands and ran record companies. He put together international tours and did things at the Fillmore with the same focus and intensity as he would do them in huge stadiums around the world. By the time of his death, he was the Cecil B. DeMille of rock, directing a cast of thousands. But he could also be a gaffer or a grip. "What the fuck is this?" he would scream at his people if he noticed something out of place. If no one was around, he'd move it himself or pick up the offending piece of trash. Then he'd go for the clipboard he always had with him, make a note, and move on to the next thing that needed fixing.

I have much to say about Bill because he was so important in my life and had such a huge effect on my career. If I had to bring it down to just one thing, I would say this: he respected the music and the people who made it. He was the first promoter I knew who fed the bands - and he didn't feed them just sandwiches, either. It might have been before or after the show, but he would always have catering ready for all the bands. Believe me, back then some of us really needed to be fed. He created a standard that put musicians first. He made sure the toilets were clean— backstage too.

I remember seeing him at the Fillmore at the end of a show. Everyone was gone from the place except a few stragglers.

He was doing one last round, closing the doors, turning off the lights. First one there, last to leave.

Bill was passionate about music, and he could be profane. I have never heard someone use the word "schmuck" as many times as Bill did. I didn't even know it was a word until I met him. Nothing intimidated him. To him, confrontation was foreplay. He would stand on the street in New York City and yell at taxis for passing him by with the same energy and language that he would use to negotiate multi-million dollar deals for the biggest acts and largest venues in the world.

Bill did not look for trouble; he looked for what was wrong or could be better. His thing was what was fair and right. I saw him argue at top volume with armed guards in Moscow who could not understand a word he was saying. In 1977 Verona, Italy, I was surprised in a hotel lobby by a TV interviewer who wanted to know how I could be so spiritual when the concert tickets were so expensive. Bill stepped right in front of me and told me not to answer that question, then turned to the interviewer and said, "Ask the Italian promoter," who was standing just a few feet away.

Bill continued, "We had a contract saying what the ticket prices should be, but he added all these expenses and jacked up the price." That guy ran for cover like a rat when you turn on the lights.

That same night, Bill jumped off the stage in the middle of our set to stop a riot. I'm not exaggerating. You could feel the excitement all around this huge energy. We started our set with "Jingo," and the crowd started pushing to the stage. For security, there was a line of policemen with machine guns right in front of the stage, which created a kind of DMZ that kept the audience yards away from the band — they still do that at many rock concerts.

The crowd was excited and running to get closer. They wanted to feel the music and boogie. Bill saw what was about to happen, and he hustled out right between us and got down in front of the guards, screaming at them to make room, to pull to the side, to let the crowd come down. It was like Moses parting the Red Sea. He defused the situation all by himself and stayed there for most of the show, policing the police.

CARMELLA FRANCESE

I was hired on March 23, 1993 as the Day Office Operations person by a gentleman named Richard Garwacki after the quickest interview in the world. I worked for the company for almost 20 years.

I don't remember who said they needed someone to work at the office of the Warfield Theatre because at that time I was working at the Kennel Club on Divisadero Street. It was one of the clubs that hosted Wolfgang's Road Show many years before. I went for the interview and was hired on the spot, as I said before. The decades that I worked at the Warfield and the Fillmore were amazing.

Bill had recently passed away, but there I was, floating through his legacy.

As a teen my years were spent getting into shows. You had to be over 18 to get in so I always had to find an adult in line and once inside I had to lay low from the adults. But then there was that one night.

I was feverishly hot and don't remember how I found myself in the front office of the Carousel Ballroom. Oh no! Bill's office! Bill wanted my mother's phone number and said she needed to come and pick me up. If she didn't come and get me, I needed to go to the emergency room at the hospital. I begged him to please wait for her to come from Menlo Park to pick me up. He did wait and that was my one and only conversation I had with him. He was concerned with all the freedom I was allowed as a kid.

At first, he seemed a bit gruff, but after hearing my story he seemed fatherly and concerned. Remember, I was a teen and wasn't really into OLD people. Thankfully my Mom picked me up.

I had the Hong Kong flu.

I continued, though, to find an adult in line at every show thereafter to get in. Bill would see me and just give me a stare as I quickly moved away from any encounter.

The last show at which I saw Bill was Lollapalooza at Shoreline Amphitheatre. James Battle and Bill were moving through the crowd and we came face-to-face. He said, "Hey kid." That was well over 20 years later. After that, I often saw him driving his Jaguar to work on Fifth Street in San Francisco. I worked across the parking lot on

Folsom Street at the Covered Wagon, a dive bar. I would often run out front and jump up and down saying, "Thank you, Bill. Thank you, Bill, Bill, Bill, Bill, thank you Bill," and then he was gone forever.

CAROL SATTERTHWAITE

I started working for BGP in 1989. My daughter, Brooke, was doing security and she volunteered me for the mixer security position. Little did I know that I would be around for almost 23 years, including time at Shoreline Amphitheatre.

My first encounter with Bill was with the Rolling Stones in 1989. I think it was the Steel Wheels tour. Bill was running around trying to reseat people nearby. I noticed he had a small notebook in his hand. He must have stuck it in his pocket without thinking. He kind of panicked when he thought he might have dropped it in the crowd. As I was watching him, I decided to approach him and pointed to his back pocket where he found his beloved notebook. I heard later that he carried it around at shows. Anyway, he was very relieved and he kept thanking me saying I had saved his night.

Another time - I think it was New Kids on the Block - Bill and his son, David, were standing off to the side near me. I could hear David complaining that the music was not good. I mentioned to them that every generation had their teenage heartthrobs. Bill backed me up and told David to listen to what I was saying and I was right. He said to appreciate all music.

Unfortunately, I did not have a lot of time to get to know Bill. He was always pleasant to me.

CASEY JONES BASTIAANS

1979-1988: BGP Accounting, including FM, then Bill's personal bookkeeper and bookkeeper for Bill Graham Management. Worked shows soon after. Moved to BG Management, 1981-1983. Office floater, 1983-1988.

Goosebump People

"As a result of these enhanced neurological communications, Sachs also concluded that people who get goosebumps upon listening to music may experience emotions at a more intense level than those who don't, regardless of whether they're listening to a song or not. "http://www.independent.co.uk/life-style/music-give-chills-spine-brain-special-research-university-southern-california-a8043416.html."

Anyone who worked at BGP knows it can be hard to explain the importance of that experience in your overall life to an outsider. Why you would stay, despite all of the turmoil, you'd just described that day. It was always simple. One of human's most sought-after quests in life is finding one's tribe, and we'd been blessed to find it early in life's journey.

We were "goosebump people," who needed to live life big, big enough to match the way that we felt inside. Big in all of the ways that music made us feel, but often didn't affect those around us. We were the people who sit in the car until the song's over. People who need to hear music really loud, because it's as close as we can get to eating it.

We did groundbreakingly big productions, arrived with big talents or potential. We had big appetites for good things like charity, and for bad things like adrenaline and excess in general. There was big ego, along with deep sensitivity. There were big inequities, including in payroll, which I did for a long time, and around the same crucial social issues that continue to plague American workplaces today.

We had a huge presence in city government and businesses, and resources extended to us, which allowed employees to get a Bank of America car loan without setting foot in the bank, or open a Paine Webber account with peanuts. We also enjoyed employee thank-you events big enough to fuel one's fading resolve for yet another year, including company picnics and parties designed by visionary, non-corporate, ambient design wizards like Zohn Artman and Peter Barsotti.

So many of the people we shared our everyday lives with were larger-than-life characters, with stories fit for books of their own. Doesn't mean we were financially rich or famous. We just led rich lives, often filled with big drama, because of our inborn capacities for emotion and fed by our chosen profession.

More than a few of us were musicians. Nothing is closer to performing than helping make performances happen. Moreover, for most musicians, the likelihood of performing your own music, with Peter Gabriel-level production, is next to nil. If standing on a Coliseum stage and being at least partially responsible for the joyous roar of the crowd is your idea of heaven, this life is, likely as close as one will get.

This same capacity for passionate feeling also led to the deeper love and lifelong relationships that still exist between many of us. We worked incredibly long hours together in often harsh situations. Working for "our lives," because "what would life be like, without this 'big'?" Marked forever, by looking into the same eyes at some pivotal moment in a show, and sharing those goosebumps after a 16-hour day. Trench-bonding.

Back in the day, our work hours took up most of our lives, even though we had outside relationships, sometimes even raising children. This meant that we shared with and supported each other in ways that went way beyond the definition of co-workers. BGP became our family, and Bill was Dad, with all of the subtleties of that role. This was reflected in many of our personal relationships, in both positive and negative ways.

Okay, maybe the BGP Christmas party, the year after Bill called a meeting to suggest that we all do Ecstasy, strengthened our bonds, just a little extra. But I'm not one to gossip, so you didn't hear it from me. All of this has meant that some kind of thread is always there, even though many of our lives have taken very divergent paths, and meant more than running into the people, drawn to Bill, or needing something from him like Dennis Quaid or a young (gulp) John Travolta or Joe Walsh.

Favorite Bill Memories

Hearing him yell for the first time, and fully expecting him to have a stroke. Ha! Knowing I needed to keep my shoes on in the office when he was in town.

Not being murdered when I didn't pay his American Express bill in full, and it was declined at a New York dinner event. "Miss, you will nevah work in this town again."

Bill disagreeing about Peter Wolf's performance skills, and promising to do "him" for me. Sure would have loved to see that.

Forgetting that he was Father Time on the GDNYE float, and refusing to kiss him at 12.

And the pièce-de-résistance: the day he mooned the entire office on his birthday with unintended results. If you were there, you were there.

We were right. Almost 30 years and several enviable careers later, nothing has ever matched working at BGP. Surrounded by people with passions so big that "even hearing a sad song is better, physically, than no song at all." Bill was the last of a sorely missed, pre-corporate, breed, and I recognize the blessing of experiencing what we did in a time now past. No matter where life takes me, I can truthfully say that I've known how it feels to be fully alive, with goosebumps. Love and Gratitude.

CHARLIE ELLICOTT

In early 1968 I was managing the Underground Uplift Limited, which was a head shop on St. Mark's Place in New York City. One day my friend, Ed, came into the store and told me, "that guy Bill Graham from San Francisco is opening the Second Avenue Theater as Fillmore East," and he was hiring. I am also a musician, so I thought maybe I could get hired on. So, I had my assistant watch the store and Ed and I walked around the block to the soon-to-be Fillmore East. We were hired on the spot as ushers.

I worked there from the opening until I moved to San Francisco with my pregnant girlfriend in late June of 1968. After driving across the country, we moved into the "11th Avenue Circus" with the Flamin' Groovies on July 4, 1968.

Bill had told me to apply for a job when I got to San Francisco, so after waiting a few months for something to open up, Bill called to let me know the stage manager job was available. So, I took the job. I left (was fired) in December of 1969 after a bit over a year.

My firing: It was late 1969. The Jefferson Airplane was headlining at Winterland. My old friend from the Village in New York City, John Sebastian, opened the show. After I got the Airplane all situated on stage, I went backstage to smoke a bone and catch up with John. Unbeknownest to me, one of our regular groupies had climbed the stage, nude, and had attached herself to Paul Kantner's leg. Bill found me backstage with John and quietly suggested I might want to get back to my stage. After the show Pat Hanks, the production manager, told me to be in Bill's office first thing Monday morning. I knew it was the end for me. So stupid.

I have many, many memories. Seeing the moon landing on a screen Bill put up before the show; waiting and hoping the hypnotist could help Robbie Robertson make it to The Band's debut at Winterland (we all know that story!); the night the Fillmore Fingers basketball team was founded after The Sons/Grateful Dead concert (that was the night Bill was dosed with Bear's best — so funny!)

Relaxing one night sitting on the sofa in the dressing room with Carlos Santana on my left and Michael Bloomfield on my right while Herbie Herbert treated us to balloons filled with nitrous oxide; the Who performing the Tommy opera with Clapton with Delany & Bonnie, Chuck Berry, Little Richard…oh my.

At Fillmore East, Jimi Hendrix was headlining. I dropped acid and at the end of his set I stood about 5-10 feet from the apron of the stage and tripped on the "Foxy Lady" finale with Hendrix torching his guitar, among other things he was doing to it.

Years later, early Eighties after I had retired from the road as Maria Muldaur's tour manager, and after having a few drinks with Bill at the old Sweetwater, I asked him for a job again. He hired me to work on the construction of the Shoreline Amphitheatre. My work ended at the completion of the venue.

Bill was my surrogate dad back in the Sixties. We had become very close and we both cried when he fired me. Imagine that. He was a deep soul. I loved the guy.

CHIP RACHLIN

Agent at the Millard Agency in New York City (1970-1972); worked with Bill as the talent coordinator for The Rolling Stones Tours, 1981-1982.

I was working at the Millard Agency, which was located on the fourth floor of the Fillmore East. I took the job because it came with a staff pass. Michael Klenfner and I were great friends and were hanging out at a Grateful Dead show one night when we decided it would be a good idea to pitch Bill on bringing the Beach Boys to the Fillmore East.

We arrived at this thought because we both loved the band and we had smoked several very powerful joints. We were under the stage at like 2:00 a.m. when we approached Bill with this "genius" idea. His response was, "Those goyish scum! Never!" They made me count ticket stubs all night because they didn't believe my sales numbers. What Klenfner and I took from this outburst was that Bill didn't think they could sell out The Fillmore.

How and why this next question popped into my head, I don't have a clue. I asked Bill if Michael and I could promote them somewhere else in New York City. He said, "If you are that stupid, go ahead." On February 21, 1971, Klenfner and Rachlin sold out (almost) one show of The Beach Boys at Carnegie Hall. Three days later, I signed them to the Millard Agency, beginning a relationship I have with them to this day. THANKS, BILL!

CHRIS ALLAN

The first time I met Bill was long before I came to work at BGP. I never mentioned it to Bill for some reason, probably because it was a fleeting meeting. It was at the first concert I attended – Curtis Mayfield and Tower of Power with the Barkays opening at Winterland in early 1973. My oldest brother was the editor and sole writer for a weekly paper in Oakland, and one of the things that came with that was tickets to concerts. I got him to take me to the show, and after picking up the tickets at the box office, he saw Bill and chatted with him for a moment. He introduced me and then we went into the hall. Everything that night seemed like magic, set me for what followed years later.

In 1983, a friend of mine was volunteering at the Warfield. She was ushering and asked me to come along for some show, and I did. I don't know what the show was – it was a show you had to work in order to work another show later. I had a great time, met a lot of fun people, and agreed to do another and another, all leading up to an Elvis Costello show.

I kept ushering – doing the ones I didn't care about to get the ones that I did and gradually moved from volunteer to paid usher. Then came a day when they needed help with the maintenance department there, and I said sure, I'd work. I came back again – extra cash was a huge plus – and the third time I came in, everyone else had quit and I inherited a supervisory job in the maintenance department. I stayed with that until the Warfield got remodeled and did some maintenance at the Fillmore the first time it reopened.

Somehow coat check got added in, first at the Kabuki, a few times at Wolfgang's and at first at the Fillmore. At the same time, I was working at a magazine company in San Francisco and doing occasional security spots like at ticket sales lines. Then I got laid off of the magazine company and, with the Springsteen Born in the USA tour, I moved to Bluecoat (BGP security). My first Bluecoat position was front of the stage at the stadium and I remember looking around at the 50,000-ish people and being amazed that there were maybe 30 of us between the audience and the stage. Bill spent part of his time where I was working and when some people rushed the stage, waded into the crowd with me to clear it.

That cemented it – the electricity and the incomprehensibility of the numbers – I had to do more. From there – booking ushers, Bluecoating, working at Wolfgang's and later booking Bluecoats and vendor coordinating for festivals, daycalls, the overnight shift, working at Shoreline…anything and everything I could find. I even served as a runner a few times on the overnight shifts at Days on the Green. I didn't make huge money, but I loved what I did and who I worked with.

Somewhere along the way, I helped out Alan Budenz with his dental practice as his receptionist and stayed there through the transition when he sold it. I also temped and picked up money to support what I came to think as my habit – working for BGP.

I stayed with BGP until 2000. At that time, I had been married for three years and was pregnant. I got put on medical leave when I was about six months pregnant, and then bed rest, and my son was born in October 2000.

Because of the amount of time I was off, when I came back I no longer had my position scheduling people for the Bluecoats, which cut my hours immensely. I worked a few more shows, but the magic was long gone and the job no longer had the allure that would compete with my infant son.

There are so many amazing Bill stories from over the years. One of my favorites happened during the time when he was filming Bugsy. It was Julianna Soumarocoff's birthday and she was one of my favorite Bluecoats. She had been engaged to Bill's nephew, so she had a special relationship with Bill. I had decided to put together a surprise birthday dinner for her at an Italian restaurant on Geary Street that was newish and a little pricier. There were 10 Bluecoats that said that they would be there and I also sent an invite to Bill without telling anyone. I didn't think that he would make it, but I thought maybe he'd send Julianna a note or something. The day of her birthday, I got word that Bill would be joining us.

I didn't tell anyone that he was coming because I know that things change all the time. So when Bill entered the restaurant after we placed our order, everyone was shocked.

He sat down by Julianna and proceeded to tell stories and entertain us for the next few hours. He had a little of some of the plates near him, bottles of wine were consumed and then he left. We sat in a kind of an afterglow for about 15 minutes before asking the server to bring the bill. She said, "You all have a great boss – he paid for it all!" I don't remember the exact bill, but there were several bottles of wine and the entrees and appetizers were not cheap. For someone who lived paycheck to paycheck, it was an unexpected and amazing gift.

Another really clear memory was very early on in my Bluecoat career: I was still the maintenance supervisor at the Warfield, and for that reason, I got asked to vacuum the theatre lobby after a Mardi Gras Parade set up. It was the Dead at Henry J. Kaiser, and they had set the parade in the lobby in the theatre on the other end of the venue, and after the parade it was a mess and needed a good vacuum.

While I was vacuuming, the theatre manager was looming around and glaring at me. Bill came in and they immediately started talking though Bill was doing all of the talking and it was at a higher volume.

My Bluecoat supervisors, I think Anne Scheer and John Kittredge, asked me to stay in the room, no matter what – just keep vacuuming. I don't know what the heck I was supposed to do, but I stayed in that room vacuuming and vacuuming the same area over again as Bill explained loudly to the man that he was NEVER to speak harshly to any of Bill's people again (I gathered that the man had yelled at Brian Auger, prompting my appearance with the vacuum).

Further, Bill educated the man on his parentage and how the whole family lacked the intellectual prowess to go to work for a garbage truck. All said at top volume and interspersed with an impressive number of four-letter words. The whole thing felt like an hour, but probably was no more than 10 minutes, 9 of which were spent re-vacuuming the same area, wondering what on earth I was going to do if something happened. In the end, the man was dismissed and Bill nodded at me with a smile as he walked out.

So many other bits and flashes – Bill wandering into the venue at Telluride during the overnight at the Harmonic Convergence. I was bundled into about 50 layers for the 30- something degree nighttime, working catering, and I heard that he was in the venue, so I wandered out to offer him some fresh coffee (catering was 24 hours leading up to the event). While we chatted, some tripping Deadhead wandered in demanding to speak to Jerry Garcia, saying that he had worked with Jerry on the Yellow Submarine. Bill raised his eyebrows to me, and calmly said, "I didn't know Jerry worked on that project!" and proceeded to chat with him, while I radioed to have Mick Jones or Steve Block come take the man out.

Bill walking out onto the floor at one of our first rap shows in Oakland at the Coliseum to break up fights – accompanied only by Jim King, and then Michelle Frink and I joined them. What we must have looked like wandering up to fighting attendees – Bill in the purple tank top, no doubt, Jim looking like biker Jesus, tiny Michelle with her big cloud of white hair, and me in my overalls. Beverly Hillbillies come to talk to the rap fans? People took one look at us, Bill trying to give them his card and inviting them to come talk to him in his office, and they ran. We were crazy white people, clearly.

Whenever Bill came into the office, I felt like we knew, without any one saying a word. He was a presence. Over the years, I met and dealt with so many famous people - presidents and a crown prince even - and not one of them had the presence that Bill did. He really was the definition of larger than life.

CHRIS CABALUNA

I first "met" Bill Graham after his death.

I was a staff accountant at Burr, Pilger & Mayer in 1991. I was assigned to handle the estate accounting for Bill Graham's estate.

It was then when I learned about the Bill Graham legacy and I've been honored to be a part of his legacy for over 20 years.

I joined the accounting department of BGP in 1996 and I currently work as CFO for SLO VIP Services. Shelley Lazar would often remind me of Bill Graham's motto: "It's not the money; it's the money!" This motto has served me well in my accounting career. LOL!

CHRIS CHARUCKI

I was working in the smaller clubs in San Francisco: Nightbreak, Full Moon Saloon, I-Beam. I knew a few of the stagehands at the Warfield: Tony B., The Captain, Zombie. Eventually they had a show that had a very large call, non-union at the time. I got on that call as a stagehand, did more shows, eventually made crew chief, eventually made head audio, eventually made production manager.

Working at the Warfield made it possible to take a lot of other Bill Graham Presents gigs: San Francisco Civic (now Bill Graham Civic), Berkeley Community Theater, Herbst, Shoreline Amphitheatre, etc., etc.

Rita's Note: Chris wrote to me in 2017 with the above information before his passing. In one of his first emails to me he said, "I never had a lot of face-time with Bill.

I started in 1989 and worked for AKG (the Club Division). Bill passed less than two years later. So, I think I'm going to pass on sending you a story." Then a few weeks later he wrote the above. I am thankful to him for his story and he is missed by so many.

CHRIS McGREGOR

There is probably something meatier having to do with learning the ropes to creating a special and, most importantly, memorable show environment for The Artist under Bill and Bill Graham Presents, or staging a successful New Year's Eve gig under Peter Barsotti that I could write, but all I can say is that's where I learned how to do so at BGP live events.

Learning from the above, I then got to go on to my own glory with bands such as Phish at arenas all over the country, including Boston Garden, Madison Square Garden and numerous massive musical festivals.

I thank Bill for the opportunity to experience all that I have.

CHRIS OLACHEA

I started with Bill Graham Presents in 1984 at the age of 16 as a Bluecoat. I eventually worked my way up to be the supervisor of the Overnight Crew. I would like to thank Molly and Steve Rigney for believing in me and for helping me to become the man who I am today.

Working for BGP was never just a job. Once you were part of the organization, you were part of a family. In fact, being the supervisor of the Overnight Crew is how I met my wife. We have enjoyed 23 years of marriage and counting.

Here is how I have always viewed Bill Graham. Bill was not just a boss. He was there any time that we needed advice or assistance. Bill was the kind of man who saw to every detail of the business. He always assured that the Overnight Crew had the things that we needed to succeed and to be the best employees that we could possibly be. I am incredibly grateful to have been part of such a great organization.

Overnight Crew: Chris Olachea, Mick Jones, Kenny Briggs ,Ken Jensen, Christa Taylor, Mike Thompson, Mike Wittwer, Chris Allan, Steve Bloch, Shawna Olachea, Gary Lambert, Athena Kirkpatrick, Dwion Gates, Rob Lopez, Mark Kraitchman, Steve Barsotti, Gil Olachea, Scott Hernandez.

CHRISTOPHER BOLEI

I'm sure many of us will remember the spectacular ARMS concerts at the Cow Palace in San Francisco in December of 1983. They were a series of benefit concerts for Action into Research for Multiple Sclerosis.

The idea for hosting the concert was envisaged by Ronnie Lane, ex-bassist for Small Faces and Faces, himself a casualty of multiple sclerosis. The concert was billed as the Ronnie Lane Appeal for ARMS and featured a star-studded lineup of British musicians including Jimmy Page, Eric Clapton, Jeff Beck, Steve Winwood, Andy Fairweather Low, Bill Wyman, Kenney Jones, Charlie Watts and Ray Cooper. The concert was particularly notable in the fact that it was the first occasion on which Clapton, Beck and Page, each a former lead guitarist for The Yardbirds, had performed together on stage.

Due to the success of the show the tour was expanded, eventually bringing it to San Francisco. Bill booked the Cow Palace for the show which now included Jeff Beck, Eric Clapton, Jimmy Page, Jan Hammer, Kenny Jones, Charlie Watts, Bill Wyman, Nicky Hopkins and I think Joe Cocker as well. There were probably a lot of other guys who I can't recall.

At any rate, at around 11:30 p.m. Bill came up to me and said to get over to his house to help Tom, Bill's house person, set up for the party. Since the concert was raging and I was in the pit, I wasn't super thrilled. A couple of hours later the vans started pulling up to Bill's house, Masada, and virtually all the musicians and support guys piled into Bill's house.

Within ten minutes a raging party was in full swing with refreshments and expensive booze all around. That's when the word came in that the Golden Gate Bridge had been closed because of the 75 m.p.h. winds! In other words, NO ONE COULD LEAVE TO GO BACK TO THEIR HOTELS. What were we to do?

Well, Bill knew what to do. He rousted the owner of the United Liquor Store on Fourth Street in San Rafael, California out of bed and sent Larry and me down in Larry's truck to get a ton of booze. It was raining so hard that we were going about 15 m.p.h. on the freeway.

Mind you, this was about 4:30 in the morning. We got back 45 minutes later just as the booze had run out and the party kicked into high gear. I remember sitting at the piano with Nicky Hopkins as he played Steve Winwood's new "Arc of a Diver" album by ear, and then later having breakfast with Charlie Watts. The party finally broke up at noon the next day.

And...a good time was had by all!

CHRISTY SHARP

My story, I'm sure, is not nearly as exciting as others. I never had the good fortune of meeting Bill Graham, unless you count bumping into him, literally, at a New Year's Eve Grateful Dead show. I feel I was lucky enough to experience him.

I spent many years working for BGP from 1999 to 2009 at the Fillmore and the Warfield. I will always be eternally grateful for all of the experiences, knowledge, understanding, friends becoming family, and posters all of which, I believe, he made possible. From the BGP holiday parties, late night Prince parties...lots of parties. Just to be able to be a small part of it all makes me feel lucky.

Even though he is gone, he is still there and always will be. Only the strange remain.

CHUCK LUTZ

Around 1968-1969, I worked in the Chronicle pressroom working on the evening printing for the next morning's readers. On my lunch break I would grab as big a pile of papers as I could carry out the door to my old ex-Examiner panel truck and, still wearing my blue work uniform with ink stains on it, drive over to the Fillmore West from Fifth and Mission Streets.

The Fillmore West security guard - it was either Leroy or Smitty - asked where I was going and I simply said, "Delivering tomorrow morning's Chronicle and would you like one?" After gaining access and going up those stairs to the desk where the apples and posters were handed out, I explained to the staff there that I only wanted a couple of posters and they could have the twenty- odd papers. I guess they figured that was okay and I even got an apple.

CHUNG KUO

I think I was only about 16 when I started working for Fillmore Fingers. We were in the middle of the six shows in seven days with Prince at the Cow Palace, which ended with U2 (they broke the barricade in front of the stage) and then Triumph.

Bill had a party at his home, Masada, for the crew and the band INXS. Fillmore Fingers did the catering. A basketball game started happening and I got to play. I only think I got to because I was so young and when the basketball went down the steep hill, I was the one who had to go and get it.

After the show at the Warfield, I was late getting back to Masada and Bill was waiting on the front porch - I think in anger. Well, I was driving the box truck up the road to his home and no one bothered to tell me that the truck was slightly too big to go through the two giant eucalyptus trees on his road. I scratched both sides of the truck and this, of course, added to Bill's anger. I loaded up the rest of the equipment from the party that was held at his home. As I was leaving, he yells, "CHUNG, GET OVER HERE!" I was like, "Oh shit!" But Bill being Bill, he handed me an envelope with $300 cash in it, all in 20s and 10s, and said, "Don't spend it all at one time."

What an amazing man. I am so grateful for all my time growing up in the family of the BGP umbrella. It has made me the man I am today, 40 years later from my first call at the Greek Theatre for Al Jarreau while everyone else was at the US Festival. I continue to this day using the many things I have learned to further my career. I am so blessed for all of that.

COLLEEN KENNEDY

I started at Bill Graham Presents as the receptionist at the 201 11th Street office in San Francisco. I was also the Assistant Box Office Manager under Sherry Wasserman. My first day of work was October 6, 1980, and I ended my work with the company 14 years later.

My favorite Bill story is that one cold morning during the holidays, Bill arrived with Alex, his son, who was about four years old, and promptly plopped him in my lap. Having been a babysitter when I was a teenager, I loved having Alex around me. I noticed that Alex was playing with some handcuffs, but I was busy answering the phones. Alex slid off my lap onto the floor. Next thing I know, my ankle was handcuffed to the desk.

Alex thought this was hysterical. After a little coaxing, I was able to get the key and free myself.

I then took the cuffs and handcuffed Alex to the leg of the couch to teach him a lesson. He began wailing. I stayed calm and explained to him that it wasn't nice to handcuff folks to furniture.

Alex just wailed in frustration. As luck would have it, Bill came down the hall from the accounting department, saw Alex and myself on the floor next to the couch with Alex handcuffed to the leg of the couch, wailing. He looked at me with question and I explained what had happened and very dryly added, "He can pull his hands out of the cuffs any time." Bill nodded and continued to his office.

CRICKET LERA

I was a post-war German Jewish orphan in Germany. I got adopted when I was almost three by an Army chaplain, and it was love at first sight. They already had three kids all about to leave home, and I lived with them in the Presidio in San Francisco.

When my father passed away, my mother became very involved with Glide Church in San Francisco and the pastor was the Reverend Cecil Williams. I guess they needed someone to watch me for whatever reason, so Cecil said, "I know who can watch your daughter. We will drop her off with my friend Bill at The Fillmore and he can watch her." So there he was, Bill, taking me under his wing. I met everybody and he was so wonderful to me. He even sat me down with Chuck Berry after he had just opened up for The Doors.

Years later, Bill wanted to see if we could find anyone that I was related to. There is more to this story - but another time.

CYNTHIA BOWMAN

One night at the Fillmore, Paul and Bill got into it. Bill huffed out of the dressing room, turned to me and said, "God put Mr. Kantner on this earth to drive me crazy."

He wasn't kidding.

CYNTHIA SAMSEL

I started working for Bill Graham Presents' Apron Strings catering in 1979 when I was 17. My close friend, Tricia Holmes's sister, Bettike Barsotti, was in charge of catering and Tricia convinced her to hire me. It was the greatest job that I could have asked for. My passion for cooking and artful presentations now had a platform that was bigger than I could have ever imagined. I learned so much during that time and have many great memories, but one memory in particular stands out.

It was the Talking Heads at the Greek Theatre in 1983 where the band's drummer, Chris Frantz, was hanging out in the kitchen (where all the artists liked to hang out) and invited the kitchen crew to come up on stage when we could take a break. Once on stage, he finished his drum solo on "Burning Down the House," and came over to me, grabbed my hand and pulled me to center stage doing the tango!

After almost eight years with BGP, I continued my career as a chef and caterer. I am forever grateful to Tricia and Bettike for giving me the opportunity and including me in the BGP Family!

D

DAL BOOTH

I can't remember the exact date of this show - it must have been sometime in the late spring or early summer of 1991.

It was Gipsy Kings at the Greek Theatre in Berkeley. I was handling production of this event and everything was running smoothly and moving along as planned. Then, on the Wednesday before the show, my desk phone at BGP rang; it was Bill calling me from Israel. He confirmed that I was in charge of production for this show and then proceeded to tell me that, "The Gipsy Kings are warm and passionate music," and that I "need to do something to make The Greek theatre feel warm," as well. I asked Bill if he had any ideas or suggestions for me to work with. He had no suggestions. He simply informed me that he'd be there on Saturday to see the show and wanted it to be special. I began brainstorming ideas for how to make the 120-foot slab of concrete at the Greek "warmer" but came up with nothing.

Later that same day, I spoke to Dan Choi who would be working this show alongside me. As we were throwing around ideas, Dan suddenly had the idea of doing something with flowers and plants. After this suggestion, the winning idea was born.

The Gipsy Kings' usual show set up was on a large Persian-style rug that only span about 20 feet on the much larger stage. The idea was to build a small forest with bushes and trees stemming from where the bands were set up on either end of the stage in order to fill in the remaining empty areas. We had asked some volunteers hand wire some tropical flowers into our shrubbery to give the stage a tropical rainforest feel.

Later on this afternoon as the show began, everything was moving along nicely and the stage looked fantastic. I was standing to the side of the stage, enjoying the Gipsy Kings' performance, when I feel a hand grab my shoulder. It was Bill. I asked his opinion on our rainforest stage and he just smiled and said it looked amazing. He then pointed to the lady standing in front of us swaying to the music and dancing in place and said, "That makes me happy." The lady was his sister, Ester, and she was having a wonderful time dancing to the music.

A bit later, Bill asked me to have Ken Freidman take some photos of the stage and performance. Ken was unfortunately unavailable (he was at another show) and we had no photographer in- house. When the boss wanted photos and there were no photographers, it was bad news for everyone.

I began frantically looking in the crowd for someone holding what appeared to be a halfway decent camera. To my surprise, I found one and I raced down to the front of the house where he was standing to ask him if he had taken any good shots and see if he would be so kind as to take some for us of the entire stage. He luckily said he had already taken some and would take more so I gave him a business card and I asked him to call me when he had proofs for us to see. He ended up dropping off the proofs for us a couple weeks later.

Nearly a month later, I received a call from Bill's assistant saying he wanted to see me. My immediate thought was, "What did I screw up now?" As I entered Bill's office, he sat me down and showed me a few framed copies of a photo from the Gipsy Kings' show. He told me he was proud of it and that he would be sending these framed photos to a few people in the music industry.

The memories of this show I carried with me throughout my long career in music. I realized that it isn't just about the show itself, but about creating a fun and enjoyable environment for the fans to enjoy and the concert-going experience as a whole. This is how Bill always approached his business and, after the Gipsy Kings' show, I finally understood why.

My time with BGP started in production in the nightclub division and ended in the concert division, these dates ranging from 1985-1991, with a lot of independent international touring before, during, and after. I am so fortunate to have had the opportunity to know, work with, and learn from some of the best in the business that also happen to be great people, too. Thank you so much, Bill, for this experience.

DAN BEAN

The beginning: As a young Jewish boy growing up in Olympia, Washington, my cousin, Dave Bean was living with my family because his father, my uncle, had gotten a new job and had to move to Denver. Dave stayed behind in Olympia to finish his senior year of high school.

Dave was in charge of putting on the dances (live music in those days) at the high school and he really gave me my introduction to music and music promoting. In fact, I put on the first dance at my junior high school that year with his tutelage.

Lucky for me, he also gave me a subscription to Rolling Stone Magazine, which was a pretty cool thing for a 13- year-old kid. In those days it came every two weeks. As soon as each issue arrived at my home, I would pore over it, cover to cover, and that's when I first learned about Bill Graham. Little did I know that Bill and I would become business partners some 20 years later.

I have so many stories about my experiences with Bill, I could write my own book. Here are some of my favorites.

When we became partners: After several years at Concerts West, I left in 1981 and started a marketing promotions business, Bean & Father Communications, to work with clients such as Alaska Airlines and Princess Cruises/Tours, among many others. Not long after that, my former tour partner and mentor, Danny Fiala, came aboard after he left Concerts West as well, and we also started promoting a few shows of friends of ours.

One day, we were sitting in the office (we had a partners desk) and our assistant, Beth, yelled, "Bill Graham is on the line two." We looked at each other and said, what? I picked up the phone and it was Rita Gentry saying, "Please hold for Bill." Then I heard the "voice." "Hey, howya doin'?" Before I could answer he continued, "Look, that fucking John Bauer fucked me for the last time. You're our partner in the Northwest from now on, okay?" I barely got out an "okay" when he interrupted and said, "You better get your ass down here tomorrow and meet with Gregg and Sherry to start planning. Pop your head in to see me first though. Talk to you later." And the phone clicked.

Danny looked at me and said, "What was that about?" and I said, "I think we just became partners with BGP." We were both kinda stunned. It's what we wanted, but wow. Not even two minutes later the phone rang again and Beth said, "It's Rita again." I picked up the phone and Rita said, "Hold on," Bill jumps back on the phone and said, "Hey, you got enough money to do this?" And I said, "I think so," and he said, "If you need help, you let me know and I will back you personally, but don't tell the others, okay?" and then he was gone… again. To say it changed my life would be a gross understatement.

Aerosmith-Tacoma Dome: We had sold out The Tacoma Dome and the multi-purpose floor there is a bit slick. The general admission crowd on the floor had pushed the barricade between the audience and the stage, up under the stage causing a safety concern. We had the Contemporary Security force try and push the kids back but to no avail. Bill seeing that it wasn't working said, "I'm going to grab a mic and have the kids move back." To be honest, I think this would have worked had the show been in the Bay Area.

The kids knew Bill there but not in the Northwest. But Bill thought he could persuade the kids. "They'll listen to me."

Well, not so much. Lots of shouts back at him, really disrespecting him, which confounded him. At one point a bunch of kids were screaming "fuck you!" at him and flipping him off. Bill immediately yells into the mic, "Look, this is okay (little finger and pointer finger up, kinda like "hook 'em horns"), this is okay (same fingers with the hand turned around, but THIS is NOT OKAY!" (flipping the middle finger). The crowd cheered and all of us backstage fell to the ground laughing. A few days later, I had an artist draw his little speech up (with fingers for each part and then a hand with a finger flipping off with a red line over it) as artwork and I had it framed and shipped it down to him. I received in the mail a week later with a picture of him holding the artwork flipping me off. Classic!

My engagement: At one of the Tacoma Dome shows, I told Bill that my girlfriend at the time, Connie, and I had just gotten engaged.

He looked at us when we told him and grabbed Connie's hand and said, "Come with me. We need to talk." I followed them as they looked at the sold-out crowd and he said to her, "I just wanted you to know that Dan has a mistress." My stomach sunk, and then he points to the crowd. "This is his mistress, it's broken up more than one marriage in this business and you need to know this. I love you both too much for that to happen." I was blown away.

The Dead at Autzen Stadium: The day before I was to fly down to Eugene for another Dead show, Bill calls and said, "Hey can you bring down $10,000 cash out of the ticket sales in Seattle?" I said, I think so and then immediately called my banker who started swearing at me. "You could have given me a little notice." I laughed because he knew that's not how this business works, but I said, "Just do it." So, the next day I got on my Horizon Airlines flight (i.e., puddle jumper) not letting them check or stow my bag of cash in the cargo hold of the plane. Upon landing in Eugene, my friend Mark Rose picked me up to take me to the stadium.

Now, Mark is a pretty short guy who loves VERY tall blondes. In the back seat of the car was one of the tallest blondes I had ever seen with him. Her head touched the roof of the Lincoln Town Car; she had to be over six feet tall. So, when we get to the stadium and parked the car, Bill rides up on his motorbike. "Hey, did you bring the cash?" I said, "Of course, right here," pointing to my shoulder bag. I then introduced Bill to my very short friend Mark (who had always wanted to meet him) and his very tall friend. Bill immediately looks at me and says, "Where'd you find the circus act?" I don't know when I've laughed harder and to see Mark's crushed face made me laugh even harder.

Memorial Stadium, Seattle: Rita, I could go on and on but there was one moment with you that I will never forget. A year or so after Bill passed away, we were doing a Santana show at Memorial Stadium together. You knew that they are one of my all-time favorite bands and you dragged me out to the mixing console to watch the start of the show. The lights go out and over the P.A. I heard Bill's voice introduce the band and say, "FROM MY HEART, SANTANA" and I remember as I am writing this just losing it. You put your arm around me and said, "Sorry sweetie. I should have told you that was going to happen." I couldn't even respond because that voice was so instrumental in who I became as a businessman and, in many ways, a man.

DAN WEINER

Agent at Paradigm Agency

I met Bill when he was promoting the San Francisco Mime Troupe in the beginning of the Fillmore days. He always reminded me that I would not let him leaflet the Bob Dylan show at the Berkeley Community Theater. I sold him bands from the beginning while I was working for Albert Grossman Management until his last show, which was Huey Lewis and the News at Shoreline.

I had many moments with Bill. When I first started selling him bands, including the Butterfield Blues Band and others, I couldn't believe how much better his offers were than any other west coast buyers. When I moved to San Francisco in 1968-1969, I discovered that the Fillmore held many more people than Bill had described.

I remember the first time I sold him a band with food and beverage listed on the rider. His words to me: "What do you think I am, a fucking caterer?" He then became the best caterer of any of the promoters. Fillmore Fingers, I believe.

It was so interesting to view from the inside the love/hate relationship Bill had with the San Francisco music community. On one hand, he created a music scene like no other in the world and on the other hand, many thought he had monopolized the Bay Area music scene.

He had many great friends and this reminds me of how much he loved Herb Spar and Jonny Podell.

DANIEL CHOI

I worked for Bill Graham Presents with ambience and production support from 1989 until 1993.

I first met Bill at the 1988-89 Grateful Dead New Year's Eve show, working in the soup kitchen. When we were done, I got my free New

Year's Eve ticket and he gave me Berna Ferguson's number to call if I wanted to work. And so, it began.

My story is from Shoreline Amphitheatre 1991 (I think). I was just hired to fill Lance Miller's old job and was on probation, trying to prove myself over the summer. I had worked the Telluride and Squaw shows and a bunch of insane hours on all of them for next to no money. Bill had this idea that he wanted to mount three Velcro pads on the wall behind the box office building at Shoreline. People could try and get the tennis balls to stick to these pads, and if they did, they could win tickets to future shows. He seemed to really like this plan.

So, we had the pads and balls and we were rushing to get ready for the doors to open for some show - maybe Lollapalooza - and Bill got me to help him mount the pads on the wall. Bill said, "Get some wood screws and the Makita out of our ambience tool box." (They called it U2.)

The pads were not made to be mounted on a wall, so we were improvising. Bill was holding one of the pads against the wall, and I was trying to get the screw through the pad and into the wall. There was a lot of pressure to hurry. And suddenly, the screw I was pushing against turned sideways and the screwdriver bit went right into Bill's finger, cutting a good gash. He was as nice about it as could be; he wasn't mad. We went on to finish the project and he got a bandage and all of that. But, for a minute there, I thought he would just fire me and I'd never get to be full- time at Bill Graham Presents. I guess I'm glad that didn't happen.

DANIEL ORLANDO

I was working at Nomad Productions after I left FM Productions. Peter Barsotti sent me plans to bid on a stage for outdoor gigs, so, we sent a bid on this request and Nomad outbid FM Productions by $30,000.

When Bill got wind of this he freaked out and Peter called us. He said that Bill was livid and that we needed to come over immediately for a meeting. Now get this, Steve Cohen (my partner) and I had just smoked a joint celebrating the $60,000 job that we just got from Bill Graham Presents. We then took off for Bill's office.

When we arrived, it started with us knowing that he was pissed and raving "How can you do this to me?" Meaning, "How can you, Steve Cohen and Jack LaFever who had all worked for me rip me off like that?"

Still raging, Bill turned to Peter who had awarded us the bid and said, "How can you do this?" Peter then whispered in his ear, "Bill, they saved us $30,000!"

His whole demeanor then changed. We shook hands and Bill said, "thank you boys…a pleasure to work with you. I've got to catch a plane."

And out the door he went. Classic Bill.

In 1985, there was a major fire and explosion in the Bay View District of San Francisco, where Nomad Production's shop was located. It was in an old slaughterhouse in what they called "Butcher Town" back in the old days. The fire consumed several blocks of wood framed buildings.

Unfortunately, there were seven casualties. This whole area remained closed and blocked off for many weeks. Nomad was lucky, because we had just moved into 20,000 square feet of a new cement block shop space and our damage was in the thousands of dollars instead of the tens-of-thousands.

Two days after the fire/explosion, as the police and fire departments had the whole area cordoned off, the police came over to us and said, "We have a person who is insisting that he has to drop some supplies off to you guys, and he won't take "No" for an answer."

We agreed to go out to the roped off area to meet this person. Low and behold, it was Bill sitting in his car, waiting for us with fourteen bag lunches from a very expensive deli. Our crew could not believe that Bill would take the time to deliver these to us personally. It was an unbelievable gesture in a time of need.

DANNY JACOBSON (aka Roadapple)

Roadapple is the radio handle I chose when I started carrying a radio as the line control "Pied Piper" at Days on the Green. I chose it as I felt like a pile of shit after working from 3:40 a.m. until the 11:00 p.m. finish. I kept the name for my BGP career of 20 years.

Job: I was a Bluecoat for 20 years, occasionally working front of house.

Date: I started on July 21, 1979 at the Monsters of Rock Day on the Green and continued until December 31, 1999. I worked 1,100 shows during this time while also having a corporate full- time job. BGP was my weekend fun job. Fortunately, I had plenty of vacation time to take off for midweek Dead runs.

Career: During my Bluecoat career I did all the jobs: searching, ticket taking, line control, fence guarding, front of stage, back stage, etc. I supervised all those areas and ran show security. Bill interviewed me for the Head Bluecoat job and Bob Dagitz for Shoreline Security Head. Unfortunately, I had to turn both down for financial reasons.

I love the music, Bluecoats, BGP and Rock Med. I know because I've been punched in the face while working front of stage at the Cow Palace. I was beat up and given a concussion by three drunks at the Allman Brothers Warfield show on September 29, 1981. Yet, I stayed to enjoy the music and people I worked with. The US Festival, Telluride, Seattle, Las Vegas, Laguna Seca, etc. and music, music, music.

Bill: Bill inspired me. If he could do it, clean up, etc., I better be able to as well. Lead by example.

At a Laguna Seca show, I was running the main gate and had all the gates open I had staff for with no reserves. The line coming in was very long. Bill came to me and wanted to know why these other gates weren't open. I had no staff left to call on. He looked at me and said, "I'm staff and there's other BGP office staff standing around." Bill and staff worked for me as I opened two more swing gates, four more lanes and used office personnel as ticket takers and Bluecoats as searchers.

I was proud but bummed one New Year, 1981. I was working at the Earth, Wind & Fire Oakland Coliseum shows, and made arrangements to meet someone. I received a call that I was moved to the Grateful Dead shows at the Oakland Auditorium (Henry J. Kaiser) after the first show of the run.

Evidently, there were issues outside the Dead show. Bill wanted to know why I wasn't there taking care of these things and thus, I was transferred. Bill knew me and valued my work!

Perks: One of the things I loved were the times we got together to relax and enjoy outside of work. Whether picnics, Christmas parties, or sports, we had fun. I got to play softball on the BGP DOGS baseball team in the Bay Area Music League. We kicked butt! I got to play volleyball for BGP against the Deadheads for show tickets, played football for David's car and Wallyball at Bill's place. The shows we got to see when available - awesome.

Sad: At Bill's house, to protect it from arsonists after the office fire; at Killer's, (Steve Kahn) house to keep bozos away after the crash; Bill's funeral and the Laughter, Love & Music show in Golden Gate Park; Jerry Garcia's funeral; the aging Bluecoats passing: Tom Howard, Jim King, Warren Piltcher, James Battle, Jr. and others.

DANNY SCHER

Vice President of Bill Graham Presents March 23, 1975 – March 23, 1999 I always wanted to be a concert promoter.

In high school I was promoting jazz concerts with Thelonious Monk, Duke Ellington, Vince Guaraldi and others. In addition, I produced the high school assemblies and dances.

Then I went to college and managed jazz vocalist Jon Hendricks out of my Stanford dorm room. As a Stanford Business School graduate student, I got the job of putting on Stanford rock concerts. I knew very little about rock and roll, but knew something about marketing and market research. I conducted polls on campus and realized that the type of music that appealed to Stanford students was different than what was happening at Bill Graham's Winterland Ballroom and other venues where he promoted.

I presented those concerts on campus and they did very well, despite Bill not even knowing since I was below his radar. That is, until two months after a sold-out Dave Mason/Journey concert in January 1975, months before my June graduation. Dave Mason was represented by the Premier Talent Agency, which had a long-standing history and reputation as ONLY selling to Bill in San Francisco. I flew to New York during the Christmas break and convinced them to sell me Dave Mason, with only a two-week promotion. Of course, they thought they had taken me to the cleaners, and I thought I had hit a home run.

When Bill heard about this show in March 1975, he immediately called Barbara Skydel at Premier and started yelling at her about the terrible job I had done, saying the sound was terrible, the gates were crashed, etc.

Barbara's response was that she didn't know what Bill was talking about since there were no complaints from the group whatsoever, and in fact she heard that "the kid" seemed okay, was graduating and looking for a job and perhaps maybe he should call me.

I believe Bill called Jerry Pompili who called Jerry Seltzer, who had just started BASS Tickets and was handling the tickets for my Stanford concerts. That resulted in a meeting with Bill and he asked how I did these shows without anyone (since he was everyone) knowing. I said it was very quite simple: I knew my market better than he knew my market. The music that appealed to Stanford students, while not as "hip" as that of the San Francisco audience, nevertheless sold out. My market was the Stanford community and not the San Francisco one.

We both agreed that I should work as Jerry Pompili's booking assistant, but could not agree on how much I should get paid, since I had job offers at Cincinnati's Proctor and Gamble selling Tide Soap, and with a prestigious Chicago advertising agency, Leo Burnett Worldwide, working with the person who had invented Charlie the Tuna. I inflated the salary they had offered, and Bill promptly offered me half.

At the Stanford Business School, we were taught that your first job and pay were very important for your future career. I got the first part right, but not the second.

Bill basically said to me, "Trust me." We shook hands and I took one of our graduating class's lowest paying jobs, but in an industry and company of which I greatly wanted to be a part, and with a person I admired and respected.

My first day as a full-time employee was March 23, 1975, The SNACK Concert.

Within a couple of years, I was in stride with concerts, doing well, and doing new types of events that BGP had never done before: Tractor pulls, mud bogs, children's shows, magic shows, theatrical shows, etc.

Once a year, Bill and I would sit down and discuss my bonus, and with it I would usually go and buy an apartment building in San Francisco. Obviously, he was quite generous and trusting. The bonus was not just based on how financially profitable the shows I booked were, but on how I got along with others in and out of the company, talent agents, city officials, and how I dealt with problems, etc.

Bill's management style was to hire people who were not necessarily skilled in one thing, but had common sense, and could apply it to other business aspects. He would often say, "Do the best you can and if you need my help, call me.

You won't get into any trouble for not asking for help, but you will get in trouble when you should have."

He often used sports analogies: "If you're on the one-yard line, don't be a star and try to take it all the way home if you could have brought me to guarantee it." He also ran the company as a good example of a profit-making company, and a bad example of a profit-maximizing company. I try to run my business and life to this day using the same principles.

I used to call Bill my "yes" man. He would almost always say "yes" to whatever harebrained idea I had, so long as it was well thought out. For instance, "Hey Bill, how about building an amphitheater on a garbage dump and using all of your money to do it?" His response was, "Will you do it right?" "Of course," I said. And, that's how Shoreline Amphitheatre came to be.

I lasted 24 years to the day at Bill Graham Presents. I miss Bill and (almost) everything about him: the way he treated me, his employees and most importantly – the public.

DANNY ZELISKO

Over the years as a kid growing up in the Sixties and learning about music and concerts, one name came up as often as any of the bands of the day: BILL GRAHAM.

I was curious who this guy was and as I got older, I would read things from afar (Chicago) about him and the Fillmore, the posters, the people doing acid tests, the Airplane, the Dead, and all the rest. It was nirvana for a kid like me! The bridge, the concerts in the street and everyone having a great time was for me.

Before I got out of high school in 1972, I made my first plane ride to San Francisco to join my high school friend, Alan, who had been living there a few months. We stayed in Berkeley a few days, did the Mt. Tilden thing and drove down to L.A. for Easter break on the way back to Chicago, as I still had to finish my senior year. I was in heaven!

I couldn't believe how invigorating it was to finally get to California. The Fillmore was gone by now, and other shows would come and go after that, but this was a great accomplishment for me, a kid who couldn't wait to see the Pacific.

Following high school graduation, I returned to Berkeley at the beginning of July with Alan and our other friend, Jeff. Jeff and his girlfriend and I got a one-bedroom rental on Dwight Way and after paying for first and last, I was broke ($300 at the time). My downstairs neighbor, Jerry, was an usher at the Berkeley Community Theater. The Allman Brothers were coming to play, followed by Yes and Edgar Winter the next night. I was licking my chops because Jerry told me he would let me in when I got there (sorry, Bill).

Shortly after arriving at the theater, I met the Allman Brothers Band's road manager, Twiggs Lyndon. He was so nice to me and wanted to help me in my quest to become one of the guys working on shows. His advice was to come round the next day and help take gear off the truck when Yes showed up. So that's what I did.

I got there early, was unloading gear, and doing what I was told by both BGP people as well as the Allman's. I was feeling it, doing good, all day, fitting in, and having my first two square meals in a week or so. I looked forward to dinner. Then Bill showed up. Everyone was happy to see him, local crews and band people alike. Then he got to me. "Who the fuck is this kid?" Everybody pointed at the other crew saying, "He's with them." Of course, I wasn't with anyone.

That's how it really started. I hung with Bill a bit during the rest of the night and got on well with him, as well as Bob Barsotti who was running the shows. I really thought I could catch on with an actual job, but sadly it wasn't meant to be, not yet anyway.

I couldn't get a gig with BGP or even the International House of Pancakes for the $1.15 minimum wage that summer and went back to Chicago, still trying to figure out a way to get into this business! I refer to this as freshman year.

Sophomore year, I was now in Arizona, and met a guy, Larry Hitchcock, working for Bill who was running the Billion Dollar Babies Tour for Alice Cooper, which was going to kick off a couple nights later. I worked the show in Tucson (front of the stage security, of all things) and met Bill again who was later engaged in a fistfight with Alice's manager, Shep Gordon.

Welcome to show business 101!

I got invited to come work the Kezar Zeppelin show the next month, and slaved away in my ongoing desire to catch on. I could do this. I made $50 at the Alice show and now another $50 at Zep's show. I was hitting it big!

By the next year, I had gathered enough money to put on a few shows, and lost the money of course, but I carried on. Bill offered me a gig in Denver, but I couldn't figure out how to make the $400 a month he offered to me work, even in 1974. So, I stayed in Arizona and became the go-to guy to do shows in Phoenix, Tucson, then Albuquerque in the second half of the '70s, followed by Vegas in the early '80s. My company, Evening Star, became a big company due in part to this encouragement in the early days, as well as my friends at Jam in Chicago, who provided some backing and partnership along the way.

Finally, as time went on, I got to co-promote some shows with BGP due to these great friendships formed with Bill as well as Bob over the years. We did the Vegas Dead shows, among others. It was my favorite show to do, especially the first year, 1991. That was the only one we got to do with Bill, and what fun we had. The party in the Beatles Suite at the Sahara Hotel was second to none! Bill made me get what was left of my last cookie allotment from a previous visit to Phoenix that I had left behind, and have it air shipped same-day flight to us in Vegas. He just wanted to see if I could do it, as he showed off a new plate of fresh cookies when I showed him my old cookies!

Salsa music, shrimp, whole turkeys and everyone having a blast after that opening night show. Could it get any better?

Sadly, we lost Bill later that year, but not before we had so much fun in those last years. Staying with him at Masada was incredible fun, noshing at all hours, enjoying our favorite entertainments. Running the lines with the Bugsy script with him, driving in too-cold weather in that damned Mercedes convertible, and many other fond memories that we can't get into here!

Although at that time it was only 17 years into my young career as a concert promoter, these gigs and friendships made me one of the guys, when I look back. And it figures it had to do with my friends from the Bay. I met so many great people during these years, who remain my lifelong friends.

Bill made an indelible mark on my life. I will always think of him in the very best of ways, and smack anyone who says anything bad about him. Without him, I am not quite sure there would be this version of me that I am rather fond of!

Cheers, Bill!

DAVA SHERIDAN

My introduction to Bill Graham was when I came to Winterland to see Jerry Garcia play with the Grateful Dead. I had met Garcia at the Keystone in Berkeley playing with Legion of Mary and we made friends fast.

I didn't like skulls and things like that, so when my friends were going into the city to see the Grateful Dead I stayed behind. I did not know that the guitar player that was showing up early at the Keystone to hang out with me was in the "bigger band." When my friends told me, I didn't believe it. Garcia confirmed, smiling, and said he was not the leader and that the bass player was always the leader of the band. Then he invited me to future shows saying, "Just knock on the back door and they'll wave you in." I started then going to shows at Winterland. I don't really remember specifically meeting Bill though he always saw me backstage from 1974 to 1978.

Often going before the doors opened, my best friend Linda and I would be standing in the big empty hall while employees there put finishing touches on what needed to be done before the doors opened. Somehow, Bill was always the same when he saw me. There was never a time when he saw me at a show that this didn't happen. He somehow would bump into me as he walked by. Whether the room was crowded, not crowded, backstage or on the empty floor. I'd see Bill and I'd turn to Linda and say, "How long do you think it will take," and we'd giggle. Bill would zig-zag across a room and, as always, bump into my shoulder and turn and say, "Oh, sorry," with a smile. I loved his way of greeting me and making me feel seen and protected under his watch. He was always very kind to me and I will always cherish and remember him for that.

I woke up when the lights went out on the 25th of October. Loved Bill.

DAVE OCKUN

My Story and Bill

I grew up in a hamlet on Long Island called Syosset, and I began working in radio from the age of 12. I was a huge Grateful Dead fan. In the fall of 1990, at the age of 14, I created The Steal Your Face Show, named after the Grateful Dead's live double album, Steal Your Face. It aired weekly on my high school radio station, Thursday evenings from ten to midnight. Over the years, I was privileged to interview many rock and roll legends on my show, including my favorite interviewee, Bill Graham.

But in 2008, long after having moved cross-country to Los Angeles, my place in Hollywood was burglarized and the majority of my archive was stolen. It was one of the hardest things for me to cope with. The stories that people had shared with me on my radio show, including some of their most intimate moments with Bill, were lost and irreplaceable. It felt like a part of my soul was taken away from me.

In November of 2014, I relocated to Las Vegas and while unpacking, I came across a couple of boxes and was thrilled to discover many of the cassettes and reel-to-reel tapes from my radio show 3/4, and they still played despite all the climate changes they'd gone through! The emotions I've gone through in finding and reviewing "The Lost Tapes" have been life-changing. It's helped me restore my roots and confirmed why Bill played such a big role in my life.

There is so much I could share with you about Bill and my life being inspired by him. Here are just four things I learned from my idol Bill Graham, both as a personal acquaintance and a music industry legend.

"Listen Kid.. Don't Waste my Time"

When I created The Steal Your Face Show, I had big dreams for it and was determined to land my first interview. But it didn't seem like getting an interview with members of the Grateful

Dead was going to happen anytime soon after speaking with Dennis McNally, the long-time publicist for the band. While flipping through the book The Grateful Dead Family Album by Jerilyn Lee Brandelius, I noticed pictures of Bill Graham and saw his name mentioned throughout the book. I didn't know who he was, but I could see he was close with the band. It seemed cool to try to talk to him about the band for my radio show so I was determined to speak to him.

I called the offices of Bill Graham Presents after coming home from school one day and spoke to Bill's secretary, Donna. I told her I was 14 and asked if Bill would be available to come on my show about the Grateful Dead.

Donna put me on hold and a few moments later came back on and said, "Dave, I'm connecting you with Bill. Please hold the line." Again, I had no idea who Bill was or the tremendous impact he had on music and society! Bill came on the phone and after telling him about the show and how I was a freshman, he said, "Okay, let's do this." I told Bill I needed to wait for my mother to get home so she could drive me to the radio station at school and after a brief pause... I got yelled at! Bill went nuclear and, with a few expletives thrown in, he shouted, "Listen, kid, if you want me to treat you like an adult, you have to be prepared and don't waste my time. Call me when you're at the radio station!" Then he hung up on me! I'm sure you can imagine my reaction: I was mortified and didn't know exactly what had transpired. All I knew was that when my mom came home from work, I told her what happened and she took me to the station so I could call Bill back. That call changed my life! He was so generous with his time.

Years later, I realized I had received a gift during that first phone call with Bill Graham. Being prepared, as well as persistence, was something I learned to be for the many interviews I had over the years after Bill's passing.

Bill's Favorite Grateful Dead Song? It Wasn't "Sugar Magnolia."

My first interview with Bill, which was in the fall of 1990, was so amazing that even though I didn't know who he was before the call, talking to him opened my eyes and helped me dream of what I might do when I grew up.

One of the questions I asked was what his favorite Grateful Dead song was. Now, if you know the stories out there about Bill and the Grateful Dead, you're most likely going to say "Sugar Magnolia." He did love "Sugar Magnolia" and always asked the band to play it at the New Year's Eve shows he produced for them. Bill also said he really liked "Iko Iko." But if he had to pick one song, or one piece when it first came out, it would be "Terrapin."

Following Bill's tragic passing in 1991, "Terrapin Station" became my favorite Grateful Dead song too, as it reminds me so much of Bill, especially the line that goes "Inspiration, move me brightly." In my eyes, that was what Bill was: an inspiration to me and to so many people around the world.

Coping with Death and Celebrating Legacy

After that first interview, anytime I would call Bill, he would either take my call or call me back. The last time I called Bill was a couple of weeks before the helicopter crash that took his life.

The Jerry Garcia Band had a concert coming up in November of 1991 at Madison Square Garden produced by BGP, and I called Bill to see if we could get together then. He told me to call him a few days before the shows. But then, on October 25, Bill died.

Hearing about the helicopter crash was incredibly hard for me because apart from my grandfather, who passed away when I was around 10, I hadn't known anyone who died. Coping with the grief was particularly isolating because nobody I knew had any connection at all to Bill. No one around me understood my feeling of loss.

The week after the accident, I called Bill's office and spoke to Donna who helped me get in touch with many artists and industry professionals who also knew and loved Bill.

On October 31, 1991, Halloween, the first artist I interviewed after Bill's death was Carlos Santana. I couldn't believe I was on the phone with one of Bill's closest friends and such an icon in music. On that call, Carlos shared with me how much Bill meant to him, which only made me want to know more about Bill from those lives he had touched. On the call, Carlos told me the last words Bill said to him: "Stay well, my friend." Carlos was also the first person I spoke to following Bill's death that gave me advice on how to cope with the pain I was going through.

After Bill's death, I decided to dedicate every one of my remaining radio shows in memory of Bill. Over the course of the next three years I interviewed many people about Bill's life and legacy, including Richie Havens, Eddie Money, Huey Lewis, Marty Balin, Paul Kantner, John Popper, Jorma Kaukonen, Jack Casady, Robbie Krieger, the late iconic producer Phil Ramone, David Gans, Ken Kesey, Wavy Gravy, Peter Albin, Peter Barsotti, Ron Delsener and so many more. I was always inspired to hear their stories because it helped me cope with the loss of my hero. I was also amazed to hear how many of them had been yelled at by Bill too! I also produced Laughter, Love & Memories before graduating high school, which was a radio tribute to Bill that aired on two additional radio stations in New York and was authorized and approved for syndication by Bill Graham Presents.

Bill Inspired Me to Join the Music Biz.

It's a testament to Bill Graham's impact on people's lives that the last 25-plus years of my own life wouldn't have happened if he hadn't taken my call when I was just a teen looking to talk to him about my favorite band. Bill was by far the biggest influence on my professional life.

When I graduated from high school, I naturally gravitated toward working in the concert industry. Among countless exciting jobs in the field, I have worked the Montreux Jazz Festival in Switzerland and Summerfest; learned from some of the best concert promoters and production managers in the business; and toured with a range of acts including Barry Manilow, The Backstreet Boys, Melissa Etheridge, They Might Be Giants and The Monkees. I was a production manager in Southern California for Clear Channel Entertainment (which spun off to become Live Nation) and a promoter representative on shows of all sizes and magnitudes from stadiums and arena to amphitheaters and clubs with everyone from Barbra Streisand to U2.

Following being a local rep, I became the Production Manager of North America Touring for Live Nation until the end of 2010. I oversaw production and operations for dozens of arena radio shows for the Pacific Concert Group and was Director of Production at the historic Capitol Theater in Port Chester, New York. I had the opportunity while at The Cap to reconnect very closely with the Grateful Dead community and had two photos of Bill in my office. Recently, I move back to Los Angeles where I formed my own company, Platinum Road, offering production services to major and independent promoters. I also currently tour manage the cast of the television show Schitt's Creek.

Throughout my career, Bill has always remained my inspiration and always will. Even when I'm working on shows today and I have the authority to decide the walk-out music, most times I'll choose the traditional folk song "Greensleeves" in honor of Bill.

There are also so many shows when I'll look out at the crowd and see thousands of people having the best time and I feel proud to have played a small part in creating that moment. Many times I'll look up and silently say in my mind, "Thank You, Bill."

Whenever I find myself in the Bay Area and time allows I visit Bill at his final resting home and pay my respects. I know my life would have taken such a different course and have no idea what I'd be doing today if it wouldn't have been for Bill. Inspiration move me brightly.

DAVID E. SMITH

David E. Smith, M.D.
Founder, Haight Ashbury Free Medical Clinic – June 7, 1967
I first met Bill Graham in June, 1967 soon after I founded the Haight Ashbury Free Clinic during the tumultuous Summer of Love.

Bill had read science writer David Perlman's article in the San Francisco Chronicle entitled, "Medical Mission in the Haight," and noted that we were providing medical care to many of the young people attending concerts at The Fillmore. I, of course, knew of the great music at The Fillmore, having attended concerts there after hearing the Grateful Dead and other bands play in the Panhandle in Golden Gate Park.

Bill told me, "You're a good cause," and organized benefits that allowed us to survive that first summer when we were an all-volunteer organization and received no official financial support. The most memorable was a benefit at the Fillmore at which he introduced me to Janis Joplin and Grace Slick.

Over the years, in times of crisis and expansion in response to the growing speed and heroin crisis, Bill was always there for us, putting together the Creedence Clearwater benefit and the George Harrison concert at the Cow Palace in San Francisco, which provided about a year's worth of funding for the clinic in 1991. When Bill passed we renamed a detox facility the Bill Graham Center for Health and Recovery in his honor.

Because Vietnam War veterans were coming home addicted to heroin and showing up at our clinic for treatment, we started receiving government support and as a result in 1972 achieved a degree of financial stability.

Soon after, Bill asked Dr. George "Skip" Gay and myself to create a program to provide medical and crisis intervention (i.e., bad trip talk down) services that became Rock Medicine. Its first concerts were the Grateful Dead and Led Zeppelin shows on back-to-back weekends in May 1973.

Rock Medicine provides services at over 1,000 concerts and other events annually with more than 3,000 volunteers. We still maintain medical services at the Fillmore where it all started.

The Haight Ashbury Free Medical Clinic merged with Walden House in 2011. Forming HealthRIGHT 360 the following year, they have gone on to serve over two million clients visit based on the founding principle that "health care is a right not a privilege," a major focus in both health care reform and the field of addiction medicine.

In a very real sense the Haight Ashbury Free Medical Clinic was a clinic built on rock and roll and owes a great debt to Bill Graham.

Bill was always very supportive of me and I agreed with his social philosophy in support of the underdog. I am very happy to share these positive social action memories to complement those of Bill's involvement in the music world for which he is best known.

DAVID FREY

Bluecoat, 1980-1988

I started working for BGP during the yearly Grateful run at year-end 1980. The shows were at the same venue that I saw the Ringling Bros. and Barnum & Bailey Circus as a kid, the old Oakland Auditorium. Appropriate, no? I sat at one of many exit doors along the hallway. Nothing exciting happened, but it was my first Dead show and my introduction to Dead Dancing. And I got paid, all was good.

I didn't work again until spring. The show was the Plasmatics, a punk bank from New York fronted by Wendy O. Williams, a former porn star. The venue was the Longshoreman's Hall near Fisherman's Wharf. It was my first experience seeing Bill go ballistic. The doors opened on time, but there was still no band in sight. They eventually showed up and did their "in" while the audience watched the band act as their own roadies.

During this Bill showed up dressed in a tux for something else, saw what was going on, the show was really late by then and went off on the band. It was kind of funny seeing these scary, bizarre looking punk rockers getting dressed down by Bill in a tux. If they had had tails they would have been between their legs. That was my real introduction to working for BGP. Incidentally, I don't believe we ever did another show at that venue, not during the '80s anyway.

As the year came to summer, Days on the Green started cranking up. I was called back again to work those and that is also when my wife, Cathy, started working shows too. For the most part I worked at a gate between stage access backstage area. It was my first experience working directly with the artists and the tour security people. One head of security that I enjoyed working with was a fellow by the name of James Callaghan. He was the best, so he was employed by the best, the Rolling Stones, the Who and other big names. The greatest challenge in the tunnel was limiting stage access. The rule was when a band was playing their set, they had full access and they could bring guests onto the stage. Once your set was done you no longer had stage access unless it was through a band higher up on the bill. This led to a number of heated conversations and bruised egos. The headliner had last say regarding stage access and James Callaghan told many a rock star "no." Those were long days.

DAVID GANS

When the Grateful Dead played at the Henry J. Kaiser Auditorium, the San Francisco Civic or the Oakland Coliseum, the Bill Graham Presents people usually conducted a volleyball tournament before the show, pitting Deadhead teams against each other and then against a BGP team headed by Bill himself.

At the Coliseum in December 1986 I was drafted onto the BGP team for a decisive game, the prize being a handful of coveted New Year's Eve GD tickets. Being a good sport and a game dude, I played. I had a good time. I didn't commit any really egregious errors, but I'm not very fast and so I wasn't exactly a spark plug. Our side lost. Bill HATED to lose.

I went back to hanging out with my pals, and for a good half hour after the loss Bill Graham and Peter Barsotti stood on the sound platform in intense dialogue. Later that night Peter's wife, Bettike, told me Bill had yelled at Peter for bringing me into the game.

And that's how I became a verb. The next day when I arrived at the Coliseum a BGP person (I forget who) said to me, "Don't Gans me, man," and giggled.

P.S. I had a GREAT time working with Peter and Bill on audio montages for the midnight festivities on New Year's Eve 1986, 1987 and 1988.

DAVID GRAHAM

My favorite work experience with BGP was in Moscow on July 4th, 1987.

Sometime in the Spring of 1987, my Dad was contacted by the organizers of the "American Soviet Walk," which originated in what was then known as Leningrad and ended in Moscow. The marchers included 200 American and 200 Russian citizens protesting the proliferation of nuclear weapons.

Dad was asked if he could stage a concert to commemorate the end of their journey. Not only was it extremely short notice, but it was only a couple of years into the presidency of Mikhail Gorbachev and still two years before the fall of the Berlin Wall. And, the walk was going to end a week earlier than planned.

The job was nearly impossible and required a series of minor miracles. So, of course, Dad said yes.

In what seemed like the blink of an eye, Dad got Santana, James Taylor, Bonnie Raitt, and the Doobie Brothers to agree to join Russian artists to perform in a stadium in Moscow. The entire American contingent boarded an Aeroflot jet, embarking on a mysterious trip to the unknown.

To properly prepare for the show, nearly everything had to be trucked in. Staging, food, crews (mostly from Hungary)

Though we had an elite skeleton crew from BGP, Dad had to rely on this "outside" help as well as the cooperation of the local authorities. There didn't seem to be too many issues that didn't require negotiations. Some things just had to accepted.

Though the capacity was much larger, only 25,000 tickets were to be distributed. And despite Dad's insistence that tickets be distributed to average citizens, it was clear that they would be given to "connected" people.

Still, it didn't take long for the site to feel like a genuine BGP outpost. Bill was in his constant whirlwind with Jan Simmons valiantly trying to keep him to a low roar. Peter and Bob Barsotti were working their usual magic putting together all the pieces to the production puzzle. Bettitke Barsotti's motherly presence set the perfect communal tone. Plus, she kept us all fed with recognizable food-a godsend for western snobs like me. Ken Friedman beautifully captured the goings on. Alvinia Bridges handled the PR with her customary grace. Ray Etzler and Arnie Pustilnik joined the Santana crew. It was truly a family affair.

It turned out that my gig was easier that I would've guessed.

I was tasked with finding and setting up basketball and/or volleyball courts. I distinctly recall a rather comical meeting with the powers that be when we suggested this in one of the stadium "boxes". To say they were a bit dumbfounded would be an understatement. But like many other requests, after some wrangling, the thumbs-up was given.

After days of great hustle and organization, the concert was set. On the scrim behind the stage was a large tic-tac-toe "board" painted with missiles (as the X's) playing against the earth (as the O's). There was one space left empty on the lower left. The caption on each side read "OUR MOVE", one in English and one in Russian. When people began filing in, Russian troops in full uniform formed a long line preventing the crowd from getting close to the stage.

Clearly this wasn't going to work for Dad. In typical style he diffused the situation and the guards relented. Given his history, I can't imagine what Dad was feeling throughout this trip.

Once the music began, it felt as close to a regular show as possible. After some hesitation, people started playing a little ball. It began as a surreal experience for all involved, but as the music went on, it felt more right and real. Regardless of how many and who they were, once the crowd realized it was OK, everyone started to truly enjoy the spirit of a rock concert.

As the show came to a close, after hours of American and Russian jamming, all the musicians joined together on stage to play "Listen To The Music." Everyone was smiling, everyone was dancing. Lots of people were crying. On stage and off.

At one point, Dad handed me a big round picture of the earth. I held it high above my head, showing it to the audience as I walked along the front of the stage. I stepped behind the drum riser and put the earth in the open spot to take the game.

The Earth wins!!!

Clearly, we saved the world that day. I realized not much later that this was a common occurrence for the folks at BGP. Miracles large and small were just part of the program. Nearly every day, at every concert, whether by Rock Med, the production staff or the Bluecoats, someone's life was saved – at times quite literally. And innumerable times perfect nights were made.

This is an astonishing gift that BGP gave to its community and in this case, the world. Of all the incredible things that Dad accomplished, I believe he'd say he was most proud of the people at BGP.

At the end of the Moscow trip there were multiple reports of a small group of Americans laughing and dancing around Red Square exhibiting "unusual revelry." All accounts of this incident, however, are classified and heavily redacted.

DAVID JENSEN

I only had one encounter with Bill, and it was a CLASSIC BILL ENCOUNTER!

Back in 1985 Bill was planning his 20th Anniversary Party at the Fillmore. I think I read about it in the Chronicle newspaper, probably an article by Joel Selvin. I had been volunteering for the BAM Archives and the BAMMIES Awards show for a few years working with the late Paul Grushkin. I asked Paul to get me on the volunteer list and he did.

Showed up that afternoon to get my assignment. I met James Olness for the first time, and he had just finished framing all of the posters that now hang on the walls. My job was to circulate and just make sure none of the posters disappeared.

Then we all broke for the dinner break and I got my tray full of goodies and headed for the side balcony of the venue. All the tables close to the edge were marked RESERVED. For whatever VIPs would be showing up. But it was early, so I sat down at the first one nearest to the door. Some other volunteers came around and pointed out that I was at a reserved table but did NOT make me move. The Bluecoats would not have been so generous. I was having a great time by myself, enjoying the view of people just arriving for the festivities.

I looked down and Bill came in on the main floor, escorting the older couple that owned the building. Somehow, I knew this, but don't ask me how or why. And then Bill looked up straight in my direction and was obviously telling the couple, "And that is your reserved table." And there I was! Holy shit! Big trouble! I could see it in his eyes!!!

But here is the Classic Bill part. He immediately left the main room, but there were fifty other people he could have sent upstairs to toss me off that table…but, of course, he came up himself to confront me as I was already moving away from the danger zone. The good news is that he did not toss me out or ask me who had put me on the volunteer list (Grushkin would generate his own problems later.)

It ended up being a beautiful night for memories and music. James and I (and Ed Perlstein) would continue to work on the archives through the '90s before they got transferred to the Museum of Performance + Design where I now volunteer. Ironically, James and I visited BGP on the morning of the helicopter crash, can't even remember why, but then we all woke up to the sad news.

DAVID KOHLS

I grew up an hour's drive east of San Francisco during the Fifties and the Sixties in Stockton, California. After graduating high school and moving out on my own in 1967, I spent much time immersed in the San Francisco hippie/music scene.

Bill Graham events and venues became my "home away from home" where I often saw and admired Bill from a distance.

He was an icon of our times. Literally everyone in the late '60s and '70s knew of him. I am honored to be able to say that in the last five years of his life he became a personal friend.

Years, life, and travels passed beyond my youth until I ended up living in Portland, Oregon in the eighties. As a musician in the Northwest music scene, I was pretty much surfing the bottom of the barrel, driving school buses, working in local staging, music and theater crews and living out of my car. Then in 1986, I started working as a roadie for a local up-and-coming band called the Dan Reed Network. Dan Reed eventually signed to Bill Graham Management (BGM) and I began to know Bill as my employer.

In 1987, the DRN recorded their first record at Little Mountain Studios in Vancouver, BC which was released as touring began in early 1988. The European tour ended in November of 1988 at the Marquee in London. So, since we were touring abroad during the Thanksgiving holiday, Bill took the entire entourage out for dinner at a fine up-tempo restaurant in the Kensington District. I sat next to Bill as we all gathered around a long banquet table where the food, drink and fellowship ran abundant. A good time was had by all.

As we left the restaurant to return to our hotel, we were one seat short in the three cabs summoned, so I volunteered to be the odd person out. "I have dreamt most of my life of someday going to England, the land of the Beatles and the Stones, Sherlock Holmes, royalty, fog, Jack the Ripper and so much more," I remarked. "Now I am here for my final night. Tomorrow I fly home and who knows when or if I will ever get to return.

It's a cool, beautiful evening, perfect for walking, so I think I'd just like to wander back to the hotel, enjoy the night and savor the experience." Bill, standing next to me smiled and said, "David my friend, you are absolutely right. It is a beautiful night for a stroll. May I join you in your wander?"

We then walked back to the hotel through Hyde Park and the streets for over two hours discussing our lives and the business. This was the night Bill Graham and I became friends. The last time we spoke was at the 1990 BGM/BGP Christmas party at The Warfield Theater, months before he passed away.

After this tour, Bill called me and suggested that I move to San Francisco where he could keep me working all the time. This I did and he put me on the crews of Eddie Money, Jefferson Airplane, Joe Satriani, Carlos Santana, Tom Petty & The Heartbreakers and many, many more. The work flowed and our friendship grew. I made many good friends both in management and the workforce. My years with BGP/BGM felt more like family than business.

Bill was an amazing man, firmly deserving of the niche he's carved in history. In those years he taught me much about work ethics, the business of show, and the ability to keep your head above water in all matters of life.

He was my hero in my youth and as an adult. I will be forever grateful for the fortune of his friendship in my life.

DAVID LEVINSON

I worked in the production and ambience departments, working many Grateful Dead shows. I worked for BGP in 1985 and 1986. I then became a union stagehand and have worked alongside BGP people even up to today, and I'm still working at Shoreline Amphitheatre.

I remember Bill having us put the final touches on the Shoreline Amphitheatre days before it opened with the act of Julio Iglesias. Bill spent the night before it opened going up and down the venue.

Late, about 2:00 a.m., the night before we opened he had us install lighting on the top of the amphitheatre bowl. I remember how late it was and how we all looked at each other, like are you insane? But, of course, Bill was "The Boss," so we did that and more.

DAVID MARTIN

In April of 1971, I was an 18-year-old senior soon to graduate from Acalanes High School located in the suburbs east of San Francisco. I was also the entertainment columnist for the school's Blueprint newspaper, keeping students informed of stories and events pertaining to their Bay Area neighborhood. I had learned guitar from an early age and was already playing clubs, school gymnasiums and outdoor shows with my originals garage band. Because of this music passion, I had frequented many concerts over the past 12 years, the absolute best being produced by Bill Graham.

I considered Bill a larger than life superstar ranked right up there with the musical stars he presented every week at different venues in the San Francisco Bay Area and New York City. Bill Graham Presents was arguably the most industrious, imaginative, and famous promoter in popular music during this era. I would often see Mr. Graham at the Fillmore West, Winterland, Berkeley Community Theater and the Civic Auditorium but was too shy to ever approach him. He would always be a whirlwind interacting with the concert- goers, and I would alternately observe the nice, warm, smiling Bill Graham, and at other times observe the angry, ferocious, in- your-face presence he could personify. If I saw his Jaguar XKE convertible parked near a venue, I was always excited that. He was in the house.

Like many people, I was shocked and heartbroken when Bill announced on April 29, 1971 that he was closing the beloved Fillmore West in San Francisco and Fillmore East in New York where incredible headline acts of all musical styles have been booked weekly for years. He also announced that he was retiring from the business (for a while) citing increased greed and declining professional standards that were "dues to be paid…no longer worth the game."

After digesting the news all weekend, I somehow got up the nerve and decided I would call the BGP office on Monday afternoon to interview Bill Graham for my high school newspaper! After getting home from school and successfully researching the office phone number with the operator, I set up a cassette tape recorder directly alligator clipped to my parents extension bedroom phone. With shaking hands, I called the BGP office, asked to speak to Bill Graham and told the receptionist I was a columnist from the Acalanes High School newspaper. When I was put on hold, I turned on the second phone tape recorder - just in case - NEVER believing Mr. Graham would have the time or interest to take my teenage angst-ridden phone call. A nearly irrelevant question was that if he actually took my call, would it be the charming or angry version of the man I had seen so many times at his produced shows.

Within a minute, to my utterly disbelieving ears, I heard the distinctive east coast accented baritone voice of THE BILL GRAHAM on the line. HOLY SMOKES! NOW WHAT!! Somehow, without prepared questions, I got up the nerve to ask Mr. Graham about his life-changing decision (personally and professionally), and went into depth about the reasons for his leaving the business, closing his very successful venues, and what plans he might have for the future. I shared with him what his work had meant to me – a kid from the San Francisco suburbs - and all the while during the call, the charming version of this famous music impresario never made me feel like I was unimportant or a waste of his time. Maybe 25 minutes later, THE BILL GRAHAM was still treating me like a valued reporter from the New York Times! I thanked Bill for his kindness in taking my call, answering my questions, and we finally cordially said farewell. I hung up the phone and the youthful adrenaline racing through my veins was about to make my body blow up! I could not believe whom I had just spoken to – and that I pulled off the dreamed of vision.

Later that week, I wrote the "Aardvark" column for the school paper about the Fillmore closings. Even though I had scored such an amazing scoop, I didn't have the editorial space allotment to write up three-fourths of the things Bill and I had discussed. Little did I know that Mr. Graham's short retirement would be followed by changing the course and direction of concert production, crowd assemblage, sound and lighting quality, staging innovation, new venue use, design, construction; world tour management, merchandising and business redefinition, and eventually a totally refined re-imagination of the golden era modern music and entertainment business.

On that Monday back in 1971, I was given the gift of an act of kindness, respect, and generosity from one of the most important figures in the music business from 1965 until his untimely passing in 1991. I was given the gift of proof that many things are possible beyond our expectations.

I was given a memory I will ALWAYS remember, and oh yes, there still is a cassette recording of my conversation with THE BILL GRAHAM stored away in an old shoe box. I will always be grateful.

DAVID McLEAN

I was a stage manager at Bill Graham Presents. My first show was Frank Zappa/Weather Report at Winterland December, 1972. My last show was the Grateful Dead at Oracle Arena, December 31, 1990.

Around 1980, give or take a year or two, Bill had two tickets to the Warriors game and asked me if I would like to go with him. I said yes, as I normally would and so we were set to go to the game. After the office closed and Bill and I were the only ones left in the building, I asked him about his experience getting away from the clutches of the Nazis and coming to the United States.

Now, at this time I had been working for Bill for about eight years and I knew he did not really like talking about those experiences; however, I knew that he knew that I had lived in Germany for six years and that I had studied that period of German history with much interest and so he opened up to me.

The conversation was very interpersonal and touching. Now, one can hear Bill talk about those experiences in interviews on YouTube. Back then it was a rare occasion when he would talk about that time in his life: getting out of Europe, being sick and stuck on Ellis Island, being rejected by prospective foster parents because of his frailty and how those experiences shaped his later life.

For me, it was a most revealing and enjoyable moment in my relationship with Bill.

DAVID RUBINSON

I met Bill in 1965. I was planning to present the SF Mime Troupe's Minstrel Show in New York, and of course, I had to meet their Business Manager who picked me up in an old green Volkswagen and drove me to San Jose. I wanted to see the show, meet the Artistic Director (the radical genius) Ronnie Davis, and to watch them again get busted for obscenity.

By the time I actually brought the troupe to New York's Town Hall (sold out), Bill had quit, transforming from a Belligerent Bronx Jew who raised a few bucks doing benefits into—BILL GRAHAM.

I was in the studio in New York and a call came through from the Columbia Records switchboard that a certain Bill something was on the phone urgently. Huh?

He was calling because I had made a hit with the song Hey Joe by the singer Tim Rose which was #1 on KFRC in San Francisco, which was the biggest top 40 radio station in town.

Bill said that he wanted to book Tim, so he had gone out and bought the record and there was my name on the label. Was that ME? Yes, I said. So, he booked Tim and we kept in contact. The same thing happened with the Chambers Brothers with the song Time Has Come Today. Bill calls, Is that ME? Well, WTF!

I went into business partnership with Bill in 1969 – The Fillmore Corporation.

Big mistake. Bill being a BBJ and me being a BBJ (Brooklyn) made it karmically and comically doomed from the get-go. Once we got our testosterone-poisoned-dick waving out of the way, we became friends and collaborators. I produced Santana and built careers with Herbie

Hancock and the Pointer Sisters, which was when Bill to accept me as a peer. Bill did not consider anyone as an equal. He had slaves and enemies.

No equals.

One day years later when Bill was just 50 (so it would have been January 1981), Bill and I were at the Automatt, the recording studio in San Francisco where Santana was recording; I was in my office and Bill came in and closed the door. He sat down and said, "David, I just turned fifty and I looked in the mirror and I wasn't there."

"I have no idea who the fuck I am."

I have always felt that Bill was always an actor playing a part and always in character. One minute he was Bill the Asshole screaming, abusive, greedy, manipulative. In a flash he could transform into Bill the Benevolent overtly caring, gentle, solicitous and enormously generous.

I can only image what profound strategies Wolfgang had to construct to protect himself from the murderous abuse that comprised his life and which he carried every second on this earth.

He was a man who could not show the slightest vulnerability and could not allow himself to breathe one unprotected open breath, lest he be annihilated. How I wish I could have hugged 10-year old Wolfgang and told him that it would be all OK…

That he could be vulnerable and soft and be safe.

Written with love….

DAVID ZOUZOUNIS

Theodore and Penelope Zouzounis opened Ted's Market and Deli located at 1530 Howard Street in San Francisco in the summer of 1967 which is located in the South of Market District of S.F. This area was referred to as "skid row" and the empty warehouses were becoming live-work-art studios. I began working with my family at Ted's Market when I was eleven and fifty-three years later I continue to carry on my parents legacy.

In 1977, I was working at the register of Ted's with my father when a man walked in wearing a grey sweatshirt, not shaven and looking a bit weary. He leaned over our open grab-and-go, pre-made sandwich cooler. My father tells me to watch that guy. That was a frequent phrase that my dad used as the area was full of characters. I turned to my father and said, "Do you know who that is? It's Bill Graham."

BGP and Winterland Productions had just moved in across the street from us. By that time, we were known for our sandwiches as my mother cooked the turkey, roast beef, meatloaf and all the salads were fresh.

Ted's was the go-to lunch and snack destination for the amazing, hard-working, dedicated employees of Bill Graham Presents. They were regular customers and the one thing my father loved was his customers that would spend money every day at the market.

One day I was trying to get to the store to work at 5:00 a.m. as usual. The streets were blocked off because of a five-alarm fire where the BGP office at 201-11th Street was destroyed. When staff began gathering, I brought over sandwiches as the day was long. When Bill returned early from Europe, he later thanked me for being there in the moment.

At Grateful Dead shows the concession stands had to change their food choices. Bill asked Ted's Market to make avocado and cheese sandwiches. I would arrive early at the venue with 1,500 to 2,000 sandwiches for each night of the shows.

A tradition at the Fillmore are the red apples located at the top of the stairs, free for whoever wants one, and I have been supplying them since 1988. I am most proud to be the supplier of those apples to this day.

A Jet Ranger helicopter crashed. I knew of only two people at that time that had a Jet Ranger in the Bay Area: Bill Graham and Francis Ford Coppola. Colleen Kennedy called me and we all met at the company office on 5th Street in San Francisco. My wife sat in Bill's office and wrote a poem.

Forty-three years later, the Bill Graham Family will always be a part of my family. Ted's Market is special because of Bill Graham and all of his employees. Thank you to all.

Dedication to Bill Graham on the day of his death. Written on my birthday, the day Bill passed, October 26th. Written in Donna's office at the BGP office on 260 5th Street, San Francisco. The office was full of flowers.

Today I Know You Well

Fires rage like hell's fury on the hilltops of California
RISING, falling, swallowing everything, everything vanishing
Before red-glazed eyes of disbelief
Where is the rainstorm outfitted chiefs danced for?
Like a curse, undeserved but inevitable
Begins invisible, then becomes luminous as a ghost
Lurking above and below, calling all to join the dance
Spirits rose, some still rising, with the deluge
On this morning of October 26, 1991
Awakened by harsh winds of a deadly storm,
I wished myself happy birthday
Extra deep breaths, extended yoga posture holds
Knowing that black outside and bellowing gales
Welcomed an unwanted fate in a wished for, tardy rain
Knowing that I needed more stamina to endure ensuing hours
As I greeted a new day of rebirth in the midst of death
When true awakening took place at 9 am radio news brief
Throwing me into a whirlwind morn
Frenzied shock-drenching tear storm
As the first Bay Area rains came to a halt
Dying down with Bill—it wanted Bill
In the peak of the night
Toppling down a legend
Carrying away with fierce force, a hero
Bill Graham, world famous music promoter, band manager,
Bill Graham Productions founder and CEO, GIANT of a man
Has left us in flesh but will forever remain for those
He loved, took care of, made happy, made famous,
Employed, made laugh, made wiser, made grateful,
Whether he helped the homeless or the prosperous
Whether he helped crack, aids or earthquake victims,

Whether he fought against war, fascism, hunger, crime,

He was a lover--a lover of life, a lover of music and dance

A maker of music, a lending hand, a healing father and brother,

A guiding light for the makers of beautiful music on any stage

Whatever the philanthropist, the legend, the great man did for 60 years

Will always be in our minds, our stories, our memories, our songs

Our literature, our walls, our posters, our photo albums, our hearts

Happy birthday to me, how sad to see you enter the eternal light so soon

Your great soul, your second life, wherever you are

By Lorene Zarou-Zouzounis - Poet, writer, artist, peace and justice activist, humanist, and wife of Ted's Market & Deli owner, David Zouzounis.

DAWN HOLLIDAY

I was the box office manager for the Club Division of BGP, which was called AKG. I started at the Old Waldorf with Queenie Taylor, Wolfgang's, Wolfgang's Road Shows, the Kabuki Theater, the Warfield Theater and the Fillmore. I was fortunate enough that I was able to work production with Rita Gentry for Days on the Green and I worked a ton of other BGP events.

I was invited to a few Beauty and the Beast luncheons hosted by Bill. Bill graciously took all of the women whom he worked with in some immediate fashion out for lunch. My God, were we ever The Chosen Ones. Anyway, you get the picture.

I knew all of the crews, the regular people in Bill's "real" circle of friends, and people who got "by" him. Kyle Brown was the only person who seemed to "always really be his guest." People who just outright ignored him and ultimately a waste of any crew's time when enforcing the house rules, and Brian Rohan, a wonderful, bombastic man, was one of those people.

The AKG staff didn't really feel like they worked for Bill. I don't even know if his name was on our paychecks. We knew he owned the company, that he was honored and certainly good, but Queenie and David Mayeri were our guiding force. I did know when I switched hats to the BGP side it was more Bill oriented.

So, speaking of Brian Rohan: I am at the Fillmore in the tiniest box office in the universe. Rohan shows up. He takes one of Bill's parking spaces in the front of the venue to begin with.

He blows past the four security guards at the front door in his brusque manner and insane look. He talks his way through Steve Ortiz at the front door. He gets to me and wants six comps.

This show is sold out. It was Santana or something huge. Bill is in the house (venue). I am NOT an easy box office person.

Rohan starts to handle me. To save myself a few brain cells and some anger, I give Rohan one comp ticket. I tell him to go find a house manager to OK his guests.

I am still in the teeny box office and real customers are coming up to the window wanting real service. At this time, I am really overweight; Rohan is out and out FAT at this time too.

Bill is not a small man either. Within two minutes the two of them were inside the box office where I am residing and both are screaming at the top of their lungs. Bill yelling at me, "Why did you let this man in?" Rohan yelling back at Bill, "It's not her fault! Just let me and my guests into the show." I really didn't care at the moment who the fuck Bill was. I physically pushed the two out of the box office, banged on the window for security to come down to help me. Security escorted the ranting and raving Bill, Rohan, and Rohan's guests up the stairs into the auditorium.

All in all, I love them both very much. I would love to relive it over and over again.

DAY ON THE GREEN by DENNIS JONES

I am grateful, always for George Harrison. The Quiet Beatle.

For a very lone and selfish reason, of which very few people were even aware existed. But for me, it is one of the repeating, lasting, memorable moments of my thirteen years as a working member of the Bill Graham Presents Family.

For many the highlight of the summer during the 70's and 80's was the

Day On The Green (DOG) music festivals, held at the Oakland Stadium. Amazing days with heavenly bills, featuring the absolute best performing contemporary rock acts of the day. The production crew would show up a week early and transform a once empty, cement cavern into a showplace: 120' x 40' stages with 60' sound towers covered in ornate, theatrical, themed sets. Concert goers would often show up 18 hours ahead of time, lining the sidewalks and streets on either end of the property to ensure the best spots possible to see their "God's".

On show day when the clock hit 9AM the patrons entering were being screened for booze, weapons and glass containers moved through the turnstiles and released into the Stadium. This is when the "magic" began. Promptly at 8:55AM I made sure I was standing downstage right with the whole of the empty stadium laying before my feet. The bands equipment was all set (sound checks having been handled the night before), the ornate scrims hung to cover the speaker stacks, and the famed BGP "Bluecoats" strategically placed at intervals between the permanent seats that usually supported the backsides of A's and Raiders fans and the 4-foot barrier fronting the stage in the baseball outfield.

From my vantage point I could see them, like ants at a picnic; crazed rock fans hurtling themselves down the cement stairs that separated the seat sections, at warp speed until they reached the grass. It was then you could find Peter Barsotti, the BGP Field General and creative production force of the family.

Standing on the downstage center edge of the massive stage, his eyes darting back and forth, from foul pole to foul pole, looking for the first ticket holding rock fan to set foot on hallowed ground.....

The Green

And at that magical moment at each of the 58 DOG's I was a part of. Peter gave the signal to the sound tech at the off-stage monitor board and the first, well-known notes to the Harrison-penned, Beatles classic, "Here Comes The Sun," would waft across the well-manicured lawn and into the welcoming arms of the concrete structure signaling the start of the day's festivities.

It was Go time! Show time! The latest Day On the Green (regardless who was playing on that particular day, the best rock and roll show on the planet) had officially begun.

The last DOG I worked (or attended in any manner) was in 1989. Almost 30 years ago. And from that day to this, without exception, no matter where I am;

in my car, on an elevator, or as background music of a movie; whenever I hear those first five notes of that ethereal tune, I am whisked back to the downstage-right edge of the stage watching Peter give the signal and the day officially starting.

The memory of that singular moment in time still floods me with an excitement and creates a fabulous sensory experience; of the amazing line-ups of music, those historic "only at a BGP show" moments, and of the beyond incredible individuals, I was blessed to work besides during those amazing wonderful years of my personal and professional Camelot, with my family.

I am far past grateful. But to Mr. Harrison, whose simple beautiful song allows me to relive that moment, the times, the finest people and most rare and memorable of experiences again and again and again, I can only say….

Thank You George.

DEBI KOBAYASHI

I worked at Bill Graham Presents with Lovester Law and we started the marketing and sponsorship entities. I believe we created the first sanctioned San Francisco New Year's Eve for San Francisco. We also worked with major sponsors on their VIP parties. What a hoot!

I am proud of my time working at Bill Graham Presents and working with all the people there. I enjoyed hearing the stories of what Bill did and would have done. Working at such an iconic company is an experience I will never forget. I learned a lot working in a grassroots, non- corporate office environment. It certainly was quite a change from working in the corporate world. Each event we held was hard work, but worth making it and seeing it successfully executed to the end.

DENNIS DUNN

I started working for Bill Graham Presents in 1981 and ended 20 years and one day later in 2002. The reason I left was because I didn't feel a sense of Bill. I hadn't felt it for a long time, but held out for that feeling again.

When I told my boss at the time how I felt, I was told that Bill had been gone 10 years. That was when I knew she hadn't ever worked for Bill, so I went back to shows and realized that every facet of the job had gone corporate and had no resemblance of what the job was to me.

On the first day of the Grateful Dead run after Christmas 1986 my brother, Kevin, had just passed away on the 25th. I was working stage stairs at Henry J. Kaiser Auditorium in Oakland, California. I saw Bill cruising backstage before the show. With a look on his face that made me glad that I wasn't in his sights, he ran up on stage. Waiting for him to pass me and unload his rage, I noticed he hadn't passed me. I turned my head to have him staring me in the eyes, and I thought to myself, "What did I do now?"

In his direct, loud voice, he asked my why I didn't tell him of my brother's passing. I said, "You are a very busy man." Bill said, "I'm never too busy for family." Those words will stick with me wherever I go, in both my heart and my mind. Bill Graham was a strong-willed person and very caring for his personal family, whether related or part of the great BGP Family.

To this day, relating this story brings me to wipe tears from my eyes.

DENNIS EROKAN

Get Famous….

If you were anywhere near the Bay Area in the Sixties through 1991 you knew about Bill. Or if you were lucky like me, you knew Bill.

While I had seen him at plenty of rock music events in my teens and early twenties, I had the chance to interview Bill right after I started my music magazine, BAM. One of the questions I asked him was, "Why are you famous?" To me, that was an important question because none of the other concert promoters around the country used their own names as the name of the company; his was Bill Graham Presents. Plus, almost every night he would come on stage sometime during the show to talk to the audience about shows coming up. All of his colleagues would send up some young kid to read off the list of upcoming shows. Bill even had his own publicist on his payroll, Zohn Artman. So it seemed like an appropriate question.

And when I asked it, his eyes lit up! He said no one had ever asked him that before and immediately went into one of his stories. He started telling me about his early years working in hotels in the Catskill Mountains of New York while going to college. The guy he worked for was constantly getting in the local newspaper about one thing or another. Bill asked him why he did it. His boss explained that he made sure he was famous in the area of the Catskills. He told Bill that because he was famous, deals would come to him that maybe no one else would get.

He explained that the hotel they were in at the moment had been offered to him to buy without going out for competitive bids, because the person who wanted to sell it knew he would be able to buy it quickly.

He told Bill that the best thing he did was become famous. "You don't need to be President of the United States, just famous around town." And then, to Bill's amazement, the hotel owner said to him, "Get famous!" At that moment Bill wondered if he would ever need to.

Of course, Bill moved to San Francisco and got involved in the budding music scene he started to make sure he got famous. And he did a good job of it! The culmination was when The Rolling Stones decided they were going to have only one promoter for their entire American tour.

They chose Bill Graham over all the concert promoters in the country. When I asked Mick Jagger why they chose him his answer was, "Everybody knows Bill Graham." Bill then went on to promote the Stones' European Tour of 1982, which proves that being famous gets you the opportunity, but you still have to be really good to get the follow up business.

After he finished telling me about his reason for getting famous and his various other stories that were always fascinating to listen to, he pointed at me and said, "So now I'm telling you, get famous!"

DENNIS JONES

While in high school, I wrote a weekly column for my local newspaper, mostly concert reviews, and when I was able to finagle one, an interview with the artist. I had arranged with Queenie Taylor's right hand, Gloria Pulido, to come into the office, talk to a few people in the different departments, see the operation from the other side of the fence so-to-speak. Sitting beside Gloria's desk, (later inhabited by Jan Wexner when she started working for Perl), was like sitting in the middle of Union Station during rush hour. I was making some notes, when Bill walked by. Gloria stopped him.

"Bill, this is Dennis Jones. He's a high school student who also writes for a local paper, here today to get a look at how the business runs."

"Hi!" Bill said, holding out his hand. "Two things. Spell my name right and don't do anything while you're here to get me arrested. What are you writing about?"

I gave him my pitch, and he said, "I'll tell you what. Why don't you come work with my security? You can still see the shows you do for your writing, see how things work from the inside, and I won't have to keep feeding you comps!" Of course, I immediately agreed. "Can you work Thanksgiving?" he asked. "Yeah, sure," I stammered, as any sixteen-year-old kid would.

Bill spun around, where David Mayeri was at his desk. "David, this is Dennis Jones. Give his name and number to Mark Lewis. I want him to work Thanksgiving." It all happened so fast. Before I could offer my hand in thanks, like a dedicated gust of wind on the bay, Bill was gone.

My first show - The Last Waltz. My last show, as a full- time BGP employee working for Peter Barsotti in the Production Department - Live Aid.

In between: closing Winterland, opening the Warfield and the Oakland Auditorium, creating Cal Expo Amphitheater, great summers filled with DOGs and Greek runs and Dead shows (oh my!), Amnesty International, ARMS Tour, the Stones Tour, Rocky Horror, the Dylan and the Dead runs at the Warfield, the San Francisco Holiday Festival, the Day on the Hill up at Masada, the annual BAMMIES shows, and so much more, all with the single greatest group of individuals I'll ever know. Not bad for a short, but miraculous career working for the world's greatest dance hall keeper. And without a doubt, the most productive interview I ever had.

There are so many great Bill stories, much more interesting than this. But when I think about Bill, the first thing I remember is how he made this incredible company of 200-plus people feel like family, and the second is how he hated to leave any situation without the upper hand. In any situation, it was almost an art form for Bill.

This is a perfect example: Bill loved to interact with his employee family, and during one particular football season, the Niners owned the world. Everyone in the office was all about the Niners, so to make the NFC Championship game interesting, Bill was taking the Cowboys – straight up – no odds or points. I got in for $25. And of course, when Dwight Clark made "The Catch" to end that incredible drive, the Niners won 28-27.

The next day in the office, everyone was jacked because of the Niners' win, but to be honest I had completely forgotten about the bet. Late that morning, sitting at a desk in the production depart-ment, making up stagehand schedules for the next month's shows, Rita Gentry placed a 7"x10" goldenrod envelope on my desk. "This is from Bill."

I opened it and found some money and a brief typewritten note.

Mr. Jones, Enclosed please find 26 dollars. Twenty-five dollars for the wager on yesterday's San Francisco Forty-Niners' Dallas Cowboys game, and one-dollar for the privilege of never having to discuss this wager with you.

Should you at any time, mention this topic, the $1 shall be immediately forfeit. Disgruntlingly, Bill.

Bill lost the wager, but walked away from the situation with the upper hand. By either never having to discuss his loss, or by my having to give him a dollar (a metaphorical win), Bill found a way to have the last word in every situation he was in. As much as any other, this story reminds me of how Bill looked at things - outside the box. That has always stuck with me.

That note, and the same, single dollar bill, remain matted and framed as a warm, vivid memory of my time working with the greatest bunch of magicians, led by the warmest mensch I've ever known.

Throughout my years at BGP, there were numerous experiences, some annually repeated, some historic one- offs, which will always nestle at the forefront of my "pleasant memories" library. None, however, have ever meant as much to me personally, or captured more accurately, I believe, the truest example of what separated our little band of merry misfits from any other live production company in the world. The moment and experience of which I speak, revolves around the opening of the house at every Day on the Green stadium concert festival, or at least those from 1975 through 1989.

Day on the Green (DOG)

To appreciate the full value of this moment, one must understand that, for a normal DOG (which clearly, did not exist), our stage builders, the local union hands, and site advance people and directors from the tour in question would enter Oakland Stadium four or five days prior, at 8:00 a.m., and begin construction of a monstrous 160'wide by 60'deep by 70'high stage, atop the once awesome centerfield bleachers. During that first day the stage crew worked their way up to stage deck level. Lance Miller and his Ambience Control magicians would begin constructing the artist's compound, with Rita in the production trailer in the tunnel. Jan and the eternally missed MFTQ, Shelley Lazar, would be assembling the last line of defense atop the ramp – where the artists and record companies sent their "guests" for tickets on the day of show (and yes, that endeavor alone, should and could be a book unto itself).

By day three we were stage deck completed and the towers on either side, well on the way, with the roof soon to follow. On day four the battalion of 48-foot semis, stacked and with enough sound equipment to defeat Putin, followed by band gear and day lights. Before sundown, the Dennis Larkin stage scrim is affixed to the front of the sound stack steel and that night Event Security is on hand to keep watch over the stage with one of Bill's Bluecoats (me, for my first two summers with the company) out on Hegenberger Road at the road racing arcade to keep the overnighters from getting into any trouble. Between 4:00 and 5:00 a.m., staff began arriving and at 6:00 a.m., the first stage crew shift begins and the gates to the parking lot opened as the drunk, exhausted fans sprint to form the first lines and wait for the stadium to open. And now it happens….

The doors to the nearly empty cement cavern opened promptly at 9:00 a.m. Rock Med, Bluecoats and the Coliseum security were all in place, the stage was set for the first act, and from the barricade infield, you could hear the din from the masses in the parking lot grow as each tick of the clock moved closer to go-time. Since the days the DOG shows had been moved across the Bay from their initial home in San Francisco Kezar Stadium to Oakland, the unofficial logo of the annual series had been this oversized sun cartoon in sunglasses. And in a manner that can only be described as "Pure Petey," BGP Production Department head, Peter Barsotti had come up with the perfect way to put the idea behind that logo – a joyous, sunny, happy day – front and center, setting the tone for the entire day.

By 8:30 a.m. of each DOG, Peter had already hooked up with the guys running the show's sound and set the plan into action. By 8:50 a.m., the sound system was fired up, and the tunage Peter had gathered (compliant with the music of the day's lineup and placed onto cassette tape (and later CDs) was ready. All that was missing was… the audience.

At 8:50 a.m. Bill, Stan Damas, Event Security Head Bruce Jenney and Bluecoat Security Lead Mark Lewis had been tooling around the outside of the stadium grounds on their mopeds for more than 30 minutes, making sure the minions were in peaceful, organized lines, to insure an incident- free entrance to the show. Peter could be found dead center on the downstage lip if the stage, scouring back and forth across the width of the lower concourse seating, waiting for those first, crazed fans to come hurtling down the concrete steps to guarantee their rightful place: smashed up against the barricade in front of the stage, with virtually no way out for the next nine hours.

Finally, at precisely 9:00 a.m., they came like ants at a picnic, headed for the platter of sweet kosher dills, concert patrons making a beeline for the grass.

Peter's hand raised into the air, one final glance to the man at the soundboard off stage left to make sure he was ready to receive his signal.

Back and forth, Peter's eyes continued to scan the onslaught of concert goers until he determined which would be first to reach the lush turf. Raising his hand slightly higher, informing his sound man the moment was at hand, as the young man in question leapt from the last step out and onto the playing surface, Peter gave the signal. As the patron's foot touched down onto the grass 100 dBs of those first five, iconic notes of George Harrison's Beatles classic, "Here Comes the Sun," blanketed the souls of every incoming guest of the day and the magic that was a Day on the Green concert had begun.

Five days earlier, 40 men walked into an empty stadium, a structure dead to the world. During the next five days more than 400 individuals - stagehands, site builders, set designers, security people, talent bookers and their staff, ticket agents, bookkeepers, caterers, vendors, sound, light and band techs, stadium personnel, rock medical, volunteers, travel bookers, artists' entourages and many others - had been working to create this event, all leading up to this one, singular, moment, a moment which less than a handful of people knew about or actually recognized, and yet was the perfect example for the company that literally invented the live concert production industry. Bill's drive and professional standard for a quality production, every show; Peter's creativity and imagination; and an entire army of hundreds of people, most who never directly met or worked with one another, over endless hours of planning, production and execution, all coming together to a single moment at the beginning of a single day and one…single…step.

I remember the very first time I met Peter Barsotti, It was the night before the Aerosmith Day on the Green. I was early for my overnight Bluecoat shift. I saw Peter standing alone on the concourse behind and to the left of the stage. He was just staring off into the empty Coliseum field. After a couple of minutes, I said, "I want your job." Peter shook his head and laughed. "No, you don't." "I'll trade ya any time." My annoying persistence tipped his patience scales. "Okay, first, who the hell are you and what are you doing here?" I introduced myself. "All right, Dennis Jones, Bluecoat. You don't know me or what I do. So, tell me, why you think you want my job."

Too young, naive or stupid (or a combination of the three) to be intimidated by the PB intensity you all came to know and love *lol*, I said, "Because four or five days ago, you walked in here and this place was empty. And tomorrow, 60- some thousand people are gonna spend the day getting their rocks off, largely because of what you do for a living.

How many people in the world get to say that? Maybe five or ten?" Peter shook his head but smiled. "Hi, I'm Peter Barsotti," he said extending his hand. "Nice to meetcha. You have a good night. I'm going home."

I stayed, stuck around for a little while, walked out on the field to take a look at the large stage set and then headed back up the ramp towards my truck and out to the Raceway. Halfway up the concrete ramp I heard, "Dennis!" Peter caught up to me, smiling. "Hey man. This was a shitty day, for a lot of reasons. I want to thank you for reminding me why these days are worth it. Come see me for a job sometime." I worked for Peter for 11 years. It's funny the things we remember.

Attitude of Gratitude – The Last Waltz

Today, I set aside an hour to reflect about the first and best career I ever had with the single greatest group of people I will ever now. Today marks the 42nd anniversary of my first day as a member of Bill Graham Presents Family at a small gathering lovingly referred to as The Last Waltz held in the family's living room, Winterland.

To go into vivid detail of everything this show encompassed, every path, good and evil, of what goes into producing an event like this, would take far more time that you have and far more first-hand knowledge of that day that I possess. Suffice to say, and I have heard this through the years from people in all walks and levels of the production industry, both in and outside the family, as well as from artists who performed that night, and who didn't. Remember there was a boss, company people, artists managers, movie production wonks (many egos involved), stage production necessities and interior design overhaul of the entire building and serving a full, four-course Thanksgiving turkey dinner to 5,000 people and having none of the above mentioned entities committing mass murder.

No one else could have pulled that event off in the professional high-quality manner: it was but Bill and Staff.

Truth be told, I thought the movie sucked. It captured about 40 percent of what happened on stage and off, virtually laying waste to what was, in fact, one of the spectacular live concert productions and performances, before or since.

My gratitude, aside from being paid to be in the building, was the first, best, greatest lesson I learned from Bill and the family, one that I have carried with me in almost every endeavor, professional and otherwise, I have been involved in since that day: "ALWAYS make sure you have a nice sprig of fresh parsley on every plate." If anyone ever wondered, I believe that single paradigm was the tangible difference between a BGP show and one produced by anyone else. Anywhere. Ever.

My eternal gratitude for this lesson is superseded only by the countless men and women who learned it, lived it, and shared it with me on a daily basis for more than 13 years. Though a comparatively short period of time, that was my golden age, my Camelot, a period from which memories and lessons were captured and learned, friends were made, and lovers cherished and fondly bid adieu. Legions of battles were fought and for the most part, won.

I am grateful to those who have moved on and now work for the Boss up in the big hall and to those who remain, whose friendships are and will always be among my most valued treasures. And for their participation in the absolute best part of what has been, and continues to be, a miraculous life, I can only say…Cheers!

124

DENNIS LARKINS

A Favorite Bill Graham Memory

Throughout the 1970s, it was my great honor and privilege to have the opportunity to design and paint the huge stage sets for Bill Graham's legendary Day on the Green festivals at the Oakland Stadium. Bill had conceived of these all day, huge-scale events as a natural music promoter's response to Woodstock, a moment in American cultural and musical history that instantly changed the lives of an entire generation! That the subsequent and equally historic Day on the Green events greatly influenced the direction and evolution of large-scale outdoor concerts around the world for decades to come is indisputable. But, for me, the most interesting aspects of these shows were the human- interest stories that happened backstage and behind the scenes.

One of my personal favorites involving Bill Graham was a "morning of show" ritual unknown to most of the legion of workers who had been toiling literally around the clock to prepare the giant stage and all of its necessary structures and equipment as well as the gargantuan edifice of my specially prepared decorations. Not only as designer and scenic artist (these massive creations were by far the largest extensions of my personal artistic expression I had ever done!), I also had the task of on-site art direction during the entire installation process to insure the best possible aesthetic outcome by showtime.

I learned early on in my time working for Bill's company that one of Bill's favorite practices the morning of the show was to time his arrival at the stadium to coincide with word that all was complete and ready for viewing. As the installation process had been going on continuously since the day before and through the night, the crew, myself included, had done everything possible to craft a successful presentation. Nevertheless, as the one entrusted to "attention to detail," I always knew intimately where the human imperfections stood out. It was because of this knowledge that a certain ambivalence and attendant anxiety accompanied the time leading up to the Great Presentation!

Bill had once told me that one of the most memorable pleasures of his earlier career had been the opportunity to commission event posters from many of the great San Francisco poster artists of the Psychedelic Era. The creation of this incredible body of work (BG psychedelic poster series) represented to him one of his greatest professional achievements. But while he certainly understood the incredible artistic value of the work itself, he shared with me that his greatest personal value of the process was the moment of seeing a new piece of incredible finished art for the first time - the RUSH! The Existential Moment! He told me that he had also come to experience the DOG stage sets in exactly the same way. That is why, except for seeing my original design drawings for approval and production, he never wanted to see the work in progress and would wait until its final moment of completion! This explains why, in designing and creating stage sets for him for so many years and so many shows through the 1970s, he never once visited my shop to see one coming together.

So it was, on the morning of the DOG show, I would notify someone that all had been done that could be done, and Bill would set out for the stadium for the "official viewing." It always happened the same way: Bill would arrive in the backstage area, be joined by his small band of lieutenants (and me), march down the backstage ramp, through the scaffolding under the giant stage, straight across the baseball field without looking back, arriving at home plate in front of the A's baseball dugout and turn around to experience the long anticipated "Existential Moment"! No pressure.

I always understood in this moment that Bill Graham would make some kind of loud noise, being the expressive personality he was. Fortunately, the relief came when that noise was almost always a positive one! Handshakes and big smiles all around!

These special moments will always hold the record as the most theatrical presentations of my artistic career!

DENNIS McNALLY

I was Bill Graham's first archivist, hired in December 1982 and let go by Nick Clainos in December 1983.

A week after I began work, I was told that I was going to supervise Bill's memorabilia booth at the Holiday Festival at Fort Mason. We had Janis Joplin's tambourine, Keith Richards' boots, and Bill's original dancehall keeper permit — his personal treasures. On the last day of the festival, which I recall as December 22 or 23, 1982, just as we were visualizing loading out at festival's end, seriously high winds were coming through the Golden Gate, to the point that traffic on the bridge was stopped.

Right in front of Bill's booth was what we called an "elephant door," a giant 25' by 25' loading door (the building we were set up in had been a loading dock for the military.) The door had been filled in with a giant plywood sheet with a people-sized door in the corner.

As the winds peaked, the door began to vibrate visibly, and I, along with the others in the area, were starting to worry. For a moment I considered leaving, and then the thought hit me that there was no way I could. Put nobly, I had already developed the personal loyalty to Bill that every BGP employee had — I just couldn't run. Put another way, I couldn't imagine enduring Bill's look at me - if not roar - for having lost his best memories.

In classic cliffhanger fashion, just as I was starting to sweat, I saw from my left a giant, a Bluecoat by the name of Dennis Dunn, run up and simply hurl himself at the door. Within seconds, a gang of slightly smaller Bluecoats joined him. Soon carpenters arrived with longer screws and power drills; the door held, and not so long after, the winds died down and we loaded out the show.

I've never gone to Fort Mason without remembering that.

DHARMA BARSOTTI

The first time I can remember interacting directly with Bill was sometime in the late '70s. I was following my dad, Peter Barsotti, around the Oakland Coliseum at a Day on the Green. I can't remember which one it was, but I do feel like it was one of the earlier ones.

Back then dad was a pretty big hot dog and took me around everywhere, introducing me to everyone and making sure I would look them in the eye and shake their hand. I met a lot of people that way, but this is not the way I recall meeting Bill. Back then, the stage was built out of old school painters scaffolding and it was a thing to behold for a six- or seven-year-old. It must have been 100 feet wide if not more, but seemed an infinitely gigantic structure.

Dad's desk, which had the chalk board with the run of the show on it, was on the stage left side of things, just outside the breeze way. I'd follow him up there and drink a ton of soda while I waited for the show to be over some 18 hours later. During that time, I'd get bored and run all over. Here's where the giant stage comes into the story. So, it was one of those moments when I was bored from waiting around for hours and having more than likely 10 to 12 cups of Coca- Cola from the jockey box just off the stage, that I ran onto the stage and headed over to the stage left wing and proceeded to climb up the scaffolding until I was about 15 feet or so up.

At this point, I had certainly heard of Bill Graham before and certainly had been introduced, but had never really interacted with him and just knew if he told you to do something that you better do it. So, here I was, 15 feet in the air, doing so without realizing that Bill was standing right there watching me climb up. Well, I guess he didn't care for it and walked up to me and with a very commanding voice said, "This isn't a jungle gym! Get the fuck down!" Needless to say, I literally jumped off the scaffolding and ran directly backstage and hid for the rest of the show. From that day for at least three or four years I didn't speak to Bill again. He was truly intimidating.

A few years later I had grown a bit and the day came when dad asked me to be one of the New Year's Eve babies for the NYE Grateful Dead show at the Oakland Auditorium (Henry J. Kaiser.) The first year was really awesome with Trixie, but we were stuffed into the top of a giant cake float and we didn't really interact with Bill on that one. The second one was with my sister, Jess, and that one we were up close and personal with Bill.

He was the presidential seal that year and dressed as the eagle from the seal. Jess and I were the New Year's babies, but this time we were to run out from either side of Bill as he stood on the edge of the balcony of the HJK auditorium and grab the red and white shield off his chest to then flip it over and reveal the Steal Your Face on the back to the frenzied audience. Bill would then proceed to fly from there across the room and land on the stage.

Well, we had practiced this and it was really scary because you had to walk out on the ledge and there was no harness or anything; you just had to make sure you didn't fall off. We had done this in the light every time in rehearsal so I didn't realize how dark it would be at midnight with all the lights off. So here comes the countdown until we start the gag and there is a big duvi curtain around us totally dark. Then it's go-time and the curtain gets pulled and there is Bill in all his glory as the eagle. I run out and grab the shield off of his chest, but as I do, Bill starts to flap his wings and almost knocks me off the balcony.

I'm dressed in a diaper and thankfully so because I almost peed myself when that happened; I was so scared.

But, I suck it up and flip the shield over to thunderous applause. I then hand over to Jess who, having not just been nearly pushed to her death, thrusts the shield out towards the sky with greater zeal and gets even more applause as she holds the shield in perfect defiance of the height at which we are both standing. But the energy of the moment is overwhelming and I quickly forget any and all trouble as Bill takes to the air over the roaring crowd and flies across the auditorium, lands on the stage just as the clock counts down to midnight and the balloon drop proceeds as the new year grows to be a few seconds old. I'm pretty sure the Dead broke into "Sugar Magnolia," but it could have been "Aiko Aiko" or even another tune. I always think of it being "Sugar Magnolia." Either way, the world is a glorious place for those intense moments and Bill was the Icon, the Front Man and the Boss and our friend - truly the best times in those innocent days.

P.S. I remember getting his autograph at Squaw and the last time I saw Bill was at the Oakland Coliseum, Metallica Day on the Green.

DIANNA ARNSPIGER

I was in college when I discovered Bill Graham. I had grown up in Southern California and been to many of his Journey shows down there, but did not truly become aware of him until I worked at a restaurant called Paloma in Berkeley where the chef had personally worked for Bill. They would often tell Bill stories, and I became fascinated with him, so much so that it helped me to discover what I wanted to do with my life.

One night, that same chef took me to a show at the Fillmore. It was the B-52s, and we had one of the small booths upstairs. I was hooked. What a magical night that was and I remember I kept staring at the chandeliers through all of the fragrant smoke.

My trajectory towards BGP was not as linear as I now wish it had been since I lost the opportunity to actually meet or work with Bill. I graduated and went to work for a law firm for a short time, and then I spent a few years working for Dianne Feinstein, the former mayor of San Francisco who would become a United States Senator. I had kept my dream of working for Bill in my back pocket, but I knew that this could help me somehow. When Dianne asked me to accompany her to D.C. I declared that I wanted to stay behind in San Francisco and work in the music business. Everyone thought I was nuts. My grandmother will never forgive me for that decision, but I will never regret it.

Being the great woman she was, Dianne asked one of her friends to get me an informational interview at BGP. My first interview was with Nick Clainos. All I can remember about my interview with Nick was him repeating the question: "Yes, but why would you want to work here?" The most exciting thing for me during that interview, however, was hearing Bill Graham yelling at someone from another room and the walls were shaking.

I can't remember exactly how much time transpired, but shortly after my first interview, Bill died. I had never met the man, and I only knew one person from the company, Steve Welkom, a bit as I kept in touch hoping to get hired. But I sat on my couch that day, watching the news and reading the paper and cried like a baby. I even went to Temple Emanuel for a public service to mourn.

Then, in 1994 on a very bad day at a short-lived job, I received a phone call from Pat Thomas, inviting me to come in for an interview. I thought, after all those years that it was one of my friends pranking me, so I made Pat repeat herself a few times.

The rest, as they say, is history. Gregg hired me and I spent six years working for him. Everything is always so much clearer in retrospect, and I had no idea how truly lucky I was there.

Gregg was a great boss and treated me very well. Even more important is that I gained a family, a huge, extended family. Anyone associated with BGP knows what I am talking about. As one who comes from a broken primary family, this means so much to me. It really did change my life and led to so many other great things.

Whatever it was about Bill that drew me to his world has stayed with me for my whole life. On the precious "big" days I've had over the years, where something great happens, there will always be a sign of Bill. I know that sounds corny, but it's the truth. The day - almost the moment - I found out a band that I managed from the ground up had secured a major recording contract, I was driving in my car and they played "I Love You Much Too Much" on the radio (and I don't think that one is often played on the radio), the song Carlos Santana had performed - taught to him by Bill - at Bill's memorial.

DICK BRIGHT

Bandleader, Fiddler and Entertainer. I came to the Bay Area in 1975 and never left.

I met Bill when I was the bandleader of the first 12 Bay Area Music Awards (BAMMIES)in San Francisco. I had a 30- piece orchestra and Bill often attended and being old school, Bill appreciated what I was doing in that Jack Benny mold.

As mentioned above, not being a famous rock star, I met Bill when I was the Musical Director of the BAMMIES. It was a bit of a Herculean task, managing a 30-piece rock orchestra and dealing with lots of rock stars and egos. When Bill would present an award, he was very complimentary towards me on mic, and I was extremely flattered and humbled. I think he appreciated my old school work ethic.

Bill got mad at me only once (and I didn't blame him). When Winterland was closing, Bill hosted a final week of spectacular shows. One of them was headlined by my friends and greatest visual rock band ever, The Tubes. Having similar senses of humor, the Tubes invited me to sing something whacky with the band, as I was currently a lounge lizard at the Red Chimney in Stonestown alongside the fabulous Bud E. Love, singing such gems as "The Theme from the Loveboat."

I had just seen the Sex Pistols a few nights earlier, and it occurred to me that what was truly "punk" was to do something against the grain, that would intentionally piss off your audience. When Johnny Rotten was getting a tepid response, he stopped the show and said, "What's wrong with you pussies? Don't you have anything better to throw at me?" Immediately a deluge of umbrellas, cameras, and large objects went flying towards the stage — mission accomplished.

So, when the Tubes asked me to perform, I wanted to go punk and chose one of my lounge

band's favorite sing alongs, Neil Diamond's "Sweet Caroline." As I launched into the song and was getting zero reaction, I channeled Johnny and stole his line. Immediately dangerous objects came flying at the stage. Drummer Prairie Prince actually took a Coke bottle to the head. I look to my left and there was Bill screaming at me, "Get the fuck off the fucking stage!" It was one of the highlights of my career.

On a very sad and personal note, I was at the Concord Pavilion watching Huey Lewis and Tower of Power that horrific rainy night that Bill passed. I so remember going backstage to say hi to the guys and got to exchange warm greetings with Bill. The fact that I got to connect with Bill his last day on earth has always stayed with me.

I know some folks had tough dealings with Bill, but not being a rock star, I never asked him for a gig or anything else, so there were never any business conflicts. I was just a working musician and I always felt that Bill had a soft spot in his heart for us blue collar working musicians. He was always warm, funny, gracious, brilliant and so much more…except that night I screwed up at Winterland.

DINA BEDINI

I found my way to the BGP family in October of 1995 at the Warfield Theater at the behest of my sister, Deborah Bedini. She recruited me to work in the security department where I started as a searcher and remained for over five years.

After putting in my time there I was able to start working at the Fillmore as a searcher of course! Back in our day you searched for a long, long time before you were allowed to do any other jobs. I loved it and wouldn't have traded it for anything in the world. At this point, I was allowed to start taking tickets at both the Warfield and the Fillmore where I continue to work to this day (now the Evil Nation, LOL). I love what we do and take great pride in running the front door and getting the crowd inside to enjoy the music! Throughout my years I've worked almost every position there is at the Fillmore, but my favorite position is the front door!

When I started working, I had NO idea how much this would become a part of my life. The people I started working with are my family. We all love and respect and care for one another so much. I have never had a job like this where my co-workers have become my extended family. Working security, you have to be able to trust the people you work with and know that they have your back. We all take this very seriously and protect one another completely. We are family, we love each other through it all good and bad. BGP has brought so much to me. I met the love of my life at the Warfield and countless friends that will always be a part of my life (1995 to present).

DITKA REINER

Bill. Bill Graham was one of those people who didn't need a last name.

I met Bill when I was just a kid in the early 1970s through my husband, Lance Dickerson. Lance was a drummer with Charlie Musselwhite, Etta James and others, a handsome man, an elegant and smooth player. He was with Commander Cody and the Lost Planet Airmen when I met him. We were married in 1973.

Rock and roll was a gnarly and haphazard business with lots of hangers-on. There were professional standout people I met at the time. The first one was Rita Gentry who worked for both the Cody band and the New Riders. Rita had been around the music scene for a while and she and I became best friends. The other was Nina Urban (Bombardier) who worked at and eventually ran the Record Plant in Sausalito and Fantasy Studios in Berkeley. We got married around the same time, we had kids around the same time and we raised our families together. We saw a lot of the music scene from the inside. When the band broke up, Rita went to work for Bill Graham at Bill Graham

Presents and that's how I got to know Bill and the team he created. We three remain just as close to this day.

When I met Lance in 1972 we moved to Kenwood (the wine country in Sonoma). Other band members lived close by so that when the band was home, we were together and when the band was on the road the ladies of the family kept one another company. We would go into the city to Winterland or The Fillmore to see our friends like the Dead, the Doobies, the Airplane, Van Morrison, everyone that was playing at the time. All the shows were put on by Bill Graham Presents and their format was pretty much the same: Bill would sometimes come out to announce the acts, but most of the time Jerry Pompili would do the honors.

In 1973, Bill started an outdoor concert series at The Oakland Coliseum called Day on the Green. They would continue under his leadership annually until his death in 1991. After that there were a few more but I never went.

The thing about a BGP show was that it was always Bill's show. No matter whom the artist was, Bill was always the star. He knew how to connect with people; wherever he went walking during the show people would stop him to talk. He had that East Coast style/presence but he did not suffer fools. If he liked you he would give you the moon, but if you pissed him off, well, let's just say you would not feel comfortable. His shows went like clockwork; he had a vision of how to entertain. If you were at a Bill show you knew who each act was, what order they came on and at what time. You could set your watch by it. He loved music and he loved the show; he gave artists a venue and on a platform that hadn't been done before. Whether it was the light show or the giant tie-dyed backdrops, his shows were meant to have fun and fun the audience had.

Backstage was a show onto itself. Each of the bands had a trailer, sometimes more than one. Bill had fantastic food and entertainment for the bands, their friends and their families: games, activities, face painting for the kids and many more depending on the acts. When the Stones released Tattoo You, he had Lyle Tuttle, famous tattoo artist, backstage doing tattoos at a time when tattoos were not commonplace.

It was a family circus and I think sometimes we had more fun than the audience.

Bill ran a tight ship with this staff, with his crew and with the artists. I saw this firsthand on June 8, 1974.

We were playing the second ever Day on the Green, first one of the 1974 season. The headliners that day were the Grateful Dead, the Beach Boys, New Riders of the Purple Sage and the opening act was Lance's band, Commander Cody and His Lost Planet Airmen.

These bands had played together many times and we all knew one another. The Beach Boys were rock 'n' roll history and the Dead were undefinable. At this show, the Dead unveiled a massive sound system that covered the back of the entire stage and was brand new to the industry. There was a bit of tension setting it up. Everybody was impressed, anxious, but excited to hear it in action. It took a bit longer to set up and timing was tight, but this was a Bill show and everyone worked together to get it ready. The Coliseum in Oakland held close to 65,000 people, and that was a really big concert back then. The audience was excited to be there.

On this day in May I was looking forward to catching up with Dennis Wilson, the drummer of the Beach Boys who had just gotten a new boat. He was always teasing about going out on the boat knowing that I didn't swim and hated the water. But he was always fun and one of my favorites. I went to find them but the band wasn't there so I went up to the stage where Lance was checking out his equipment and then we went up to see the sound system.

We were at the back of the stage behind the speakers and perpendicular to where we were standing there was an open concrete tunnel, probably 20 feet wide, with equipment and other stagecraft on either side. You had to walk through this short tunnel from the stage to get to the backstage area where the trailers, food and games were. On the other side of the tunnel was the back gate for the artists and families to enter. I had seen Bill pacing up and down, as he often did, then sitting on a case, then getting up again and constantly checking his watch.

I knew the Beach Boys were late and they were going to be in trouble!

A few minutes later Dennis, Mike Love, Al Jardine and a fourth person I don't remember came through the gate and started down the ramp in the tunnel. They were laughing and clearly having fun. When Bill saw them, he started yelling; I could hear him clearly from the stage. "Where the fuck have you been? You were supposed to be here at XX hour!" The guys were a bit taken aback and thought that he was joking, and so they laughed about getting stuck in traffic and something else, which I didn't hear because Bill didn't let them finish. He said, and I'll never forget, "You are playing at a Bill Graham show because I let you. Your name may be on the marquee today, but my name is on there every day. When I say that a show starts at a certain time, that's when it starts. This is my fucking show and I expect you to show up on time, and if you ever come late to another of my shows again, you will never play a Bill Graham event ever again."

Those guys couldn't wait to get out of there. They mumbled something and scattered back through the tunnel to the trailers.

The next year 1975, the first Day on the Green was on May 24th. Chicago headlined and then it was The Beach Boys, Commander Cody and the opening act was The New Riders. I watched as the bands rolled in, I think the Beach Boys beat everyone there. They were not going to be late for another Bill Graham show.

DONNA GOLDMAN

Like Mick Jagger, Bill's voice proceeded him. I first "met" Bill over the phone. "Michael Ahern please," was all he said. I knew it was him. "One moment please." I placed the call on hold.

"Michael, it's Bill Graham on the phone." My calling him Michael had already gotten his attention as I typically called out to him as "Ma." Additionally, I had pushed my tall director's chair back from the old wooden drawing board that served as my desk to announce this call to Michael who was in the back office, not that far for every day calls, but for this call I got up to tell him so.

It's too long a story how and why I knew I wanted to be in the concert production coordination or working in this field, but suffice to say, I knew of and had Bill and Michael in the crosshairs of my very focused, beaming with intention, bright, young mind.

My first break came when I met and quickly befriended Paige Kevan's niece, Glynis. We met working answering phones backstage at the Police concert at Shea Stadium in the early eighties. Within days of this, I was knocking on a 12th floor apartment door of a large Upper West Side pre-war building. A disheveled Michael Ahern answered the door that morning. Paige lived and worked out of this apartment, which at the time was like the Batcave of the international rock 'n' roll touring "industry" – in my humble opinion.

Paige was the queen of hotel logistics for such acts as the Rolling Stones, Fleetwood Mac, Bruce Springsteen, Billy Joel and John Cougar. I was her typist. I also had the honor of working on Live Aid with Paige.

It was the fall of 1986. I was returning an airline ticket for Glynis to a brokerage agency in the Fisk Building, a famous West 57th Street building, when lo and behold Michael Ahern was walking to the same central revolving door of the building, just as I was.

I hadn't seen Michael in three, maybe four years, when this fateful moment happens. When we were both in the lobby, Michael explained that he had taken an office here and said, "Why don't you stop by when you are done with your errand."

It wasn't 20 minutes later that I passed by Michael's new office. It was a great large space with two separate work areas. Michael sat behind a desk on a large black swivel chair I guessed came with the space. It was so not him.

Then he explained that Bill rented the office for a couple of months while Michael helped him with the Crack Down (On Crack) benefit concert that Bill was producing with Ruben Blades. Hence began the greatest tenure of my life, working as Michael Ahern's assistant which inevitably and thankfully had me meet and work with Bill on various events along the way.

I never met Bill during this time, but I did meet Rita Gentry and Eleonore Hockabout following the show in a hotel room where we discussed the emergence of rap music because Run-DMC had created such a stir or mini-frenzy that night. Then came a call a while after this, I think from Eleonore, who hired me to scour the city for the largest pumpkin I could find for the Grateful Dead's Halloween concert at The Lyceum Theatre. Again, I didn't meet Bill.

The first time I really got to work with Bill was when we all started out helping with the Amnesty International world tour. The BGP gang helped produce Amnesty International's A Conspiracy of Hope tour a few years earlier.

There was a knock on our office door, which was now a small, loft-style apartment in a five- story building on West 56th Street. "Who's there?" "Bill," again, the voice before the man. I opened the door. Large, but mellow is what I remember now. I think we shook hands then and there. This was the first time we met each other face to face. I too had pretty much always been proceeded by my distinctive voice.

What a great day that was. I remember it like it was yesterday. Bill and Michael had made amends after some horrible arguments during Live Aid. The three of us had lunch together. Bill had a liverwurst sandwich. Most likely Michael had grilled cheddar with extra crispy bacon and me, my faithful provolone cheese sandwich on a roll with mayo, o&v, l&t, s&p.

I've been a Tibetan Buddhist practitioner since my late teens. At around this same time, early on in the coordination of the Amnesty International World Tour, I learned that a group of Tibetan Monks were creating a sand mandala at the American Museum of Natural History. I mentioned this to Bill and about my interest in Tibetan Buddhism, and much to my surprise he joined me for a visit to the museum – clearly, a memory I hold on to fondly.

It must have been the summer of 1991. Michael was in Europe with the Rolling Stones' Urban Jungle Tour when Bill reached out to see if I could hold down his New York office as he was going to try to produce a Harry Belafonte show at Yankee Stadium. We had one meeting at the East 64th Street townhouse, but all I remember is him talking to me about his business strategies and relating that to how to play chess. We also talked about my passion for documentaries and wish to produce and direct them. The Harry Belafonte show never happened. I was preparing to move to San Francisco in January, but Bill's untimely death in October brought an abrupt ending to a dream I was so close to seeing come true.

Which brings me to remembering October 25, 1991. I'm sure it was before 6:00 a.m. EST that my phone rang. The time of the call was not alarming or unusual as Michael was in Europe. Back in those days, calls came in 'round the clock but when it was Shelley Lazar on the phone; that was unusual.

She told me what happened then asked how she could reach Michael because they did not want the story on the news until certain people had been notified. I ran to fetch the small, plastic ring- bound paper itinerary for whatever tour or project Michael was on at that time. I remember, Michael was in Germany. Shelley of course called to tell Michael about the horrible accident that claimed Bill, Melissa, and Steve "Killer" Kahn – another BGPer I'd become very close with. It wasn't a half hour later that Michael called me to see how I was doing. I remember him saying he can imagine I must be very upset because of how close I'd become with him.

There are no answers for the ways we've seen. I'm thankful now to share a few words and memories about Bill and to reconnect with these life-long friends I've made along the way.

I can't help myself but to sign off as Bill did… Cheers!

DORE COLLER

The first time I met Bill I was 13 going on 14. I was going to see the Jefferson Airplane's first show at the Fillmore East. I had been to con-certs and peace marches in New York City already, taking the train down and back, but my Dad wanted to drive me down from the sub-urbs for this show because he had gone to NYU and wanted to see his old college haunts, obviously trying to protect me in his own way.

We're talking about the East Village in May of 1968, a total freak show. All street people and colors and the Electric Circus on St. Marks Place, where two generations ago my relatives were the scions of the Yiddish Theatre (check out what Michael Tilson Thomas says about his grandfather, Boris. They were the Barrymores of that scene.) We walked around, gave money to panhandlers, bought a copy of the East Village, ran into Buffy St. Marie on Second Avenue and Third or Fourth Street right below the Fillmore East. I was starstruck; one of my favorite albums at that time was Fire Fleet and Candlelight, and she was so beautiful! I was delighted by the whole scene and my dad kept up a decent front which I will give him total credit for that.

Anyhow, he leaves me in front of the Fillmore East in line with my ticket and I see Bill hanging out. He had on the cap he liked to wear back then with a couple of cornflowers about six inches long sticking out like an antenna in front of him.

He was relaxed, just enjoying the scene, really just about three months in for the Fillmore East.

Being the bashful fellow that all know so well, I wanted to meet the guy at the center of this amazing new scene. I decided to go up and ask Bill when he was going to have Cream, my favorite band at the time, play the Fillmore. Bill was gracious, not condescending towards some kid bugging him and told me that he hoped to be able to book them soon, but he wasn't sure he could get them. They only played in New York twice after that: once at Fordham University and, of course, the farewell show at Madison Square Garden that November. Bill never did get them back at the Fillmore East. Don't know what the relationship with Robert Stigwood was, but apparently not good enough. I would love to know the inside story from someone about that, maybe Jerry Pompili.

So, first impressions, first time at the Fillmore East. Went there many, many times after that and pretty much all of the Dead, Airplane and Tuna shows and a bunch of others.

The next time I met Bill was outside of Winterland, December of 1973. I had just seen the Dead and my face, hair, neck and arms were painted completely silver. I had been at a friend's house getting high, playing with his Etch-A-Sketch and it broke. When I saw what was inside, I decided to smear it all over my face and hair and be really freaky for the show. Nothing short of a miracle that I didn't die of lead poisoning, right? Anyhow, it was after the show, which was a rainy, rainy night, and I was out front crying out if anyone wanted to take a space cowboy home. Bill saw me, rolled his eyes and helped me find a ride to my friend's place.

My first show as a Bluecoat was the Rolling Stones at Candlestick Park. Ann Krcik via Davis Baltz got me the gig. It was the first time BGP had hired up so many Bluecoats. I was assigned to Johanna

Lewis' crew. She put me in the scissor gate, the entrance to the huge guest seating area stage right.

I was the worst Bluecoat imaginable. I was too nice and people would walk right through me, and I was so terrible that the people sitting around the gate working tried to help me. They told me to put on sunglasses saying that my eyes are too nice, don't talk, just point, because your voice is too nice. I did everything wrong; anybody with some pot or mushrooms could bribe their way in. On my breaks I went backstage, ate at catering, walked into Peter Barsotti's tent and asked for some backstage passes for my collection. He stared at me in utter disbelief and then in shock gave me a handful - just the worst. But I didn't abandon my post and I learned.

I learned from all my Bluecoat brethren, but also from Bill - by example, from his conviction, from his presentation of integrity, from his presentation of bad-assedness. Remembering those speeches before a big show, they made a strong impression, really instructing us on how to act, how to carry ourselves, how to address and deal with the crowd.

Something I learned from Bill and BGP employees was how to turn the tough guy on and off, like there was a little switch inside me. You could be talking to a patron in a friendly manner, dealing with an issue graciously, and if things with someone else suddenly turned sour you could switch it on and deal on a totally different level. That sort of instant diplomacy switch is something I learned from Bill Graham.

I'm not a big guy, couldn't control the results of a fight very well by myself, but I was a strong factor to deal with and anyone coming at me would have to think twice because they might be able to take me, but not the other six to ten BGPers who would come to my aid.

I remember one time at a Rush show at the Cow Palace in San Francisco (why did they insist on seats at a general admission show? Such an awful crowd!) A couple of big guys were tussling with me and when they did, Ross Cascio came up from behind and flattened them and said, "Yeah, but at least we get paid to be assholes."

Another remembrance was working with Bill at the Fela Kuti show at the Berkeley Community Theater. Fela had just gotten released from prison and it was his first time back to the United States. Mayor

141

Lionel Wilson gave him the key to the City of Oakland before he started to play. A momentous, prestigious show and Bill was proud to have it and wanted it to go without a hitch. I was positioned center aisle at the entrance to the orchestra pit trying to keep things smooth right up front.

About halfway through the show there was a young hippie guy just off the aisle who wouldn't sit down (in front seating was Bill, Jerry Pompili, Steve Rigney and Molly Frink - everyone I wanted to make sure had a hassle-free musical evening.) We tried speaking to this gentleman, but he was acting like he was very high, in a trance and wouldn't even acknowledge that we were talking to him. After a while Bill came up and asked us (it was Andy Zacks and me) what was going on. Bill went up to the guy and tried to talk to him, trying to get his attention, but to no avail. The last thing any of us wanted was a security scene in the middle of this show. After awhile with this guy ignoring even Bill, Bill motioned to us to take him out. We had to drag him up the center aisle, no fun, but we did it as smoothly as we could. That's what we were there to do - to deal with whatever came up. Of course, when we got him outside he stood up, brushed himself off and said, "Hey, it was worth a try." We didn't kill him.

Over the years there were lots of interactions: How Bill would appear in an aisle you were trying to clear, with his notecards (the clipboard was too big after a while). Or at the front of the stage (where a knife got thrown at him and Randy Bushner blocked it!) Or hanging out at the office after Live Aid when he had us all over to share tales of the event. I remember him telling me the biggest prick he dealt with at Live Aid was not any of the stars but Dick Clark. Or encouraging me to make extra sure that my crew kept the crowd from standing on their chairs at the Rolling Stones. I still have one of the sweatshirts somewhere we had that said, "Don't Stand on the Seats!") Or playing ball at a Bluecoat picnic on the courts at Masada, Bill's home. Or hanging out at the stage left pass gate at Henry J. Kaiser in Oakland with Bob Hope as they toured the Concert for Care shows after the Loma Prieta Quake.

Bill liked to be everywhere on all levels and he always added an extra touch and an extra piece of class even though other people might consider it pearls before swine. Bill knew how to enhance the events to make sure everyone had a good time and felt like they had experienced a special event, even the artists. I remember right after Bill passed, we had a show with Ricki Lee Jones at the Palace of Fine Arts in San Francisco. Rita Gentry had to bring a velvet robe that Bill had purchased as a gift to give to Ricki Lee Jones. It was a perfect example of that extra attention that Bill gave to things and we all felt it. Sure he was gruff, but he had a huge heart and wasn't afraid to put it out there and make something good happen, whether it was a concert or politics or something for his people, which I still consider an honor and a privilege to have been one of.

DOUG WENDT

One of my favorite stories of working with Bill Graham was the time I was waiting at the top of the stairs for African reggae great Alpha Blondy to arrive to the 260 Fifth Street office.

The Ivory Coaster was in town for another packed BGP performance and Harry Duncan, Gary Lambert, and I, of special BGP world music promotions, had wrangled Arts Editor Joel Selvin to do an interview in advance.

Alpha was on time, so we cooled our heels waiting for Joel to walk the couple of blocks from the Chronicle office to ours. Bill was strolling through the main booking "war room," spotted Blondy and came over, inviting us to his corner office. I don't think he was aware of exactly why Alpha was there except that he was in town to play for Bill.

Once inside Graham's office, I immediately spotted two Alpha Blondy albums on top of his desk: Alpha's top-ranking masterpieces Apartheid Is Nazism and Jerusalem, the latter recorded with Bob Marley's Wailers after his passing, with the hauntingly beautiful title track sung in five languages, all for unity. Bill mentioned he'd been listening to the CDs that morning driving into work and how much he loved both creations and listened often.

He said, "Alpha, I'm going to be touring Africa for the first time this year with the Amnesty International benefit concert and need your advice on where it's okay to play." He spread out a large map of

Africa on the floor on his hands and knees, motioning for Blondy to join him.

I watched in amazement as Alpha, also on all fours, went over the map in great detail with Graham, describing various countries he'd had concerts in and where it had been the most problematic. He was effusive, from being forced to do special unpaid private or other performances to being held hostage for renegotiated terms and more strange shenanigans he'd confronted just trying to play for, and survive, various governments, kings, and bigwigs. He concluded by recommending places that could be relied on to act honorably. As usual Bill got right on it and soon Amnesty's big annual tour safely made its first ever concert visit to the motherland of mankind and music.

I remember saying at one point, "If folks really want to help Africa outside of special crises fundraising events, it's way past time to just start exposing and playing its artists and music regularly as a major part of all outlets, festivals, media and special occasions." After a few minutes, Selvin arrived and Alpha had to go. Youssou N'Dour from Senegal was a major act on that worldwide Amnesty International tour.

Bill Graham was an unflappably committed advocate of the thriving the world music scene from his deep love of Latin sounds through his get-go Fillmore days to the worldbeat Bay Area bands of the late 1980s and early 1990s. Bill's death was an incalculable loss for that global momentum.

When the lights dimmed across the Bay Area just as his helicopter hit the tower in that terrible rainstorm, I was on the floor in my San Francisco apartment reading a Rolling Stone article on the first ever major rock festival just held in Russia. It was very poorly presented on some inadequate airport tarmac. I had been recalling Bill telling me how pissed he was that he didn't get that gig, that big corporations had no idea of how to do it successfully, and it would be botched. Just about the time I thought, "Oh gawd, what would the concert world be like without Bill?" the lights flickered. We all soon found out what that world is. I was devastated.

As the proverb says, "Where there is no vision, the people perish: but he that keepeth the law, happy is he." The latter reminds me

144

of another great Graham episode which I'll save for later. My Greek Theatre lunch with Bill where I found out exactly what the San Francisco Chronicle had dubbed his "wild west" rule in 1960s San Francisco was all about. Soar on high big guy. Many are called, few are chosen. Love up....

DREW HOLMES

I contemplated what would be interesting, what would be beneficial, and what should the populace need/want to know about my experiences with BGP and catering. Needless to say, I have a lot of standouts. The odd ones are the shows I had to do myself without my sisters, Bettike and Tricia, because they were working other shows on the same nights at places like the Cow Palace, Winterland and even the San Francisco Opera House.

Bill had booked the Chinese Opera for three weeks at the Warfield Theater in San Francisco. I worked these shows by myself. Wow! I never in my life saw so many people consume large amounts of sugar. All the donuts that I would place out were gone in seconds flat, as well as all the sugar packets. Mind you, no coffee was consumed. Oh, and they kept coming back to the kitchen to see if I had any more sugar or pastries. I then had to say, "no" to the manager who was the only one who spoke English, a Mao Tse Tung guard if you will. But these people were incredible athletes, contortionists, magicians, gymnasts and I really wanted to get to know them. In the course of three weeks with huge language barriers, I did connect with the whole troupe. Hey, they knew I would be bringing the donuts!

My mom had Bettike first, a year later my brother John came along, and a year after that I entered the world. Our brother John was visiting California for a few weeks. The Grateful Dead were playing the Greek Theatre in Berkeley and Peter put my brother John down as stage security.

Jerry Garcia comes up and brother John says, "You need a laminate to be on stage, sir." Jerry was actually very amused and said, "I'm with the band." John had never seen the Dead no less was a fan if you will. John said, "Well, you still need a pass sir." Obviously he took his job very seriously. Just then Peter B. came up and introduced John to Jerry and the band played on… LOL!

I sure do miss my family members Bettike, Peter, Tricia and Lord knows how many others…

E

EDAN MILTON HUGHES by Rita Gentry

Wikipedia – Edan Milton Hughes (1935-2015) was an American art dealer and collector of California art. He wrote the definitive work on California artists.

For over five decades, he researched and collected early California art. His three-volume Artists in California, 1786-1940, is the standard reference book on the subject. Until his passing in 2015, he collected some of the most well-regarded early California artists. Edan has donated Artists in California, his lifework, along with all future income and publishing rights to the Crocker Art Museum in Sacramento.

Lastly, he was for many decades the night janitor at all Bill Graham Presents offices. Sometimes working very late at the office it was so wonderful to have them there with me in the background.

Dianna Arnspiger has kindly passed on a story about Edan as he is no longer with us.

Dianna says: One night, I was working late at the office and Edan Hughes, a long-time staff member who kept the office clean, was the only person there. He came by my desk and we talked about how we were both there late and he said, "Bill used to always be the last person here."

We got to talking and Edan told me a great story. He said that one night he had been having a rough time, and was really worried about his finances. He really needed a thousand dollars and was wracking his brain as to how he was going to come up with that kind of money. He was off vacuuming in a room across the building and assumed Bill was in his own office. Suddenly, Edan felt a presence behind him

147

and turned around. It was Bill, standing in the doorway just staring at him. The two did not exchange words, but Bill opened up his arms towards Edan and they embraced.

Bill slipped something into Edan's back pocket. After he left the room, Edan looked and it was a thousand-dollar bill.

EDDIE PALMIERI

From Bill Graham I learned that punctuality is class. He told me my music is always in the pocket.

Loved you Uncle Bill!

ELEONORE HOCKABOUT

How I Became a Part of the BGP Party.

It was July 1967, in the Summer of Love, when I came to California from Vienna with my American husband and pregnant with our first baby. We settled into my parents- in-law's house in Alameda, the small town with a feeling of the gone-by Fifties. Years later, in 1989, when working at the Bay Area Music Awards (the BAMMIES) one of the Oakland blues musicians asked me where I lived and, when answering, Alameda, he smiled and said, "Ah, Kansas of the East Bay!" Wink…

When still in Europe I was aware of the civil rights movement, Mario Savio in Berkeley, the tragedy of the Vietnam War, had felt the shock of the Kennedy assassination. I was a huge fan of Bob Dylan and The Stones, but loved continental music also, the Greek sirtakis, the Portuguese fados, the French singers Aznavour, Brel, Piaf. My years as a flight attendant took me from Vienna to London, Paris, Rome, Moscow, Beirut, Cairo, Athens and all over Europe and the Middle East. I had an adventurous life.

Now part of a conservative family, without a car, alien to place and culture I found myself far from where the action was, where THE music happened, Winterland, the Fillmore, the Haight, the hippies, Berkeley, the Mime Troupe and Bill's doings. Between 1967 and 1981, I enjoyed being a mom to our two little boys, to play and discover with them. When they were in elementary school, I returned to college and graduated from Oakland's California College of the Arts in Environmental Design in spring 1981. Ha, I had my car by then, a VW Rabbit.

My love of rock and roll had never stopped since I discovered it in the '50s and grew when I met students at the college who had formed bands and played in the small clubs of San Francisco and Berkeley. In 1976, I saw A Star is Born with Kris Kristofferson, of whom I was a big fan.

When I came out of the theatre, a strange thing happened to me. Above in the dark, clear night sky I had the vision of my pianist grandmother, translucent and luminous, whispering: "Where is the music in your life?" This was one of these eureka moments, one of sudden clarity for my path ahead.

During my studies, I had felt confusion about working in the corporate world of office and commercial space design. The movie had made me curious about the behind-the-scenes production work of rock concerts. I began to book the small college band I knew into clubs, trying myself at managing without having the faintest idea of what I was doing. I know it was fun to climb up the fire escape to get to a booker's office at the Keystone Corner in Berkeley. I stayed until the early morning hours at Mabuhay Gardens to pick up "peanuts" from Ness Aquino long after the band had gone home.

Dirk Dirksen, the tough guy promoter of the space up a long flight of stairs at the Mabuhay told me, "Well, Eleonore, the band is not bad but you have to do better publicity to get a bigger audience!" We rarely got weekend dates or headliner gigs. At one time, my dance buddy friend Minoo and I thought of promoting Blue Mondays at the Keystone Corner. We had paint available, asked people to paint their face blue - small success on a Monday night. But I loved these nights, the live music in the clubs where smoking was still allowed, the audiences, the darkness of the clubs, the whole scene. Still, management skills needed major help. Overall though, always a night owl, this work fit me perfectly and my family put up with me.

Bow to them.

After graduation in May 1981, I was offered a job at a major architectural firm in San Francisco. I had dressed up appropriately for the interview: olive leather suede top, olive straight gabardine skirt, heels and portfolio in hand. This was the fork in the road, I loved this firm and their work, but something in me said, "NO!" I felt nauseous, weighing a career path with income versus the unknown, worse even, the possibly frivolous. I had a few months before my job would start, so I continued my music connection.

It was October 1981 when I had arranged a meeting with one of the musicians to go over the sketch for a stage backdrop. I waited and waited in a café on Fillmore and Steiner Street in San Francisco, but the guy did not show up. Daytime appointments were never easy for the night- loving types. I knew The Stones were coming into town and decided to drive out to Candlestick Park, hoping to catch a glimpse of the stage prep.

I parked in the vast empty parking lot on a brilliant, sunny fall day, grabbed my clipboard and pencil, my "security props," hoping to look professional, acting as if I belonged there. At that time, I did sketch in clubs, artists, for the late Jim Carroll, people in the audience, at the bar.

A car pulled up beside me, a Volkswagen bug, stuffed so full the guy could hardly see out of any windows other than the front one. He stepped out of the car, approached me and said, "Hi, I came from Colorado. I worked on the show there. I came all the way looking for work here. Do you know where I need to go? You look like you'd know." I guess my props worked. I told him, sorry, I did not. In a flash I thought, "Well, maybe I could find work here too?"

I pointed to him where I thought the staging area was, and he walked off. I, instead, found my way into the upper tiers, the stage far down in the distance from me. I sat for a while seeing men building high up on the scaffolding. I just watched, no sketching at all, sat for a while longer, and then decided to go down to the construction site. The workers looked pale and tired to my pampered eye. I asked them where I might get a job. They were friendly and pointed to the trailer behind me. I turned around, walked up the stairs and knocked on the door.

When I entered I saw two men on the phone. I waited, stood there not wanting to interrupt. One of the men got up (it was Peter Barsotti) approaching the door, I suddenly blocked his path, stepped in front of him and said point blank: "Hi, I'm Eleonore. I am a designer. Do you have a job for me?" He stopped, looked at me with a twinkle in his eyes and said: "Too bad, I gave it away this morning, but give me your name and number, and we'll call you when we have something." I noticed he was a fast talker and very to the point. "What the heck!" I thought. Why would I think it could be so easy to get work here? I walked down the stairs, Peter walked off towards the stage.

Just then, I heard someone shouting after me: "Come back! I might have something for you!" I returned to the trailer and the man (I wish I remember the production manager's name) asked, "Do you want to be a runner?" "What's a runner?" I asked. Well, you get us anything we need. Wow! "Yes!" I said, heart pounding. And I said, "I can start right now and I can work 24/7." Hmmm? "Do you know the city?" he asked. "Oh yes!" Not true at all, but I had a map, my VW Rabbit and that's all I needed. By the way, the man in the parking lot was hired as a stagehand.

I was introduced to Ron Schaeffer, who told me only recently that he was the man in charge of provisions. This seemed like heaven. I called home using the crew phone and told my guys the news. "Imagine! I got a job at The Stones concert! But I won't be home until late and don't really know exactly when." Nevertheless, my three males sounded excited too.

I filled in some form, was given a sticker pass, and sent out to pick up stuff right then and there. On my second day, Peter Barsotti gave me a design project on top of my runner tasks, to construct a 3' x 3' x 3' cube out of foam mattress material. A store on the corner of Geneva Avenue in San Francisco cut the foam pieces to size. I built this object bit by bit between runs, gluing the layers together and adding black dots to make it into a die - the tumbling dice to be thrown off the stage when the song came on.

Hahaha - no farther out than 30 feet this thing was torn to shreds by the raucous, ravenous crowd.

SO THAT WAS IT, the beginnings of my slow slouch into the BGP family. I caught a glimpse of Bill once as he walked up the incline behind the stage. For me it was now all about working behind the scenes in production, to get to know the inner workings of these events. Bill was The Guy, the best in the country and beyond in those times. What luck to be in his territory.

It took a while to become a full time "family" member. For months I was on the phone bugging production with, "Do you need a runner, do you have work for me?" To earn money, a friend and I did manual typesetting for a tech company on the peninsula. Several times a week I walked out to the telephone booth in the yard during my breaks to make my squeaky-wheel calls to BGP. I must mention that I had cancelled my job offer at the architect firm. When there was work, I was the runner, but began to get on backstage projects with Lance Miller, too. At The Cow Palace, Lance asked me to be on the carpentry crew with Art Kimura. As I hammered together a railing, I hit down on my thumb hard, ending my carpentry career in agony. I had taken one semester of woodshop at CCAC, but gave up when the saws gave me the chills. Drawing up plans with materials lists and cost proposals became helpful to production and led to more assignments. The runner position was now a job done often by me rather than the stagehands only.

My husband was an early Macintosh savvy guy and suggested a system to help with the stagehand booking and scheduling in support of production management. I proposed this to Peter Barsotti and was given the task in addition to my other activities. The latter earned me the "Babysitter of the Year Award" at one of our Christmas parties.

Smile! My workload got bigger. I became part of the out of town teams, Cal Expo Amphitheater in Sacramento, Shoreline Amphitheater in Mountain View. I had to leave scheduling behind when I was sent out of town more and more. The runner job was taken over by some young and excellent newcomers.

The middle '80s with Bill became the defining time for me with the many benefits around social justice on a global scale from Live Aid to Amnesty International and the Moscow Peace Concert, the shining beacons. By then I had been hired full time and was going out of town often. I had no official title while doing production design and managing, art direction, most projects being site related, designing minor stage sets, reconfiguring spaces. What a joy the fantastic New Year's celebrations and various Grateful Dead events were!

The awareness how my early life connected with this NOW still blows my mind, all was meaningful, made sense and was full of joy in spite of the hard, often exhausting teamwork. Out on the road, my silly teenage dream of running away with the leather-clad carnies in my hometown had become reality too. Springsteen's Asbury Park and "Sandy" ringing in my ears.

It may be hard to grasp what I felt in my heart working for Bill as a gentile immigrant from Austria born in 1940, unharmed by the war, coerced to share our house with Russian occupation soldiers, having survived the horrors of my time by pure luck. Yes, I had felt guilt. For me, Bill Graham was the ultimate MENSCH, a bright light encouraging, empowering, generous in spirit, the one who, together with Peter Barsotti, gave me my first job in the United States and put my New World roots deeper into the ground.

Thank you, Bill Graham; thank you, Peter Barsotti, and thank you to the whole BGP Family in the office and the teams out in the field and in the venues, all those it took to paint, as Bill said in a letter to me, "the big murals" he cherished. I am forever grateful having been part of the BGP family.

ERIC BLOCKIE

My start with Bill Graham Presents was June 26, 1982, at a Day on the Green show with Journey; I was a kid from Hayward, California who was lucky enough to know Mick Jones through a mutual friend that got an underaged kid a job working at the mixer. I became a full-time employee in June of 1988 until the date that the company was sold to SFX Entertainment.

I met Bill Graham working as a Bluecoat early in my career, but did not develop a close relationship with him until I became the assistant office manager at 260 Fifth Street in San Francisco, consisting of giving breaks to the main receptionist for lunch and her breaks, taking care of things that needed to be done at the office and answering the office phones after working hours. This would be from 6:00 to 6:30 p.m. when most of the staff had gone home. Calls would come in for

Bill after 6:00 p.m. and after I found out who was on the line, which could be anybody from an agent, manager or even a superstar (especially when Mick Jagger would call). I would then contact Bill to see if he wanted to accept the call.

At 6:30 p.m. I would go to his office and tell him I was leaving for the day and we had many short, but very rewarding conversations on life and how to treat people and how not to take any shit from people and to stand your ground if you were truly passionate on the issue at hand.

My favorite story about Bill is when we were producing In Concert for AIDS at the Oakland Coliseum and I was working with the Special Events Division. We had a VIP area behind the stage that the public could buy into that had food and drinks that raised $150,000 as a standalone event and he was so proud of the event and personally thanked me in a letter after the event.

On the 25th anniversary of BGP, we received a BGP jacket that Bill had made for us. He would call you into his office to present it to you personally and we (all full-time employees) received a one-time bonus of $1,000 for each year of employment. My bonus was $5,000. I was so moved by his encouragement. He wanted me to buy something that I always wanted and not to pay off credit cards. I bought a 1969 Corvette that I still have to this day. I grew up in Hayward, California and had no relatives that worked at BGP, but I figured out a way to survive and he always, in passing, acknowledged my presence, which I am grateful for today.

I held various jobs inside BGP, but the most interaction I had with Bill was when working as the assistant office manager at the 260 Fifth Street office where I worked with all the departments and Bill Graham himself, as directed by Rita or Jan, to do errands, from taking Bill to the bank and picking him up at the airport in the company station wagon.

I had the pleasure of working at Masada, Bill's home, to park cars for fundraisers for Bread and Roses and a few other events, but when I was called to help clear a fence line in the brush down from his house I caught a severe case of poison oak. I didn't know it, but I transferred it to his dog, and only realized this when I noticed calamine lotion on his desk.

Reading the Bugsy movie script into a tape recorder and leaving his line out so he could practice in the car while driving was a fun time.

The private conversations that I had with Bill - good and bad - are what made me today the best that I can be in public assemblage.

I could go on and on with stories about playing sports with Bill, such as the BGP softball team or the BGP football games against Bob Weir and Woody Harrelson in Golden Gate Park, but that's another time.

Thanks to Bill, I now work for the City of San Antonio programming the Alamodome, Illusions Theater and Sunken Gardens Amphitheater.

ERIC CHRISTENSEN

I first met Bill Graham when he did the Mime Troupe Benefits before the Fillmore. I had attended a couple of those shows along with two of the three nights of the Trips Festival for which Bill sold tickets and ran around with a clipboard trying to make order out of all the chaos. I documented this in my film The Trips Festival. I was just 17 years old, but had been working after school at Autumn Records and Tempo Productions for Tom Donahue. Donahue had put on shows at the Cow Palace featuring all the top forty acts of the early 1960s, and The Beatles' two Bay Area shows, one at the Cow Palace and one at Candlestick Park, which somehow turned out to be their last live show. I worked at those shows and was so turned on to rock music that I managed to go to every show I could possibly attend. I became friends with Bill and some of his early staff, and somehow managed to get on the guest list.

As a student at UC Berkeley in the late 1960s, I was a political activist and a rock and roller. These two merged when, in May of 1969, I worked on building People's Park, an act that defied the University of California's plans for a vacant piece of land near the campus. When the police arrested hundreds of protesters, there was a need for a bail fund. I called Bill and told him of the situation.

155

He quickly replied, "You get the acts, you can have Winterland free of charge." I immediately called Rock Scully of the Grateful Dead and he talked to the group and they said yes. The same with Bill Thompson, manager of Jefferson Airplane and they also said yes. Other groups soon joined in - Creedence Clearwater Revival, Santana, the Elvin Bishop Group, and Bangor Flying Circus rounded out the bill for a sold-out concert on May 28, 1969.

In my opinion, that was the most star-studded lineup Bill had put on, only to be eclipsed by The Last Waltz at Winterland. Part of Bill's incredible legacy will be the number of benefit concerts he produced, from Farm Aid, the Loma Prieta Earthquake, Amnesty International and for many more worthwhile causes.

The guest list thing became more official when I became Program Director for KGO-FM and KSFX from 1970-1972. I first actually worked with Bill and his staff when I produced the closing of the Fillmore radio broadcasts on KSFX, and later as Arts and Entertainment producer from 1972 on KGO-TV. I became the go-to guy for BGP at the television station, and I often was the one to interview Bill and coordinate coverage of BGP events.

I also became friends with Chet Helms and was on the guest list for his Avalon and Great Highway shows. I knew Bill was going to be financially more successful because in those days I would go to the Avalon and there would be a short line to the left of the box office and a long line along Sutter Street to the right. The short line on the left was to buy tickets and the long line was for the guest list. The opposite was true at The Fillmore.

I was always impressed with how Bill would book shows that often had a jazz act play with the Dead or Airplane, or a blues legend on the bill with one of the top rock acts.

Bill helped the careers of those artists and exposed them to a whole new audience. The most impressive show Bill pulled off was The Last Waltz, Thanksgiving evening, November 25. Not only did The Band play what was billed as their farewell concert, guests included Bob Dylan, Eric Clapton, Ringo Starr, Ronnie Wood, Muddy Waters, Neil Young, Neil Diamond, Van Morrison, Bobby Charles, Dr. John, Paul Butterfield, Emmylou Harris, Ronnie Hawkins, Joni Mitchell and the

Staple Singers. A sit-down dinner with turkey and all the trimmings was served to all who attended. That was easily one of the best evenings of my life, and to those of you who helped make this happen, as Bill would write, "Cheers!"

In the mid-seventies, Bill hired Dave and Dell Furano to help expand the scope of what BGP did. Out of that came Winterland Productions and a film division that I became staff producer of for a short time. During that time, I did a promo film for Focus on Fitness, Bill's ill-fated attempt to get involved in the fitness craze. I also did promo videos for Santana and Eddie Money, acts that Bill managed. But most importantly, I produced and directed A Day on the Green July 2 and 4, 1977. My three-camera crew shot both days with footage of Peter Frampton, Lynyrd Skynyrd and Santana. The Skynyrd footage of "Freebird" and "Sweet Home Alabama" has been viewed by millions of people on YouTube and used in a couple of documentaries about Lynyrd Skynyrd. The numerous Oakland Coliseum Days on the Green shows were part of an amazing legacy that Bill Graham created, and just to have called him a friend and have him as a mentor in many ways, makes me think about him often and how he impacted my career, all with fond memories.

ERIC WILLIAMS

Geologically speaking, you can't speak about this industry unless you speak of its foundation and in the case of performance, Bill Graham is the rock upon which our church is built.

Over a thousand people are better to speak about BG than I, but my connection to him brought me something special so I'll bend your ear with this story.

It all began on what I will always say is the hottest day in our nation's history, July 13, 1985, Live Aid. My entrée to that event was REO Speedwagon and serving as the assistant to Tom Consolo, the band's tour manager. I helped the band through our 18-hour stop in Philly. Flush with our success with the number one song, "I Can't Fight This Feeling," we played a day show in Cleveland, jumped the jet to Philadelphia, checked into the Ben Franklin Hotel and were immediately presented with the summons to appear before the event's godhead, Bill Graham.

Trundling the entourage to the production HQ at the Embassy Suites, we were met by the XXXL persona of the Man-In- Charge himself and ushered into his suite of offices.

Meeting him was big enough, but if that wasn't enough, I was momentarily stunned by his incredible assistant.

Extracting myself from the moment, I was doing my very best Bogart to say hello in a somewhat meaningful way to Rita Gentry. The band caught the level of impact and suggested that I refocus on the subject at hand, but I had been hit.

The next day was large and after our performance in front of many, televised to many more and captured on tape forever, we were thoroughly engrossed with the effort. I even got to sing backup on "Roll with the Changes," a moment that makes me smile to this day. But I still remembered that pretty girl.

Fast forward to 1993 and I am in Hollywood and my company, The Special Services Group, is doing well, staying busy and providing production support worldwide. A friend at the time calls and tells me that he's got a gig for me. He says that there's a show he's running at the Masonic in San Francisco and he wants to know if I want to stage manage it. Flight to SF, lodging at a cool and groovy psychedelic shack in Berkeley, a great dinner with equally cool and groovy folk and a guaranteed great time would be had by all. I thought, "Wow, sounds great." I then wondered aloud why he wasn't getting someone locally and he dropped the bombshell of the benefit factor. Having some free time and anticipating the fun part of the deal, I said, "Sure, why not?"

All things going swimmingly, I arrived at the venue and walked through the night's rundown with bands and crew. At some point, I ended up in the production office and who did I see? That girl. She wondered aloud had if we'd met before and after piecing it together, we finally figured it out. I made many excuses to visit production during the day and during that time heard her negotiating with her daughter, Gina, regarding the acquisition of a pet rabbit.

The show was a blast and the visit promised a future second act to the re-introduction process, and so I was left with the conundrum of the grand gesture that would be required to provide maximum impact. The next day allowed for little productivity towards the cause as I only had so much time pre-flight, and I rambled across San Francisco to find a pet store to find the elusive rabbit. Who knew, certainly not me, that a recent piece of local legislation had prohibited rodent sales in the city and after visiting the only two pet shops I could cover, I was told that my quest was impossible. Not by a stretch was I to be to shut out, so I bought a small fury brontosaurus and thought that the kid, and more importantly her mom, would be impressed and dig it immensely. Nicely I note that Dino is still property of Gina Belle. I had it delivered to BGP headquarters and BARTed to the airport.

There was further courtship: me working Woodstock 1994 and we had an incredible vacation trip to Belize together, coming into an agreement that we would move in together in San Francisco. A beautiful apartment in the North Beach/Wharf area and life was magic.

One of the greatest gifts Rita gives is granting membership in the Gentry family, something that I still enjoy. Her mom and dad, Betty and Jack, and her brother, Lee and the wonderful Ruth and four daughters were the best you could ever hope for. Family holiday times were incredible.

So, this is where my submission to the book really begins….

Somewhere along in 1995, Rita calls home and says, "Guess who is playing the Fillmore tonight? Little Feat!" I love Feat, and if you don't, you have no business reading this book, so off we went. As the ultimate Production Babe, she had advanced our arrival and, due to the sellout, was told we would be seated in the spotlight nest. We loved that idea and soon made ourselves comfy. The manager du jour (or more accurately, du soir) came over and said that Carlos Santana was there and that he was coming over to sit with us.

Now, this was during the time when the Santana Express was in a holding pattern, a concept that nowadays seems rather strange and Carlos was kinda just floating around town.

Intermission comes up and I ask him what he has been up to. Now, if you have ever sat with Carlos, and most of you have, he has the rare gift of making you feel like the two of you are the only ones breathing for miles.

So, Rita and I are transfixed listening to him tell this story about getting fax transmissions from Bill up in heaven. Bill is sending him a message to produce a show about the Dead. I asked how and he pulls out a thermographic fax paper, like the kind we used to use, and shows us the transmission. I said, "Let me see that." He explains that the strange lines were tones that he transposed to music. What he didn't realize was that it was just electronic fuzz from a loose fax cable. I asked him how often this happened and he said like every now and then. The stage manager popped in and told him that the band wanted him to jam and off he went.

The night was great and the show was so good. We jumped in the car and started to drive home. Rita looked at me and said, "Give it to me." I played dumb cause that's what guys do in that situation. Fax pages often had the header with sender/receiver info on it so for the next six months or so, at midnight, I faxed Carlos some unintelligible gibberish. I felt like I was somehow participating in the creative process.

Life being as it is, somehow Rita and I lost our way and I left San Francisco for New Orleans and running a cigar store. Rita left BGP and went to work for Santana Management. Carlos, as everyone knows, rebounded quite nicely and the ensuing album was a smash. The hit went to number one and Rolling Stone published the obligatory cover story. Rita called me in New Orleans. "Tomorrow the Rolling Stone issue comes out with Carlos on the cover. Run down and buy yourself one. Read the article and call me immediately." In the article, Carlos mentioned his receiving fax transmissions from the Angel Metatron on a consistent basis leading to the inspiration for the songs on Supernatural. Suddenly I got lightheaded.

I called Rita and she immediately said, "Carlos is in the next room. If he hears me start to yell at you, I will kill you. One word to anyone about those stupid faxes and I will never speak to you again." (I should have filed for royalties, but then I wouldn't be telling you this story, would I?) Looking back on that hard-won love, I could never, ever want to be on the bad side of that girl, so this is the first telling of the story.

Sometimes if I listen closely while reminiscing, somewhere in the background, I could hear Bill saying, "It's not about the money, it's about the money."

ERIN GRAVELIN DHRUVA

Getting an internship at Bill Graham Presents right out of college was a dream come true for me. I was able to work in Bill Graham Management and it was a learning experience like no other. Not only did I learn about the business, I learned about Bill and how things had been before I'd arrived. I will never forget the first day. I walked into the offices on Fifth Street and wound my way down the hallways, trying to be cool and composed while passing all of the concert posters and memorabilia on my way back to the archive department. This place was pulsing and buzzing with activity and energy and I was exactly where I wanted to be. I would end up working in multiple departments and would leave the company and return a few times, but one thing would remain over time: the connection, the caring, the personalities, and the fun. I have so many memories of that time, but there are a few that stand out.

When I was still an intern in Bill Graham Management, my dad died very unexpectedly. He had visited the office a few times and had attended a few concerts so the people in management knew him, but not very well. After I got the news of his passing, I traveled down to Southern California to be with my mom and help with the planning and loose ends that needed to be done. My dad had been enamored with New Orleans and the music scene there.

He was particularly fond of The Preservation Hall Jazz Band and the tradition of the "first line" and "second line" jazz funerals, so we thought it would be fitting to hire a band to perform something like this during his Celebration of Life.

I had asked a few people in the management department, I believe it was Kevin Burns and Laura Fraenza, if they knew of any New Orleans-style bands near where the celebration was to take place. Not only did they get back to me with some suggestions, but they ended up booking and managing the details for me.

Bill Graham Management paid to have the band perform, for Kevin and Laura to attend my dad's Celebration and my return flight back to San Francisco. My mom and I were absolutely bowled over and eternally grateful for everything that was done for us. The band ended up being fantastic. A perfect way to say goodbye to my dad, and to have the logistics and fee taken care of for musical excellence at his Celebration was just incredible, for which I will always be grateful.

An incident that still cracks me up to this day was my Tom Petty encounter in the BGP office on Fifth Street. It was slightly after hours in the office and I must have been wrapping up some work or maybe working late before going straight to a concert. I don't remember. I was walking back towards the management department from the direction of the art department and as I rounded a corner there was Gregg Perloff giving Tom Petty a tour of the office. All of us were startled, as the offices were pretty quiet and there were barely any people still there, and we all sort of just stood there for what felt like a very long time (in reality, it was probably just a few seconds). I was semi-star struck and unsure what to do which manifested itself in me doing a mini tap dance for the two men. I guess it worked to break the awkward silence because they both laughed. Gregg introduced the two of us, and we all went about our respective business. It was a day I look back on with a simultaneous shaking of my head and laughing my ass off.

ERROLL JACKSON

When I think of Bill there are so many things that come to mind and yet, it becomes very clear who, what and why he became the legacy that he is.

It is an honor to be an alumnus of what I affectionately call the "Bill Graham University." It was highly selective, efficient, innovative and groundbreaking school that I was more eager to attend, be a part of, and to learn from. Being around the BGP scene has been so critical as to how I've been able to forge long and lasting relationships that I can call on to this very day. The people I've been able to learn from have been an endless resource of knowledge, experience, and support.

At BGP we were more than just colleagues; we were one big family where everyone was afforded every opportunity to grow and become the best. Bill encouraged us to push ourselves to the limit with the support of being surrounded by just everyday good people.

I remember vividly how Bill and I met. Phil Casey of ICM had recommended my partner and I assist BGP with Street Marketing for some upcoming shows at Shoreline.

Lyor and Russell (Lyor Cohen and Russell "Rush" Simmons) asked us to help on a Run-DMC show at the Oakland Coliseum Arena.

Once we got involved, tickets started trending at an accelerated pace and everyone wanted to know who are these guys (meaning my partner and I)?

I remember Bill leaning up against the wall outside of the production office. I walked up to him and introduced myself. Bill and I ended up talking for a good 30 minutes. He told me we had done a great job and we should talk more.

Bill said, "look, you guys are going to be successful with or without me. However, I think I have a few things that can help you and I know you guys have some things that can help us." I was stunned, to say the least. The Godfather of the entire live entertainment experience had just told me he wanted us to form a business relationship.

I immediately shared this great news with my partner about what Bill had shared,

However, we waited for about three weeks to get back to him. We did this because we didn't want to appear to be too anxious. We called Bill's office and they scheduled a meeting with us the same day. We arrived in the late afternoon and in attendance was Bill Graham, Gregg Perloff, and my two partners. We met for over two and a half hours and I could see and feel my life's trajectory changing with each passing moment.

After the meeting, Bill stated, "here's the way we should work: We'll be 50/50 partners and you have the full support of my company. Whatever agreement you will need we can have drawn up for you to feel comfortable and I will sign it. However, your word and your handshake are good enough for me."

That arrangement was the way we did business throughout our time with BGP. After Bill's passing and still to this day, it hasn't changed with all the folks from BGP who I still interact with.

I remember speaking with Bill about his success and this is what he shared.

"People think I'm powerful, but it's the people that I have around me that makes me much more powerful that I really am. That comes from working with great people and treating them right."

I was fortunate enough to be chosen to be part of something that shaped the entire global live events and concert industry. I am forever grateful, and I will always be aware of my responsibility to uphold the excellence of creating memorable experiences and to share what I have learned with those I work with, teach and mentor.

I will never forget the wonderful lessons that I learned from my mentor, business partner, teacher, friend and a major influence in my life.

Thank you, Bill.

You were the Best Act!

F

FRANK ANDRICK

Here we go….my KSJO/U2/Bill Experience…

Over the years stretching from high school there were the Fillmore and Winterland shows especially the Dead, Quicksilver Messenger Service and even the Sex Pistols. I had evolved to facial recognition with Bill Graham. Having gone from college radio days at KZSU to a music department position at KSJO and co-hosting the Modern Humans program of alternative music sounds…

I now spoke with Bill at shows quite frequently. I cherished that position as an outsider. Then one day coming into KSJO Radio Station from lunch I was informed "Bill Graham for you on line 9."

Bill is calling ME! How cool…I went to my office picked up the phone.

Jan who was Bill's personal secretary said, "Frank…Bill Graham" and

Bill said, "You little son of a bitch! Who the Fuck do you think you are?"

This was not what I expected.

I stammered, "Bill…I have no idea what this is about…but, if I did something wrong…I did it so I can fix it." "What are we talking about here?" The issue was I was bringing in the band U2 into San Jose State for a free concert ahead of BGP's debut of U2 in San Francisco and my show was impacting the sales for the second U2 show. Plus, my very aggressive promo onslaught had caught his attention and that fueled by my contact and love of the band in those times was hurting BGP no matter what my personal passions were. I offered to tone down my promotion, understanding his position and would offer hundreds of promo mentions to promote his show. After all my show was free and his was a paid entrance show and I had unknowingly violated his 50-mile rule of No Competition.

So, we can do this…and we did.

Bill's demeanor changed right away. He complimented me on my putting together of the show, my passion manifested and thanked me for working it out.

We were cool and he would see me at the Old Waldorf show. Whew and Wow.

Queenie Taylor then got on the phone saying, "Bill wishes you the best on your show and says, "If you had not used KSJO stationary to promote your show he would have had no problems. Then you would have just been a private citizen promoting your event." I said, "So, why did he run me through all the yelling and all that?" Queenie answered, "He just wanted to see what you were made of."

I asked humbly, "Did I pass the audition?" She answered, "With flying colours!"

In short, the San Jose show leaned into the legendary 1,200 free tickets given away; the band stomped and went wild themselves. The earthquake safe floor bounced 4 to 6 inches; the band was amazed. The Old Waldorf shows were sold out and amazing too…and my relationship with Bill Graham was forever changed.

G

GAIL HELLUND BOWLER

I worked for Bill Graham in 1969 at Shady Management, which was a band management company in a little walk-up office/apartment on Union Street at Divisadero above a liquor store. (Bill was not present on site.) The office was run by Gretchen Glanzer and Chuck Ream (band managers) with me as secretary (not a dirty word in those days). During my tenure, our clients included bands like Sanpaku, Cold Blood, Elvin Bishop, Lamb, Aum, and a few others. Just prior to that, the client roster had also included Santana and the Grateful Dead, both of whom went off on their own.

We were a happy little family at Shady – lots of activity, and people coming in and out. We were all still young and we used to go to gigs almost every night. I liked to frequent the performances of the bands we represented – just to show solidarity with them. And I also went to the big gigs, too, at the Fillmore, Avalon, and Winterland. Music was our focus. For fun, I posted a list of my top ten favorite songs on my bulletin board each week as a springboard to discussion. It helped to have something to talk about as everyone milled around the office for hours waiting for something to happen. It was a hangout. I made some life-long friends while working there: Dixie Swanson, Richard (Taco) Madrid, and Hewitt Jackson, among others, with whom I have enjoyed both professional and personal friendships.

For my birthday, Gretchen and Chuck presented me with a huge plastic embossed sign that read, "1969 Psychedelic Sweetheart of the Rodeo COSMIC GAIL." It hung over my desk at Shady and later at the Grateful Dead's office. Sam Cutler used that name for me on the back cover of Workingman's Dead.

167

However, my most interesting memory of Shady was when I quit. Lenny Hart, then manager of the Grateful Dead and Mickey Hart's father, came into the Shady office one day, complaining about the situation at the Dead's new warehouse/office/practice studio located in an old auto parts warehouse near Hamilton Air Force Base in Novato. He said he needed someone to work there who could get along with the "crazy" people and asked Gretchen if she could recommend someone. What Lenny didn't know was that I was already firmly entrenched in the Grateful Dead scene partly because of my prior relationship with a prankster named Bill Laudner, road manager of the Airplane, with whom I'd worked before. The Dead was a perfect fit for me. I already knew everyone in the band as well as the extended family, so I chased Lenny down the stairs on his way out, and asked him if he might consider me for the job. He was surprised, but said, "YES. You would be perfect," and hired me on the spot. He had no idea I was one of THEM. Then I had to go back upstairs and tell Gretchen. She was cool – she knew of my connection with the Dead. She passed the word on to Bill, who immediately called me into his office.

Bill was cordial at first, but you have to remember he was furious with the Dead for leaving Shady. He had a big emotional investment in the Airplane, and the Dead, and Santana. He didn't like losing his big clients. They were his friends. He felt betrayed. So, when he asked me why I was quitting, I didn't have the guts to tell him the truth. I knew he would flip out. So, I told him that I was quite happy at Shady, but they had just raised the toll on the Golden Gate Bridge by 50 cents (I lived in Mill Valley) and with the cost of gas, etc., it was more economical for me to work in Marin – closer to home. Calmly, he asked me where on earth I thought I could find a job in Marin better than the one I had at Shady. I hemmed and hawed. I knew he would flip out if I told him I was going to work for the Dead. But I also knew I had to be honest. Finally, I said that I had, luckily, already found another job.

Bill placed both his fists on the top of his desk and pushed himself up slowly, working himself into a rant. "Yes. I know. You fucking traitor! You're going to work for the Grateful Dead, aren't you?" I calmly said that I was, and he started screaming obscenities at me. "Fucking GOLDEN GATE BRIDGE TOLLS? Come ON! Do you think I'm an idiot? Do you think I don't know what's going on in this town? I KNOW EVERYTHING. EVERYTHING. Go ahead. Quit. God damn it! GET THE FUCK OUTTA MY OFFICE. OUT!"

I can't say I was surprised, but still, his wrath could be pretty overwhelming. But even with that little blip in our background, we remained friends for many years to come. We were neighbors in Mill Valley (we lived on the same street) and he even came down and surprised us (my roommate Jacky Watts [Sarti] and I) by making us breakfast one morning, as a thank you to us for helping out one of his friends. He served it to us naked – well wait - he wasn't totally naked – he was wearing a bow tie.

GARY RASHID

Bill manufactured an amazing life that thrived on the relationships he shared with so many incredible people. I was slow to offer any of my experiences with Bill because they just seemed so personal and relevant only to me that I didn't think would be of much interest to anyone else.

Some of the most remarkable experiences I was so fortunate to share with Bill were like watching an incredible movie that I didn't write the script for. Trying to craft a detailed remembrance from these events is difficult because it was such an "in the moment" experience.

My initial relationship with Bill in many ways was so normal. Being around Bill, either as an office go-fer or as Carlos' best friend, Bill always treated me the same way - he was always friendly, kind and generous, never too busy to take a minute to ask me how I was doing. As infamous as he was for his temper, in all the years that I knew him, he never had as much as a cross word for me; I was never the target of his ire.

Having been an enthusiastic patron of the Fillmore West, gaining employment at the BGP office on Howard Street was an unimaginable miracle. Becoming a part of the "Bill Graham Family" was like running away with the circus or joining a cult. It was filled with adventure and you knew you had found a place with like-minded people.

In my six years of working at the office there was never a day that went by that I wasn't impressed and moved by the memorabilia on the walls of the office, offerings from other concert attendees just like myself, so affected by their experiences at Bill Graham events that they were compelled to express their feelings or offer a gift of gratitude. There were so many letters from people who, while attending a concert, met their significant other and at that moment began the journey of their future lives.

Bill touched so many peoples' lives; it was hard to be unimpressed.

Going to the office was never like going to work, it was an adventure! I remember the sheer entertainment of hovering near Bill's office door, intensely amused by those infamous phone calls with some agent or manager, Bill expressing in his inimitable dramatic style his disenchantment with negotiations and after LOUDLY voicing his displeasures, inevitably slamming down the phone with enough force as to require a replacement.

There was a time Bill threw me the keys to his beloved convertible Jaguar XKE on a beautiful summer day to run some tape down to Neil Young's ranch in Santa Cruz (about a five-hour excursion). Considering at the time I was a car crazy 20-something, that was a level of trust I still can't believe.

As I became affiliated with Santana, I was able to enjoy a more intimate relationship with Bill as a friend rather than an employee. As such, I was the beneficiary of some incredible shared experiences with Bill.

Bill was, as everyone that knows him well would say, a master storyteller. There were times when he would join the Santana tours and would entertain us with dramatic tales of everything from escaping Nazi occupied Germany as a child to become an orphan alone in the U.S. to his touring adventures with The Rolling Stones. His stories were fascinating and always told with the presence of a great actor!

I was too young and distracted to really appreciate many of the incredible experiences I had the unique opportunity to share with Bill. Going to Israel and spending the day at Masada with Bill as a personal tour guide for the band or going to the Wailing Wall just seemed like more daily adventures that I certainly didn't realize the real significance of in the moment.

Bill was a generous man who loved sharing with his friends and strangers. So often he exploited his entrepreneurial skill to create a special environment, event or situation for the sheer joy of creating unforgettable moments for those around him. I was the beneficiary of more than one of these occasions. Being with Bill in Israel during a Santana tour was amazing and there were so many more precious, incredible moments.

On one European tour with Santana, we crossed the Hungarian border enroute to Budapest for a show where we arrived at our hotel at around one or two in the morning. Due to extreme travel requirements that day, Bill assumed that we would appreciate a good meal upon our arrival.

The dining experience Bill arranged could have qualified as a scene from a Martin Scorsese film. At the hotel, in the most lavishly set dining room, Bill had arranged an exquisite offering of authentic Hungarian food along with an incredible Gypsy band that serenaded us as we enjoyed this fabulous meal in the middle of the night (like 2:00 a.m.!). Of course, Bill joined us for what was truly an unforgettable night.

There was another time Santana was booked for a show in upstate New York. I had heard something of the Catskill recreation area, but I wasn't fully aware of its history at the time. Knowing where we would be, Bill made a special arrangement to book us into the Concord Resort Hotel.

The Concord Resort Hotel (pronounced KAHN-cord) was a resort in the Borscht Belt part of the Catskills, known for its large resort industry in the 1950s, 1960s and 1970s.

Located in Kiamesha Lake, New York, the Concord was the largest resort in the region until its closing in 1998. At the time, unbeknownst to me, I came to learn that Bill had actually worked as a waiter in this hotel back in the 1950s!

The dining room at this hotel sat 1,500 people and served three Kosher fixed menu meals a day. The head waiter took great pride in serving us, and was the very same head waiter that was in place when Bill had worked there so many years ago. We were all hysterically amused when the head waiter would stop at the table to grab Bill gently by the cheek and affectionately announce, "Billy, Billy, Billy," as if he was some long-lost son finally returned home which Bill graciously tolerated. As soon as the head waiter was clearly out of sight and out of earshot, Bill turned to the table and stated in his inimitable way, "I always hated that motherfucker!"

To top the night off, we were all invited to the hotel nightclub where the evening's entertainment was Buddy Hackett! I never laughed so hard in my entire life. This once-in-a-lifetime experience was an incredible gift, all thanks to Bill.

I have to pinch myself regularly when simply thinking of that fact that I enjoyed a personal relationship with a man who seemed bigger than life. It was such a fortuitous blessing.

Bill was a huge personality with so many admirable qualities and although he mingled with the most significant, famous celebrities of our generation, if you were his friend, no matter your position in life, he never treated you as someone less important.

One of my most precious possessions to this day is a note from Bill written on a page from his desk pad, which had the printed title at the top "From The Desk Of God." The note thanked me for a very modest pen set that I had left in the office for him to commemorate his birthday. For Bill to take the time from his ridiculously busy schedule to acknowledge that small gesture was hugely significant to me.

I was so blessed to know Bill and to have shared so many mind-blowing experiences with him.

GENO LUCERO

Memories of Bill Graham

To appreciate Bill Graham for who he was and remains to this day is to share the backstory of how I came to know him.

Like so many teenagers in the early Sixties, one particular Sunday evening in February 1964 had the most significant cultural impact of my young life: The Beatles played on the Ed Sullivan Show.

Suddenly, nothing fascinated me more than popular music, not only that of the British Invasion, but the overall abundance of live music from around the globe. A transistor radio soothed the lust for the latest acts' offerings, from surf tunes penned in Southern California to Motown's sultry, sensual soul and R&B music.

San Francisco was already primed for this explosion, with its post-WW II jazz scene in the Fillmore district, often referred to as the Harlem of the West, as well as Elvis' early dates stirring a young crowd's fever. Live music was all around, but neither readily nor consistently available to all-age audiences until a young eclectic entrepreneur presented regular concerts to the City's hungry masses.

Bill Graham was not merely a promoter. As an arbiter and maestro of live entertainment, his impressive pairing of artists on the same bill was something few people had rarely experienced. He was by no means alone in his efforts to highlight acts from the burgeoning local music scene, with competing shows by Chet Helms under the Family Dog moniker.

Bill was savvy enough to see the bigger picture. His determination to improve the overall experience in live music helped launch local related support industries to set new standards in production. His legendary company, Bill Graham Presents, enlisted a cadre of talented individuals who always found a way to turn his vision into reality.

Watching his hands-on approach alongside the efforts of his crew at both The Fillmore Auditorium and nearby Winterland Ballroom/ Arena was an education in attention to detail. It would take over a dozen years from those early days as a patron to finally cross paths with Bill's organization on a professional level.

One of his production/stage managers, Mick Brigden, was most accommodating to me in my capacity as a crew member of Little Feat for the first of two Winterland shows in December 1975.

The band was planning a European tour and Mick told me that the Who's UK production enterprise, ML, might be able to provide rental equipment or tour support.

Ever the visionary, Mick kept in touch and told me about two separate opportunities to fill crew positions for both Peter Frampton's current and Paul McCartney's upcoming Wings Over America tours. Long story short, I declined the Frampton offer because it paid the same as Little Feat. I was two days late in deciding to make the leap to the Wings tour.

Eventually the end of a personal relationship in early 1976 was impetus to move from L.A. back to San Francisco. I kept one foot in the door in L.A. as an independent Hammond B-3 tech, leading to work with Dave Mason and Bad Company.

Mick Brigden remained in touch, however, and in early 1978 asked if I was interested in working with Ronnie Montrose, an artist signed with Bill Graham Management. Mick scheduled a meeting at Bill Graham Presents' offices at 11th and Howard Street.

Santana's production manager, the late Steve "Killer" Kahn, with whom I crossed paths on separate Rolling Stones and Dave Mason/ Little Feat tour dates, asked why I was there, and said I should instead "come work with Santana and see the world." Mick and Steve agreed that I was a better fit for Santana's crew, and introduced me to the band's manager, Ray Etzler, who hired me on the spot.

Years of honing live production skills had finally led me to the inner circle of people working with Bill Graham. It would expose me firsthand to the vision, talent, and resources of rock music's greatest impresario. What will always be remembered was Bill's generosity, often for causes he deeply cared about.

A limited but distinct memory of some benefit concerts he championed follow, the latter two which I worked:

1975 - S.N.A.C.K. (Students Need Athletics, Culture and Kicks) - Kezar Stadium to offset budget cuts by San Francisco's school board to address a deficit. Only Bill could get Marlon Brando, Bob Dylan, and some of the Bay Area's top bands (Grateful Dead, Doobie Brothers, Santana, CSNY, Joan Baez, Larry Graham's Graham Central Station, Jefferson Starship) to pack this venue, in spite of the school board later claiming a smaller deficit due to inaccurate accounting on its part.

1986 – Crack-Down - New York City (Madison Square Garden and Felt Forum) to raise awareness of the negative impact on his old Bronx neighborhood's culture that prolific use of the illegal substance had fostered.

1989 – Earthquake Relief Benefit – Watsonville, CA – One of a series of three events co- produced with public TV station KQED in the Bay Area to raise money for victims of the 7.1 Loma Prieta earth-quake. Bill flew over the concert site in a helicopter piloted by Santana's production manager, Steve Kahn.

While Bill was known for saying, "It's not the money. It's the MONEY," I always had serious doubts that he would have ever allowed BGP to be bought by SFX Entertainment. After SFX was subsequently purchased by media conglomerate Clear Channel Communications, that entire concert and theater division was spun off as Live Nation.

Bill would often join Santana on domestic and foreign tour dates.

In Paris, he treated the band and crew to a spectacular cabaret show at the famous Lido Theater on the Champs Élysée. A cops and robbers segment featured a suspended helicopter theater prop and simulated machine gun bursts. The evening's highlight was the superb choreography of its fabled showgirl dancers.

Bill would also influence Santana's bookings into small clubs, i.e., Manhattan's Bitter End and the Old Waldorf in San Francisco's Embarcadero Center. Packing a concert stage production into venues a fraction of that size created load- ins and load-outs rarely appreci-ated by the crew. It validated both Bill's ego and desire to create not merely a show, but an entertainment event. We survived it.

Ray Etzler, who remains a very close friend and mentor, con-fided that he was often the voice of reason if Bill's booking sugges-tions failed the smell test whereby necessary travel logistics and mon-etary rewards weren't worth risking the safety and well-being of the Santana band and crew. It wasn't difficult to notice that he understood Bill's passion for Latin music and entrepreneurial showmanship, yet was able to keep some of Bill's ambitions in check.

Ray thankfully knew when to say no to Bill.

Truth be told, I've always felt that if Steve Kahn had done the same, he and Bill might still be with us today, as well as Bill's compan-ion, Melissa Gold.

One of the saddest days of my life was an early morning phone call in late October 1991 from Ervin Grinberg, who worked with the trucking company Santana used, Roadshow Services.

He was kind enough to ask me first if I was sitting down.

GISELE "GIGI" MALINOFSKY PAUL

Thank you, Bill.

A million times over, thank you, Bill.

My life is sweet and almost of all that is directly related to Bill Graham Presents starting with being a part of the Bluecoat Nation. I had a boyfriend who worked as a Bluecoat. He was gone almost every weekend. I finally said, "We are over unless you quit BGP or get me a job with you." Well, I guess he liked the job as much as he liked me because he didn't quit, but he did set me up with Molly and Steve Rigney to book some shows and that was that. I was in and I was hooked, and I loved everything about it.

My first call to work was at the Oakland Coliseum for the Rolling Stones and I was working a gate with Diana B. All I can remember from that day was laughing the entire 18 crazy hours or whatever it was. We became fast friends and are still best friends to this day.

While working a Steven Wright show at the Warfield Theater in San Francisco I met my husband in the bar while giving someone a ten-minute break. We've been married 27 years. Like I said, "thank you, Bill!"

I have had too many good times, great times, heartbreaking times, adventurous times and crazy times to list while working at BGP. Where else in the known universe would I learn to drive an 18-wheeler (Cal Expo Amphitheater), cut a hundred pounds of fruit salad in two days (thank you, Bettike), be a Santa's elf at the Holiday Festival (RIP Randy Bachman, my sidekick elf!), get carpal tunnel punching in numbers on a calculator for hours on end (Shoreline Amphitheatre), nearly have my ass burned off while watching Steve Winwood (again, Shoreline and the infamous methane!) and the list goes on and on. Maybe at the next Bluecoat Reunion we can all do a story swap.

And last, but not least, a big thank you to you, Rita Gentry, for spearheading this amazing project. I know you have put in a ton of hours and work and I, as well as others I'm sure, are extremely grateful.

GLENN RASWYCK (RAZ)

Rock Medicine 1980-2006

There was an old Rock Medicine (RM) saying that "you were not a Rock Medicine veteran until you were puked on, bled on, or yelled at by Bill Graham." I worked a lot of shows and he never yelled at me. Now, the Grateful Dead palace guards and Bob Barsotti is another story, but that is for another collection of tales.

I think the reason can be explained in this Bill Graham story. I had just finished telling some new volunteers about an RM worker who just had to talk to Bill during a show. Bill snapped around and yelled, "I know you are doing a good job, but if I had to stop what I was doing and talk to everyone who wanted to talk to me I would never get a god damned thing done. Now go do your goddamned job!" I explained to them that I learned in the Army that you never talk to generals, they talk to you.

Twenty minutes later, in walks Bill as usual checking RM, his barometer for how the crowd was doing, and asked how everyone was. The entire staff stood up at attention and did not say a word. Bill looked at me and said, "You need to give your staff more Gatorade."

So, in many ways, that is the reason I watched Bill at a distance. Bill at the US Festival, Bill at Masada, the gracious host after the US Festival, Bill at the Sahara Hotel in Las Vegas, again the gracious host in Frank Sinatra's old suite, Bill at meetings and at the planning and opening of Shoreline.

"Bill this place is a dump." No, sez Bill. Look closely and you will see the future of rock and roll production. Jeez, was he right!

Bill and Peter Barsotti looking at the New Year's Eve gag that he was going to ride over the crowd on. Bill looking VERY quizzically at it and saying, "So Peter, this is going to fly and not kill me, right?"

Bill running into our galvanized steel storage shed/medical site at Cal Expo in Sacramento at a Dead show where Bob Barsotti had come down with food poisoning from a fatty kind of burrito. Bob thought he was going to die until he saw Dr. Skip Gay was taking care of him and ordering up an ambulance. Bill comes running in and goes to the back exam room. He comes running out and yells, "Where's the phone and it is hotter than hell in here, open a window!" I say to Bill, no phone (before cell phones), no window. He sends someone for something, goes back in the room. He comes out again, yelling: phone, window…same answer. He sends another person for something else and now we have a crowd of runners. Third time, he says, "I know, no phone, no window, but goddamn it, I know there is going to be both in here real soon. They were installed by the next show with a swamp cooler to boot. Bob recovered.

My last and favorite Bill story was the Squaw Valley Music Festival. Thousands of people moved up and down the mountain chair lift. Bill and BGP had always been a leader in reasonable accommodations for the disabled. How to do this? The chair lifts at the top are designed for snow levels of five feet and above. When there is no snow these lifts are way up above ground level. Lance Miller and the BGP crew built ramps for the disabled to wheel down to the concert site. At the last week before the show, Squaw pulled the plug on putting the disabled on the gondola because of what they said were safety concerns of evacuation in lift stoppage, even though they took disabled people up before.

I heard Bill suspected extortion for more money. Bill got in touch with Charley Diamond, the Rock Medicine Director, who lost his leg in the Korean War and knew what being disabled meant. Charley got in touch with all his Northern California and Nevada disabled veterans and they showed up with a fleet of disabled vans. They drove the disabled up a very long access road. That road was slow going up and brake-eating coming down. Between BGP and the vets, they burned out a whole bunch of brakes, but no one complained, except for U-Haul who threatened not to give us any more trucks. At the end of the second show we had run out of vans and Bill said, &%*^ this and said bring them all up on the goddamned ramp that I paid for and put them at the front of the line and I dare anyone to say anything to me about it. When the disabled were all up there he bought them all a round of drinks at the bar. He later commented that he did not know they drank so much.

After the show was over and all the pilgrims were off the mountain I was called out to the main medical tent. There I met up with

Jim King and saw that the winds had flattened the tent with all the equipment inside. We straightened everything up the best we could. We were dragging our tired asses around when up pulls Bob and Peter Barsotti.

They asked if we were okay and we said we were done and they invited us both to an after party. We both thanked them but sleep sounded better.

I related a story to them. A little disabled kid in a wheelchair was waiting for a van to go up the hill. I apologized for the wait and he said, "Ya know, I've been denied access to a lot of things, including a bathroom, all my life. The fact the Bill Graham and Rock Medicine made these accommodations to go to a show on top of a goddamned mountain brings tears of joy to my eyes. God Bless Bill Graham and everyone else who made this possible." I said, "Make sure you tell Bill." Out of the dark back seat I see Bill and he said, "I've been told, thanks." This still brings chills when I think of this story. Bill died two months later.

As I wrote this story I also thought about the fact that Jim King and Peter are also gone. Please, more events for the hell of it rather than memorials.

GORDON TAYLOR

My story might be a little different than many. I never worked for Bill while he was alive. I started about a year after. But I'll back up.

Years before, I was running my college radio station at a small college in Connecticut and wanted to get an interview with him. I was a young Deadhead and knew all about him and had always admired how he put on concerts. So, I called the office.

Whoever answered was gracious and actually put me through to his office. I didn't expect that. Even more unexpected was that his assistant who answered at this office actually put me through to Bill. I couldn't believe it. I asked him and he was so kind and politely declined to be interviewed, wished me luck and we hung up.

A year or so later, I found myself on the west coast for my first visit and wound up at Kaiser Auditorium in Oakland for a Grateful Dead show. I was staying in San Francisco and decided to leave just before the encore. As I walked out to a beautiful moonlit sky there was Bill, all by himself, clipboard in hand, leaning on one of the grand columns there at the entrance just looking up at the moon. I realized it was him and immediately stopped to thank him.

Slightly startled, he turned to me with a big smile and thanked me instead for coming out to the show and shook my hand heartily. I had just met THE Bill Graham and I was elated. As the next years wore on, I found myself at Grateful Dead shows, sitting behind the stage watching the crew and local stagehands do their thing. I wanted to be one of those people. More than that, I wanted to work for Bill Graham Presents someday if I ever decided to move to San Francisco, which had been in my thoughts a lot.

Forward to February of 1992. Bill had died a few months earlier and I found myself trekking across the country to begin a new life in San Francisco. I took a small job as a bartender on a tourist cruise ship where I met a friend who was working for BGP as a stagehand. He then introduced me to Berna Macfadyen who began to put me to work. I was finally doing one of my dream jobs!

Let me just say that from day one that I started, Bill's presence was EVERYWHERE. He was in every person I worked with who had worked with him during his life. He was in every show I worked, and in every instruction I was given. I could absolutely feel him in everything.

So, while I never worked for Bill, I worked for everything he started BGP for. I was a proud member of that company for a number of years as a stagehand. I learned production from the best of the best and although I haven't done stagehand work full time as a career for many years now, the times I had with BGP and the friends I made while I did are still some of the best friends and most memorable times I've had in my life. It was the honor of a lifetime, cherished for the rest of my days.

Bill, thanks for being such an integral part of putting on all those shows for the years you were there. I'm not just an ex- BGP staff, I'm one of the many beneficiaries of your work.

GREGORY MALLOZZI

My Odyssey from High School Teacher in the Bronx to BGP in San Francisco

In 1972 I was in my fifth year of teaching English and Stage Design at Christopher Columbus High School in the Bronx. During my summer vacations I drove out to San Francisco to hang out with friends who had already relocated there. I loved San Francisco - back then it still had quaint little distinctive neighborhoods, which were fast disappearing in New York.

Of course, there was also the weather - the summers were almost always sunny and not hot and humid. In addition, you were never far from being reminded that the man-made environment of the area is dwarfed by the spectacular geography of the region: the hills, the mountains, the rugged coastline and the clean blue skies. Definitely very different from New York.

I liked my job pretty well; the kids were smart and inquisitive. I was also lucky that I was able to teach what I loved best - stagecraft. My students designed and built the scenery and lighting for all the stage productions at the school.

In my spare time I worked as a lighting designer, sometimes paid, usually not, at off Broadway productions. I tried, but did not succeed, at getting into the stagehands union.

I frequently fantasized about moving to San Francisco permanently, but the reality seemed too daunting. I had a good secure job. My family and friends were in New York. I was also in a long-term relationship with a woman who had been my high school sweetheart, Barbara. On my summer trips to San Francisco, it was my longing for her that cut my trips short to return home.

Early in January of 1972, Barbara died suddenly at the age of 25 as a result of medical malpractice. I was shattered by the loss and could not find a way to rebound and continue my life as it had been before. I requested and received a leave of absence from my teaching job, gave up my apartment, and drove to San Francisco to stay with friends until I could sort things out.

Soon after arriving, I began to look for work. My former professor of Technical Theatre at Hunter College was living in San Francisco and he got me little temporary gigs with ACT and the opera, but it really wasn't a living. I went through the want-ads in the San Francisco Chronicle every day looking for work. After a month of looking I came upon a help wanted ad for a lighting designer in contemporary music productions. I sent in my resume to the listed post office box. Within a week I received a phone call from FM Productions asking me to come in for an interview. I didn't know what FM Productions was, but I guessed it was probably something to do with ballet.

I met a man named Barry Imhoff in a warehouse on Golden Gate Avenue. He explained that FM Productions was the newly created technical branch of Bill Graham Presents, which had recently been revived after a long hiatus following the closings of the Fillmores in 1971.

I knew who Bill Graham was, but I had never been to a rock concert in my life. What I knew about the rock scene I picked up from my students. There was a sizable group of them who disappeared for a few days every time a band called The Grateful Dead toured in the Northeast. Barry Imhoff hired me as a lighting designer and I started the next week at a place called Winterland. The headliner was Van Morrison with two or three opening acts. Rock and roll lighting was very different from the jobs I had done in off Broadway theatre. This show was especially strange as Van Morrison insisted that no lighting should be focused on his face.

I was asked to work in the shop at Golden Gate Avenue, as there was a lot of activity going on developing sound and lighting systems. It was there that I met Jay Drevers, Ed Stewart and Steve Gagne. Steve was working by telephone daily with the former head sound engineer at the Fillmore East, John Chester. John was an electronics genius and he was designing new sound mixing boards for FM.

John just sent schematic diagrams of the circuits he designed, but building all the components and assembling them into a mixing board was a challenge left to the shop. I was asked to help out on the project. My dad had started an electronics subcontracting business in 1958 and I spend a lot of time after school and in the summers working for his company. I learned a lot about soldering, wiring harnesses and the mechanical assemblies that house electronic devices. I shared my skills with Jay, Steve and Ed, and I was no longer a member of the lighting crew. I became a part of the sound crew.

I didn't know much about audio in general, let alone serious sound reinforcement for large concerts. As I helped to construct these systems Jay, Steve and Ed were great mentors to me about the bigger picture of technical concert production. Soon, I was mixing stage monitors for most of the shows at Winterland and learned the complexities of live sound mixing - the convergence of technology, music and the art of dealing with rock bands and their crews.

As I was working on stage at almost all shows it was inevitable that I interacted with Bill on a pretty regular basis. At first it was pretty scary, but eventually he began to have confidence in my abilities and slowly I became a trusted member of his team.

It was during the Days on the Green concerts that Bill and I got a chance to know each other on a more personal level. We were both from the Bronx. We attended rival high schools in the Bronx, he from DeWitt Clinton and I from Evander Childs. He went to City College and I went to Hunter College.

We shared a love for old films and often discussed them in the backstage environment, recalling great scenes and reciting memorable dialogues from classic films of the Thirties and Forties. One of our favorites was Grand Illusion, a 1937 French film about World War I. Erich von Stroheim played an aristocratic German major who, when informed that a French plane had been shot down and the two French pilots had been captured, tells his young lieutenant, "If they are officers, invite them to lunch."

I continued to work for BGP for several years, transitioning from a technical work to administration. I left the organization to pursue a career in the straight world, eventually starting my own telecommunications company, which I still run.

But my ties with the BGP Family really never ended. I became a vendor to the company and have maintained my friendships with former colleagues some forty years later.

The years working for Bill in that crazy, dynamic company and the memories of the challenges and teamwork remain for me as the defining experience of my adult life.

H

HAROLD HOOGASIAN

Rita, when you contacted me about your book with stories about Bill, it sent my wheels spinning like an old slot machine. My mind has been whirling since. I have so many hot memories, it is going to need chapters. I need to tell a story about a young kid who walked up to the Fillmore one evening, probably around 1970, and was turned away as there was a private party going on that night. Disappointed, he walked off and imagined a time in the future when he might gain admittance to a private party at the Fillmore. Could he have imagined the heavy heart and life experience recalled each January when he walks up the stairs for Bill's birthday celebration? I can tell you, no. Beyond that, he could scarcely imagine that, not only would he have known Bill personally, but also the larger than life guy, Bill, would eventually know him!

Chapter 1 – The World of Plants

In the fall or winter of 1975, I met a lady named Sandy Furano (Dave's wife, as I recall). She came by my flower shop at the Cannery and solicited our participation in The World of Plants at the Cow Palace. There was a huge green plant craze going on and Bill, I guess, knew how to capitalize on it. It was scheduled for February 11-16, 1976. My family thought I was nuts to participate in an exposition during Valentine's week, a very busy time in the flower business. At the time, the Cannery was ground zero in the world of spin and tourism. I knew all the things that might actually sell, and they did; we actually made money! It set the stage for us to participate the next year. We blew all the restraints and had a large booth in the center of the main arena. Larry, my brother, went crazy on the design; he had just graduated from Cal with a degree in architecture. We won first prize! The blue ribbon hangs on the wall at Hoogasian Flowers to this day.

That was the year I met Peter Barsotti. I could not believe this guy was my age and would shortly have enough kids to have his own basketball team!

The original official host of the show, Euell Gibbons, passed away unexpectedly just before New Year's. Bill subbed as the show host and actually manned the host booth during posted host hours. After the show, I wrote Bill a typed letter and asked for his flower business. It worked! That was the start of a long, beautiful story.

Chapter 2 – Amnesty International

The relationship with Peter and later, Bob Barsotti, was one of mutual convenience, insanity, work, play and, occasionally, drugs. It was not unusual for Peter to bring me into some venue and start waving his arms. I loved it! It was always like we were kids ready to push the envelope on what everyone else considered work but actually was a lot of fun. In this particular case, I was not familiar with Amnesty. Peter wanted the stage to be filled with flowers along the front and we obliged. We never discussed budget until I presented the invoice. Peter said it had to be "a lot less" on the order of less than half of the $2,000-3,000 the work was worth. I made out another invoice for $1,000 and told Peter he owed me. A few months later I was backstage at Henry J. Kaiser in Oakland and realized the perfect payoff was a lifetime annuity of Dead backstage passes for my crew and me. Done!

Chapter 3 – The Rolling Stones

This one, I have always felt, could have been a Saturday Night Live sketch. I was visiting New York for a florist conference (1980?) and Peter was touring with The Stones. Bill was doing the tour, but not the shows; more on that later. We figured out we would be in the area at the same time. He told me to call him at the hotel and I did. He arranged for Nikki, my wife, and me to go to a show at The Meadowlands Arena. We got to the stage door entrance and gave our names. We were not on the list and were thinking on our feet. I said to the guy at the gate that we should be on Bill Graham's guest list. Almost before I could utter the words "Bill Graham," I was informed that this was "not Bill Graham's show." I guess there was some questionable energy from the local promoter's side to say the least. I was mentioning names like crazy and was told to wait.

Shortly, a babe with a very short, tight dress, high heels (and, well, she was perfect for the part) came out from inside. She asked our names and said, "Follow me," which we did. She got us to the seats and we were happy to be there. The stage was very close and John Sullivan, Marie Mandoli's first husband, was there, spied us and got us backstage.

It was not a typical BGP backstage experience. No hundreds of people, only a few dozen. Bettike Barsotti took Nikki to show her where the band was doing whatever they do to prepare. I came back upon the two ladies and saw a group of guys that looked like The Stones, but I was trying to be glib, so I said something that today would be like "look at those posers." I looked at Nikki and Bettike, they looked at me, then Mick looked at me and I figured out what a dummy I was as it was clear it WAS the band and they figured out what a dolt I was. At the time, I was wearing a yellow winged baseball cap for FTD, and Mick was in a yellow jumpsuit. It would have been a perfect addition to his look, but I was too embarrassed to offer him the lid!

Chapter 4 – Nelson Mandela

When Nelson Mandela was freed, it was a HUGE deal everywhere. He toured the U.S. and Bill, of course, put together a great event at The Oakland Coliseum. Peter told me that Bill wanted flowers all over the stage: garlands suspended above the backdrop and all over the front and back stage areas. He must have remembered the Amnesty deal as he told me up front that the job needed to be done gratis. I was worried that the cost of goods might be a problem, but I was pleasantly surprised as EVERY single supplier donated all we needed. We had a crew under the stage for three or four days doing all the labor. I worked closely with a member of the crew who was called Smokey.

It was, as you would say Rita, "a beautiful thing."

I was especially thrilled the next week when Peter told me that there was going to be a meeting of all BGP staff at the 260 Fifth Street office and Bill wanted me there. I was a little bit shocked when Bill told those assembled that the Mandela event was "the most important thing we have ever done." This was after he had brought Rock to Red Square recently. He even mentioned my flower crew and me. Pitter, patter; be still my beating heart. All the hard work and sweat was totally validated. This is my most retold Bill story, or at least right up there with "Box Office," below.

Chapter 5 – Box Office

On one New Year's Eve (don't ask me which one!) at the Civic, Peter asked me to make myself available after midnight. I am up for just about anything at a Dead show. (At a different NYE in Oakland I actually climbed up above the arena and helped The Balloon Lady's staff with the balloon drop.) I met Peter in the lobby after midnight and he invited me into the box office. It was just Peter, Bill and I raising a glass. Wow, was I stoked to be included! We are BS-ing and drinking. I look out through the window and see security dragging one of my student employees down the sidewalk. It was surreal. I had to excuse myself to see what could be done. He was (and is) a good kid and I wanted to see if I could salvage his experience.

The Bluecoats told me they caught him trying to sneak backstage. I was able to cool the situation down, the kid got back in the show and I returned to the box office and we all had a good laugh. I don't remember if I pointed to the box office at Bill and Peter as they were interested in seeing this play out, but that would have been a perfect play.

I'm sure this is a lot to take in, but I couldn't resist memorializing these moments of my life. The lives of the Hoogasian family have been enhanced and enriched by Bill Graham and the BGP Family.

HEATHER GILL

I started at Bill Graham Presents in the accounting department as an accounting filer and when I left I was the director of accounting (1996 to 2007). Unfortunately, I never met Bill, but heard wonderful stories about him. I feel very blessed that I was a part of the wonderful BGP family.

My favorite memory of being with the company was getting to see David Bowie at the Warfield Theater as a reward from the management department; being front row at the Fillmore seeing the Cure, being able to work with people like Rita Gentry, Shelley Lazar, Ray Etzler, Mouse, Mick Jones and Chris Cabaluna.

HEWITT JACKSON

Bill helped so many people in large and small ways. Those who knew him were witness to his many unpublicized acts of kindness. I got to know him through my association with the band Sanpaku. In early 1969, they played a Tuesday night audition at the Fillmore West. After their set, Bill came backstage to find out more about them. When he found out the band had no management or booking representation, he offered both on the spot, which was readily accepted.

At the time he was managing Santana, the Dead, Aum, Cold Blood and various other groups. We all became pretty close friends playing shows together and hanging around the management office on Union at Fillmore Streets in San Francisco.

Fast forward to December 1969 and Sanpaku disintegrated due to most of issues that plagued many young bands, immaturity, clashing egos, excessive psychedelics and alcohol usage, and not listening to Bill's advice. The musicians scattered back to Sacramento and Lake Tahoe. I was broke and with few prospects, but elected to stay in San Francisco. Bill and the BGP folks kept me alive with odd jobs of all kinds and I was willing to work. I moved office furniture, helped various employees move from one house to another, including a brick kiln from San Francisco to Mendocino. I think, Santana's road crew, the Villanueva Brothers, brought me along as a third roadie when they needed one.

In mid-1970, Bill convinced (I found out later it took some convincing) the band, It's A Beautiful Day, to try me out as a roadie. My first show with them was the last week of The Fillmore West. I went on tour with IABD for three years and learned how to take a rock band out on tour, which began a 14-year career in the business. I will be forever grateful to Bill and to many of the BGP employees who had faith in me and were willing to give me a chance.

Thanks again, Bill!

HONEY GREEN

I started working for Bill Graham in 1966 as his private secretary and worked for him for the first two years. I left law for rock and roll.

On Monday mornings, Bill would come in and just be in awe of how many kids came to see, hear and dance to the music. They shared what they had with each other and a community was formed. The press called it the "counterculture" and coined the term "hippies." That is when Bill started putting different styles of music together for a show. To him, it wasn't just about the business, it was the music! He found his niche in the world and little did he know what was to come.

Another memory I have is the story of Bill, Chet and the Paul Butterfield Band. It was the end of the summer of 1966 and Bill called Albert Grossman in New York about booking Butterfield's band. In that conversation, he also asked and was granted an exclusive, meaning that Chet Helms and the Family Dog could not have access to them. A contract was put in place. Earlier that year, he and Chet produced the Paul Butterfield Band together.

When I got to work that day, Bill was on the phone with Chet and what I heard was, "If you got up earlier than noon, you could have done this." What happened is that Chet also called Grossman, but way too late because he wanted to do the same. Later that day, Chet came by to see Bill and my memory is that they were at the bottom of the stairs talking. Bill explained how business worked and that Chet was not a businessman.

The glaring statement is, however, the one above. "If you got up earlier than noon, you could have done this. I called New York at 6:00 a.m. because it was 9:00 a.m. in New York." I know that this story has been told countless times over the years and I am a witness to it.

J

JACAEBER KASTOR

I have a very funny and long list of official and unofficial associations with Bill and Bill Graham Presents. In one guise or another, BGP has kind of woven in and out of my life since 1965 or so.

I grew up in Berkeley and a number of my friends went to work for him right out of high school. I met Bill directly while trying to sneak into a concert at the Berkeley Community Theater (I didn't get in…that night. Ha-ha!)

Later on, in the mid-1970s, I drew some paychecks from him (FM) and had business dealings/contracts in the 1980s (BGP). But the work I did with posters, art and artists was my favorite due to my gallery, which was called Psychedelic Solution in New York City.

The best project that I worked on so diligently was The Art of the Fillmore.

JACKIE KALKANIAN MILLER

Laguna Seca, Grateful Dead/Los Lobos and others in July, 1986. It was a three-day run - Friday, Saturday and Sunday - and for some reason we "found" more tickets made available for sale several hours before the gates opened on the first night. It was me, Colleen Kennedy and I think maybe Sugar Sims selling the released tickets out of the makeshift box office that was a rented RV. Colleen had stocked us up with everything we needed for the three days, as usual, including large fanny packs for holding cash and tickets since there was no ticket window.

After word got around to the hundreds of Deadheads that had been looking for a "miracle" that tickets were now available, needless to say, we were inundated with waves of humans for several hours - and it was of course cash only at that point.

The three of us were working so hard and fast that as soon as our fanny packs were filled with cash all we could do was run into the RV, dump the money we had collected in our packs into a box and then go back to continue selling tickets. Even with Bluecoat Security helping in managing things, it was a complete circus with the three of us and several hundred people trying to get a ticket before they were gone.

At some point it just became ridiculous to keep running into the RV to dump cash, so I began to stuff the money into the front pockets of my shorts when the fanny pack became too full to try to limit the trips into the RV to dump cash. At some point I felt an arm go around my waist from behind me and in a flash, there was a hand jammed into my right front pocket. Instinct took over and before I turned around, I reached into the pocket where I felt the hand and dug my fingernails into the flesh as hard as I could, which probably wasn't that hard as I had a handful of tickets. As the hand pulled out of my pocket, I whirled around fixing to say some choice words and there was Bill grinning at me.

I remember thinking, "Holy shit! I just stuck my nails into Bill's hand." I think I sputtered "oops" or something like that, but he just kept smiling and I swear his eyes were literally twinkling. He turned, got on his motorcycle that he was riding the grounds on and off he rode.

To this day I've always wondered if he was just joking around with me as he did with everyone on occasion, or was he trying to send me a message of, "Don't even think about pocketing any of my cash; I see you!"

Another story takes place a day or two after the San Francisco 201 Eleventh Street BGP office was firebombed. The staff was allowed to go inside for a few minutes to collect whatever belongings of ours that might still be salvageable.

A side note: Lance Miller and I had been drinking at Hamburger Mary's, which was near our office, the night of the bombing.

That night just happened to be on one of our early date nights. We had our respective cars parked in front of the office and we went back to get them around 11:00 p.m. at which time I drove home and Lance decided to sleep for an hour or two on the couch in the office before driving back to the East Bay. He left the office for home around 12:30 a.m. The arson squad later said they determined the bomb had been thrown sometime between 1:00 and 1:30 a.m. Yep!

On the day we were allowed to enter the office building we all had to put on a yellow hard hat before we could enter. I remember feeling just gutted emotionally when I went in and saw what had happened to beautiful memories, so very many of them, that Bill had made sure would live forever. I was furious, sad and sick just like everyone else. On top of everything else, the office was like a family home to us. Like sleeping it off there before you drove home.

On the way out of the building, a reporter ran up to me and thrust a microphone into my face and said something like, "As an employee, how do you feel about what's happened?" And I replied something like, "Devastated, it's an absolute shame what has happened here." And they ran it that night on their news broadcast. Unbeknownst to my somewhat naïve 24-year-old self, we were not supposed to give any statements to the press. I had not gotten that memo apparently. Which is why I guess all they had to run with was my comment.

Bill was still overseas making his way back to the States at this point. I later heard from one of my co-worker friends that she had heard a couple of other BGP employees talking about how my comments had made the news broadcast (meaning the insignificant clerk from accounting I suppose). I remember feeling bad and embarrassed like I had done something wrong.

When Bill got back there was a meeting where we all came together. I can't remember where we were, maybe Don Ramon's Restaurant next door, and Bill spoke to us. I also remember feeling really scared that I had misstepped, knowing that Bill had reviewed all the print and broadcast press on what had happened. After he was finished speaking to us, I remember he walked across the room to leave and had to pass where I was sitting. I remember glancing at him and as he passed by me, he put his hand on my shoulder and smiled just long enough to say, "You look good in a hard hat kid," and kept on walking. That's all I needed to feel like it was okay. That's who he was.

193

As I approach my sixtieth year I have never known anyone like him and I'm confident I never will. I loved him deeply. We all did.

JACKIE MILLER LEOS

I remember how it all started. A friend of mine, Timmy Ochoa, was working at Bill Graham Presents and I asked him if I might get a job there. He told me, "You would never last, the work is too hard. I don't think you are strong enough for this sort of work." Well, I went the next day to Shoreline Amphitheatre and hung out with Timmy all day. Someone finally asked me what I was doing there, and I said I was hoping to get a job with BGP. I said, "Tell Bill Graham I am working for free today," and I continued to help Timmy and his friends the rest of the day. We painted white safety lines on every single step in the Amphitheatre. At the end of the day they were in need of an extra stagehand for the show that night and I said I was the stagehand that they needed and that's how I got hired at Bill Graham Presents.

Once I was at the Warfield Theater with a Bluecoat by the name of Mick Flaire and Friends. Bill let Mick shoot a video with his band and I went along to help with makeup, hair, etc. We had a great time. I wonder whatever happened to that band.

While doing a Grateful Dead/Santana show at Angels Camp in Calaveras County, I wanted to take a picture of a couple of friends located on the side of stage left. I asked the Grateful Dead people if it was okay and they said, yes! Well, just as I was starting to take a picture, here comes Bill Graham and he stops and looks at me. I froze. I then grabbed him and asked if he would take a picture with me and he said, yes. I then gave my camera to my friend, Joe Sagara who worked for BGP. Joe took the picture, but just before he took the shot Bill yelled out, "Stop!" He turns to me and says, "I need five dollars first." So, I mailed a framed copy of the picture to his office with a five dollar bill inside it. I always wondered if he ever hung that picture up somewhere.

JAGE JACKSON

During the early 1970s I lived in Venice Beach in Los Angeles working for Irving Azoff's Frontline Management. I was primarily a roadie for the Eagles. Over the years I was associated with several of Irving's acts before I saw the light and moved - first to Dana Point and subsequently, to the Bay Area where Pam, my wife, and I finally moved in together continuing our long relationship.

I think Bill always harbored the memory of me as being one of Azoff's goons, even as I worked as a stagehand for BGP and attended company functions under Pam's wing.

I have always considered highly successful promoters and artist managers to be what I refer to affectionately as "Master Bastards," the Best People in the World to work with and the Worst People in the Universe to work against. Bill was a Master Bastard.

It was a sunny Day on the Green in the late 1970s. The all-star line-up for the day's festivities included Boz Scaggs, Fleetwood Mac, and the Eagles. It was a flawless, sunny afternoon, with not a cloud in the sky, load in and set up going as usual. As pre-show sound checks were being completed, Bill Graham held court with his staff members and the visiting road crews, exchanging war stories and telling the occasional joke. He was master and commander – totally in his element.

As the stage was being prepared for the opener's performance, Bill was engaged in a conversation with one of the production managers and a few of the various road crew's members when, out of the corner of his eye, he sighted a wanna-be patron, probably short on cash, climbing over the rear barricade approximately 80 yards from the stage. Bill exploded into motion, leapt down the backstage stairs and took off at a dead run, finally seizing the unlucky interloper in what can only be described as an iron grip, and escorted him unceremoniously to the nearest yellow-shirted security person for ejection from the venue back into the throngs waiting to enter through the gates.

We all stood rooted to the spot, jaws agape as Bill, hardly winded, returned to the stage and rejoined our astounded group. He said: "Hey guys, 15 bucks is 15 bucks!"

JAMES BATTLE, JR.

Security Administrator for Bill Graham Presents

Rita's Note: This was submitted to me by Lonie Battle, James' wife. James Battle, Jr. passed away on March 31, 2016.

James Battle, Jr.'s journey to Bill Graham Presents was quite simple, but it became an extraordinary event in his life. One of James' coworkers, Lenard Priestly, worked part-time at the backstage door of Winterland as a security guard. He urged James periodically to attend a concert and take a look. He would be making extra money, but he would also have the opportunity to hear great music.

So, having made plans for a vacation to Mazatlan, James decided to take Lenard up on his offer. The concert that James and I attended was a Grateful Dead concert. As we entered the arena, what we saw was indescribable. It seemed as though the whole arena was dancing, swirling or gyrating. All I could say was, "Oh my God!" but that very night in 1972 James Battle, Jr. was hooked and became a Deadhead for life. He also embarked upon a new career in the concert business.

With his aptitude for handling potential volatile situations, James' leadership abilities became apparent to Bill Graham Presents and especially Bill Graham himself.

He made many suggestions that became policy for improving concert security. James believed that preventative measures were better than wading into an already happening situation.

After working with contracted security companies such as Event Security and Staffpro Security, Bill approached James with the statement, "I want to go in-house for my security. Can you establish our own security department?" James' answer was yes! He established procedures for hiring, recruiting and training for all security personnel. Bill Graham security became the model for crowd control across the country and is still in effect today, thanks to James Battle, Jr.

JAN SIMMONS

Assistant to the Boss (as it said on my business cards). Started working at BGP January 4, 1978 and left April 30, 1990.

Favorite Bill Graham Story

It's hard to pick a favorite story about Bill, so let me just start at the beginning.

I was hired initially as production assistant. My desk was located in the middle of the production office where I was surrounded by concert bookers, the marketing department and production people. Bill's office was off to the side of the main room.

Queenie Taylor and Greg Mallozzi had hired me while Bill was out on tour with Santana in Europe. Danny Scher later told me that Bill did NOT like it that a new employee was hired during his absence. He was protective of his inner circle. But I didn't know that; I was thrilled to be working there and was trying very hard to do a good job.

I had barely had any interaction with Bill yet, when one morning during one of my first weeks on the job, I arrived at work to find a note from Bill stuck in my typewriter. It read, "Remember to turn off your typewriter when you leave at night. You left it on last night," and signed, "Bill." As if an afterthought, he had added the word "please" at the beginning of the note. I knew it was added because "please" was written in a different color ink than the rest of the note. Bill was a nit-picker, to be sure, and always had a critique on whatever the subject. But I never did forget to turn off my typewriter after that!

By that fall, Bill's secretary had quit and I was asked to move into her position. I'll never forget the first time Bill screamed into the telephone when I was sitting there, just outside the glass window that opened between Bill's office and my desk. He had been on a minutes-long tirade towards someone, and then literally THREW the phone down onto its cradle. Without a beat, he looked up at me and winked. I don't think Bill's blood pressure had risen one iota, although I suspect the person on the other end of the line needed a cold drink when the call was over.

Bottom line: Bill was a great actor. He had moves. He knew how to intimidate. He knew just how to slowly begin to remove his wristwatch in such a way that the person he was staring down would become very afraid of this madman and back off. He'd puff up his chest and bound through a crowded aisle of rabid music fans in such a way that no one would dare interrupt him. He loved old movies, especially with John Garfield, James Cagney and the like, and I believe he learned many of his moves from actors of that genre.

After surviving a harrowing childhood, Bill wrapped his arms around life and embraced it for all he was worth. He had boundless energy, tremendous intellectual curiosity, and an unlimited imagination. He was aware of what was going on in the world – he read the newspapers daily, and magazines like Newsweek and U.S. News and World Report every week. An avid sports fan, Bill could discuss game strategy for hours on end. He was shrewd and had an uncanny way of sizing people up. Not a lot got past him in the course of a day.

Take my typewriter, for example.

JAN WEXNER and DAVID HAYA

I'd been working as a Bluecoat for some time when I officially met Bill. He had just landed from his trip to Egypt and came straight to the Oakland Coliseum Arena for the Boston concert. Earlier that evening I had been punched in the face. I didn't see it coming, but quickly got away as soon as it happened. The man who did it was then hit over the head with a baton by an Oakland Coliseum guard. We called them the Green Coat security. They had been sitting behind me, in front of the stage and had seen it very clearly. I was called into the security room, and of course Bill was now there, and involved.

He asked me what happened and then to identify the man. His head was now bandaged and still bleeding. I felt badly for him; he was probably just too high to realize what he was doing. Fast forward two weeks and I'm in an interview with Bill in his office for the position of secretary, as we called it back then, for Gregg Perloff. Bill says something like, didn't we meet recently at a show, and doesn't your boyfriend work as a Bluecoat too? And that is how I started working in the production office.

When Bill got excited about ticket sales he would fly out to the main floor of the office and demand the count. No computers back then. We had to get counts on the phone from the rep at BASS. For Days on the Green we had to keep hourly counts on paper. I learned to keep them handy.

Bill's generosity to his employees was always amazing.

I haven't been to many musicals in my life. I'll always remember getting to sit with Bill and Jan, when they offered David and me tickets to Evita. We weren't up front, but it was amazing to be there at all at that time in our lives.

Bill enjoyed taking all his ladies out to lunch for Secretary's Day. It was our special time to share stories with him without the guys around.

When Bill found out we were getting married he asked where it would be. I told him what we were trying to do. He then insisted we do it at his house and grounds called Masada. We had a beautiful ceremony with 200 friends and family. Bill set up the tent from Egypt for us to put the gift table in. He had Gary help us serve cake and be our logistics person. Bill even got in some photos with my sisters and mom in a bedroom where he let us get dressed. When the champagne didn't arrive on time due to logistics problems, he brought out some boxes of white wine he had to use in the interim.

David always enjoyed sports. A benefit of being a Bluecoat was if we were ready before it was time to open the house, they got to play. At one basketball game with Bill, before a Dead show at the Oakland Auditorium, David was on the opposing team. No one else was willing to guard Bill, so David got to. No idea who won, because even though Bill always cared, or pretended to, no one else did.

We both played on the Bill Graham Dogs softball team. Bill came when he could and joined in. We knew if he showed up we better win; best not to make any errors, with him there. My last game with the Dogs I was six-plus months pregnant and got out before I could waddle to first base. Luckily, Bill wasn't at that game.

David was the Bluecoat supervising backstage at a Day on the Green when Bill came up to him and said, "Someone has to work this door." David said he was waiting on folks to come in from out front. Not the right response. Bill said "Well, I'm not going to do it," in his matter-of-fact way, and you knew you better do it. So David did.

Whenever Bill left the country there was always a nervous receptionist. I covered as one on a couple of occasions. The reason for the nerves was we didn't have the greatest phone system, and if we had to transfer Bill and the call dropped it was very bad, or at least we were led to believe it would be. You also needed to recognize his voice and not put him on hold. Since receptionist positions are often new employees, it's not always that easy. I was more comfortable in the main office than as receptionist.

JANET RITZ

Running Into Bill Graham

I met Bill Graham on my first day transferring into Berkeley High School. Or re-met him, as I had met him years earlier. My mother, a reporter and sketch artist for CBS and Associated Press, threw a party that he attended with a lawyer named Bill Coblentz. My mom commented how striking Bill seemed to her. A far better-looking and taller Edward G. Robinson was how she described him. I remember that he looked unforgettable.

I transferred into Berkeley High School in my junior year two weeks after the start of the semester, with no idea of my classes, or where to go to get them. I had wandered the lower floor of the Berkeley Community Theater, which is on the high school campus, and ran into some boys who began hassling me. Bill was there. He was putting on a show. They ran on just his raised brow. He asked, "You okay?" I nodded and followed him to the stage where I watched in wonder as high school kids and recent graduates, his crew, set up for that evening's concert.

Those classmates and those that had graduated worked for Bill after school or full time by that point. I can't remember a time in my late teen years where I wasn't around someone who worked for him. I was working in recording studios by that time, singing, arranging music, and later, writing. I ran into Bill a few times in those places, and he always remembered me, and was polite to me.

I was nineteen when he came to speak to students at a music school in Marin County. I sat cross-legged on the floor with the others in what became an honest and close discussion. "I cheat," he started.

It was clearly for effect. "I cheat when others cheat me," he elaborated [paraphrasing here]: "When the Rolling Stones take the limo that I ordered for the airport all the way to L.A., I charge them for it with their M&Ms." It was funny, hysterical, but also — to me — shocking. My father was a CPA. I knew bookkeeping.

He was asked a question that would resonate with me years later — how someone could get a job with him. He suggested they start by volunteering at a radio station, sweep the floor, whatever. Get experience.

The school had made a tape of the event and I had a copy at the time. I had made a copy for a friend from high school who worked for him. I don't know if he told Bill I had the tapes or if the school did, but he wanted them, so I gave them to him. We got to talking, and he remembered my parents, and how we seemed to run into each other.

He then asked about my father who'd been reserved with him at the party. I told him he had served in the Second World War, and was, in my opinion, a hero. Bill spoke to me about his experience in World War II. I learned his real name, Wolfgang Grajonca (also spelled Grajonza), that his father had died just after he was born, that his mother had died in the Holocaust — as had one of his sisters — that his other four sisters had hid or survived the camps, and that he had escaped as a young boy.

I stayed in my car after I left. You never really know someone. That's what I thought at the time. This dynamic, unmissable man was the young boy who had run through France. Trauma does that. A part of you stops at that age and becomes imprinted on your soul. That was Bill. That was Wolfgang. It was his anger, his self-destructive tendencies, his covetousness, his kindness. That was the insight I had.

Not long after that, one of his employees, Mick Brigdon, reached out to me about writing lead sheets — sheet music — for copyright for the acts Bill managed. I started with Santana, using his guitar solos as melodies on instrumentals, and Eddy Money, and used a calligraphy pen to draw the notes by hand. I was sitting at the desk in his offices when Bill saw the Santana lead sheet for a song he liked, he asked for a copy. I had to redo it, so I offered it to him. He looked back at me with an interesting look that I would see again another time and walked away with it.

My experience of Bill Graham was that this man, for all his anger, was kind inside. I told him once, much later, that he reminded me of an inside-out version of my father whose job in the war was to train soldiers to kill with their hands. My gentle father. He was sweet, and kind, but, if anyone tried to harm someone he loved, holy cow. That's how Bill seemed to me, but with his kindness more often on the inside, and the anger out.

I worked in the office for a while, temporary, manning phones or a desk for employees who were overloaded. I remember a day that Bill came out with a jacket — a present someone had given to him -- with his name embroidered, emblazoned, on the back. He held it by the hanger over his should and asked his lawyer what he thought. The lawyer, seeing a risk, formed his hand into a gun, pointed at the name on Bill's back, and said, "Yeah, Bill Graham, boom." Bill left with the jacket, and I never saw it again.

I was offered a job at a recording studio called The Automatt when Rita Gentry, who worked for Bill, referred me to the owner. It was a wild ride at a time when the business was wild in general, but the memory I have that's related to Bill was when I received a call from his office inviting me to a Christmas Party. It was at Wolfgang's which was run by one of my former high school friends, and the employees were doing musical numbers on the stage while Bill served the drinks at the bar.

Bill laughed at my drink (I don't drink), which was orange juice and soda, and poured it for me when, suddenly, the music to "Putting on the Ritz," which includes my last name, started, and an employee — I think it was Jerry Pompili — in white tux and top hat, performed the dance from "Young Frankenstein." The employees shouted "Putting on the Ritz" each time it came up, and Bill grinned at me ear-to-ear. No one, not Bill, not anyone, ever said that it had anything to do with me, but it was wonderful.

Another time, not as wonderful, was when I was asked to work on a Christmas Fair that Bill wanted to put on at Fort Mason. I became involved because I knew many of the craftspeople at the Renaissance

Faire. I reached out to them, and that led to a request to attend a meeting and write up a proposal for the Fair to be held at Fort Mason.

I spoke to my mother at the time. She warned me that Bill had run into problems early in his career with what she called "stiff suits" at Fort Mason. Knowing that, I drew up a prospectus, a proper business plan with everything a "stiff suit" would want to see. I turned it in at the next meeting. Bill made a comment (paraphrasing), "this is what you get from someone who knows how to do this."

I was asked to attend the meeting at Fort Mason. Bill wasn't there. Some people who worked for him were, and they sat there as the suit from Fort Mason said, "I wasn't going to agree with this but when I saw proposal [insert name of a guy who worked for Bill] put together, I had to say yes."

There could be reasons for it. They may have wanted whoever was running the project to be on it. I could understand that. But finding out that way bothered me enough that I left the project. I began to receive calls from the crafts people. They were worried that I wasn't there. I then received a call -- I was at Disneyland, I'd gotten out of town — from the guy who'd put his name on the report. Someone had asked him to find out where I was and get me back. I agreed to come back, and then heard nothing. I didn't attend.

I ran into Bill at the Bay Area Music Awards (the Bammies) about three years later. I was working backstage and he asked what happened. When I told him, he became quiet. Later that night, in the Hospitality Suite, he handed me a surprise orange juice and soda. We didn't talk about it again, but we were back to striking up a conversation when we'd run into each other.

One of those times was at the Menorah Lighting ceremony in Union Square. Ronald Reagan was president and was going to lay a wreath at Bitburg Cemetery where SS officers were buried. For Bill, this was fascism in his time, with his mother's death, the horror of escaping across France, the loss of his sister being all for nothing. An American president was honoring their murderers. Bill spoke out against it at that ceremony and took out an advertisement in the paper against it.

Then, when Bill was in Europe on a business trip, someone threw a Molotov cocktail into Bill's headquarters on Howard Street, and it burned to the ground.

The papers reported the first two questions Bill asked, and in this order: "Was anyone hurt?" "Is anything left." Not much was left. The iconic offices that had so much of Bill's personality in them, and not just in the memorabilia, the few pictures of his family (some of which extraordinarily survived the fire), how the place felt, was gone.

The company ended up taking temporary offices in North Beach. I remembered they made me sad. The building construction, the coldness of the design, it wasn't Bill Graham Presents. I was unsure anything would be again, at least at that time. It also led, as change does, to certain employees taking more control, and others backing off. I didn't know what that meant at the time. I did know the company felt different.

I again moved on. I was hired in production by the astonishing Roz Blanch, a longtime CBS executive who ran the multimillion-dollar CBS Marketing Convention in what was essentially a two-week party at a different location each year.

That year it was in Honolulu, and I was at the front desk at the Sheraton Waikiki — I remember the breeze felt like it was caressing my cheek, the gardenia-like flowers, and a mouth-watering combination of fresh pineapple juice mixed with guava juice — when I overheard the desk clerks laughing about a request from the televangelist, Billy Graham. I asked, "Since I don't think Billy Graham is attending a music conference, is it possible you mean the rock concert promotor, Bill Graham? If so, what did he want?"

The clerks looked up his request and become worried. They knew me as Roz's aide, and that she could move the whole show if she wanted and would. They apologized, said he wanted a suite, and they didn't have the one he wanted. I asked what they did have. The reply was the presidential suite. I told them to give that to Bill and charge him what they were going to for the smaller suite. And to add flowers for laughing at him.

I walked away with that queasy feeling you get when you apply power you're unsure you have, don't quite know the consequence, but at least know it was fun to do it.

When Bill arrived later with his entourage — a hotel employee relayed this to me — he immediately balked at the size of the suite and said he wasn't paying for it. The bellboy assured him it was covered, and that "Janet" had taken care of it. Bill didn't know who the bellboy meant but accepted the suite, flowers, and gift baskets.

That night, as Bill sat at a table with CBS power players, he looked like he might get whiplash watching someone familiar run around with a clipboard and headphones, while Sade, Bruce Springsteen, and Carly Simon performed. After the show, as the guests exited, I sat on a table swinging my feet that didn't reach the floor beside Roz, enthroned in a white wicker chair. Bill came out and paid his respects first to Roz. He thanked her for the show and then turned to me and asked, "what are you doing here?"

Roz answered for me: "She's running the show, and how do you like your room?"

Roz was amazing. I hadn't told her about the room, but of course she knew. All my fear of going too far faded as she continued to misrepresent me as the person in charge and blew Bill's mind. I miss her, and him.

The next morning, Bill came by the production office, again to pay his respects to Roz, then came over to my desk. He was clearly curious. This was not the same girl who'd walked out on his Christmas production. Not the gawky teenager he'd seen at school. I was putting on a multimillion-dollar show — it was only me and Roz in the office at that moment — and it was going off without a hitch.

I told him immediately that it was nice of Roz to give me credit, but Roz was in charge. Bill came back after he'd had breakfast, and we got into a conversation. He told me his reasons for being there. He wanted to manage Sade, wasn't getting through to her, and wanted to know if I could set up a meeting. I told him I would bring it to Roz, and I did. He went on to say he'd come to see his son who lived with a former wife or girlfriend, I wasn't sure which, and seemed sad about how that was going. He looked, honestly, lost.

After I returned home, I received a call from his office with an appointment to see Bill. I didn't know what it was, but I went to those North Beach Offices. I sat in the small padded double chairs that served as a waiting area with Howie Klein, also there to see Bill. I'd known Howie for years and liked him. At the time — this was before he would go one to become the head of a large record company responsible for the careers of iconic stars — he was involved with Punk music scene in San Francisco.

Howie told me he'd overheard a someone at the Oasis nightclub across from the burned offices brag about setting the office on fire because of the advertisement Bill had put in the paper protesting Reagan's flower-laying at the SS graves.

I sat there while he went in to see Bill thinking about that would mean to someone still so traumatized by what had happened to his mother and sister when he was a boy.

Bill was distracted when I went in to see him. He blurted out — I don't think he would have been blunt if Howie hadn't gotten to him first — that he had told his employees he wanted to hire me when he got back and was surprised when they balked.

I wasn't. Bill had this powerful and insular top layer in his company who perceived me as the person they knew in high school when I was struggling to fit in. I had transferred in mid-year. It was a horrible time and had it followed me. I thanked him and moved on.

I went to work for Saul Zaentz Films/Fantasy Records. If there was a place that Bill was considered the enemy, that was it. Saul was involved in a lawsuit with John Fogarty for copyright violation on songs Fogarty wrote after he had left their record company. They said his songs were too much like songs he'd written in Creedence Clearwater Revival.

To say the suit outraged Bill on principal was an understatement. The idea of suing an artist for sounding too much like himself was too much. Like with Bitburg, he made his opinion known, and Saul Zaentz, who looked but did not act like Santa Claus, was having none of it. He let me know, when I came to work there, that I didn't work for Bill Graham anymore. I tried to say, I never did, not really, not more than as a temp. We just have this way of running into each other. Saul wasn't in a mood to listen.

It wasn't where I wanted my career to go, but it was a steady paycheck, and I had cool office with a blue corduroy couch the director, Philip Kaufman, had given to me.

I remember getting stuck in the elevator and Ralph Kaffel, the head of the record company, shouting into the barely opened doors to wait until they could reach someone, and pushing through a vintage life magazine for me to read.

It was fun.

I went back to work at the CBS Convention annually — that was how I used my vacation time —and saw Bill there. We took walks and talked mostly about his life, not mine, and he would put in a good word with Roz about me. He was still always kind to me.

He told me about a 25th anniversary event that was coming up for his company. I got there after it started. The event is available on YouTube, and I recommend it. He was funny, engaging, and incredibly poignant at times.

There was one point when someone raised their hand and asked him the same question someone had asked when I was seated cross-legged on the floor at music school. "How does someone get a job working for you."

Bill answered differently: "It's still run by all of those people who started those many years ago. In order for somebody to come into our company, it would be very difficult because we ain't going anywhere." Bill stayed talking to people afterward. I didn't stick around though I saw him glance at my direction.

I ran into him last at an event for the Holocaust Oral History Project at the Jewish Community Center on California Street in San Francisco. They were honoring Bill for his contributions with an audience made up of Holocaust survivors. It was mid-afternoon on a holiday, and the Center, which had put food on tables covered by clear plastic, was not to allow people to eat until after sunset.

When elderly man with a tattooed arm seated next to me said, "I am so hungry," I went to Bill who was speaking with the actor, Peter Coyote, about Bill's performance in the movie, Bugsy (which I also recommend), and I asked if he could spare a minute. He said, "I'll talk to you when this is over." I don't know why that made me angry, but it did. I went over to the food, ripped off the plastic, made a plate, and brought it to the elderly man. Others got up when they saw that and went and got food. I have no idea if I was going pay for it with religion or from someone there mad at me, but I felt better for it.

I went outside and sat on the high curb — as tall as a chair — outside the center. It faced an inline road next to the busier street, and it was a warm night. Bill came out and sat next to me. I asked how the event was going. He grinned and said, "everyone is eating." I laughed and it broke the tension. He asked what I wanted to talk about. I replied that Holocaust survivors had food issues, and they needed to eat.

I asked him about his comments at the 25th anniversary event about his company, and if everything was all right. He said, "It's become a business for business's sake, and I never got involved with that side of it. I didn't attend meetings about the taxes, or the budget. They do that."

I said that meant he got to do the fun stuff. Bill replied, "until it wasn't fun."

One of his employees, Steve "Killer" Khan, was a buddy of mine. His number was first speed dial button on my fancy white phone with lots of buttons, and we would talk about everything from my job at Fantasy Records which was on the other side of the divide of the politics of the business at that time, to his love of flying. Steve was Bill's pilot and considered himself a hotshot, which scared me. I would not fly with him. If you don't think of the worst that can happen, then it can. It didn't change that we were buddies. But, when he called me and said he'd gotten a helicopter, I worried.

When my friend, Cindy Sterne, who had once dated Bill, called me up in tears to tell me his helicopter had crashed, I sat in front of my fireplace in total shock, and then seemed to see Bill out of the corner of my eye, looking back at me with what I finally recognized as regret. I knew I was imagining it, but it felt real.

When I read reports in the paper a week later of people who'd attended a concert at the Fillmore Auditorium, Bill's first main venue, that spoke of seeing Bill looking back at them as he walked way, I still couldn't believe it was real. But I know the regret I felt when I thought I saw him. He had so much more to do I went on to work as a record producer and did well at it, and then in the film and TV studios where I still work. That's where I was working one day when an older gentleman reached out to me on social media and asked if I'd known Bill Graham and told me he and Bill escaped through France as part of the One Thousand Children (OTC) program.

His name was Ralph Moratz.

Ralph had found out, after Bill died, that he was his childhood companion, Wolfgang. He had photographs, including one of Bill's sister, Tolia, who died at Auschwitz at age 13. Bill had thought she died on the road with them in France. Ralph explained that was a Russian girl who was part of the OTC. Together, we researched the history of both their families. Ralph's had died horribly. He knew most of that.

I found out that Bill's mother, Frieda, was sent to Riga, Latvia, where she may have died in the Rumbula Forest Massacre or in Auschwitz. Ralph described her as a tall woman with a strong presence. I think she must have been incredibly strong, but her story broke my heart. She lost her husband, as Bill told me, when Bill was two days old. Frieda was left with six children and no husband two years before Hitler took power.

I read with horror and fascination, though the records at Bad Arolsen and Yad Vashem, how Frieda tried to get her children out. Rita fled to Shanghai. Frieda applied for the family to follow with no success. Evelyn and Sonja finally fled to Hungary and Vienna and worked under false identities as a singer and dancer.

Frieda put Bill into an orphanage that was arranging to move the boys out of Germany. Tolia, her youngest girl, went to one that was not making those accommodations. Frieda had no choice. They had no food. She said goodbye to Bill and his friend, Ralph, in Berlin. The boys were taken out of Germany, and Bill never saw his mother again.

Esther left in search of her sister in Hungary and was caught and sent to Auschwitz.

I read Tolia's and Frieda's "declaration of means," the form they had to fill out when called up for deportation. They had so little, it was heartbreaking. But what I did find out was that Tolia spent some time in the temporary housing for those who were going to be deported and was remembered as a bright presence who helped the others there.

Bill never knew who killed his mother and sister. I'm sure he would have liked that information. I don't know if he would have found solace in the knowledge that Alois Brunner, who signed the order that sent his sister and mother to the East, died in squalor in Damascus. To quote Robert Graves from I Claudius, "it's some justice."

Ralph ended up speaking at events for Bill. His focus was on their relationship, as it should have been, on where Bill's propensity for providing apples at his shows came from — Bill and Ralph would gather apples when it rained because that was when the Nazis wouldn't come out, and on what Bill's life had been like before he'd become Bill Graham. But Ralph had also been an extra in Judgment at Nuremburg and East of Eden.

Another extraordinary boy who'd become a man.

Ralph gave me an understanding of the loss I would see in Bill's quiet moments that was from that boy on the run in France, the one who didn't know what had happened to his mother, though he knew she was dead, or who'd done it, that the word "Holocaust" was so big, that it was made up of so many who perpetrated it, that he would have been surprised to know there was one name, and that man was dead. What he knew was that that it if it could happen, it could happen again. Bill told me that, and I agree with him.

He spoke often of wanting a new society, that it was what drove the music when he became involved, and decried the lack of leaders to make it happen, that we were on a road that worried him, and that was why he'd had so much more to do.

He was right. That moment when everything seemed possible in San Francisco was down to him. I'm not sure he realized he was the catalyst bringing all together. It became obvious after the helicopter wound its way up a power line into a pole. More was lost than Bill, or his companion at the time, Melissa Gold, or my buddy, Steve Kahn.

The essence and the energy of the time, when the music – while making astonishing money for both good and bad people – was a creative force for change, with Bill and the people around him, my friends from high school, and those who weren't friends, were, all of them, the ones making sure it was heard. They were an effing miracle, all of them.

Rest in Peace, Bill.

JAY BLAKESBERG

I was a kid from New Jersey and Bill Graham was a legend in my mind! My first Bill Graham experience was a New Year's Grateful Dead run in 1979. I called the BGP office from New Jersey and was told I could send a blank money order to Bill directly for my tickets, and that is what I did! I still have the receipt from the bank where I spelled Graham wrong (only one A).

I took a Greyhound bus to San Francisco for those shows. Crashed with some hippies in Berkeley I met in Colorado the previous summer and basically had my mind blown by the whole California experience. Bill flew across the arena as a giant butterfly that New Years and I got the picture!

I moved to Oakland in 1985, and by going to many Dead shows I figured out who Peter Barsotti was. I was trying to figure out how to make a career as a photographer, and by keeping my eyes and ears open, I concluded that Peter was a man in charge and could possibly facilitate me working for BGP. New Year 1986-1987, I got the call from Peter. He wanted me on his photo crew. Of course, there was no money involved, just access and opportunity. I jumped! Ken Friedman was probably not happy! But that was Peter's specialty, pushing buttons to make people work harder and be better. I shot Bill rehearsing his midnight flight as an eagle. I shot the balloons on the floor before they hung them from the ceiling. It was an amazing experience. I was slowly floating over the barricade to the other side. I kept pushing to shoot more shows, develop my skills and trying to get paid!

November 11, 1987 was my day! I had been shooting for a variety of music publications, mostly small-time pubs, but that day I got the call from Rolling Stone Magazine. My first assignment for the venerable rock magazine. They needed me to shoot the free U2 Concert at Justin Herman Plaza. My big break! Peter Barsotti was scrambling around and Bill was a major presence. By then, I was seeing Bill all the time at shows, but to me he was still a legend and larger than life. He created the magic that I was photographing week in and week out.

A month later, January 23, 1988 was the Blues for Salvador benefit at the Henry J. Kaiser in Oakland. Cynthia Bowman was the publicist and I was on assignment for Rolling Stone Magazine. It was probably my third assignment for RS. I still had A LOT to prove. I scurried around everywhere looking for the unique shot. I got many! But at one point between sets, I saw Bill walk through a door just to the left of the stage. So, I followed him not knowing where he was going or what was behind the door.

I found Bob Weir and Jerry Garcia in their nifty Hawaiian shirts (they had both just flown back) with Bill. I said, "Can I get a shot?" Bill sat in between them and I took four quick photos. I GOT THE SHOT! That was my first truly memorable Bill Graham photograph even though they are just snapshots. That was about the level I was still at in terms of shooting pictures off stage. They still, to this day, hold a very special place in my heart!!!

JAY HELGEDALEN

I started working for United Production Services (UPS) in 1983 at the second US Festival. A handful of BGP guys were there with us. I first worked with a full BGP group at my first Day on the Green show in Oakland while we were on tour with David Bowie.

The first time I remember dealing with Bill on a one-to-one basis was when I was building a stage at Meadowlands in 1986 for an Amnesty International show. They were overseas and I talked with Bill over the phone from our production office. He was telling me what he wanted with the front of stage and ego thrust. I was young, maybe 24. I took very specific notes and built what he had told me. When he arrived at the stadium he called for me to see him downstage and proceeded to chew my ass out in front of the entire crew. I know that I built what he told me over the phone. But it was "Bill Graham, king of live events," so I sat there and took it. I assembled my crew and rebuilt it how he wanted it.

One of the things that always stuck in my mind after doing tons of shows with my BGP family is that whatever he was worth moneywise, he would always grab a bunch of patrons after the show and pick up garbage alongside of them.

He kind of made up for the ass-chewing the following year. A couple of months after we shot the video for the Grateful Dead's "Touch of Grey" song, I was in the middle of another Bowie tour and was supposed to go home the following weekend and got a call that I had been requested to jump on the Grateful Dead tour. My wife at the time was not happy. So, UPS flew her out to Telluride, Colorado for our next show. The BGP gang had gotten wind of our marital issues and a mandatory meeting was to be attended. Very strange but I grabbed my then wife and off we went. Sitting at our table was Bill Graham, the mayor of Telluride, Peter and Bettike Barsotti. During the dinner party, Peter stood up and proceeded to explain to my wife how much they appreciated her and how they needed me because the band was comfortable with me building their stages and how they consider me as part of the BGP family with a big nod and a thumbs up from Bill. I was floored.

Love my BGP family!

JEFF LEE

It all started with a chance encounter with Joyce Van Horn at my brother's house in Pacifica. I'd been pounding the pavement, handing out my resumes in my chosen field of computers…and failing, bit too cocky, thanks to great grades and landing on-campus computer jobs. I stank in the interviews. So, I was stopping by my brother's house to destroy a few brain cells.

There I met Joyce Van Horn who was dating a friend of my brother's. While there, I noticed Joyce had that odd tilt to her head/neck that told me she had some shoulder pain issues. I offered to remove the tight muscle and she accepted. I told her I'd just graduated and was job hunting. She mentioned I should apply at the Fillmore Fingers office on Cypress in Oakland. Working together, Joyce and I became an item. This was good and bad. She could keep an eye on me, but the sex, drugs and rock and roll lent to an atmosphere where boundaries got fuzzy.

Pragmatically, I wouldn't/couldn't get into anything while working having been royally burnt/face-shoved-in with a workplace romance – nevermore! As I worked more venues, managers would clamor for me because I followed orders, was early, never late and was older.

One test was the "drop this off at (name of superstar here)'s room." This time it was Phil Lesh and a plated request. I knocked, entered, left the plate, bowed and exited back to the kitchen. That I didn't stay, try to get an autograph, take a souvenir AND came right back meant I would get to work Dead shows. As an urbanite, I was sequestered/sheltered from life in the hopes I would NOT stray from the path of achieving great wealth by my parents. So, I never got to hang in the Haight, etc.

Exposed to a hippie counterculture now, it was the beginning of an end.

One phase I heard at BGP venues was, "You're lucky to work here. There's a line for your job at he door." This was true. It was also true that good workers are hard to find. If you wanted to work, don't complain. Doing so would mean fewer hours until you quit coming around. So, I put up with breaks when/if you could, long days on the road, heavy lifting and an occasional opportunity to shine by achieving something they said couldn't be done, such as maneuvering a U-Haul BIG truck in/back on the upper tier of the Greek Theatre to deliver soda cans without hitting anything; hats off to the manager who allowed me to do it as it saved TIME!

Working that hard alongside others is a bonding. At Fillmore Fingers I met hard MF working people I respected and would take a bullet for. Neil Marquis is one. The son of John Marquis, a renowned psychologist of Palo Alto.

Neil could have gone into a "clean hands" profession (fork, knife, spoon, pen or phone are heaviest things encountered.) Instead, he showed me "the challenge." One has to hold a fully loaded 16-inch sauce/frying pan on a fully extended arm WITHOUT quivering. Ah, the macho- BS/initiation of craft trades; don't get me started about boilermakers. This Tonto needed two hands so I was relegated to second class by default.

Still, it was a time when I could endure the blood, sweat and tears of working that hard. Working at Fillmore Fingers gave me the gumption, strength, drive and faith in myself that I could survive 24-plus years of working in a corporate prison environment. I'd just remember 36 hours ON THE JOB with breaks when and if you could get one was my record, but it was a Grateful Dead New Year's Eve show and you can't get memories like those ANYWHERE.

"Our greatest glory is not in never falling, but in rising every time we fall." "There is beauty in everything but not everyone sees it." Confucius

JEFF TRAGER

Over the span of probably 20 years I must have played for and against softball games that Bill Graham played in. He always played one position that I can remember and that was the pitcher. I think he fancied himself as softball's version of Sandy Koufax being both Jewish and left- handed.

One day we were playing a game at Rossi Playground in the Richmond District of San Francisco and Bill brought his son whom I helped by working on his outfield skills. This day, I was playing for Bill's team and in between innings we would just chat about nothing in particular and then out of nowhere he says, "Okay Mr. Hotshot record guy, who do you suggest I put on one of my upcoming Day on the Green shows?" I said, "How about Def Leppard, The Scorpions and Pat Travers." All of these bands were on the label that I worked for Polydor Records. He then asked me, "Who is Pat Travers?" I told him that he had sold more than 5,000 albums in one store alone in San Jose, California on Bascom Avenue. He is huge down there and will give you San Jose, the hottest rock market in the country, which will be great for you! "Interesting," he said. "I never heard of this guy, this Travers, thanks." That summer or maybe the next year, he put on one or two shows using all three of those acts, adding on Blue Oyster Cult and AC/DC if I am not mistaken.

It certainly endeared me to my record label, the manager of each act, and I think (no, I know) my relationship with Bill improved immensely because we spent hours after the show talking about the different bands that I was involved with. Before that I don't think he trusted a lot of local record promoters and music promoters in general for some reason. I know he banned me for at least a year from his venues because of a misunderstanding over a fundraiser that I threw at the Family Dog using one of my opening acts. It took KSAN's Tom Donahue to make peace between us one night when I found myself in a room alone with Bill at the radio station. His comment after we shook hands was, "Yeah, I guess a year is long enough to hold a grudge, you little prick!"

JENNIFER LEINSS

I was eight years old attending my first real rock concert, Day on the Green, at the Oakland Stadium. I knew, even at that young age, who Bill Graham was and what a special concert experience it would be that day. My father and stepmother took my younger sister and me to the full day festival.

My dad alternated between my sister and me who got to sit on his shoulders for a better view of the stage and to see all of the smiling faces in the audience. I'll never forget what an awesome experience we had and knew then I wanted to be in the live event industry when I grew up.

Day on the Green #1: Oakland Stadium, Sunday, May 28, 1978. Tickets $11, The Beach Boys, Linda Ronstadt, Elvin Bishop, Dolly Parton, and Norton Buffalo.

Both my sister and my stepmom have since passed away. My father and I cherish the memories of the four of us having the best day together, especially when we hear songs by those artists that rocked Oakland Stadium for us in 1978.

I vividly remember every staff member being so nice, eager to help and told us to "enjoy the show" at every turn. Another reason why I knew that I wanted to be in the live event industry: of the many concerts I have attended over the years as a guest, I always felt respected and part of the whole experience at BGP shows.

I was honored and lucky to see Bill with his sisters at a San Francisco Marriott while promoting his biography, Bill Graham Presents. I was honored and humbled by the stories he told about his childhood during WWII and his perseverance as a young adult to make his mark in the world. After his speech that day, I was even more enamored with him, BGP and the live event industry creating experiences. I ran into him in the hallway after he spoke and told him I wanted to work for him. He was kind, smiled, said thank you and that I should apply for a position.

The news of his death shook the Bay Area community (and the music industry worldwide) like an earthquake!

I attended his unforgettable, amazing and spiritual memorial in Golden Gate Park, Laughter Love and Music, on a beautiful sunny day. It was a fitting tribute to Bill being honored by thousands of artists, family, friends and fans. I felt great sadness that this legend had died too soon and yet how blessed I was to have met him and how honored we were as a community to have attended amazing concerts he and his team had produced.

I was hired at BGP in 2000 by Shelley Lazar in the Special Events Department. This was my dream job, dream company and my dream had come true. Even though Bill was no longer there physically his presence was always felt from the office walls adorned with his personal notes and letters, his MTV Award in the conference room for anyone to touch, the framed NYE floral crowns he wore every year, the posters and pictures of past performances.

Most of all, his presence was felt in the souls of everyone who worked at BGP, past and present. From the day I started working at BGP I felt like I found my family and those relationships I made will last a lifetime and beyond in rock and roll heaven.

I feel so honored and blessed. Thank you, Bill. BGP family forever….

JERILYN LEE BRANDELIUS

Bill came to my birthday party in the mid-1970s when I was living with Mickey Hart at his ranch. He told me we were the first people in rock 'n' roll to invite him to their home. I felt like saying, "Well, if you were nicer, maybe you would get more invites." But I didn't because I really liked Bill and had known him since the time I worked for his competitor, Chet Helms. I wanted him to feel welcomed, so my heart spoke and I told him, "We think of you as family and you are always welcome in our home."

As the years went by, he invited us to his home for holiday parties and in 1978 he came to Egypt with us as a friend instead of the band's promoter. That's another amazing story.

He loved the Grateful Dead folks and we loved him. It was a wonderful connection.

JERRY POMPILI

Bill and I go way back. I began working at the Fillmore East as an usher in May of 1968. A fast- talking New Yorker, I describe myself as "bossy" and "pushy." So, it wasn't long before I took charge, becoming house manager in August and soon after, starting the Fillmore East show program.

Bill suggested that I come to California and at the end of 1969, I found myself at the Fillmore West. I then went on to booking shows at Berkeley Community Theater, including Jimi Hendrix's final appearance in America. I booked and ran San Francisco's Winterland Arena through the '70s and I think I made a lasting impact on the makeup of Bill Graham Presents when I hired several "Berkeley High boys" who became mainstays to the company. After Winterland closed I moved into artist management at BGP, signing Eddie Money to Bill Graham Management.

I was the Master of Ceremonies at many BGP events, including all of the Days on the Green. In my latter years at BGP I focused on wiring the company for computers and organizing the company's extensive archives.

A problem arose on the 1988 Amnesty International World Tour featuring Bruce Springsteen, Peter Gabriel, Tracy Chapman and Youssou N'Dour. Bill had offered BGP's services in producing a show in New Delhi, India where there was no local concert promoter. When BGP's advance team arrived in New Delhi, they discovered that their promotional partner, a large newspaper, had represented the Amnesty event as the newspaper's 100th anniversary event instead of the important political statement that it was.

Bill was outraged and sent me out to contact every news media outlet I could find. I systematically contacted each and every news outlet in New Delhi in order to correct the perception of the event. By the time the tour arrived in New Delhi, I had succeeded in turning things around so that the event was reported accurately and Amnesty International signed on some 50,000 new members that week in New Delhi.

Shortly after Bill's passing, I was part of the original group that formed the Bill Graham Foundation in Bill's memory. That foundation later re-organized into the current Bill Graham Memorial Foundation in 2008.

I have now retired from show business. I am a very happy husband and a stay-at-home dad to two sons. I still act as MC at our annual Bill's Birthday Bash and am an active member of the BGMF board.

JESSIE BARSOTTI

Early Days

In the mid- to late 1970s when the Grateful Dead used to play Winterland in San Francisco, my brother Dharma and I were the only kids there. Our parents being so young, both in their twenties, they were the only crew members with children. David Graham would show up every once in a while, but Dharma and I were at every show. It is incredible to think that at three to five years old I was running around Winterland unsupervised, before, during and after shows, with my five- to seven-year-old brother. We knew that building inside and out. We would climb up onto the rafters in the ceiling and up on the large air ducts behind the stage. We would be front of house and backstage, under the stage and on the stage.

In those days there was no kid's room, so we had to fend for ourselves and we had a blast doing it. I learned to effortlessly weave in and out of the spinners and the floaters as we called them. It was pretty easy because I was so small at the time. I can still navigate any crowd with relative ease due to all the early training.

Often Deadheads would ask us if we were lost or where our parents were because honestly, I think we were the only kids in the building. That was before people started bringing their kids to the show in any great number. I remember being so annoyed by them asking us this, as if we needed our parents around at age four at a Dead show… pleeease. I would roll my eyes and say, "No, we're fine" and run off. Looking back, I can't imagine leaving my kids to navigate any show at that age, but it was a different time then. And don't judge my parents too harshly. God rest them both, they did the best they could and always put us first, despite how it may seem to outsiders. BGP and the crew were like a family to us. We had a happy, safe, interesting, joyful and fun childhood and I wouldn't change it for the world.

Sometime later, the kid's room was established with Wavy Gravy at the helm. I remember Mountain Girl, Hidden Mountain and Calico all there with us, among others. Most of my memories from the kid's room are from The Oakland Auditorium, which later became the Henry J. Kaiser. We were at the Oakland Aud, as everyone called it back then, all the time. My mom's kitchen was right off the parking lot in the back and we spent a lot of time there too. We would run around the building and loved to hang out in the theater area behind the stage.

Wavy would play bingo for prizes and the blackout bingo had the best prizes. One time Wavy announced that the prize for blackout bingo was going to be a skateboard. Dharma and I were determined to get that skateboard to use to skate down the switchback halls that lead from one level to another. Halfway through the game, it seemed that we were not going to win our skateboard because we had few pieces on our board. That is when I came up with an idea.

Wavy never checked your card, he would always ask you to read out your card to verify the win. I had a very good memory, so I decided that I would just remember the numbers he called and then claim that I had blackout using a few added numbers from my memory rather than what exactly was on my card. I didn't tell Dharma. When I had the right amount of numbers covered and memorized, I shouted, "bingo!" We got the skateboard and we were off. We sped down those halls for quite a while until finally we whipped around the corner and who was there? Bill!

We nearly ran him over. He was not happy, and he yelled at us. Somehow Bill was always there for the bust. It was uncanny.

Another time in the Oakland Auditorium I was sitting on a fork-lift backstage drinking some juice. I decided that I didn't want the juice anymore and I poured it on the floor. Of course, Bill saw me and he rushed up to the forklift and yelled, "Who do you think is going to clean that up?" I was paralyzed with fear and shrugged my shoulders. He looked at me and I jumped down to get a paper towel. I always think of that moment when I do something that someone else would have to deal with. Bill was a great teacher that way and I learned a lot from him.

When the Oakland Aud was transformed into the Henry J. Kaiser a lot changed. The whole building was upgraded and the theater in the back, which I believe was called the Calvin Simmons Theater, was totally redone, or created I can't remember. I do remember it got new carpets and chairs and huge chandeliers were installed in the main hallway. One day, David Graham, Bill's son, was there and suggested we play football in the theater hallway. Of course, a few passes in, the ball hit one of the chandeliers and the crystals came crashing down. And of course…Bill walked around the corner shortly after-ward. Another tongue-lashing from Bill, but I felt okay because David was the main target of his wrath that day. I can't say Bill was ever wrong about our bad behavior and he wasn't too mean either, just intimidating.

We knew Bill well because we saw him at the shows all the time. We would see him at the office and we also spent time at his house in Marin, Masada. He would invite us over there and often we would play sports or swim. As everyone knows, Bill loved competition. One time we were at Masada and Bill challenged my dad to a swimming contest. The teams were Dharma and my dad against Bill and me. When Bill made the teams, I don't think he knew that I was not a strong swimmer.

Each person had to swim from one end of the pool to the other where they would tag their teammate who would then swim back to the other side. Bill went first. He had a substantial lead over my dad when he tagged me. I jumped in and began to do the breast stroke because that was the only thing I was really confident doing. Mind you I was probably around eight or nine years old. The whole time

I was swimming back to the other side, Bill was on the side of the pool yelling, "Go faster! Why are you swimming like that?!" Dharma quickly overtook me, and we lost. Bill was disappointed, but my dad was happy to win because he was just as competitive as Bill.

JIM GAINES

One of my memories of Bill Graham: I was recording vocals with Buddy Miles for a Santana Band record at The Plant in Sausalito, California. Bill came in and stood behind me at the console while Buddy was singing and proceeded to spread his arms and wave them, sort of like angel wings going up and down, while instructing Buddy to sing as if a wild horse was running along a beach and Buddy was about to land on the horse's back. Sort of a slo-mo thing. I looked at Buddy, who was looking back at me with his eyes wide, pleadingly asking, "What the hell does he mean?"

Another memory: we were recording my first Santana project and we had a large vocal booth off the main floor and Bill was in it negotiating some kind of deal. Whomever he was talking to was not making him very happy. He's yelling into the phone so loudly we had to stop the session because he was being picked up by the drum room microphones. That was my first experience of being around Bill in the studio.

To me, Bill was a huge personality and a genius. Sometimes we just couldn't understand his interpretation. Still, loved him!

JIM MATZORKIS

I started working for Bill Graham Presents as a Bluecoat, stagehand and backstage ambience beginning in 1974.

I was working security at the Paramount Theater in Oakland on November 20, 1976 for the Jackson Browne show. The Paramount was a recently renovated classic music venue.

Jackson was playing an acoustic set. The theater and audience were very orderly and respectful of the music, except for one person that insisted on standing in the aisle in front of the stage directly in front of Jackson.

There were three of us working security for the show:

David Steidel, Bob Christenson and I. We made several attempts to politely ask this person to return to his seat. He continued to return to the front of the stage, dancing wildly and disturbing the show. The three of us gave him a final warning to sit down or be escorted out of the theater. He refused to sit and continued his wild behavior.

David, Bob and I grabbed him and began to escort him up the main aisle away from the stage. He struggled with the three of us, but we were able to contain him and walked him towards the exit. When we were part way up the aisle with this guy in tow, David and I looked at each other and said what happened to Bob?

We looked back at the stage where Jackson was playing his quiet song on his acoustic guitar. Evidently in the struggle to contain the uncooperative customer, we bumped a button where the encounter took place that raised the orchestra pit. Bob had been standing on the pit as it was rising to the stage level. As we looked back we saw all six feet, six inches of Bob hovering over Jackson Browne as he sang. Jackson gave Bob a quizzical look. Bob shrugged his shoulders and hustled off the stage. Jackson never stopped playing. David and I laughed hysterically as we removed the guy from the building.

JIM MATZORKIS

Led Zeppelin Story

I expected July 23, 1977 to be another typical day working for BGP. Actually, the expectation was that it could be a challenging day because of an early-arriving, sold-out audience that would likely be a potentially raucous group of Led Zeppelin fans. I could never have imagined what would take place that day.

My role for BGP was to work in the backstage ambiance crew in the days leading up to the concert and to be the on- stage security on show day. The best aspect of working in the Bill Graham organization was the close friendships amongst the staff and the closeness that many of us had established with our boss and leader, Mr. Bill Graham.

Organizing and managing large public assemblage events required this tight-knit staff. We always had each other's backs.

We worked for several days in advance of the show to build a backstage area, which included dressing room portable trailers, a catered crew and guest meal area, and a game area for the backstage guests, all with a show-specific décor. This would become the scene for what would become an infamous story in rock history.

It was late afternoon after the show had ended. My work as on-stage security was done for the day and I was in the backstage area doing the after-show cleanup. The band and guests were still there.

As I was performing my routine tasks, I noticed that a young boy had removed the Led Zeppelin dressing room signs from the trailer doors. These were wooden plaques engraved with the band's name. There was a second show the following day, so we needed the plaques for that show.

I approached the boy and told him that we needed the plaques for the next day. I didn't know who he was, only that he was a backstage guest. I told him that he could have them after the second show. He initially said no, but eventually gave them to me. I took the signs to our production trailer.

I was in the trailer a few minutes later when I heard someone call to me from outside the open door. I turned to see that it was John Bonham, the band's drummer. I walked out to the top of the small raised landing outside the trailer door. He told me that the boy was Peter Grant's son. Mr. Bonham was extremely agitated. He yelled at me, accusing me of hitting and harming the boy in the process of retrieving the signs. I told him that I hadn't touched him and that it was a misunderstanding. He grew angrier. He said that he could get me fired from my job. I replied that he couldn't have me fired (I knew that I would always have the support of Bill Graham).

He then walked up the three or four stairs to the landing where I was standing. Then, without warning he kicked me in the crotch. I was totally unprepared to defend myself. I was in extreme pain. One of the Led Zeppelin private security members ran up the stairs and got between Bonham and me. I was bent over in pain. The security guy whisked me into the trailer. I was in shock and severe pain. He knew me from my role as the on-stage security. He was clearly protecting me from Bonham who was in a rage. He whispered to me to get back and asked if there was another exit from the trailer.

He guided me out the back door and took me to a mobile home, which was situated just outside the backstage compound. He thought I'd be safe there. Some of my coworkers had seen the incident. They followed us to the trailer and told me they'd find Bill and bring him there. I was recuperating alone in the trailer with the door locked.

A few minutes later Bill came to the door and I let him in. He asked me what happened. I told him what had just taken place. He was very disturbed when hearing the story. He told me he was going to take care of it and asked me to lock the door and wait for him to return.

A short time later there was a knock on the door. I saw that it was Bill and let him in. Peter Grant, Led Zeppelin's band manager, accompanied him. Bill said that Mr. Grant was there to apologize and began to introduce us. Before he could complete the introductions, another man entered the trailer (I later learned that he was John Bindon, a band bodyguard). Grant and Bindon forcibly removed Bill from the trailer. He tried to resist but was overpowered by the two men. Grant was an extremely large and powerful man and Bindon was a bodyguard by profession.

They locked the door and approached me. The area inside the trailer was very confined. They began to violently assault me. They repeatedly punched and kicked me. I didn't try to fight back. That was useless. I was in full self-defense mode. I did my best to deflect their blows, but I was taking quite a beating. A punch to the face knocked out a tooth. Then Bindon reached for my eye socket attempted to rip out my eyeball. At that moment, I had a huge rush of adrenaline. I was young and strong. Using all of my adrenaline-fueled strength, I managed to push them aside and make my way to the door. I could see Bill through the trailer window. He was trying to get to me but there were Zeppelin security guards keeping him back and holding the door.

I unlocked the door, but it was being held closed by their security. Grant and Bindon were also trying to pull me back. I knew my life was in danger. These guys were out of control. I used all of my strength and somehow squeezed out of the door. There were many

BGP officials there along with many of my close friends from the BGP security detail. I remember seeing James Battle, Rudy House, and others approaching the trailer to rescue me.

Bob Barsotti, a BGP production manager and close friend, escorted me to his car. He then drove me to the emergency room at nearby Highland Hospital. I was bleeding from my face and mouth, was missing a tooth, and was severely bruised over my upper body.

I was treated at the emergency room. Several BGP co- workers, including my girlfriend Beverly, Peter Barsotti, and others soon accompanied me. I received a call in my emergency room bed. It was Zeppelin's road manager, Richard Cole. He had found my whereabouts.

After introducing himself he proceeded to offer me an immediate cash settlement to waive all charges and suits for the incident. I was still dazed from the beating, but I instinctively told him I wasn't interested and not to contact me again.

Soon after the call, Bill Graham joined me in the emergency room. My wounds had been treated and I was preparing to be discharged. At that time, I was told more frightening stories about other similar events that had taken place throughout the Led Zeppelin US Tour. There had been a number of violent incidents with several other victims.

I told Bill that I was concerned about going home. I thought I was potentially vulnerable if the Zeppelin folks wanted to track me down. He offered for Beverly and me to stay at his home in Marin County. I was familiar with his property. It was gated and very secure. We stayed with Bill the next couple of days. Later, on the night of the incident, I was sitting next to Bill in his home when Richard Cole called him. He wanted to know my whereabouts so he could speak with me. Bill told him he didn't know where I was.

There were subsequent discussions between Bill and Zeppelin regarding him releasing them of all liability for the incidents that took place (there were two other assaults that day involving BGP employees Bob Barsotti and Jim Downey). Zeppelin threatened that they wouldn't appear for the second show if he didn't sign. Bill eventually signed the release after being assured by his attorneys that the release was signed under duress and wasn't enforceable. The threat to cancel the second show would have resulted in the 50,000 ticket holders showing up the next day to a canceled event.

Bill wanted to have them served with criminal charges. I agreed. We knew that if they were arrested that night, it would have created an uncontrollable scene with disappointed and angry patrons at the event the next day. Bill offered me the option. If I gave the word that night to press charges, he would initiate it. After some discussion I suggested we wait until after the second show to have them arrested. Bill Graham had a well-known reputation. He could be an extremely volatile businessperson who had no hesitation to use intimidation in his negotiations and business dealings. He was also a very principled man and a loyal friend. He was willing to accept the significant financial loss if the second show was canceled. He was very angry that his staff (and close friends) were abused by Zeppelin's arrogant and hateful behavior.

Bill and his attorneys arranged for Bonham, Grant, Bindon, and Cole to be arrested at their hotel after the second show. They were scheduled to leave the Bay Area the next day, but there was concern that they might leave that evening in case criminal charges were forthcoming.

Bill had a plan. He was communicating with the local police captain providing band security, and the band's limousine driver to alert him if there was any movement indicating they were leaving the hotel. Later that evening they were served with the criminal charges. There was also a subsequent civil suit filed by Barsotti, Downey, and me.

The event had a significant impact on rock and roll history. The Zeppelin defendants eventually negotiated a plea bargain and received a suspended sentence and probation. The lawsuit was subsequently settled out of court and the three of us received a cash settlement. There were efforts made to prohibit the four Zeppelin defendants from getting visas to enter the US going forward. The original Led Zeppelin never performed in the US after the 1977 incident in Oakland, California.

JOE EHRLICH

He didn't want to watch the donkey and so he quit. They needed to hire a replacement. That's how I got my job as a Bluecoat.

Bluecoats were otherwise normal people who resembled peers of the ticket holders. This was a counterpoint to traditional concert security that had typically been recruited from college football teams, had flat-top haircuts and no social skills. We were called Bluecoats simply because our nylon windbreakers were blue. The jackets had "STAFF" printed on the backside, since we were not, by law, actual security guards. We did everything from taking tickets, keeping fire aisles clear, protecting the artists, arranging steel barricades, and occasionally watching donkeys.

It's hard to fathom now that back in the mid-1970s, there was an indoor plant craze gripping the nation. Everyone in the USA had decided that they required green potted ferns and climbing rhododendrons in their homes. Bill Graham must have seen an opportunity. The Cow Palace was rented and booth spaces were sold. It was advertised as The World of Plants. Besides plants to buy, there were things to gawk at. As you entered, where would normally be calf roping and tractor pulls, there was a large, erupting volcano that had been erected right in the middle of the floor. Somewhere else, there was a display that required the services of a donkey and a Bluecoat. I was never assigned donkey-watching duty. I don't remember exactly what they had me do, but I do remember meeting Joe Carcione that day. Joe Carcione was a local radio personality who talked about produce and had a gravelly accent.

I was off at college then, had no seniority and didn't get called unless they were really desperate. I recall once working the perimeter of the fence at a Cal Expo show in Sacramento. It was very hot and my task was to fend off fence-jumpers. The bill was odd: The Cars, Bebop Deluxe and the Marshall Tucker Band headlining.

I also worked occasional shows at the Winterland Arena. As the low man on the totem pole, both literally and figuratively, I searched ankles. I was tasked with finding half-pint bottles of liquor that had been tucked into Frye boots and then confiscating the bottles. Sealed bottles were then put into milk crates. When the milk crates were full, they were returned to the corner liquor store where they had originally been purchased. I also remember that Grateful Dead shows there went on seemingly forever (this was before their "concise period" of the 1980s) and fluorescent paint that glowed under blacklight on the ceiling. I remember little else. One time, I was put in a chair upstairs to guard a stairway. Another Bluecoat wandered by and handed me a rolled joint. I thought that it would be an ideal time to light it up, right there on the job. Suddenly, I was too stoned to work.

This would not be the last time that I exercised poor judgment at work.

During my salad days, I was enrolled at Chico State University, an institution that I was entirely unprepared for. Soon, the university and I parted ways, and in 1979 I returned to the Bay Area and started begging to work - anything and everything.

The Bluecoat ranks in those days were slim; most were from Berkeley and many were attending college there. The pay was minimal, but I didn't care: I was there mainly to meet girls and get an occasional free T-shirt. I had better success with the shirts. It was exciting to be at a concert, to be an actual part of it. The rush of the doors opening, the house lights dimming, the overpowering stench of vomit; it was all exciting to me.

Unlike most of my Bluecoat co-workers, I was not really enamoured of live music or concerts. Although I grew up in Berkeley, I never went to any concerts before I was employed by Bill Graham Presents. Occasionally I would sneak in to a jazz concert at the Greek Theatre (with the help of a senior BGP person who shall remain nameless), but I was primarily a record a collecting nerd. I didn't like to stay up late even then (and in my dotage, 8:00 p.m. is the time to get ready for bed, not for a for rock concert to begin).

Most of the shows I was working were crap anyway. People always wax eloquent about wonderful concerts in those days, but I was nowhere near them. I didn't have the seniority at that time and I wasn't one of the "cool" Bluecoats. Instead, I mainly got sent to the Cow Palace to work shitty metal bands (and Journey, which was just plain shitty). I remember once being assigned to work behind stage at

The Cow Palace for some loud and boring excuse for entertainment, but I don't remember who it was. I do remember that it was warm, very loud and since I was behind the stage, very dark. While guarding a section of roped-off seats I fell asleep (for a song or two) at about 120 decibels. That's how boring these bands were. Nobody even noticed.

Speaking of loud music, I still have bad tinnitus. The ringing never stops, ever. We were always issued yellow EAR Brand earplugs which claimed to knock out 35 db, but to effectively communicate with a patron in hopes of explaining to them why they should not stand on their chair, you had to remove the earplugs. Been there, done that, got the T-shirt, got the tinnitus too. Quite often, I was sent to work front of stage. Front of stage is where most of the time nothing much happens. The Bluecoats that liked the band would make themselves available right in the middle so that they could catch a glimpse of the show. I would always stand off to the side, thereby finding myself right in front of the speakers. The low notes would seemingly go right through my bones. Standing to the side meant that I could not see what was happening on stage; all I could see were sweaty kids from Concord and Fremont. Occasionally, some drunk girl would pull up her shirt and flash the stage. Somehow, I was always looking elsewhere. After the house lights came up, the Bluecoat guys would all elbow each other. "Did you see THAT?" they would exclaim. But no, I never saw whatever suburban breasts were on display.

BGP did concerts wherever there was an opportunity. We once did a run of shows called Takin' It to The People, where unworthy and pathetic acts played in small, municipal venues around California. Sacramento Memorial Auditorium one night, Stockton Civic Auditorium the next, etc. After the show in Sacramento, we camped, late at night in a state park in Rio Vista and really annoyed the park rangers. The next morning, we were off to Stockton to work some another half- witted show.

One regrettable venue was the T-Car Speedway in Carson City. The concert was, as I recall, a disaster. And without any prior knowledge, skillset or competency, I had been assigned to lead a bunch of similarly employed idiots in parking cars. The "lot" was an irregularly

230

shaped area of deep sand. Cars got stuck, but nobody was injured. Again, nobody noticed, so I still remained employed as a Bluecoat.

Eventually, business improved. BGP was now doing several shows at once on the weekends. They needed more Bluecoats and started heavily recruiting from the suburbs, from exotic places with fancy names like Fremont and Hayward.

The Day on the Green concerts are a painful memory. The call time for Bluecoats was 3:40 am. Due to pre-show excitement, I was never able to get a good night's rest beforehand, so I was always a mess during the long, long day. We started way too early in the dark and ended our day in the dark.

The patrons lined up outside the gates the night before. When the gates were opened, harried Bluecoats with bullhorns arranged them into lines about five people deep that snaked throughout the Coliseum parking lot. The concertgoers came with the intention of having a bitchin' party right then and there and were equipped with all sorts of recreational substances and illegal fireworks. They did not share the recreational substances, but they generously shared the fireworks by throwing them at us as we patrolled the line. I learned to despise fireworks.

With more concerts to staff, I was working a lot more shows. It actually became possible to pay my rent by working concerts.

Eventually, I became one of the supervisors and got paid a princely $10.00/hr. There was little training, guidance or oversight given to new supervisors and I stumbled often, but after a decade or so I figured out what to do. Sadly, I had left the company by then.

When the Rolling Stones came to town, Bluecoats were sent to SFO on the cargo side of the airport to wear our blue staff jackets and greet the Stones' airliner out on the tarmac. I suppose that was someone's idea of rolling out a red carpet: "send the Bluecoats to reassure them!" On show day, I was assigned to supervise backstage security at their Candlestick Park show. I have no idea how I got through that day. We also were sent to demonstrate our security antics at The Rolling Stones shows in Los Angeles and San Diego.

At the LA Coliseum, the opening act was a then-unheard-of skinny guy wearing a black leotard and a black cape. This was the first time that Prince had ever performed before such a massive crowd, one that had come to see the Rolling Stones, not a diminutive guitarist dressed as Batman. They showed their appreciation by pelting the stage with liquor bottles, one of which beamed Prince right on the head. He panicked, abandoned the still- playing band, ran off the stage and got about halfway down the ramp. Luckily for him, a very angry Bill Graham was walking up the ramp pointing and yelling. Prince went back and finished the set. Bill had undoubtedly saved Prince's career.

I spent a lot of time at the Warfield Theatre. As a small venue, it was an entirely different atmosphere from what I was used to (arenas and stadiums.) Once, we did the Grateful Dead there for 15 nights, though I only worked 12 of those shows; they sent me to work other concerts for three nights just to give me some variety. The Warfield was also used for legit theatre shows that I worked, such as Rocky Horror Picture Show Live and Little Shop of Horrors. For Christmas one year, we did an entirely absurd Nutcracker on Ice featuring Dorothy Hammel with the most ludicrous little ice rink that you ever saw. Unfortunately, the stage lights kept melting the ice during the show. Dress code for that run was tuxedos, which Bill had bought for us.

One time, Peter Gabriel and his band needed the Warfield to do a secret rehearsal. I was sent down there by myself and instructed not to wear anything that would alert anyone that anything was going on inside. Eventually, the band broke for lunch. Being secret, there had been no thought as to hiring catering. They came up to me and inquired about nearby restaurants. I panicked; this was the Tenderloin! No place suitable for big rock stars!

They said, essentially, "We don't care. Where would you eat?" I told them that I would probably go to Original Joe's, but that it wasn't appropriate for the likes of them. They scoffed. Peter Gabriel and band all marched up Taylor to Original Joe's. They loved it. They came back and thanked me profusely.

At Winterland, the Grateful Dead had not yet been the phenomenon that they were to become. We started doing Dead shows a lot more often. I was usually assigned to work before and during the shows, to hang out with the Deadheads. Shows were often at the Oakland Auditorium where I attempted to keep a handle on whatever was going on outside in Deadhead-land. One time, I was one of two Bluecoats sent out to work a Dead show in Park City, Utah (where the front of stage "barricade" was only a split rail fence!) It also seemed like we were sent down to the Ventura Fairgrounds too often. There, we worked alongside a local security crew who were completely inept while their management overcharged us.

Once, we did three days of the Dead at the Laguna Seca Raceway in Monterey County. The regular operations guy was out on paternity leave, so they shuffled me in to handle the task. One of the chores was inspecting the facility beforehand for damage, as one would with a rental car. All the fences and buildings were intact. Afterwards, we were charged over $10,000 for damage that the concert fans had done. The Laguna Seca shows were difficult for everyone, Deadheads and BGP staff alike. We all camped right there at the venue, which was a new and novel experience for much of the production staff. The weather was dense fog at night, bright sun and windy during the day.

Everyone was exhausted by day two. Thankfully, we had plenty of medicinal help. One evening, we cleared the concert area. The patrons dutifully went back to their campsites and heavily imbibed. Then, we were told to let the now-peaking patrons back in to the venue so as to provide an audience to a video that they were shooting. The fog machine effects of the "Touch of Grey" video were not needed; natural fog rolled right in on cue.

After that video was released, the popularity of The Grateful Dead greatly increased. The runs of shows were longer and in bigger venues. The parking lot scene at the Oakland Coliseum was a mess, and I (the designated "outside" guy) started bringing more concerns to my bosses about what I was seeing out there.

Without explanation, I was switched to the work inside. For the remainder of my time, I supervised the backstage security at Dead shows. I was well equipped. I had two electronic leashes: one walkie talkie from BGP and another from GDP. Either company could (and did) yank my chain at will. On the plus side, I was very well fed; Jerry Garcia once playfully called me a "porker."

I was not a very good Bluecoat. I screwed up a lot and got called into Bill's office several times. He always called me "Joseph," and he must have fired me two or three times. However, whenever he entertained at his house, I was the one who was trusted to stand at his front gate with the guest list.

I left BGP, sort of, in 1990. The North Face had hired me, thanks to another Bluecoat who was in management there. But one doesn't ever really leave Bill Graham Presents. When he died, I was immediately called in to do security at Masada, Bill's home. I was no longer on the payroll, but that didn't matter. I think that we stayed for two or three nights, just keeping the crazies away. There was also a show at Golden Gate Park. I worked that too. It was the least that I could do for all that Bill Graham had done for me.

JOE PAGANELLI

Office Assistant in AKG to General Manager of the Fillmore 1993-2005.

I did not know Bill, but as I say in my book, I got to know him through the people, through the stories, the pictures on the walls. Through the posters, the velvet curtains at the Fillmore, the solitary mic stand on stage when I introduced a band. Everyone had a Bill Graham story, even the guy who printed the posters.

Two stories come to mind, but I cannot speak to the accuracy. One may have come from the Barsotti brothers or Ray Etzler; it was a concert in Russia. Everything was challenged: the production, the security, stage, you name it. Starved for entertainment, for an opportunity to express themselves fully due to a lifetime of repression, the crowd rushed the stage and the environment became dangerous.

There were soldiers in the crowd. They wore weapons, they seemed nervous. Bill got on stage and asked the crowd to stop pushing, to stop crushing each other and the stage.

It wasn't enough. The soldiers as security became more anxious. A state of emergency seemed imminent. Finally, he had them kneel down. Get on your knees. Move slowly. One knee at a time. And they did. And it saved the day. And I don't know if it's true, but I'd like to think it is. The Bill Graham I heard about, believed in, was capable under such conditions of getting that done. Maybe in the end it was

Peter or Bob Barsotti who got this done. But it makes me think of the herculean charisma and power Bill had to control a crowd.

Bob Barsotti told a story by the water fountain at the BGP office on Fifth Street near David's office – the crossroads between the management department, the archives office and AKG. The show was Rush, a sold-out crowd for two nights.

Bill felt he owed them an introduction. Bob said it wasn't necessary, but Bill didn't listen and went up on the stage to do it anyway. Before he went up, he was yelling and distracted and trying to do three things at once; you know Bill. On the stage, he took the mic and went into his practiced routine: Ladies and gentlemen, we are delighted to have them here for you. Your friends and ours, E-L-O!!! Bob said, "Ohhhh Bill, no." Bill came off the stage. He went into a rage. Bob said it was okay. So the next night, Bill finds Bob and says, "I have to go up there and make it right!" Bob says, "Bill, it's okay, they don't need an introduction tonight. You don't have to go up." Bill goes up anyway. "Ladies and Gentlemen, it is our pleasure to introduce to you, the best in the business: EEE-LLL-OOO!"

And then my true story, that night I left for The Fillmore. The name of the band escapes me. He was an indie hipster, one of those artists where it sounded like two last names. He didn't have a "band name." His music was in a movie called Good Will Hunting. Elliot Smith! I didn't know who he was. I asked several times about the name. People told me, but it vanished every time. I took to the stage. A solitary microphone. The crowd sold out, San Francisco's most critical hipsters, shoe-gazers, who cared little about Fillmore fanfare. "Ladies and gentlemen, our friend and yours, it's my pleasure to introduce… CHRISSSS ELLOTT!"

In the crowd, one face stood above the very rest. He was a tall guy. I could see his face, the only one through the hot white lights shining down on my defeated face. Nobody in the room made a noise. The man's face looked offended, like he had just been raped by a cat. And then…"BOOOOOO!"

JOEL SELVIN

Pop Music Critic, San Francisco Chronicle, 1970-2009

I am a proud three-time member of Club 86. "You're not in until you're out," is our motto. We have some surprising celebrity members, such as Janis Joplin. When I told Mickey Hart about the club, he said that he and Jerry also belonged.

To qualify, you must be thrown out of the show by Bill himself. And these banishments were always permanent - "He can NEVER come to one of my shows again" – until, of course, they weren't.

The first time I joined was early in my days at the Chronicle, like two or three months on the job, 22 years old, still wearing neckties to work, although in my mis- guided fashion scene, I was sporting those ridiculous large bow ties that were briefly popular in the early 70s. It was Friday afternoon when I got the call from Bill – "You can NEVER come to one of my shows again." I have no recollection as to the specifics of the offense, but that never mattered with Bill.

I hung up. My career was over. What possible use could I be to the Chronicle if I couldn't attend Bill Graham concerts? I looked around for some brass to report my sorry state, but being Friday afternoon, none of my bosses were around. I finally located Stanleigh Arnold, editor of the Sunday paper and the features syndicate. I slumped into a chair in his office and told him my story sadly. "Wait a minute," he snapped, picking up a phone and dialing an extension.

"Hal," he barked into the phone, "You got Bill Graham's ads down there? Well, pull them until I tell you otherwise." Stanleigh hung up and turned to me. "They can't do that to one of our guys," he said.

About a half hour later, my phone rang and I received what passed for an apology from Bill. He never really went straight at the apology thing, sort of walked around the side of it and patted it on the butt as he went past. Bill Graham apologies were always special – just ask Dave Furano – we all remember Dave Furano, right?

So early in his heyday at BGP, Furano was dispatched to advance a big weekend deal in Phoenix with Barbra Streisand and her "A Star Is Born" movie. When Bill arrived and found that Furano had rented luxury cars at the top of the card, he busted a gut and blew it out on

Furano. Monday morning, coming back to the office, Graham walks by Furano's office and thinks, "Hey, I was a little to rough on him I really owe him an apology." He stops in Furano's office and starts his apology. However, in explaining why he was upset in the first place, Graham got all worked up a second time and found himself holding Furano by his collar and shaking him. "Dave, it's not the money...it's the money," he said.

I've always considered that the quintessential Bill Graham quotation and it should be used as an advertising slogan for a bank.

Anyway, back to Club 86. My favorite ejection was poor Steve Rubenstein, who was sent to cover the early part of The Last Waltz for Cityside in his second or third week on the job. He would be writing about the scene Bill had created at Winterland – the potted plants, the waltz orchestra, the turkey dinner with all the trimmings for five thousand. With all this lavish display of hospitality, there had been only one small glitch. They packed the apple juice with too much dry ice and all the beverages were frozen solid. Rubenstein, the intrepid 24 year old cub reporter that he was, finds Bill.

"Mr. Graham, Steve Rubenstein, San Francisco Chronicle. Mind if I ask you a couple of questions?"

Graham is in one of his famous expansive moods. Grinning broadly, spreading his arms out, he says, "Shoot."

"What happened to the apple juice?" Rubenstein says.

Graham does not even look at him. He turns away to find the nearest blue jacket. He points at Rubenstein.

"Him," he says to the blue jacket. "Out."

JOHN FOLLANSBEE

I worked as a Bluecoat for Bill Graham Presents.

I was working at the Cow Palace mopping floors in July of 1984 when I asked one of the security people how I could get a job. She pointed out a gentleman by the name of Richard Cicchetto to me. I told him I wanted to work security. He asked me if I was crazy. I replied, "Yes." He said, "You're hired."

My first show was Julio Iglesias on July 21 at the Greek Theatre in Berkeley, California. I was so amazed at the behavior of the women who were coming out of his dressing room. They acted like they were 14 years old and at a Beatles concert. They were saying things like, "He touched me – I'll never wash my hand again!" It was really crazy how he charmed them.

I was with BGP for a total of nine years, my last show being New Order, July 24, 1993 at Shoreline Amphitheatre in Mountain View, California. I worked approximately 675 shows for Bill Graham Presents; about a third of those were Grateful Dead related.

One of my most cherished moments was while working Bob Hope's dressing room at the Earthquake Relief concert in November of 1989. David Crosby wanted to meet him and when he did, he threw his arms around Bob and said, "Hope and Crosby – together again." It was hilarious!

It was the best job that I ever had and I wish it never had to end. Working for Bill was a real honor.

JOHN FRANKLIN

Mike Thompson invited me to start working at BGP. My first stadium show was Steel Wheels with the Rolling Stones and I was working the first aisle behind the first section of stage left and on my way to my break. Bill was dealing with people who were doubling up on seats. So, he grabs me and gives me a couple and says (yelling), "Take those people and walk them out now!" I didn't know what to do other than just say to them, "follow me," and I got them away from him. He was obviously very agitated and worked up. I just asked the people to walk up the steps with me and halfway up the steps, they showed me their tickets. They were the actual tickets for those seats. I informed them that I wasn't going to escort them out. I made an executive decision which could have ended my whole career right then, but Bill had the wrong people and I wasn't about to throw them out. So, I said, "Have a beer up here, and then go back to your seats and he'll be somewhere else and I will tell the person in the aisle that these are your actual seats and you have the tickets."

This is what I did in that situation and I never heard another thing about it, but I was sure worried throughout that show that it would come back and bite me hard. I always thought that situations like this were what separated Bluecoats from Staff Pro and other event services; more of a personal compassionate approach,

My other story has to do with Shoreline Amphitheatre working a Grateful Dead run during a daytime show. I was at the top of the steps behind the main bar dealing with some radio station winners trying to get in through the entrance and I was directing them back to the 200 seats bar, and all of a sudden, I realized Carlos Santana was standing behind these people. I stopped for a moment and ushered him in and went back to directing the people where they needed to go. About two hours later I was doing the same with another group of winners and when I was done I realized that someone was standing behind me; it was none other than Carlos Santana.

I looked up and said, "So, is there something I can do for you?" and he politely said, "No, I just wanted to thank you for letting me in earlier." My jaw pretty much dropped and I just looked at him and said, "You know, you kind of helped build this place and I think you'll always be welcomed." I just wanted to note the humility that man possesses. The idea of him waiting all those minutes for me to get my job done just to say thanks is unbelievable.

I will always feel thankful and very fortunate to have had my BGP experiences.

JOHN HUTCHINSON

Tired of traveling from Los Angeles to San Francisco to attend Dead shows, I moved to the Haight in 1979 to be closer to the action and attend San Francisco State. Fast forward one year to the Dead's 15 Year Anniversary run in October of 1980 at the Warfield Theater. Attending 13 of the 15 shows, I became acquainted with many of the Bluecoats working the events. Chatting with them pre- and post shows and during breaks, I found the connections to ushering shows, which sounded like an awesome way to attend shows for a broke 21-year-old student. So, I did, then quickly worked my way to the "big time" of a paid Bluecoat! This led to the nightclub world of AKG and the Old Waldorf.

Scheduled to work a Dave Mason show on July 11, 1981, Dave had to cancel. I was asked to go help stamp hands next door at the

Punchline Comedy Club. That night changed my BGP employment path, for I stayed there for the next 19 years. There I was, 21 years old and working at what would quickly become one of the most popular comedy clubs in the United States. I was privileged to be hanging out with some of the funniest people to ever perform stand-up during the heyday of the '80s and '90s comedy scene. The Punchline S.F. was kinda off to the side from the rock venues, big stadium and coliseum shows, but held a special little corner in the world of Bill Graham Presents.

Back to the Beginning

Last night of the Dead's run at the Warfield, we had talked with Bill a few nights earlier about presenting the band with a cake before the show. Bill arranges for me and a few others to walk down the aisle as the band takes the stage and hand them our homemade Skull and Roses decorated cake, which we hand to Phil to much applause. Good fun!

As the night progresses, I'm dancing on my chair and notice a flashlight from the stage coming from behind some equipment, hitting me in the eye. It's Bill motioning me to get down from standing on the chair! After the show in the lobby I stopped to thank Bill for letting us present the cake. And using his best Bill voice he says, "Don't ever dance on my chairs again!" He scared the shit out of me… couldn't wait to work for him!

JOHN NASH

On a cold December morning just prior to this Christmas, I walked past the front of the old Fillmore East and the vacant space where the old Anderson Theater stood two blocks down the street, where the ghosts still haunt the alleys with no place to call home. New York City in the bite of winter seems eternal!

My part in this play started on February 23rd and 24th, 1968 when my band Pearls before Swine, flush with the momentary success of our first album, came to NYC from Florida and played the Anderson Theater with newly formed The Electric Flag opening, Pearls as special guest and Country Joe & The Fish headlining.

I was 17 and scared to death to follow Michael Bloomfield. It was Jerry Pompili's first show at the Anderson Theater as well. Pearls folded after the Anderson shows and I did not return to Florida with the remains of the band, but remember well the bitter winter and spring that cut to the soul of a misplaced Florida boy.

I went to work at Danny Armstrong's Guitar Shop on LaGuardia Place, went home with a waitress from the Café Wha and settled into a flat on Minetta Alley.

Bill Graham and Jerry Pompili opened the Fillmore East and it was heaven. I witnessed rock history parade across that stage nightly. I left NYC in 1972 when the heroin epidemic was at its worst, moved to Atlanta and worked the Southern rock scene. I became an audio engineer and production manager in those years and landed on the West Coast at the end of the Isley Brothers/Graham Central Station Fight the Power Tour in late 1977.

Kenny Rogers had just had his huge crossover hit with "Lucille," and Bill had taken on Bobby Bare in an attempt to do the same. Bobby had relocated to San Francisco from Nashville and was miserable there. BGP needed a tour manager who could mix audio, production manage and most important…speak Southern.

It was Jerry Pompili who got me the job. A string of U.S. dates and a package tour of Europe followed. Bobby just wanted to go fishing. When we returned from Europe, Bobby left Bill and Bill Graham Management and I was about to be without a job when Eddie Money punched out his tour manager, Jerry Bergh, and Arnie Pustilnik handed me the project, saying I wouldn't last two weeks. Five years later I had worked for every act in the stable.

I loved the office at 201 11th Street, and the management offices in the back; Bill's Mercedes convertible and Carlos' green Volvo sports wagon in their parking spaces.

I still hear Bill Graham, Mick Brigden, Jerry Pompili, Ray Etzler and Jerry Pompili in my sleep. Bless you Queenie Taylor for talking me down a hundred times (especially after the Madness show at the Old Waldorf on March 12, 1980.) My life was never the same…ever… thank you all!

Note: Eddie Money was my best man 30-plus years ago. We stayed close up to his death.

JOHN "JT" TOOMEY

Over the years there has been a lot said and written about Bill Graham. His life story has been dissected and discussed through the many articles, interviews, video documentaries and even two different books. There is nothing that I could possibly add to tell his story any better.

What I would like to do is to give some insight into the man from my own perspective and personal observances. As one of his employees at Bill Graham Presents for almost ten years (1988- 1997), I was fortunate enough to work with and share some rather private moments with this man.

Several things come to mind when remembering Bill, his associates and other employees whom I worked with at both Bill Graham Management and BGP. I saw Bill's insight and wisdom about the need to build a team around him to fulfill his dreams and aspirations while making BGP into the powerhouse business that it became.

Bill understood the importance of hiring only the best people for each position. He attracted these kinds of talented, loyal people to build his base of operations and some of his closest employees have been with Bill since the middle sixties.

They grew as he and BGP grew together as one cohesive team.

In some respects, everyone who worked at BGP was a pioneer in their own field of expertise and many innovations in the promotion and production of live events can be directly traced to their demanding work and insightful input into the company. Everyone had their place and there was a place for everyone inside his company. Bill's business thrived in no small part due to the work and progressive thinking of many different people. This was one key to Bill's incredible success. It takes a village to make this happen and many of these villagers who came into Bill's orbit usually stayed there for a while and some for their entire careers.

Secondly, part of Bill's success was his passion to create and present the best possible production night after night to the multitude of customers who came through the various venues' doors. Bill would do whatever it took to ensure that they all had a most pleasurable experience at his shows. I often saw Bill go toe-to-toe with someone who didn't agree or understand why this was so important to Bill.

He would spend countless amounts of time discussing why a camera that was set on stage would interfere with the audience sightlines, or why an overzealous security staff could intimidate and infringe on the space that the patrons had paid good money for. Bill always understood that these patrons were the key to the establishment and growth of the rock 'n' roll industry and he did everything he could to ensure that their best interests were represented...always!

Was Bill egotistical, self-centered, unrealistic, greedy and perhaps more than a little inhumane as many people have often said about him? In certain ways he was probably a little of all of these things. He had a way of eventually getting what he wanted, but sometimes this rubbed people the wrong way. Bill was a human being and, like anyone, could exhibit some nasty character defects. On the flipside of that coin, Bill could often be kind, forgiving, generous with his time, energy and money and he was funny as hell. He could tell a story like no one else that I've ever known and leave you laughing until your sides ached.

Bill just had that charm and unique gift which enabled him to switch from one character to another before a person could catch onto its subtleties. Bill was a truly gifted storyteller and character in his own right. Bill had a lifelong dream to become a successful stage actor, but after some initial failures at that, including character roles in several well-known movies, he abandoned the dream and focused on the work at BGP instead.

At some point, Bill had an epiphany and realized that the entire world could be his stage and he could switch roles daily. Once he understood that he was free to be Bill Graham, the great actor on the largest stage ever available - the whole wide world!

It was a thrill to daily observe Bill perform his greatest roles. Oftentimes he was better than any movie actor known to man. He relished this newfound outlet or his talents and energies, rehearsing it every day for the rest of his life.

Bill taught us all through his actions that the human condition that we all lived under was of utmost importance to insure our continuing existence on this planet. Perhaps this happened as the result of his very rough and scary childhood, but Bill seemed to never forget that helping others was so especially important. He would often put his energy and monies into many events that had a profound and long-lasting effect on his fellow human beings. Sometimes these were big and loud, generating massive amounts of media coverage and raising a lot of money for a cause. Other times there were more private with hardly any notice given, but they all had Bill's imprint on them, and they all had the same result for Bill and everyone else who benefitted from his work. Promoting a large show that highlighted the worldwide plight of poor, starving people or raising awareness of some social injustice was not any more important to Bill than a local show to raise funds for a new school bus in Oakland to insure the safe transportation of children to their schools and back home again.

This was the kind of man Bill was. He took great internal satisfaction in helping "the little guy" on a local level, as well as the "bigger guys" on his world stage. He had made an obligation and felt he needed to contribute something to make what he felt was wrong… right! If you feel so inclined to find out more about Bill, I suggest you read the book Bill Graham Presents written by Bill Graham and Robert Greenfield.

My concluding thoughts and words on this man, Bill Graham, are that I am so very thankful to have been given the opportunity to work with, and in a small way, get to know Bill. I am also proud to say that I knew and cared for this individual and held him in the highest esteem and regard.

The last time I saw Bill was when we were together in Israel doing a couple of huge outdoor shows with The Neville Brothers, Joe Cocker, Jack Bruce and Ginger Baker. During those ten days, Bill was very peaceful and serene, which were not two words that were often used to describe Bill. I stood alongside Bill when Teddy Kollek, the Mayor of Jerusalem, thanked him for helping to bring these bands to Israel. As Mayor Kollek said, "Our people are like camels in the desert; we need some well-deserved relaxation from our tribulations as the camel also needs water."

Three weeks later while I was in Germany, Bill was killed in the tragic helicopter accident while returning home from a local Huey Lewis and the News show. When I first received the news of this event I literally broke down in tears. My grief was shared by everyone at BGP as well as all the others who had ever attended one of Bill's shows.

I feel that the years I spent working at BGP were the "jewels in the crown" of my career. I wouldn't trade any of my experiences with Bill and BGP for anything.

I will forever be grateful for that time and I will never forget Bill, the man who inspired me and countless others to always do our best and to carry with us the lessons we had learned by his steadfast influence over us.

Thank you very much Bill We all miss you every day And as your usual salutation simply stated, CHEERS!

JOHNNY COLLA

It's the summer of 1967 and I'd just turned 15 years old (yikes)! Thanks to Bill and Chet Helms over at the Avalon, a kid like me could fill a car full of bodies, be in the City an hour later, witness an amazing variety of music and musicians at each venue, and be back home that night just a little late (I was telling my folks I'd fallen asleep at the local drive-in; they had no idea I was bipping off to San Francisco every weekend).

I spent a lot of time at the Avalon, but we were soon spending more time at the Fillmore because of the musical diversity. One particular night I was standing in line working my way into the venue, when all of a sudden Bill comes charging out fuming, virtually dragging a kid by the collar, where he unceremoniously tossed him out.

As he's walking back inside he gets right in my face and looks me dead in the eye. "HOW OLD ARE YOU?" he bellows at me. With the best poker face I could muster up, I told him I was 16 years old. Bill gave me a strange little smile, turned around and walked back inside, knowing damned well I was lying through my teeth.

Decades later, performing at a BGP show in Monterey, California with Stevie Ray Vaughan, I had gotten to know Bill good enough to share my story with him, to which he responded, "Sounds about right!"

JON HAMMOND

The very last time I saw Bill was about three in the morning. I went into the Carnegie Deli on Seventh Avenue back when the Carnegie was open all the time. I felt like a corned beef sandwich. So, I came into the deli and there was Bill standing by the counter. He looked a little rough around the edges, unshaven and like me, sleep deprived.

So, we stood there talking for a while. He said he had been jonesing for a corned beef sandwich too. I didn't know Bill real well, but he knew me well enough that he would give me recognition and talk to me.

The first time we talked at any length was at Eddie Mahoney's (aka Money) wedding reception – the first one, to Margo - at the Claremont Hotel in Berkeley, California in 1984. I flew in from New York City to attend the wedding. Bill spoke at Eddie's reception and I was talking with Bill about Hammond organs. We had spoken before about this subject because I knew he had to pay for renting a B3 quite a few times, which wasn't cheap, so I knew he must have dug the B3 I had.

When Bill was giving his speech at Eddie and Margo's reception, he kept taking a cassette box out of his jacket and kind of toying with it while he was talking (I had given him the tape.) I dug that. I had just bought one of the first gray market camcorders from Sony. They didn't even have consumer camcorders in those days; it was a Sony Betamovie camera. I was new at using it and so I filmed the whole wedding thing and I thought I had turned it off, but I had about 30 minutes of my shoes when I had the camera hanging on my shoulder. LOL!

It was a formal Catholic wedding and I noticed a lot of Jewish people in the audience. My folks were there with me and my mom was even crying at the wedding. They even had bridesmaids and all that kind of stuff. Quite the wedding.

I didn't see Bill for quite awhile after the wedding party. I had my Silver Streak Trailer parked at Lucky Drive in Marin at the RV park for eight years and I used to go to Uncle Charlie's, a club in Corte Madera, California. One night I ran into Bill there and he told me that he dug the tape I gave him and he kept it in his car. He was driving an old Mercedes back then.

Note: When the Carnegie Deli closed on December 31, 2016 there was a note on the door that stated the following: Along with my daughter Sarri, and in honor of my late father, Milton, I would like to sincerely thank all of our loyal patrons, tourists, dignitaries and New Yorkers alike who have visited the Carnegie Deli over the past 80 years. Since my father took over the deli in 1976, this has been a second home to me and it has been a true privilege and honor to serve you. Although this has been an incredibly difficult decision to officially close Carnegie Deli New York (854 7th Avenue), we thank you for your letters, notes, visits and sharing your stories.

JORMA KAUKONEN

Bill Graham was one of the most interesting people I ever met. He was older than I and a World War II refugee and survivor. That carried a lot of weight and set him apart from other folks in the music world.

I first met Bill when we did the Mime Troupe benefit.

He was already in such command of the situation that I never questioned that he knew how to get it done whatever it was. He attacked tasks like a dog going for a bone. He would not be denied.

We didn't know anything about the music business at all back then (I'm not sure I do today). Our identities and careers were works in progress, but Bill was always there to give everyone focus as he saw it. There could be an oppressive aspect to his personality, but like it or not, more often than not everything would come up roses.

As right as he might be most of the time, he could also be tyrannical and at some point, the disparate characters in Jefferson Airplane could not tolerate this and we went our own separate ways. All that being said, we were always friends and we always shared mutual respect!

247

Bill would always be looking for a bigger stage for his evolving shows.

The Airplane would simply continue to try to solidify their collective identity and there was no longer a place for Bill in this quest. We would continue to work for him as individuals or as a group, but the intimacy of the early years would never be recaptured again.

Of course, I would see Bill every time we worked the Fillmore or one of his other venues, but our relationship just naturally grew distant. Things are only new when they're new.

I was more than shocked when I heard of Bill's death.

He was one of those larger than life guys you would presume would live forever.

Writing here in 2022, it seems like he has been gone a long time because he has been gone a long time.

I still miss him....

JOSEPH SAGARA

I started working with Bill Graham Presents in production in 1985. Candace from the Grateful Dead hired me to assist her in delivering a "lighting texture" for the Henry J. Kaiser Auditorium in Oakland, California. Working there, I met Peter and Bob Barsotti and Bill Graham.

I reckon I passed the audition because my calendar filled with many moons of magical Bill Graham Presents gigs, and a lifetime-long friendship with Peter, Bob and Bill.

Once at a show at Mountain Aire in Angel's Camp, California my friend Jackie hands me her camera as she snuggles up to Bill asking me to please take their picture together. Bill then holds up hs hand to the lens of the camera and turns to Jackie with his other hand out, "That will be five bucks." Jackie was shocked, dazed and confused as Bill snuggles back and I push the button.

JUDE HELLER

Director of Advertising at BGP

Bill Graham never had a reason to yell at me so far. It was early 1985, and Gregg Perloff, Vice President, walked into my office midday on a Wednesday.

"Jude, we just booked (name of big artist). It's going on sale this Sunday and has to be in the Pink Section."

"Gregg, the deadline for this Sunday is closed – no way this can happen." "Jude, it's gotta happen – call them and get it done."

I called my rep at the SF Chronicle, Dean Leary, and begged. BGP was a big advertiser in the Chronicle. Back then we had an annual contract of 52x page twos in the Chronicle Datebook (that's the inside front cover of the Sunday Datebook), a considerable contract for the concert division, plus we had print ads for the club division for The Warfield and Punchline. Dean got it cleared, but they needed it within the hour. Art Director Arlene Owseichik had the ad in my hand in half an hour and literally I ran it two blocks up the street to the Chronicle. Whew!

Sunday's Chronicle published and the ad was way back on page 52. At least it was right next to the horoscopes so I knew it would be seen, but I knew Gregg would not be happy. The next day Monday, I got a note – the dreaded, "See me, Bill," a rubber stamp in Bill's hand-writing stamped onto a Post-It note dropped into my in-box. Oooh, I knew I was in trouble. I walked over to Bill's office and he waved me in. He was on the phone, apparently in the middle of a negotiation for a show, and he was yelling phrases like, "What's $100,000 between friends?" As I listened in silence, the phone conversation got more heated. I tried to shrink smaller and smaller in the chair across from him, knowing I was next. He ended the call with, "Show me you're a man, hang up on me – I dare you!" and slammed down the phone. Once that was done, he turned and gave me a big smile.

We had a six-word conversation as he brought out the Sunday Pink Section, dramatically thumbed through it, turned to the offensive ad and held it up to me. "Jude, never again." "Bill, never again." And he waved me out of his office.

JUDY WHITT

On December 1-3, 1983, Bill donated the time and efforts of the Bill Graham Presents staff to continue support of the Action into Research for Multiple Sclerosis (ARMS) concerts at the Cow Palace in San Francisco, a benefit for Ronnie Lane who suffered with MS, to raise money to combat the disease. Months of planning, days of execution and hours of the most incredible music of the time and to top it off.

Bill invited the BGP crew and all of the musicians to his house for a party. No one else invited— if you didn't work it, you didn't go. How many people can say that they sat in a living room and had a conversation with Bill Wyman, Joe Cocker and Jeff Beck? I left amazed and humbled by such talented, giving people.

I don't know if others saw it that way and I don't care. This is how it impressed me and to this day I carry this memory.

I have a son that was diagnosed with severe onset MS and the impression this all made on me and my continued fight for my son's life was fueled by seeing so many people I knew and worked with willing to give time and effort to support such a worthy cause.

I worked for BGP and I made lifelong friendships. I know Bill had a big heart and the money that was raised with those benefit concerts supported research that keeps my son alive today. Thank you, Bill!

JULIA WINSTON

I started working at Bill Graham Presents on April 10, 1987 and stayed for 12 years. My jobs consisted of A/P and payroll for Fillmore Fingers and A/P and A/R for Bill Graham Enterprises.

It was Friday, February 27, 1987 before Paul Simon's Graceland concert at Berkeley Community Theatre. The evening was a culmination of almost one year of going to shows, watching staff and noticing when Bill was in attendance. I'd quit my job as bookkeeper for a San Francisco law firm to pursue my passion to work in the music business. It had become apparent over the prior two years managing a local band in my spare time that music was most important and I did the work well. My mother died in 1983 and I felt I had to make a change. So, I went to as many shows as I could, mostly at Wolfgang's,

Bill's nightclub, and the Warfield Theater. I was hoping to learn how to book the venues or work in management.

A friend invited me to the Paul Simon concert and I knew this was my opportunity. I knew Bill would be there and I would give him my resume. That day I labored over my cover letter on my electric type-writer. I was getting ready for my friend to pick me up at my home in Sausalito when the phone rang. My friend's car had broken down and he was stuck at a gas station in Daly City. He said we'd miss the show.

"No way," I said. "I'll come and get you." I drove from Marin to Daly City in record time. As we were crossing the Bay Bridge my friend kept saying, "We're not going to make it." I told him to shut up; we'll get there in time.

As we approached the theatre, a car pulled out and I pulled in. We'd arrived with 20 minutes before the concert was to begin. We walked the foyer and lo and behold, there was Bill in the center of the foyer. He was talking to three older men, I assumed to be Paul Simon's management. I positioned myself a respectful distance, but in Bill's sightline. As soon as they finished their conversation and the other men walked away, I walked towards Bill, extended my hand and said, "Hello Bill, I'm Julia Winston and I want to work for you." Bill shook my hand with a quizzical look on his face. He replied, "You do?" and I said, "Yes and I have my resume here," and showed him the manila envelope.

He made another face and said, "You don't expect me to schlep that around all night, do you?" I said, "No."

He said, "Here's what you do. Put a note saying we talked tonight, send it to my office, and I promise we'll read it." I thanked him and went to my seat. We were in the last row of the balcony, but I was so high from my Bill encounter that it didn't matter. The concert was magical, still ranks as one of the best concerts I've ever seen.

I followed Bill's advice. I updated my cover letter and mailed my resume to BGP. Weeks went by and no word. It's now March 26th, which would be my mother's birthday. I went out to Stinson Beach to meditate and commune with Mother Ocean. In my meditation, my mother came to me and said it was time for me to dance on my own. I left the beach feeling a lightness I hadn't felt since my mother passed.

I was telling my roommate what happened when the phone rang. It was Pat Thomas, asking me to come in for an interview with Steve Welkom. I didn't tell her that it would be my birthday, but I just knew this was it. The next day my 32nd birthday. My mother was 32 when she had me. This was it!

My face hurt I was smiling so much, telling Steve Welkom how much I wanted to work at BGP. He called Arnie Pustilnik and Mick Brigden to come meet me. We talked, but it was clear that I didn't have the experience they wanted. I don't remember exactly how, but I got referred to Frank Rockwell, the CEO. I interviewed with him another day and he told me there was an opening in accounting with Fillmore Fingers, which would fit my prior job experience. I made an appointment to meet with Nick Nicora at the Fillmore Fingers office in Oakland. The interview went well and Nick hired me. I was ecstatic!

I arrived at Fillmore Fingers on April 20 and was sitting with Nick at the computer when Steve Welkom called. Nick told him I was there. I heard yelling on the other end: Nick said, "I was supposed to let Steve know what I thought first, not hire you." "Well, she's here now!" And that's how I got my job by meeting Bill.

This truly was a dream come true. I cherish the almost five years with Bill. I forged friendships with coworkers that have lasted beyond my time at BGP. I count myself extremely fortunate to be a part of the BGP Family.

Bill taught us all so much and I carry his words, "It's the parsley on the plate," with me in my daily life.

K

KAREY MARENGO

I started working for BGP in 1981 as a Bluecoat. Through the years, I worked my way up through to assistant on call.

One story I remember was that I was sitting at the front desk at the BGP office being the fill-in receptionist and we had Paul McCartney in town performing in Berkeley, and we also had a skating show tour going on at the same time. We were getting over 300 calls a day and I remember somebody told me that Bill counts the rings it takes for the person at the front desk to pick up the phone at the office. I decided to take two seconds to check with Pat Thomas in the office to make sure that I was sending the skating calls to the correct person due to the hundreds of calls that was coming in.

Sure enough, the next call on the line was Bill while I was talking to Pat. And when I do pick up the next call, Bill in his stern voice said, "The phone rang 14 times before someone picked up. Way too many times. The phone can't ring that many times!" All I could say was, "Bill who do you need to talk to?" Well, after his call I started to cry. I was kind of mad at him. Then the next evening when it became closing time, I was talking to Toni Isabella at the front desk about something and Bill comes walking up the stairs to the office and again says in a soft voice hello looking at Toni and I say to Bill, "Ya know, I just want to do things right." Well, needless to say I wasn't mad at him anymore and I understood how things were.

That man was incredible and is missed dearly.

KARI THOMPSON

How I Became a Part of the Bill Graham Family

My next-door neighbor and friend told me there was a position at Bill Graham Presents. Before I met her, embarrassed to say, I didn't know much about this man, Bill Graham. Listening to her stories and knowing her, it sounded like a great place to work. The job was in the accounting department. After three interviews, I was hired.

My first day: I was introduced to many, many people. One of the moments I remember is this one man, Gregg Perloff. After being introduced, he stated, "I spell my name with two Gs." My intuitive response was, "What?! Ggreg?" I thought he should have said three.

It's been over 35 years. I worked for six, back in the early '80s. Things I Remember First football season – the first memory of many. The "boys" loved

to play football - tackle football. Growing up with five brothers, well, I wanted to play, too. Standing on the sidelines, I inquired as to why none of the women wanted to play. "Oh, no; it's the guys' thing." Hmmm. Not knowing Mr. Graham at the time, I timidly approached him and asked why women were not allowed to play. He looked at me and said if you want to play, you can play. I was so eager!!! Oh goody! I was put on the defensive line and was told to attack the quarterback. Bill was to protect him. Hike…BOOM!!! Bill had knocked me right on my tail end with one precise blow. He reached out his hand to pick me up. "Are you done?" he asked. "No, I'm just getting started," I replied with a humph! This time, I was ready for HIM!! Hike…BOOM!!!! AGAIN!!!! The hand reaches out. Big ol' fat grin on his face. I was moved to a less physical position with no plays. That was my first real introduction to Bill Graham – and my first lesson.

Next: Ah, yes, the US Festival in San Bernardino. Still getting my feet wet with the veteran folks at BGP. I was not only new with the company, I was also a little green around the ears. Okay, totally clueless when it came to being cool, hip or any semblance of being worldly. The memo stated anyone interested in attending the festival was invited – you just had to pay for your own airfare. I wanted to go. Staying in the sidelines backstage, I observed my comrades in action. I smiled, said hi, offered to help and mostly tried to stay out of the way. It was noted that someone in the parking lot was selling counterfeit backstage passes. The powers that be decided that a decoy was needed to sabotage the ring and I was chosen to be the decoy. It was mentioned that I could pass as a ditzy groupie and I was a sure in.

It happened as planned. The offer was made and the bad guys were caught. Honestly, I was frightened out of my wits. It did lead me to feeling more part of this wonderful family. Bob Barsotti took me on a tour around the event, introducing me to the Hog Farm Family and many others. I soaked it all up. It was also the first time I was invited on stage. Joe Jackson was playing and I'm sure everyone remembers what happened with ZZ Top…oops! My flight was paid for and on the way home I was introduced to part of the FM Production crew.

What a great, exhausting weekend.

Being the BGP Sports Director (dubbed by Bill himself), it all started with softball. Being horrible with names, I honestly don't remember all the bands we played against. I think Bob Seger's band might have been my first and I remember playing against The 5th Dimension. Then the Crackers (BGP employees) created our own team and played in the Entertainment Industry League, which is where I eventually became captain of this team. Three years in a row, we won the championship. We were the team to beat.

Bill Graham was unable to make most of the games, but there is one I will always remember. Not sure where we played – Marin somewhere and if I had a year or two, I might remember the band. It might have been Santana's. Bill was there and I was informed that he liked to pitch – so pitcher he was. Now, it had been a while since he played, let alone pitch. By the fifth batter, the opposing team was swinging at anything to offer some sort of excitement/entertainment to the game. Fellow teammates were glaring at me to do something. OMG!!!!! I have to pull Bill Graham. VERY nervous indeed. I walked up to him from first base and shook my head apologetically and ask him to give me the ball. He nodded his head yes, and walked over to first base. Now, I know this isn't a great story; however, it does simply show how intimidating the man could be.

As his sports director, I even assisted at personal events – Chabad was one. There were many lovely events at his house. He loved challenging me (and always won) to games of croquet.

While working at this inspirational place with this man with nonstop energy, I, too, was inspired. The early '80s. Reagan was president. The Cold War was on and the nuke arsenal was piling up. I participated in the nuclear freeze movement. Then I thought: a benefit concert! I cautiously approached the "big office" so I could share my Grand Idea with the Big Guy. He had a moment to listen. He thought it was a Great Idea too. He looked at me and said, "So, go do it." His point was well taken.

Years later, I was directing and promoting a children's theatrical performance, my own adaptation of Fantasia. The staging was elaborate. Timed lights, fog machines – the works. Sixty little ones, ages 5 to 11, performed. At the last minute before the play was about to start, I realized I had to get out there in front of the audience and introduce the event. Once again (OMG!!), I stood there in front of this packed house and said: I would like to dedicate this performance to two people who have been very inspirational in my life: first, Walt Disney, who taught me never stop dreaming and to Bill Graham, who taught me "So, go do it!"

KATE POTT

Terry, my husband, and I met in Cleveland and loved music. We moved to San Francisco mainly for the music scene in 1975.

Terry knew of Bill Graham long before we got to California; he was his idol. A year after we arrived, I met Jan Simmons (my Gem Sister) at a law firm in San Francisco. We shared the love of music and dancing and became BFFs. Jan left the firm and started working for Bill Graham Presents and became Bill Graham's assistant.

Terry and I were blessed to have met Bill, to have met my other Gem sister, Maggie Pinatelli, Rita Gentry, and so many other wonderful people at BGP. We were so blessed to have experienced the sheer fun at all the Dead shows. Thank you, Jan – who insisted we needed to see them live.

Seeing Bill standing at the side of the stage smiling at all of us having so much fun! Those Dead shows with all our friends, dancing as one with the music, were the highlights of my life! The New Year's Eve Grateful Dead shows were over the top with Bill's entrance as Father Time at midnight. Bill loved blowing people's minds. He loved it! Bill, thank you for creating that experience that allowed that fun to happen.

In 1984, Bill blew our minds by sending Terry and me as Jan's playmates to London and Dublin to see the Bob Dylan/Santana shows. He sent a limo to the airport to pick us up with a spray of flowers in the back of the limo and a bottle of champagne!

We felt like royalty. He was so generous and always had a smile for us and so charming. He loved "holding court" with us, showering us with so many wonderful stories. One day he took us all to Windsor Castle for the day and he imagined that he could put on a Grateful Dead concert at the castle. He took us all out to dinner with the Rolling Stones' office staff to a Russian restaurant where we drank too much frozen vodka. Then came the phenomenal shows at Wembley Stadium in London where a few local musicians came to see the concert and were hanging out with Bill and Jan (like Mick Jagger) and then to Slane Castle near Dublin, which was the coolest place to see a concert. We were totally blown away. This was one European trip to go down in history for us all because of Bill's generosity and kindness.

My Gem sisters and I often say "Thank you, Bill," to this day. Thank you, Bill, for all the great times and great shows and especially the Fillmore shows too. He was in his element at the Fillmore.

What a gift and privilege to see a concert there and then to receive a free poster before leaving the venue. Our home is full of those posters and a constant reminder of Bill and all the wonderful memories.

Thank you, Bill! You are a legend and so very missed.

KATHY BISHOP

I started working at the Old Waldorf early in 1983. Also, did some cocktail waitressing and bookkeeping at the Punchline until Wolfgang's opened. I was the day box office person at Wolfgang's until Marge Piane suggested that I apply to BGP to temporarily help with promotion of Little Shop of Horrors, a production BGP was presenting, while she was away. It became a permanent position, which I loved, until I moved to the East Coast to work in New York City in 1985.

Not one of my favorite stories, but Bill had this reputation in some circles of being this hard-ass, pain in the keister (which we know he was not.) One time after we heard him bellowing at someone on the phone, he strode out of his office, shaking his head like a horse, laughing. He said, "That felt GREAT!" The consummate showman.

I never told this story to anyone, but Bill offered to pay for me to go to acting school. He said, "Just sign up and tell them to send me the bill." I had no idea how to deal with that generosity. I came from a background of taking no help from anyone, so I never followed up. It wasn't until Bill died and Rolling Stone Magazine featured so many stories about him that I realized he meant it, no strings attached. I met Harvey Weinstein in Bill's office one time. Since then, every time I saw Harvey's name I kicked myself so hard for not following through with the acting school offer. Ha-Ha! Until recently right? Everything happens for a reason.

I will say for the record, Bill saw something in me that I didn't see in myself and knowing this it has gotten me through a lot of tough stuff.

For the first year after he died I couldn't say or hear his name without crying. Then I had a dream where he told me he was doing just fine and keep on being me.

KATHY SUHY

May 30, 1970

After much cajoling, Barry Imhoff finally let me accompany him to see Jimi Hendrix at the Berkeley Community Theatre. I was looking forward to the experience with great anticipation.

When Barry and I arrived, the crew was in full swing, readying the equipment for Jimi's shows. Bill was everywhere, making sure the experience would be perfect for everyone. The energy was palpable, both inside and outside the venue, and even though it was still morning, there were huge crowds gathering outside the BCT.

It seemed like we waited for hours for Jimi, Mitch and Billy to arrive for soundcheck. Bill was nervous, as he didn't tolerate tardiness, especially since these shows were being recorded, and he wanted to make sure both shows would go off without a hitch.

Jimi, Mitch, and Billy did eventually arrive, and the first show was brilliant. There were many familiar faces and happy hippy vibes all around. The day was manifesting beyond anything I had imagined.

Barry and I were hanging out in the dressing room with the band between shows when we became aware of some disturbance. We heard breaking glass, yelling, and people running around, so I left the dressing room to find out what was happening. I was told the sound truck outside the theatre, which was recording Jimi's shows, decided to open their truck doors so the hundreds of Hendrix fans, who couldn't get tickets to either show, would be able to listen to the live show. BAD IDEA!!! Many fans started climbing up the building and breaking windows to get in to see Hendrix. Fans were coming in through the roof.

Security was scrambling.

I was wandering around backstage watching the events unfold when I ended up standing inches behind Bill at exactly the moment he chose to go totally ballistic. He started yelling and swearing at the top of his lungs about how inept and moronic everyone was and how he wanted to fire everyone.

I had known Bill for awhile, but I had never seen this side of his personality. Being only inches behind him, I was frozen in absolute terror. I was sure I would be the first person Bill would throw out, if for no other reason than being in close proximity to him.

After standing there motionless for what seemed like an eternity while I was covertly checking for an escape route before he noticed me, Bill stopped yelling. He turned around, looked me directly in the eye and said, in the most casual and friendliest of tones, "Hi! How are you?" before he walked off to deal with the drama. I can only imagine the look of fear and total shock on my face at that moment.

Over the following years, I witnessed more of this type of behavior from Bill, and I came to realize Bill could be a raging tiger on the outside when he needed to be (and he definitely scared the shit out of everyone), but he was all heart on the inside.

KEITH GABRIEL

Master Electrician at the Warfield Theater. I started with Bill Graham Presents in 1979 and was with the company for 28 years.

I first met Bill covered head to toe in dust after changing some of the light bulbs in the ceiling that were burned out for a good 20 years. He was impressed with the dedication I had in trying to restore as much as I could of the original lighting that was no longer in working condition.

I guess one of the best stories I remember about Bill was one time when we had Guns N' Roses performing at the Warfield. As per usual, the band took their time, and in those days would never get up on stage at the scheduled set time. This performance, they were already an hour late from going on stage and Bill went down to Axl's dressing room to get them up on stage. After talking with the band, Bill then left the dressing room walking down the dressing rooms hallway. Axl came out of the dressing room and threw a chair down the hallway towards Bill. Bill turned around looked at the chair, then Bill pointed to the door that lead to the stage and said, "You get up there now or you will never work in this country or anywhere again." Bill turned back around and left; you never saw a band move so quickly to get up on the stage after that.

Another story I remember was about Bill and his son, Alex. Quite often Bill would bring Alex to the Warfield with him. Alex was in his early teens at the time and since the shows would often run quite late, Alex would end up tired out. I ran into him one night and he could barely keep his eyes open. I suggested to him that he go into my office and take a nap. Later that evening, Bill was looking for Alex and asked if I had seen him. I told Bill that Alex was probably still in my office. When Bill found Alex, he was sound asleep on my couch in my office. After that night my office became Alex's regular resting place and Bill knew where to find him at the end of the night.

KEN FRIEDMAN

I started shooting photos for Bill Graham Presents on December 31, 1979 at the Cow Palace where the headliner was Blue Oyster Cult with Montrose and SVT.

Story One – The famous Alice Waters decided to put on two benefit shows with BGP that would be called Aid and Comfort. The first one was held at Fort Mason with the San Francisco Ballet. The second show was held at the Greek Theater in Berkeley, and Alice made a secluded area at the top of the venue for VIPs where there was to be food served by famous chefs of her knowing. It was a gourmet meal served on a beautiful evening with a beautiful view. But there were large clouds forming around the venue. The venue was decorated beautifully even to the point where all the Grecian columns were draped in a gauze material with wonderful spotlighting effects on them. The acts that I can remember were Herbie Hancock and Phillip Glass.

The clouds keep rolling in and as soon as the first act hits the stage it starts to rain, not lightly, but very hard. The first act finished and the rain stops. The second act hits the stage and it starts to downpour once again.

Imagine this, Herbie Hancock playing his piano with four stagehands holding a blue tarp over his head. The rain kept on all night with each act. By the time the last act was going to play about 90 percent of the audience had fled for dryness and left the venue. Bill came on the stage and did something that was really inspiring. He walked to the middle of the stage speaking into the microphone the following: "Anyone who will stay to the end of the show, you will receive two tickets to any show that BGP produces through this next year." He walks off stage and about 15 seconds later walks back on the stage and says, "Except for Grateful Dead New Year's Eve." I must give credit to the tremendous amount of work that was put into this production by BGP employees making it a great event even though it was raining. The show must go on!

Story Two – In Sacramento, Bill Graham Presents built a venue called Cal Expo Amphitheater. One day, BGP employees, the crews and Bill were in the area directly located behind the stage where the

BGP production office and the limo drop-off area was, and where a football game was now taking place. I was on the opposite team from Bill.

I was guarding Bill. He got behind me and caught the pass, and before he could even slow down or look up after catching the pass, he ran full speed ahead into a wooden trellis that was eight feet high and separated the loading zone from the backstage area. Everyone that was playing went running to see if he was okay and he was…lying there on his back with the football still clenched in his arms.

No one even spoke a word (like saying, are you okay?).

Well I guess we knew he was fine because he still had the ball and didn't seem injured and didn't ask for help. But what was funny to me was that all of us just turned around, walking away, going back to work.

Lastly, a couple of the most memorable shows that I got to work as a photographer for a BGP event was Live Aid, the Russia Freedom Concert, and Laughter, Love and Music.

KENNY WARDELL

I first met Bill Graham when I worked at KZAP 98.5FM in Sacramento, California. In 1968, Bill had recently moved his Fillmore concert business to the Carousel Ballroom at Market Street and Van Ness Street in San Francisco and he renamed the venue Fillmore West. Wednesday nights were when Bill had band auditions at the Fillmore West and hopeful musicians lined up to play on audition night in the hopes in making it to a Saturday night slot with their name up on the Fillmore West marquee. Bill started his Wednesday night shows with a "celebrity basketball game" where BGP staffers would go up against invited teams from bands, radio stations, and the like.

I was doing morning drive and was the music director at K-ZAP when I got the call from Bill's office inviting us to field a team at the Fillmore West to play basketball against Bill and his boyz.

Everyone at the station wanted to go to San Francisco that Wednesday night for a chance to meet Bill and shoot some hoops. I had a VW bus back then and I must have had 10-12 people going for the ride.

Unfortunately, none of us could dribble very well, let alone shoot a basket. It's funny that over the years, I have had scores of old K-ZAPPERS tell me they were on the bus when there was no way in hell I could have had that many people in my bus.

To be on Bill Graham's Fillmore West basketball team you had to be good. Bill was no sloucher either, and when you got to know him you saw how competitive he was even on the indoor basketball court located right in front of the stage going right to left. The hoops stayed up all week long and I'm sure Bill ran practices and team tryouts to get to wear a Fillmore West basketball jersey!

By now, you probably know the outcome of a busload of Sacramento radio hippies going home after playing basketball against the Harlem Globetrotters of rock and roll. It was a slaughter after the first tipoff. It still was a legendary experience and Bill and I became friends after that basketball throwdown.

In 1972 I left Sacramento to go to San Francisco to become RCA Records Regional Promotion Manager. I was a huge Jefferson Airplane fan, who were on RCA, and I had already made inroads with Paul Kantner, Grace Slick and the rest of the band, band management, and other staffers when I came to town. In many ways it was a perfect fit for me at RCA. I had Elvis Presley, David Bowie, Lou Reed, the Kinks, Waylon Jennings and many others in addition to the Airplane. One of my first stops after getting my RCA company car was certainly to Bill Graham's office. BGP back then was a little office on Golden Gate Avenue in San Francisco. I dated a couple of women that worked for Bill back then – one named Mary Roach (I think it was her real name) and one named Dilly Dally (pretty sure it wasn't).

We all remained friends even after the dating stopped. Needless to say, I logged a lot of time at Bill's office and got to see first hand what made Bill tick and what made Bill go off!

In a world of peace and love and the Vietnam War, Bill's legendary temper was something to avoid at all costs if you wanted to stay in the San Francisco music business. I was very successful at that for a very long time and our friendship flourished. When BGP moved to 11th Street, I could walk right into Bill's office and talk to him if he wasn't busy.

He had a huge concert calendar of all his upcoming shows on the wall outside his office and Bill explained that only the shows in ink are confirmed and concerts in pencil were still being worked on. This really was the epicenter of Bill's concert planning and as a music promotion person I had inside information that few outside his staff knew about.

Now, let's fast forward a number of years to when I was working at KFOG 104.5FM as Promotion Director and Assistant Program Director. I learned that Bill was bringing Paul McCartney to the UC Berkeley Memorial Stadium for a grand stadium concert that sold out immediately. KFOG was playing classic rock from the 60s, 70s and 80s back then, and McCartney was one of the station's core artists with the Beatles, his solo albums, and later, Wings. His catalog of music attracted fans from all walks of life. This show had to be one of the quickest sold-out concerts of Bill's career.

At KFOG I had commissioned an East Bay solo airplane company named American Airlights to run night time advertising for the station over drive time traffic, big time events, including concerts before the shows and as concert goers were going home. Bill knew KFOG had this promotional tool in our bag of tricks but for the Paul McCartney concert, I saw him run out from behind the stage charging up the middle aisle yelling at someone, "Help me find Wardell!" My seats were two in from the aisle and I slid down in my seat to avoid being seen by him. He ran by me a couple of times, but I was lucky that he didn't see me or I would have been kicked out of Memorial Stadium and would never see another concert in my life again.

What I had done was to schedule our American Airlights plane to run the line, "KFOG WELCOMES SAUL McCARTNEY!" There was a noticeable gasp, laugh, and audience buzz right after the plane's first pass over the stadium before McCartney took the stage. That's when Bill went looking for me. The lights at the concert were going down and the plane headed for the airport. I loved the concert but figured my music career in San Francisco would be toast after I heard from Bill. What saved my sweet ass was that the legendary San Francisco Chronicle newspaper columnist Herb Caen wrote up a great little item in his column about the KFOG plane's "airborne type!" According to a couple of my BGP friends in the office, when Bill saw Caen's column he got a big laugh out of it! It might have been Bill's Jewish heritage that made him laugh about Saul McCartney and let me continue what has been an extraordinary career.

KENT SIMMONS

Office Manager at Bill Graham Presents and also usher, Bluecoat, stagehand, T-shirt maker, Rock Shop manager. I began in 1971 and worked for 23 years if you count all the shows I worked before I went full time.

My favorite things about BGP: Christmas party skits, Days on the Green as a Bluecoat, Days on the Green as a fan, carpooling from Marin after the earthquake, Mr. Clyde Williams, bourbon balls, Mrs. Bell, Grateful Dead shows and Deadheads, Mick Jagger at Skywalker Ranch, Prince at the Warfield, the Ethel Mermans, the sign over the urinal, meeting Katarina Witt (thanks, Tom), watching shows from the catwalk above the stage at Berkeley Community Theater, Edan Hughes, the park scene at the Oakland Auditorium during Dead shows, Gary and Harry intimidating Bill at Winterland.

I've been away from BGP for 24 years now, which is curiously about the same amount of time I was around the company. The size of the extended family is amazing and was so much fun, so much music and so much love. I feel so lucky to have been a part of all that. It's hard to explain it to people where I am now. I could talk almost indefinitely about what we all shared there.

My BGP experience always has two sides: one being in it and around it and the other being how Bill and the company influenced me as a music freak growing up in the Bay Area. I thank Bill often in my mind for exposing me to so much music I never would have heard if he didn't conjure up those amazing combination of bands, and that experience makes me find something in my heart for all musical genres.

KERRY RIECK and SHERRI RIECK

I have a couple of memories to share that all relate to Bill's generosity. I first started working at Bill Graham Presents part time at the end of 1979 with Kerry Rieck on the maintenance crew at the Warfield Theater. Kerry had started working for BGP at the Rock Shop a year or so before.

In 1982, Kerry and I were in a car accident on our way to work at an event that was being held at Fort Mason in San Francisco. Someone ran a red light and hit us, totaling our car. We were both injured, but Kerry's was so much worse and he needed to have knee surgery. He was unable to do any physical work. He still supervised his crew, but no hands-on as he tried slowly to recover. At one point, it was determined that he needed more physical therapy because he wasn't healing. Not being a full-time employee, he had no insurance to cover this needed medical attention.

Bill paid for all of his physical therapy and we were told that he was not to be paid back. It was a gift.

Another time two of our maintenance crew members were involved in a motorcycle accident and they had no insurance; they too were pretty badly injured. It was decided that we would hold a benefit to raise some money for them. Bill let us use his house for the benefit which was so kind and more than generous. Bill had set up transportation/ride back to San Francisco via a van from his home in Corte Madera, but unfortunately, when we were ready to return home to SF the van that was supposed to pick us up broke down on the Golden Gate Bridge. So Bill drove us home in his Mercedes.

Talk about going beyond the call of duty!

Rita's Note: Sherri, Kerry's wife, wrote these beautiful stories as Kerry passed away on June 17, 2010.

KERRY WATKINS

Shoreline/BGP taught me the experience in the details, etiquette and impression.

I was a parking lot attendant starting at 15 years old, and would watch Bill walk the lots. I saw Bill at the Monsters of Rock show jump over the barricade and go into the large general admission crowd.

I was "Check-in Gal" when I was 17 to 18 years old. Sitting on the counters, Bill would drive by and he would always tell upper management that we did not look professional.

Working the Earthquake Relief Benefit in Watsonville, California is where the suburban girl gets an education in being a Bluecoat and that women can have beards.

Assistant House Manager at 19 years old. The Center Stage Bar at Shoreline Amphitheatre was a place of feedback from Bill on cleanliness. Once, his helicopter was landing and I noticed the cup debris amongst the rails and did a clothes line with one arm with a garbage can in the other to quickly clean. Bill told us that Shoreline should look like our home not littered with cups along the Center Stage Bar.

Odd moment for me at the age of 19: Alex Graham makes his friend turn in his all-access pass for abusing its privilege.

Rita and the rolodexes…those rolodexes were so big and intimidating.

Rita-ism: WWWWhhhhatttevvRRRR, with a fantastic eye roll. Making men stop with a pointed finger, "I've got to talk to you," as the VIP did the peepee dance.

WOMAD – Golden Gate Park Production Office: Rita and I are chatting across an eight-foot banquet table while working the show as another employee joins us and begins to rant to us while one of his teeth pops out of his mouth and onto the table and keeps on with his story. Rita taps her nail on the table near the tooth and says, "I believe this belongs to you!"

KEVIN BURNS

I first came into Bill Graham Presents with Eddie Money in 1976. Wasn't offered a job. When Eddie's first tour began with the release of his first album in 1977, I went on the road as a drum roadie, guitar roadie, conga player and truck driver. As time went on I kept moving up with more responsibilities.

After three years of touring I had to get off of the road - too crazy. I was offered a stagehand gig from Peter Barsotti but I turned it down. I started a booking agency called the Entertainment Clinic.

When the 201 11th Street BGP office fire happened, I volunteered to help out in Bill Graham Management at the temporary North Point Street office where Bill offered me the job with BG Management. I started looking in the clubs for new bands. I brought Joe Satriani into BG management. I went on the road as tour manager for Paul Collins Beat.

I spent the next 14 years as management partner. Too many stories during those years, always finding new bands to work with.

I left Bill Graham Management in 2000 after the company was sold.

KEVIN CHISHOLM and LYNN CHISHOLM

Lynn started at the Old Waldorf as a waitress in 1977 when Jeffrey Pollack owned it. I believe it was only a couple of months later that Bill bought the club. When David Mayeri and Queenie Taylor came in, I remember hearing the theory that Bill only bought it to use as a tax write-off because it did not do that well.

Well, that changed fast; the place took off and they also opened The Punchline. After a year I was also working there also partnering with Robbie Taylor as heads of sound and production. We had and worked the Old Waldorf, the Punchline and the Kabuki Theater. Then Robbie went back to work with the Grateful Dead, I took over the production and that is when Bill bought the lease to what became Wolfgang's at 901 Columbus Street, San Francisco. I was then in charge of the rebuild and the budgets for the Wolfgang's project.

I think it was around 1981 Lynn then moved from head waitress to in being charge of all bookkeeping for the clubs. She was tremendously proud of working for Bill and David Mayeri and she continued in her role for over 25 years until her passing. One of Lynn's favorite Bill Graham moments was when our son Ryan was born and we were just finishing the rebuild of the Fillmore in 1986 and Bill presented us with an engraved baby silver spoon set. I had many great moments with Bill and his 3 x 5 cards with thoughts on what I could do better.

My favorite was while on the stage in Moscow in 1987. We were getting Santana ready to play and Bill started yelling at me that we were taking too much time. I turned to Bill and looked him straight in the eyes and said, "Carlos' rig is not complete yet and besides I don't work for you anymore. I work for Carlos." That discussion was picked up by one of the American TV news shows saying, "Here is Bill yelling at one of his employees." I never corrected them because I always felt that I still worked for Bill!

L

LANCE MILLER

In 1981 we had just finished the west coast swing of the Tattoo You tour in San Diego, Los Angeles, San Francisco and Phoenix. Peter Barsotti called and told me to pack my bags and bring some cash because we were headed to New York City for the Stones Madison Square Garden show with David McLean and Bob Barsotti.

I was put up in Bill's apartment for a couple of days and then into a hotel when he got to town. The night of the show we arrived backstage preshow. At some point we were ushered into a dingy storage area where there was a basketball hoop and Bill was standing there, as well as four or five tough-looking IATSE stagehands. Soon, Bill, David, Peter and I were engaged in a brutal half court game. We were fouled and hammered mercilessly, and it became clear that fouls would not be called as we fell behind by 10 points in a 24-point game. The four of us gathered and Bill let us know we could not lose this game!

We gathered our resolve and fought back, and Bill was especially tough, and we played hard defense with Peter and David pouring in the points. We came from behind and narrowly defeated the shocked henchmen.

Bill looked at their leader and said, "So you wanna play ball?" They had history over rules Bill wouldn't accept when he first worked in The Garden. They were settled with a basketball game back in the day.

Now I knew why I was treated to a wonderful trip to New York City.

LARRY HOOGASIAN

It all started for me at the World of Plants 1977. The star of the show was supposed to have been Euell Gibbons, but unfortunately, he had passed away.

I was fresh out of architecture school and my brother Harold and I entered the booth design contest (We won first prize). The other exhibitors didn't like us much because our booth put theirs to shame. I remember trying to borrow a couple of finishing nails to put the last piece of wood on and no one would give me any. They told me to go out and buy some if I really needed them.

So, I'm now on the defensive at this point and then I hear some-one say, "My, my my…Never seen a pile of sticks look so good." I was looking down from the top of the gazebo and I will always remember that day.

Here I was, so pissed off at everyone over a couple of finishing nails. When out of the blue I get a compliment from some guy that I had no idea who he was. I would later find out that it was Mr. Bill Graham. Harold and I continued yelling at each other as brothers do. I remember Bob Barsotti checking us out and smiling. I think he could relate to this whole situation since he and his brother Peter worked closely together at BGP. These similarities bonded us with the BGP brothers Peter and Bob Barsotti.

During the show we went around handing out roses to the attend-ees (trying to spread peace, love and groovy). We fit right in.

After our initiation into the BGP family we began having many things going on and bonding with the company mainly in regard to flowers.

I will always remember the emergency calls for flowers. Hoogasian Flowers nicknamed BGP "Last Minute Productions." No matter what, we always came through and got whatever needed to be done…done.

I learned so much working with Bill Graham Presents. The main thing was getting impossible things done in a short amount of time and in an excellent manner and…

First Thing…The Show Must Go On…Party Later!

271

I remember being at a Grateful Dead show at Shoreline Amphitheatre. Somehow, one of the staff found me in the crowd and I was escorted to a backstage trailer. Bill wanted to talk to me. In my head I thought I was thinking that I was in trouble (not that I wasn't an angel at the shows). Anyway, I walk into the trailer and Bill is on the phone screaming and yelling at someone. He is really telling them off. It was kind of scary. He then turns around putting his hand over the receiver and smiles. He says, "Don't worry, this is just business." I felt so relieved.

After he hangs up on this caller, he asks if Harold and I (Hoogasian Flowers) will be able to decorate the main stage for the upcoming Nelson Mandela concert to be held at the Oakland Stadium. I went from shaking in my boots to being so very happy and feeling very special.

LARRY SANTOS

Back in the day I did meet Bill Graham a few times going to shows. Nothing memorable - just cordial greetings.

However, when I was a lad of about 15 or 16 years old I went to the Fillmore with some friends. I was approached by someone selling a ticket for the show and I bought it from him. When I got to the door Bill was taking tickets and immediately recognized that the ticket was a forgery.

He spent the next minute yelling at me for being so stupid (in sort of a fatherly way) and let it be known to everyone around us that only an idiot would be so stupid to buy a ticket from a stranger off the street.

He REALLY let me have it! Then he let me in.

LAURA FRAENZA

Bill's Lists

"All you have to do is sit beyond the drums, I give you a half a cookie, you go to heaven."

Bill is on the phone with the legendary comedian and actor Robin Williams, coaxing him to come to the BGP Christmas party that this year was to be more a celebration of 25 years of the company he created, and a couple of weeks after that, to the upcoming Grateful Dead New Year's Eve show, where Bill, done up as a witch doctor, would descend from the rafters to ring in 1991.

I am unexpectedly in Bill's office overhearing this conversation, and quickly took notes as he was talking, just so I wouldn't forget this detail, a snapshot of Bill.

I happened to be there not for just this moment, but for two full weeks to witness all kinds of things that would transpire every given day in that southeastern corner of 260 Fifth Street in San Francisco.

In a way it was kind of karmic; the whole reason I ended up at the BGP offices in May of 1990 was that Bill was considering trying out a range of different assistants and I was in the cue. It turned out I never ended up meeting him face-to-face before he decided to stay with his current assistant, so I floated around the company until a job opened up in Management, which ended up being right where I should be, after all.

But at this point in late October of that year, a deliriously creative time for Bill, he needed extra assistance and I was there as a notetaker, keeper of lists, and catcher of thoughts as he spewed them. He was energetic then and flying high, thrilled to be celebrating 25 years as the head of BGP and arguably the best-known concert promoter in the world.

Bill had recently gone Hollywood, having just wrapped Barry Levinson's film Bugsy, playing Lucky Luciano, a character he reveled in, and also producing The Doors movie directed by Oliver Stone and starring Val Kilmer as Jim Morrison. It was soon to be released.

Bill's dramatic trajectory itself was a movie, a story to be told. Right then he was collaborating on a book about his life in rock and roll and all that came before and what perhaps would come after.

At 59, Bill was at once forever young and older and wiser than his years, beyond us all, it seemed. It can probably be said that without a doubt, everyone who showed up daily to 260 Fifth Street, Shoreline, the comedy and music clubs, and anywhere the company put a stake in the ground were all elated to be part of the extended BGP family at that time.

But probably no one more than Bill.

With so much going on, he needed an extra hand to take notes and keep track of it all. Since I was one of the newer assistants and somewhat expendable for a bit, I was summoned to his inner sanctum, taking a seat diagonally across from his desk, helping him organize the ten thousand things he was trying to keep track of, and just as soon as he thought of them.

Right in the middle of the daily whirlwind, I observed Bill in his brilliance, with his quick mind and incessant enthusiasm for music and musicians, songs he loved that were stuck in his head, pairings on stage or dinner parties he imagined, future shows, things he had to buy (like his concert uniform of purple shirts from the International Male catalogue), issues he had to address with certain staff members, things that sparked him, and ideas for the future. It was all fascinating, but what I found most striking was his quiet generosity.

The job really was more listening than watching Bill work; I had to quickly capture each word or phrase or name or plan on its correct list out of the dozens of steno pads sprawled before me and not miss a thing, while words and thoughts flew across the room. Keeping up with Bill's New York pace and getting it all down as fast as he spit it out.

At the end of each day, I'd type every list on its own page, each item in ALL CAPS, unless it was a duplicate, then in lower case. After that, I'd hand the day's lists back to Bill for his review.

Only once did he challenge me, but I prevailed. "Bill, how could I make that up?" I asked, terrified for what would come next. "You're right," was all he said.

Beyond those lists were a few illustrations of Bill at work that stand out, detailed in my memory.

In his mail one day was a letter from a Noe Valley neighborhood mom, whose daughter had worked all summer in the Little League Snack Shack so she could save up to buy front-row seats to Day on the Green with New Kids on the Block.

The woman wrote in her letter that she wanted to know: Just what does it take? The New Kids were coming back to the Cow Palace in a few months and please, how do you ever manage to get a front-row seat to a concert if you can't get one by being first in line, waiting overnight, like her daughter had done at Tower Records in North Beach?

I can hear him marveling out loud; something about the girl's hustle and the place she worked all summer got to him. With his ever-present accent straight from the Bronx, punctuated by his bushy eyebrows, Bill peered up over glasses perched low on his nose, and read the letter aloud to me. "Listen to this. The Little League Snack Shack! She worked all summer in the Little League Snack Shack. Can you believe it?" I didn't quite know what it was about that unique element of her letter, but it sparked him.

Bill gave me the mother's name and asked me to find her number. The internet did not yet exist. You had to dial 4-1-1 and hope to get lucky. We did. I called her up, and when the mom answered and heard, "Bill Graham is calling," I could tell she was shocked.

Bill picked up and spoke for just a few minutes, laughing with the mom and lauding her daughter for dedicating a summer to a place like the Little League Snack Shack so she could go with a friend to see the hot new boy band. He'd make sure that her daughter would have two tickets, front row, center for the upcoming New Kids' Cow Palace show. By now that girl must be in her 40's, and I bet she still shares that story.

I also remember the letter he dictated to Paul Simon, after hearing Rhythm of the Saints, Paul's just-released album full of Brazilian beats. Bill was deeply moved, not by the spirited single Obvious Child, but by the much quieter She Moves On and Can't Run But, songs he placed on another of his lists, and was listening to on repeat.

A line in the fax he sent to Paul stayed with me: "I've started swimming to She Moves On, over and over, and suddenly my strokes are so much easier."

Bill wasn't too cool to let a rock star know he was a big fan of his brand-new music. Bill didn't hesitate. He just did it.

I also got to witness his humanity when he quietly picked up the phone to generously donate $10,000 to Dr. David Smith and the Haight Ashbury Free Clinic. And when he also called up Reverend Cecil Williams to give 200 turkeys to Glide Memorial for their annual Thanksgiving feast for the homeless.

The lists linger as a glimpse into the workings of a man with a great mind, and a unique and legendary character, who was both a pioneer with decades of experience in the music business, and also a music fan with the loves and enthusiasms of an energetic and down-to-earth younger guy.

Probably the most important list at that time was filled with plans and directives for the holiday party he was planning at the Warfield Theater: Lucky's Silver Bash. It read:

DRESS CODE – LIKE YOU'RE ON A HOT DATE

DOC'S COOKIES – BUT IT MUST BE FROM ME

PRODUCING TEAM: BG – JERRY, PETER, BOB, MICK B, ARLENE, SHERRY,

DAVID M., PAUL KANTNER, KEVIN BURNS – BG MUST SUPERVISE

NO KNIVES (for Food)

RESERVE TABLES FOR SPECIAL PARTIES – i.e. TABLE 1: GARCIA, BARSOTTIS, CARLOS, RAY

NO OLD TIMERS WORKING

HOUSE MUSIC – BONNIE SIMMONS – FIRE ON THE MOUNTAIN – OTIS REDDING

The party list included Bill's wide circle of business associates including Mike Peranian, Carole Kinzel, Herbie Herbert, and Dell Furano, and friends like Ken Kesey.

Carlos Santana and Jerry Garcia of course were invited, and so were Pete Escovedo and Neil Young. Joe Satriani and Eddie Money, two artists the company managed, were asked to be there too.

A page titled KILLER was for the loyal and intrepid pilot who would leave the world with Bill, included things that might make sense only to the two of them:

THE LINCOLN CONTINENTAL

OUTSIDE CHESS BOARD

SABRETT'S

MUSHROOM, EGG & WORLD REPAIRS, which likely meant the upkeep required of the Grateful Dead's New Year's props that Bill kept at his Masada home.

POPPER referred to the lead singer of Blues Traveler, the band Bill's son David was managing at the time as they teetered on the brink of their great success-yet-to-be.

Bill dictated the names of artists and albums including Otis Redding and Aretha Live, Carmen McCrae, Sketches of Spain, and Traffic, likely who and what he wanted John Popper to listen and pay close attention to.

PROJECTS included things that never came to be:

MAMBO NIGHT AT ROSELAND-RALPH MERCADO-AUDIE & MARGO & ANDY

PHOTO BOOK WITH PETER was the birth of a list of images that were to become a coffee table book on the company's history. JEFFERSON AIRPLANE-HOLLYWOOD BOWL and GRATEFUL DEAD-EGYPT-7-UP ACID TRIP were just two.

MASADA was filled with imagined dinner parties, complete with guest lists like PASS-AROUND FOOD ONLY with PAM-COLLEEN-BILLY-KENT-MICK JONES, and another with JAN-RITA & GEORGE-LANCE-LEE-GREGG.

I remember just scribbling all these things, not questioning anything unless something didn't make sense.

On the BG PERSONAL list, #11 is "TOOLS OF POWER-KNOWLEDGE-VIOLENCE-WEALTH". What exactly did that mean to Bill?

His son David had his own list with things like PHONE USE, PHISH, CHEAP FLIGHTS AND SAVINGS and so did Peter and Bob Barsotti, with notes about New Year's Eves to come, the Dead in Arizona, and Jerry in Telluride.

THE BOOK listed THE REAL MANDELA STORY first, and second, THE REAL STONES STORY. Third on the page was simply LED ZEPPELIN, and we all know that story.

Bill's BOOKING AND SONGS lists were my favorites, with shows he was planning to book or perhaps confirm, from IGGY POP at the CREST Theater in Sacramento and DANCE, DANCE at the CIRCLE STAR, to SOUL II SOUL and DEEE-LITE. (Bill delighted in Deee-Lite and correctly predicted their first record would be a smash).

His love of Latin Music led to a desire to book it. A long-antici-
pated show with Juan Luis Guerra y Grupo 4.40 at the San Francisco
Civic in November 1991 would sadly take place a month after Bill left
us.

SONGS was a disparate and short list of music he loved like My
Blood by the Neville Brothers and Peter Gabriel's In Your Eyes. State of
Independence had place on this list, and not the original Jon/Vangelis
version, but the Donna Summer cover that was also a favorite of mine.

Broken Wings by Mr. Mister was there too, and Bill noted it as a
possible song for Carlos Santana to cover, also placing the name of the
song on a separate call list so he'd remember to discuss it with Carlos
when they spoke.

For Bill's 25th Anniversary I made him a mix tape of 25 songs–
one from each year–that included some of these.

It was such a captivating couple of weeks. Besides the great honor
of being next to Bill at his desk during a grand time in his life, it was
a true gift to have the chance to get a daily glimpse of how the man
worked, who and what he thought about, and who and what mattered
to him.

I vividly remember being on the dancefloor at the Warfield on the
night of Lucky's Bash, at one point right next to Bill and David, in the
sea of employees who'd been there for decades and making a silent
vow to be there forever.

"I'm gonna die with this company," I thought, dancing with a
dose of magic cookie that sent me to that heaven Bill had talked about
with Robin.

That wonderful night was my first of what were known to be legendary BGP Christmas parties. None of us had any idea that that special holiday celebration at the Warfield would be Bill's last. He was
flying high, in love and seemingly in love with the life that he lived,
the world he created, all of us in the company, that room full of people
he cared for. And, of course, like every one of us, he was deeply in love
with the music.

It was a lightning strike of luck to have had that chance to be in
Lucky's office by his side for those two weeks, as he celebrated his

25th anniversary, capturing his thoughts and plans and dreams and desires, being a witness to it all while he worked.

LAURA GREENBERG

BGP Family Forever!

There are two stories that stick out the most for me with my time at Bill Graham Presents from 1994 to present day, and let me tell you that there have been MANY incredible experiences over my 26-year career there. Needless to say, BOTH of my stories for these purposes are about the one and only Shelley Lazar.

I will relay one of them here. The other was about the time when Shelley flew five of us New Yorkers/baseball fans to New York to see Game Five of the Subway World Series in 2000 (Mets vs. Yankees) with a few hours notice – she just said meet at the office at 5:00 a.m. and pack a bag. We flew to New York, magically appeared at Shea Stadium, got our faces painted outside, watched the game sitting next to Wayne Gretzky and Jerry Seinfeld, (the Mets lost) went to White Castle and flew back to San Francisco.

Phew!!! What an experience that was!!!! It was a magical night for all of us involved. However, she did something even GREATER than that.

Shelley was on the board of the Rock and Roll Hall of Fame. She knew I was (am) a HUGE Bruce Springsteen fan. In 1999, it was Bruce's turn to be inducted. She asked me if I would like to work the event for her. I did not hesitate one bit when I immediately responded with a resounding YES!!!!!

I was flown out to New York with a co-worker, Julia Winston, who was also invited by Shelley because of her love for Sir Paul McCartney, who was also getting inducted that year. Julia and I were blown away at Shelley's thoughtfulness and generosity.

We were put up at the world-famously beautiful (and expensive) Waldorf Astoria, where the Hall of Fame ceremony was taking place. My parents were married there, so it has always held a very special place in my heart. That alone should have been the highlight of our trip. We were there for a few days, ordering room service, watching dress rehearsals, learning about our roles for working the event and getting Mavis Staples "HOT" tea.

The big night was upon us. I had tried to find the coolest, most rock 'n' roll outfit I could, which ended up being just a simple black suit with a silk blouse (#wardrobefail).

The ballroom filled up with every person in the music industry I had ever seen or heard of. Elton John, Paul McCartney, The Staple Singers, Ray Charles, Bono, Billy Joel, Neil Young, Robbie Robertson, Jan Wenner (Rolling Stone Magazine) Paul Schaeffer, Chris Isaak, P. Diddy, Lenny Kravitz, Lauryn Hill, all the inductees and their families and then some. It was mind-blowing...I felt like I was in a dream.

Then the man showed up with his family and all of the E Street Band, and all of THEIR families in tow. I'm pretty sure I was having a massive out-of-body experience, but because I was working and reasonably professional, I (think) I kept it mostly together.

My role was to wrangle the performers out of their seats and organize them on the side of the stage when it was time for them to get inducted. Then I would have to take them backstage to get interviewed. I was assigned to Mavis and Pops Staples and Bruce and the E Street Band.

When it was Bruce's turn, I went from table to table gathering everyone up (there are A LOT of E Street Band members) and shuffled them to the side staging area. I recall having an issue with Clarence Clemons – he was all up in arms about having his sax in the exact place (they were to play after the induction) with the exact mouthpiece - he was drama, but it was epic.

Bruce went up on stage after Bono inducted him and the band.

I was standing in the midst of all the E Streeters when Bruce singled out each one of them to thank them (only Bruce went up on stage for the ceremony.) I felt like an actual band member. I couldn't believe what was happening – it all went so fast and I was so stunned to be standing there in the middle of it all. When that was over, the whole band went up and played a few songs.

It was a fabulous evening with lots of incredibly delivered speeches and music and laughing and crying, not to mention that I got to hang out with Mavis Staples for two days!!

The night went on with other people getting inducted and when the magical night was over, Julia and I were asked if we wanted to go to a party in Bruce's suite. Um, DUH!!!! Yes, please.

We approached the door to the suite. We told the security guy that we were invited to the party by Shelley. Without any hesitation, we were let into the party. We walked in and got a drink and looked around. We were the only non-rock stars/ famous people in the room. Tom Hanks and Rita Wilson, Danny DeVito, Neil and Peggy Young, Lenny Kravitz, Stella McCartney, Bruce's MOTHER and aunts and so on. I went into the dining room part of the suite, where the whole table was COVERED with food and drink. I started to grab some food, and shove it into my face, when right then, Bruce walked in. I almost lost it. He looked at me like I was a complete interloper, which I was. We met eyes, and I as he was picking up a plate to grab some food for himself, I blurted out, with my face filled with food, "I'm all about the pasta." OMG – what the hell was that!?!? He just looked at me, made a weird face, nodded, grabbed some food and went into the next room. I just about DIED right there on the spot. What the hell did I just say, with my mouth still chewing??? I knew I'd NEVER live that down, and my friends that I have relayed the story to still have never forgotten to give me crap about it to this day, 21 years later.

We hung around the party for a bit, yapping with the aforementioned people. When we finally realized we didn't really belong, we got the hell out of there, only to find ourselves at Phil Spector's party down the hall.

Phil's party was lightly attended, but it was clear we missed a pre-party of some sort. Everyone who ever mattered was at Bruce's party anyway. We decided to call it a night, and I'm pretty sure we were not able to fall asleep for the days to come. It was such an incredible experience.

I honestly have to admit that it's all a blur, but what I DO remember is that it was the most magical experience of my life and nothing will ever top it. Thank you SHELLEY with all the madness in my soul!!!!

BGP family forever!

LAURA HERLOVICH

It was the first Grateful Dead show at the Silver Bowl in Las Vegas with Danny Zelisko and Bill Graham co-promoting. I was helping Danny and was backstage in a trailer and couldn't believe I would be in the same place as Bill Graham. He was an icon and someone I idolized.

It was warm out and the trailers had an air conditioner. As I sat there cooling off Bill walked in with a plate of food to eat. He was by himself and here I was with a chance to meet my idol. I thought carefully about what I should say to have a moment with him and not be too intrusive. I said, "I like your socks, they're cool." They were tie- dyed print scrunchy socks and they were really cool. He said, "Thanks," and something else about the weather and was eating a piece of fish; it was oily and all around his mouth was a shine of oil from eating so quickly. That was it – my Bill Graham moment!

Many months later I was driving on the Las Vegas Strip heading north at Flamingo to turn west in a turn lane. My husband called me on my cell to tell me that there had been a helicopter crash and Bill Graham was dead. I put my car in park and sat there for a long time weeping at the news.

It seemed like a long time, but strangely no one behind me honked or seemed to care while I was missing the turn lights. They were probably busy staring at the sights around them and had no idea that my hero was gone.

LAURA STEWART KAPLAN

Bill Graham Presents taught me how to work. BGP was a family and we took care of each other. Some of us did not have such a great upbringing and BGP was the surrogate family where we learned how to work, how to cooperate and how to communicate.

Most of my time with the company was as a production runner or backstage manager at the Warfield, Fillmore and Shoreline Amphitheatre. It was my job to keep the visiting production manager happy, get what was needed for the show and at the smaller venues create the dressing room environment, then fill the coolers with ice and keep the potato chips fluffed.

The stage crew at the Warfield under Paul Majeski was a tight crew. Paul was our guiding light. The few times I actually met Bill Graham it was backstage at the Warfield. Bill was larger than life and we were very proud to be working for him.

BGP was the first job I held that mattered and it was the skills that I learned during my time with the company that have carried me through the rest of my life. We are the people no one sees, doing the jobs no one knows about and providing the hospitality so that the headliner is happy when they hit the stage and the visiting crew is well cared for.

That was one of the most valuable things I learned from Bill. Take care of your performers, take care of the staff, create a vibe that allows the headliner to relax and enjoy their time with us and make memories.

It was always the small details that stood out. Taking the time to find out what wine they liked, what specialty chocolate they raved about in a recent interview, finding the clues and creating the scene. Making sure they had a little bit of San Francisco to take with them when they left.

From the origins of the bagged breakfast he handed out at Winterland or the apples he handed out at The Fillmore, the backstage hospitality was an extension of that. We took our cues from him and created ever lasting memories.

Laura (Stewart) Kaplan
Volunteer Usher 1985-1990
Rock Medicine Volunteer   1985-1990
AKG Backstage Production   1990-1998
Shoreline Production Runner 1998-2001

LINDA NYGARD

I started working for Bill Graham Presents in 1980 as an usher during a Grateful Dead run and did the following jobs: runner, runner coordinator, production secretary, ambiance, usher and barista at the Warfield Theater and in the accounting department. I departed in 1991.

My story: Madonna and Sean

It was Christmas of 1985. Employees and guests were assembled at the annual BGP Christmas party waiting for the skits, songs and parodies to start. Each department and individual rehearsed his or her performances in advance.

Past years had seen the likes of Danny Scher singing "I Didn't Mean to Burn Your Lawn" (sung to Robert Palmers' "I Didn't Mean to Turn You On"), an homage to Shoreline Amphitheatre. The Bitch Goddesses were made up of women from the office staff. One year, Jan Simmons sang "Wedding Bell Blues" to Bill Graham, then the Bitch Goddesses came onstage to change her mind.

That particular year I dressed up as Madonna. The makeup department gave me the signature birthmark/mole above my lip. Extra blush was brushed into my belly button to highlight it and my see through midriff lace top.

Jerry Pompili introduced the number. "Every year that dynamite singer from production gets up and does a little number. But she couldn't make it this year, so, we have the Material Girl herself - Madonna!"

I came out onto stage and sang Madonna's "Material Girl." The band consisted of Dave Carpenter (of Greg Kihn fame) on guitar, Stevie Barsotti on bass, Scott Donaldson on guitar and Joey on drums (of Stoneground fame). Toward the end of the number Tom Howard came onto the stage dressed as Sean Penn. (During that time period Madonna and Sean Penn were a couple. They famously filled the tabloids.) Tom (aka Sean) came up from behind me and tried to get my attention. I continued to sing and dance and act as if I was unaware of his presence. Tom/Sean interrupted me and said, "Madonna, I'm hungry! Who do you care more about? Me?"

He then pointed out to the audience and said, "Or them?" I looked up into Tom's eyes, and then looked longingly out into the audience and then back to Tom, "You dear," I replied. Tom looked out into the audience, pointed at Bill Graham and yelled "Graham! Philadelphia!" (Sean Penn had previously had a run in with Bill at Live Aid in Philadelphia.) Tom/Sean grabbed me/Madonna by the arm and began to pull me off stage. Pompili got on the stage and said, "At least somebody rehearsed!"

Some time later during the next year I was working at the BGP office and heard over the office intercom: "Linda Nygard and Tom Howard please come to Gregg Perloff's office." As Tom and I were walking up to Gregg's office we looked at each other and said, "What?" We had no clue why he would call us to his office.

Tom and I stood in the doorway of Gregg's office. A gentleman was sitting on the couch in Gregg's office. Gregg raised his hand in my direction and said, "Madonna." He then pointed to the man on the couch and said, "Meet Madonna's manager." Madonna's manager looked up at me from the couch and said with a smile, "I saw the video." I just about died! Madonna's manager had just seen the Christmas party video where I parodied Madonna and Tom made fun of Sean Penn! Inside my brain I was screaming, "Oh no!" Madonna's manager continued on. "Do you want to do what she does?" I was speechless and stunned. However, inside I was screaming, "Yes! Yes!"

Tom and I walked away from Gregg's office feeling giddy and blown away. This has always been one of my fondest memories involving Tom Howard. Note from Rita: Tom Howard passed away unexpectedly on January 5, 2017.

LINDA WALSH

I remember my first show as a Bluecoat. I got to work New Year's Eve in 1980 and UFO was the headliner. I had a blast working it as I was a very shy person and working these shows brought me out of my shy self.

Every time that I walked by Bill I would say, "Hi." I really never got to know him on a one-to- one basis, probably due to the fact that he always had so much going on.

My husband, George Walsh, got me the job and from then on it was history. I met a lot of nice people with BGP and I worked a lot of great shows. The Grateful Dead shows were the best to work on New Year's Eve.

I stopped working in 1989 when we moved to the Valley. Eighteen years later when we came back to the Bay Area we got the news that Bill had died. We were so saddened by this because no one had let us know about this tragedy. We think of him often and the people who are with him now.

He was a very kind soul and may he and everyone with him from the past rest in peace.

LIONEL BEA

I'm Lionel Bea of Bay Area Productions. Growing up in Oakland, California as a young man I was always interested in music. I played the alto saxophone and the drums in grades six through eight. I attended many concerts in my youth and it seemed that every one of them was promoted by Bill Graham Presents. The very first concert that I attended was a show entitled Funk on the Green. It was held at the Oakland Coliseum Stadium. The featured groups were Parliament- Funkadelic, Bootsy's Rubber Band, Rick James and the Stone City Band, Barkays, Brides of Funkenstein, Con Funk Shun, Sister Sledge and Parlet. I was 13 years old at the time. It too was promoted by Bill Graham Presents.

Around 1983 I was attending the College of Alameda where I saw an ad for a seminar entitled, "So You Want To Be In The Music Business?" As I was interested in promoting concerts after having spent the last couple years promoting large dance parties, I signed up for the seminar and attended it with my partners. I believe Herbie Herbert, the manager of Journey, was there as well as Bill Graham and a few other music industry executives. I learned a lot about the concert business from attending. At the end of the seminar, Bill Graham offered up his telephone number to any attendee that wanted to ask him questions about the music business. I took him up on his offer and called him on the following Monday. I was very excited to speak with him. I remember saying to him, "People think you have a monopoly on the concert business in the Bay Area." He responded by saying, "I do not have a monopoly. Anyone can rent the Oakland Auditorium or the Oakland Coliseum." He went on to say, "I can't help it if acts want to play for me." The conversation lasted about 15 minutes.

Around 1984, I ran into Bill Graham once again. It was at the Prince Purple Rain concert at the Oakland Coliseum. I approached him outside on the plaza and I introduced myself to him and asked if we could set up a meeting. He asked what about? I told him I wanted to discuss the business with him. He said to me in an exacerbated tone, "If I met with everyone that wanted to discuss 'the business' I wouldn't have time for anything else." Later that evening, I saw him inside the concert; I approached him once again. I wanted to ask him a question. When I attempted to speak to him that time, he scolded me and said, "Dig yourself man, can't you see I'm working?" It was obviously bad timing.

That same year in 1984, my company promoted our very first concert. The show featured Run- DMC with Egyptian Lover and Uncle Jamm's Army. Uncle Jamm's Army was the premier dance party promoter in the city of Los Angeles. They featured some of the best DJs in the world. The show was a success. We then felt that rap music was going to have a big bright future.

In 1986, the management team for Run-DMC was run by Russell Simmons and Lyor Cohen. A decision was made that Run-DMC would headline their own national tour. The year prior, 1985, Run-DMC headlined the highly successful Fresh Fest Tour. We were very interested in promoting the Oakland date as we were the first to promote Run-DMC in the Bay Area. Lyor Cohen asked if I had $42,000 for the artist guarantee. I did not. He then said that he would sell the date to Bill Graham Presents but that he would have us work together with them on the shows that summer. Lyor spoke with Stan Fieg from BGP and told him that we were the best street promoters in the country. That summer of 1986 we helped Run-DMC sell out two shows at the Oakland Coliseum - one show in June and another one in August.

At the June show I met Bill Graham briefly and we had a very short conversation after I introduced myself to him once again. When Run-DMC played the second show that summer in August it was a different story. The night before the Oakland show we played Fresno, California. I walked into the production office backstage. Lyor Cohen was on the telephone with Russell Simmons. Lyor handed me the telephone to speak to Russell. He congratulated me on doing a great job. After handing the phone back to Lyor, he proceeded to tell Russell that he was having lunch with Bill Graham at his home that next day and then said, "Lionel doesn't know that Bill Graham wants him to be his new business partner." I was totally blown away.

On the very next night in Oakland, we had the second sold-out concert with Run-DMC. This time the conversation with Bill Graham was not a brief one. He saw us and said, "Hello." We talked for at least four hours. At the end of the conversation he said that he had never made so much money on a Black show before. He said he would help us in any way he could. If we needed him to make a phone call, he would or if we needed his assistance or if we needed money just give him a call. Keep in mind that we had prior knowledge as to what his intentions were.

After Bill's generous offer we waited two weeks before phoning him. I didn't want him to think that we were desperate. When we finally phoned him the very first question he asked was, "What took you so long?" We met with him at his office soon after that phone call. After a lengthy conversation he was ready to make an offer. He said that I reminded him of himself when he was my age. He then offered us a 50/50 deal to essentially be the urban music extension of his company. We would co-promote R&B, rap and Black comedy concerts together. The relationship was born. I never reminded Bill about our previous encounters. However, it wouldn't have surprised me a bit that he remembered our prior encounters and didn't say anything.

As the relationship with Bill Graham began to grow, he was very supportive with everything we wanted to do. He was always able to lend some advice to keep us going in the right direction.

Most of all, Bill gave us the freedom to be creative and to make mistakes and fix those mistakes and do a better job the next time. He was a music giant, but behind the scenes Bill was a compassionate but firm man who believed in giving people an opportunity to flourish. That's a great leadership quality to have.

Bill paid attention to the details which obviously made him successful. One night at a show in Oakland, I saw Bill Graham and he asked me about the show that took place on the previous night. He asked me, "How did it go?" I told him that it went well and that we made money. He said, "I know that, but how was the catering?" That was Bill Graham, paying attention to all the little things, the details.

That was the Bill Graham that I knew. He always carried a pen and pad in his back pocket. He took detailed notes at every show and he would tell you what mistakes were made and how you could do it better next time.

I knew that Bill wanted us to be successful. You could tell that by the time that he took with us. He told me to always remember that "this is a business of relationships." He talked about how to build relationships with managers and artists and help them succeed, and by doing so they would always want to work with you. He taught that "you should treat an artist as if they were a guest in your living room."

Bill shared a few intimate stories about his personal life. His story of escaping Nazi Germany really touched me. I knew of the Holocaust, but his stories brought it to life. We had a few discussions about race relations in America. He said that people are always complaining about things, but that they should "get up and do something about it." He also shared many stories from the road. He talked about the Rolling Stones, the Grateful Dead, The US Festival. He once introduced us to the legendary Harry Belafonte, a giant in the civil rights movement.

In 1990 Nelson Mandela was planning to visit the United States. It was his first visit to America after being freed from prison in South Africa after 27 years. This was going to be a historic moment in U.S. history. Unfortunately, Mr. Mandela was not planning to visit the Bay Area. It was the Bay Area dock workers who first refused to unload ships from South Africa as a protest to apartheid. Bill and others went to Washington D.C. to make the case for Mandela to visit the Bay Area. They were successful in their efforts.

Bill included us on the committee of about 20 people that helped put the event together. The Mandela visit would take place at The Oakland Coliseum Stadium in June of 1990. We met several times in the BGP conference room to discuss the details of the Mandela visit. What made Bill great was that he would listen to other people's ideas and he never came across as a know-it- all. I found that refreshing. We were able to book rapper KRS-1 for the event. Mandela's visit went off without a hitch. It was a great opportunity for us to be a part of a truly historic event. Bill made this happen.

Another special moment with Bill was when he was being honored by the American Friends of Hebrew University. Bill wanted us to attend the dinner. It was at a San Francisco hotel. It was a very powerful evening. I remember that Ted Turner and Jane Fonda were in attendance. Bill received an award that night. I was honored to be invited.

Bill once invited us to the Warner Brothers Records Music Convention in San Francisco. He felt that it was important that I meet some of the power brokers in the record business. He introduced me to Mo Austin who was the president of Warner Brothers Music at the time. Also present was Benny Medina. Bill introduced me as his business partner which was big at the time because Bill knew that would lend credibility to our joint venture. Bill was always the smartest guy in the room and he never made a move that was unintentional.

One day we got a phone call from Bill's office saying that Bill would always spend a special day with people that he liked. Bill invited us to fly on his private plane to Los Angeles to attend the James Brown tribute concert at the Wiltern Theater. James Brown had just been released from prison and the music community wanted to pay tribute to him with a star-studded concert. Bootsy Collins, Rick James and many superstars were in the house. I remember seeing Jesse Jackson, MC Hammer, football legend Warren Moon, and I believe The Greatest - Muhammad Ali was present.

Almost every Black celebrity that I could ever want to meet was there and Bill made sure that we were in attendance. It was one of the best nights of my career.

I was in Bill's office one day and noticed that he had two stacks of baseball tickets about a half- inch thick on his desk. He asked if I wanted to attend the American League playoffs. Of course, I said yes. Bill then peeled off a pair of tickets each for my partner and me. When we got to our car, I noticed that the ticket said the Oakland A's vs. National League Champion. I realized that these were World Series tickets. I immediately returned to Bill's office to return the tickets. Bill looked at the tickets and said, "What an honest guy. Most people wouldn't have said anything." To this day I'm not sure if Bill Graham was testing me or not. If it was a test, I guess I passed.

On October 25, 1991 I was telling that exact story to Lee Smith at the BGP office. I had run into Bill a few minutes prior and he said hello to me. I told Lee the World Series tickets story and I said I'm not sure if Bill was testing me or not. Lee said, "Well, Lionel you'll never know." At that exact time Bill was in his office yelling at someone on the phone something like "I dare you, be a man and get on an airplane. You come up here and say that to my face. I dare you. Be a man. Come say it to my face. You'd never say it to my face." I looked at Lee Smith and said, "Wow! Why does he still do this?" I'd seen Bill get angry before, but he was giving this guy the business. Lee said to me, "Lionel, you and I will never be as driven as he is." That was the last time that I saw or heard Bills Graham's voice. That evening I was having dinner with some friends and one asked me how I'd met Bill Graham. I told them a few Bill Graham stories. After returning home I got a phone call at about 1:00 a.m. from my then business partner informing me of a rumor of the Bill's accident. I called Gregg Perloff at 7:00 a.m. the next morning. He confirmed that Bill had passed away in a tragic helicopter accident. I was floored. He told me "that Bill wanted me to be successful and that our relationship wouldn't change."

Attending Bill Graham's funeral was a very sad day. I lost someone who shared my dreams and did what he could to make them come true, someone who believed in me. That was pretty hard to take and has impacted me to this day.

Bill was a larger-than-life figure, a real-life living legend. He was a mentor and a friend. I think of him often. He's greatly missed.

It was a pleasure to work side-by-side with Bill Graham and the wonderful people of Bill Graham Presents. For that I will forever be grateful.

LISA HANSEN

I never really met Bill, but I saw him arrive in his helicopter many times at Shoreline Amphitheatre. I started my adventure with BGP at Shoreline in late '80s as a parking cashier. I then went to balancing parking lot cash once lots were full and then security at different venues.

As a parking cashier I recall a Whitney Houston show. We'd just finished parking duties when she canceled her show (supposedly her voice, we were told.) The food vending was open and cooking, warm-up band about to go on, everyone parked, when it was announced. I will never forget the angry patrons and the confusion as everyone was coming at us demanding their money back. Most of us only had large bills at that point, so it was very difficult to refund their parking fee, which I think was $7.00 at the time. People had come from miles away, really angry and flooring it out of there. I remember getting welts on my legs from the stones the tires threw up when they floored it. I do not recall ever seeing her booked again under the BGP organization. The money she cost BGP.

I worked a lot of security at Oakland Coliseum, mostly for the Dead. One time, another Bluecoat and I were placed at the backstage nosebleed seats. They were never sold, but we were to guard them and not allow anyone to cut through. We both had a huge area between us. This one Deadhead, out of nowhere, came flying past the other Bluecoat. I tried to get to him, when he stood on the railing overlooking the backstage area and leaped onto the stage, out of both of our reaches. I could not believe how fast this guy was, but he was clearly on something and it had to be a 20-foot drop! Tons of security came from everywhere to retrieve him. I thought we would be in trouble as I was fairly new, but the guy was so fast, not sure any experienced BGP staff would have caught him in time.

My last is the final Dead show I worked. It was the Mardi Gras show at Oakland Coliseum in 1995 and also Jerry's last Mardi Gras. I'd never worked one before. I was stationed at the sound stage, keeping it secure. What a thrill and my most cherished memory there. For three days I watched floats being built. I was told I did a great job the first night and they requested me for the remaining two nights. What an honor. The last night - I will never forget those bay doors opening and the crowd was parted, and the floats came by to the music, throwing beads and candy, I get goosebumps telling the story. I can still close my eyes and see it. What a thrill.

The best job, to date, I ever had.

LORI GATES

I'm a fourth generation San Franciscan. I graduated from high school in 1979 and listening to music had been a part of my world since my early teens. I remember getting my first transistor radio (AM and FM) up at a place on "top of the hill, Daly City." It was round and green. This was the first time I had control of my own music. While in high school, around 1976, I started going to as many concerts as I could afford, standing in line at midnight at my local Record Factory to buy tickets. My first major concerts were Days on the Green in July of 1977 when I was 16, Peter Frampton with Lynyrd Skynyrd, and then later that month, Led Zeppelin's last

U.S. dates ever. I needed more music in my life and concert-going became my "thing."

Eventually I went to San Francisco State University and participated in a London Semester in 1984. It was there at a party that I met a roadie for the Thompson Twins and an artist named Annabel Lamb who had a song on the British charts. I'd never met anyone in the music business before; in fact, I'd never even thought about there being a business of music. Game changer. When I returned to SFSU, I worked with a counselor who helped me get an internship at 415 Records with Howie Klein. Then I took classes at State taught by Joel Selvin (Rock I and Rock II) and he took me under his wing and helped me network. I wanted to work in the music business.

I first met Bill Graham in September of 1985 at a Bruce Springsteen concert at the Oakland Coliseum. We were not introduced. I was attending the concert, sitting in a folding chair on the lawn. There he was: Bill Graham, walking in my general direction. The man. The myth. The legend. The man who brought music to life for me. I had to say something. My heart was pounding in my chest and up into my throat. I was going to do it. As he walked with extreme determination, I said, "Mr. Graham, this is amazing to have Bruce here. Thank you so much." OMG, I did it.

He acknowledged me and said, "You're welcome."

Little did I know that the following year I'd be receiving Bill Graham Presents paychecks. Seriously. With Selvin as my mentor, I met so many industry folks at his Tuesday evening parties at which the only food served (food?) were barrels of glowing-orange Cheese Balls - San Francisco band managers, artists, publicists, agents, promoters and more.

And then there was me, about 26 years old and eager to be a part of this community. I was a kid in a figurative candy store. I got my first paying job in the Industry working for the Bay Area Music Archives and then the BAMMIES. I was the associate producer for a few years. This was only for half of the year, so I needed to fill in with another job. Roger Clark, one of Joel's friends, worked for BGP in the marketing department. He was looking for an assistant. Yes, please. So, during half the year, the extended crazy summer season, I had the extreme honor to work with the Minister of Propaganda, Roger Clark and the San Francisco legend, Jude Heller. I helped them during the day and then many evenings I worked at the shows with the production crew. One of my favorite jobs was assisting the photographers get their much-needed shots at the gigs. I'd meet them backstage and then escort them to the front of the stage while the first three songs were played. They would take their pics and then I'd escort them out.

Metallica, however, had a different set of rules — photogs got to shoot the LAST three songs, after the set had been accumulated and they were at their best.

Another of my jobs was to proofread the plethora of concert posters that came from the world of the uber-talented, now retired, Art/Creative Director, Arlene Owseichik. She would churn out these fantastic pieces of marketing art, send them over to our department, where we'd proof them and then they'd head off to the printer. Well, one day I was the only one in our little glassed-in room, just off the main area of the office in San Francisco. Bill usually stayed in his corner office and dealt with all the necessary phone calls. This time, however, he bounded over to the marketing offices and came bursting in the door. He looked serious, more so than usual. He walked over to me and held up a recently printed poster, aiming it right towards my face. "WHAT'S MY NAME?" he yelled. I thought I was going to die. "WHAT'S MY NAME?" he repeated. "Bill Graham," I answered as I looked up at my highly respected, bigger-than-life boss. "What is missing from this poster!?" His voice grew louder. Oh, holy crap. Missing at the top of the Fillmore poster was an empty spot where the BGP logo was supposed to be. I answered that BGP was missing and as he turned on his heels, he reminded me to never let that happen again.

And that is the time Bill Graham yelled at me. While I was horrified and scared to my toes, it is a great memory I will never, ever forget. Oh, and I never, ever forgot to check for the BGP logo on every poster I was asked to proof.

LORI SUN-LOOK

Project Manager, March 1986 - March 1999

I started working at Bill Graham Presents in 1986, a few months before the opening of the Shoreline Amphitheatre in Mountain View. I reported directly to Danny Scher, who at that time was the Vice President handling corporate sponsorships and events, and was also responsible for building Shoreline Amphitheatre and other facilities. I was actually introduced to Danny by my cousin, who was working with Danny on some computer-related projects. Shortly after Danny hired me, he left for vacation for a few weeks. Due to a Shoreline Amphitheatre construction issue, one of my earliest memories of my time at BGP was trying to track Danny down as he climbed the ruins in Machu Picchu, Peru.

Not long after he returned from vacation, Shoreline Amphitheatre opened and with it, the very successful and long-running New Orleans by the Bay, created by Danny, who frequently visited New Orleans for both the music and food. New Orleans by the Bay would eventually become one of the biggest projects on my to-do list. During the months leading up to NOBB, when the normal work day ended at 6:00 p.m., I would put on some Barry White in Danny's office to get energized, crank up the music, and with a krewe of BGP employees and interns, start pulling together the elements for this fun, family-oriented food and music festival.

While I can't quite remember when I first met Bill at the office, I certainly can't forget (as I'm sure other women in the office will agree) how special it was to be invited to Ladies Night Out with Bill! There was a definite excitement in the air as we got ready for the night, putting on dresses and freshening up our makeup. I still remember the limo ride (and getting a little carsick!) and heading up to the San Francisco Fairmont Hotel for dinner, followed by an evening performance by Tony Bennett. And somewhere I know I have a special photo with Bill, handsome in his suit, stretched out on the office carpet surrounded by a bevy of glammed up BGP women!

Thirty-four years later, I'm still working for Danny and even sometimes trying to track him down as he bikes the scenic roads in Europe and Asia. And for that I am forever grateful to Bill Graham, for allowing me to become part of the Bill Graham Presents family so many years ago.

M

MAGGIE SICHEL PINATELLI

I am a San Francisco native. I grew up in the Sunset District. I got my driver's license in 1971. From then on, my friends and sisters and brother and I went to every show at Winterland. We were the kids out in the driveway turning our transistor radios this way and that to get the best reception we could.

I have always been a music lover.

After awhile, I realized that I saw Bill at every show. Somehow, I would always see him walking by or yelling at someone or coming in or going out. I always saw him. So I started trying to catch his eye. Then I started saying hi to him. Sometimes I got a nod or a smile.

Life went on. I left town to go to college. I had studied piano throughout my childhood and thought I wanted to be a music major. The first day, I discovered that you had to sing out loud to be a music major. Well, I was much too shy for that and had to change majors that same day, but I was still a music lover. By then I was a Deadhead and met my husband, Tom. We veered off the straight and narrow path and onto the bus. We moved to San Francisco and I got my first account-ing job and I realized that even music promoters had bookkeepers!

It took awhile. Dennis McNally had introduced us to Jan Simmons already. They produced our wedding reception and used skeletons from the Warfield on the walls and drove us from the ceremony to the reception in Bill's Mercedes.

Then we moved to Santa Cruz. Then my Dad had a stroke and we moved back to San Francisco. The very day that I returned to San Francisco, I got a call from Steve Welkom at BGP saying the accounts payable clerk had had a meltdown and left in a hurry. Could I start working at BGP the next day?

So I did. I was the first person hired at the office that was not interviewed by Bill. I remember Jan thanked him for hiring her friend; it must have been okay.

Bill loved my son Tony. Gary Orndorf, Bill's house manager, gave Alex Graham's toy fire engine to Tony. Bill tried to get Tony to pick up garbage at Laguna Seca…that was funny!

Everyone that worked at BGP loved Bill. We may have not always agreed with him or thought he was doing the right thing, but we still loved him.

I remember how he would always bring the ladies of the office gifts from his adventures around the world…and they were nice things: Beautiful earrings, scarves and bracelets. One time, Owsley came in to sell some jewelry pieces he had made because he needed money and Jan made Bill give me a belt buckle! He loved her so much and it paid off for me!

Bill loved all of us too. I remember at the Bay Area Music Awards when he was awarded something, he made all of us stand up and told the audience he couldn't do it without each and every one of us.

I've never been in another workplace like that. Never!

Anyone who worked for Bill could go into his office and talk to him about their work issues at the end of the day, after hours…and he listened.

It was the best job ever, because it was our life, not a job. It was the best of times….

MALVINA SUGAR SIMS

My first encounter with the Bill Graham Company was when I was hired by Bruce Jennings who was the owner of Event Security. Bruce was a good friend of Bill Graham and helped in the making of a great security company. We got things done.

My first show was The Last Waltz.

In the city of San Francisco at the closing of the venue Winterland, I worked my first Grateful Dead show. I had never seen anything like it before. All the people were crammed into the building and on the outside of it too. There were so many people looking for that "miracle" ticket. Working outside of the building my job was to check bags and bodies as they entered the venue. I would say, "have your tickets out and ready." No cans, bottles, everyone is subject to a search. Part of my job was to search the women and the men for any of these items.

It was a job that is not for everybody to do. I found out that you need a special gift to be able to pat down hundreds of people before the show starts. It was quite a feat.

From the very start I knew that this was the job for me.

I got to finally tell people what to do.

I became part of a family that took me on so many wonderful journeys. Coming from a little town called Oakland (the eastern part of Brookfield Village), I was one of six children (5 girls and 1 boy). Being the oldest, I left home at the age of 16 thinking that I knew just about everything and I knew nothing at all.

If I could rewrite anything, it would have been to continue with my art classes in school and staying in school. But, as life goes on I chose to venture out on my own. In my day, you were seen and not heard…you stayed in a child's place never letting one's own thoughts to be heard.

I went through a lot and learned a lot about being on my own. After a very bad relationship I moved to San Francisco to get away from the abuse. My friend, Jackie Robinson lived on Divisadero Street where I met Ms. Freddy Hinkle. She worked for Event Security which was a company that was employed by Bill Graham Presents. There weren't very many black women on the staff at the time. You worked just as hard as the men and you definitely had to hold your own ground. Through Event Security I got a chance to travel and work with The Grateful Dead and many other groups.

I also got a chance to work at The Fillmore, The Warfield Theatre, the Paramount Theater in Oakland, The San Francisco Civic Auditorium, Concord Pavilion and Shoreline Amphitheatre.

If I had not come into contact with Bill Graham Presents, I would have never had been able to experience the following:

A promoter job with Sugar Sims Comedy and Music Review, which was held at the Last Day Saloon in San Francisco.

The chance to see what it was like to fly First Class to Telluride, Colorado being the only black woman on the staff of the Telluride Music Festival. After the show I ended up at the only radio station in Telluride and spun them some Soul music especially the song, California Dreamer by Frankie Beverly with the group Maze. What a treat that was at 3AM in the morning.

The chance to work at the following shows: Working at the Rolling Stones Concert at the Oakland Coliseum while also being able to babysit my granddaughter as well, and Meeting Tom Petty and the Heartbreakers for 27 days. Also being able to sing and dance with Tom Petty and the Band at The Fillmore, and Sting at the Greek Theater in Berkeley and the list goes on.

I give thanks to being part of the Bill Graham Presents family which is such an amazing and wonderful group of people. BGP made it able for me to meet all of the different people involved with the behind the scenes in the production of a concert/show. These people that make it all happen are as stagehands, caterers, front of stage, behind stage staff, security, runners and even the cleanup crews.

I want to thank Bill Graham, Bill's immediate family and the Bill Graham Presents family for their friendship. If I hadn't had Bill and Bill Graham Presents for about 30 years of my life, it would definitely had been a very boring existence.

If I could rewrite my life, I would not change a thing

MARC MARGOLIS

So, a neighbor of mine gave me a recipe for gefilte fish with homemade horseradish, a traditional food for the Jewish holiday of Passover.

I made both the fish and horseradish for the first time and it came out quite tasty. I decided to wrap up a piece of fish along with the horseradish and some matzoh. I dropped it off for Bill at his office with a short note.

A month or so later I was at the Grateful Dead show in Las Vegas backstage at the end of the show. I saw Bill striding by me and said, "Hey Bill, how was the gefilte fish?" He stopped dead in his tracks and turned to me and said, "Fish was a 10." "And the horseradish?" I asked. "A 9." I think he liked it.

MARC WENDT

My experiences were one degree of separation from Bill Graham directly, given that I didn't begin working for James Olness and Rebecca Nichols until after Bill died. However, prior to that, I got to experience the generosity of Bill through my uncle, Doug Wendt. Generosity is an often-overlooked form of magic and in my case, Bill's generosity was expressed in my being able to attend amazing world music, reggae and Day on the Green shows.

As a result of Bill's awareness of diversity of music, my life as an audience member was enriched enormously in a spiritual way.

What Bill Graham produced were rites for the soul. What his generosity did for me was create an extraordinary vision of the world of possibilities. Fostering the growth of my imagination, the depth of my compassion, and a vision of what it meant to create experiences of a transcendent nature. Bill rendered into existence communal experiences that reshaped the spiritual landscape of our community. He did it without the ego of a guru, but with the twinkle in his eye reflecting that of a magician, a showman, a non-denominational priest of magical musical possibilities.

His generosity inspired and fueled my posthumous contributions as an intern in the BGP archives (1992-1994). I had visceral access to my memories of his dedication to quality, and I poured that into my work at BGP and it was evident in every other BGP person I met while I was working. Bill's bobblehead sits on my desk as I type this, a potent reminder of what it means to pursue greatness relentlessly through joy and generosity.

MARGE PIANE

I started my career at Bill Graham Presents in 1980 when Steve Welkom hired me to help Peaches O'Reilly paint and install the window décor for the Grateful Dead's October series of shows at the Warfield Theater in San Francisco. On one of the installation days Bill came over to where I was working from high on a ladder and introduced himself! I don't remember what he said, but I'm fairly sure I was totally tongue-tied.

After having a great time working with Peaches on many, many outrageously creative windows and dressing rooms at the Warfield, Henry J. Kaiser Auditorium, the (then) San Francisco Civic Auditorium and some Day on the Green shows, I got an office job as Gregg Perloff's assistant that included getting venue availabilities (by phone!) for all the booking agents, putting shows on sale with Ticketmaster and — the best part — sitting at a desk facing Jan Simmons and across from Rita Gentry.

And that's where I was sitting one morning when Bill came in, went into his office and came right back out. He stood in the middle of the room, called everyone around, pulled down his jeans and showed us the brace or cast (cannot remember) he had on his leg. What I noticed, though, was the fact that his underwear was full of holes! I immediately called Gary Orndorf and asked him what size underwear Bill wore and passed that info around to all the women in the office. We were about to have our annual "ladies lunch" at Don Ramon's Restaurant for Bill's birthday, and the idea was for all of us to buy him a pair of underwear. Bill opened, maybe, the third package when he realized where the stack of gifts was going. He could absolutely take a joke and we all got a great laugh along with our usual great meal.

Once I became director of advertising and had my own office, I had what I'd still call the best job ever. Not least because it's where I met my dear friend and sister in creativity, Arlene Owseichik. Our collaborations on Prince's dressing room at the Cow Palace and a mini- Stonehenge for Spinal Tap at Wolfgang's were so much fun! (One of my last and best efforts at BGP was convincing the decision makers that it made fiscal sense to create our own art department and bring Arlene in-house).

And finally, one of my most treasured mementos from Bill was lost in the fire. I had given him a case of homemade dill pickles for Christmas and his hand-written thank you note said:

"You have automatic tenure for life — 'Pickles' Graham." I had it framed on my desk and still wish it had been true!

MARIE MANDOLI

I, The Balloon Lady, had a contract with Bill Graham Presents to drop 10,000 balloons every night for indoor shows and release 20,000 balloons for every outdoor show during the 1981 Rolling Stones U.S. Tour.

We were at Madison Square Garden and during the show I was sitting backstage. There was a rigger lounging on a couch and Bill was sitting on a chair nearby. A security guard came and asked for Bill, saying, "There's a woman at the backstage door. Her name is R and she says that if I ask Bill Graham he will let her in." Bill looks up and says, "Don't let her in."

The security guard goes away. He comes back a few minutes later holding a woman's wool coat in is right hand. She says, "Give him this!" Bill looks up and I think he's about to yell at the guy. Bill just tells the guard to leave the coat and go tell her, "No." The guy comes back in ten minutes with her scarf. Bill throws the scarf on to the coat. Next comes the sweater. When the guard brings in the high heels Bill just shakes his head and groans.

"I better go get her before she's naked!"

New Year's Eve, Grateful Dead, Oakland Coliseum. Bill was afraid of heights — very afraid. But he was a true showman through and through, and in the most dramatic way. He was to make a theatrical entrance and ring in the New Year.

Part of getting ready was being rigged into a harness, dress into his themed costume for that year, floating over the crowd and landing on the stage to bring in the New Year. He always played Father Time. There were New Year's Eve babies, indoor pyro, confetti, flowers, lots of balloons and then "Sugar Magnolia."

This year, Peter Barsotti's plan was to create a huge nest, which had people in it dressed up as baby chicks. There was pyro set up on the nest to be cued when Bill descended from the ceiling in a bright yellow chicken costume. The day before the show we had our visit from the City of Oakland Fire Marshal. Not our favorite guy. Rocky Paulson from the company Stage Rigging was the only person Bill trusted to rig him for the New Year's Eve extravaganza. Don and I met with the fire marshal and explained the plan for the midnight surprise. He asked to see the nest, the pyro set up for the nest, the baby chick costumes, the father time and the on-stage babies New Year's costumes...and The Chicken Suit. He put a flame to the chicken suit and the feathers instantly turned to ashes.

Nope. This chicken suit was not going to fly anywhere in this building. We asked him, "What about if we fireproof the suit?" Would he come back the day of show and let us try again? We spent the next 24 hours soaking the feathers with fire retardant and drying it. We passed! The show must go on and as everyone knew, Bill really did not understand the word "no."

MARJI BLEA

I often call my time at Bill Graham Presents (BGP) as a Bluecoat a "butterfly" flap in my life. Thirty-plus years later, I still keep in contact with many of the Bluecoats. I am blessed to have them as Friends!

I have so many memories and I've had a difficult time writing it all down. I would get blocked when I would sit to write. I decided to put a bunch of thoughts in a list. This isn't all of them, but here is what I have remembered and written.

Wavy Gravy as Santa Claus at the BGP Christmas Party

Volleyball against the fans at Grateful Dead shows

Mardi Gras Parade at the Henry J. Kaiser (Oakland) Grateful Dead show

Day on the Green's – Funny story.

The Wham and Scorpions shows were back-to- back.

Bill told us if we could find someone with a ticket to both shows, he would give us tickets to the Grateful Dead

New Year's Eve show.

Of course, we all knew we would be working those shows anyway. I did find someone with tickets to both shows, but I never told Bill.

Laguna Seca shows – Highlight was working the Touch of Grey video shoot

Working front of stage at the Frost Amphitheater when the puppeteers came to observe the band in preparation of the Touch of Grey video

Bluecoat College put on by Bill

New Year's Eve shows – Always special

Singing at the BGP Christmas Party on a boat on the Bay

Bill telling a group of us that he would have been a waiter if he wasn't a promoter

U2 at The Embarcadero in San Francisco

Amnesty International Concert

One of my favorite memories was the night I was on the New Year's Eve Float in 1987.

I was supposed to be working the Stevie Ray Vaughan show for New Year's Eve. I was working day calls at the Oakland Coliseum the week before the New Year's Eve show.

I was stationed in the catering hall and I was helping to de-thorn dozens and dozens of roses for the show.

While doing this task Eleonore Hockabout came up to me and said, "Bill would like you to be the Indian Pocahontas on the float." Of course, I said, "Yes!"

There were Bluecoats on the float: Mick Flaire and Julianna. David Graham was on the float and Larry Bird. Larry Bird was at the show.

We really didn't know what was going to happen once we were on the float. I remember I was standing with Mick.

The lights went down and I Left My Heart in San Francisco started playing as we moved into the Arena. Then the music got louder, and the float began to spin to Helter Skelter. We had buckets of roses and big balloons to throw out to the crowd. I remember thinking, "Those are my de-thorn roses."

It was being filmed for pay-for-view and there were boom cameras moving around the front of us. I have always wanted to find someone with the footage.

The countdown to midnight started and Bill as Father Time began to rise up. The balloons and confetti dropped from the ceiling and the cheers were deafening.

I was SO happy. Everyone in the Arena was smiling. Mick and I just kept laughing and smiling.

It was SURREAL!

The float docked at the stage. Mick and I didn't know what we were supposed to do so we got off of the float and onto the stage. The float started to move away, and we were still on the stage. Someone handed us champagne.

Later I was changing in the RV which was a trailer located backstage. Bill was in there too and he said that he had lost his Live Aid necklace somewhere in the Arena.

I always wondered if the necklace was ever found.

Late in the evening I saw Bill backstage and thanked him for choosing me to be on the float.

I hugged him and told him that I will NEVER forget the experience that he gave to me. I remember that night like it was yesterday.

MARK BETHEL

I worked for Bill Graham for the first time at Winterland in February of 1974. I worked as a stagehand/Bluecoat from February to April.

I started at FM Productions* in the FM Shop in April of 1974 as a carpenter. I went out on tour with CSNY setting up the P.A. from June thru August of 1974, then went out with Santana as a carpenter from August through September 1974. Then, the George Harrison tour October through December, 1974.

I became a lighting technician in 1975 where I learned that trade by FM Productions. I ended up working as a lighting guy either going out on tour or at Winterland, Days on the Green and other shows of that liking. Took on Production Manager in 1978 doing The Commodores tour. I ended up leaving FM at the end of 1978.

I worked as a promoter rep from 1979 until 1982, including being the site coordinator for the first US Festival.

I don't really have a good story about Bill. I don't think he liked me much.

*FM Productions was a company owned by Bill Graham which was the first rock and roll lighting, staging, audio and scenic company on the West Coast.

MARK WHITE

In 1986 I got a job at Shoreline Amphitheatre as an assistant electrician, so to speak. My first job assignment was to spread coco chips on the hillsides outside the wind screens to quell the smell of the impurities in the methane gas that was permeating its way out of the ground as the amphitheater was built on an old dump. They wanted it to smell like chocolate!

My first show was the first Bridge Benefit Concert. I watched Bruce Springsteen do a two-hour sound check. I played a video game backstage with Rob Lowe on my break and I was in awe of Bill Graham and everything that was going on around me that day. Not a bad first day to start for BGP.

Between the 1986 and 1987 season they were installing a two- million-dollar methane gas extraction system underneath the lawn seating area. I had been doing a lot of electrical work with Jack McKeown, Steve Hummer and crew getting ready for the season. Besides the tent ripping and other unforeseen things going on around me, one day I was asked to come into the office for a meeting. I came into the office and in that meeting, I was told I had been chosen to be offered a permanent position.

The job would be all year round as they needed someone to operate and maintain the new methane gas recovery system.

I took that job as it was security and I also knew I would be working every single show and given a lot of responsibility to ensure the safety for the facility, workers and patrons attending the venue. I was honored they chose me. I did that job until I left in 1993. Not only did I do that job, but I was also a stagehand, truss spot operator, musician and many other doors opened for me. (My nickname at Shoreline was "Gas Man!")

My band even got to play a set at the BGP Christmas party downstairs at the Warfield Theater one year. Made many memories and lifelong friends working for BGP. I met Bill a few times and also got invited to his house a few times for parties, etc. I am forever grateful for my time working for such a great company! It changed my life forever.

I'll never forget working on top of the bowl one day. Stevie Ray Vaughan was rehearsing all week as they were starting the tour with Joe Cocker at Shoreline. Stevie had taken a break and was walking around the venue. He came up to me and we started talking a bit. He asked me, "Hey, is this place built on an old dump?" I said, "Yes, it is." He said, "Cool man," and took a swig off his Corona and went on with his walk. I thought to myself, "This is my job?" I'm a lucky guy!

MELVIN McGARR

January 7, 1954 – September 8, 2014

Written by Dina Bedini on the sixth anniversary of Melvin's passing.

Melvin McGarr was born in Tennessee and moved to San Francisco when he was five years old. There he went to school and graduated from Balboa High School in 1971. Melvin started working security for Bill Graham at Winterland in 1974 and soon became friends with Bill and thus started his career in the Bay Area music scene.

Melvin worked at Winterland until its closing and then went with Bill to continue working security. He worked at the Warfield Theater from 1979 through 1997 where he eventually became a security supervisor. Melvin worked all of the other venues where Bill would promote shows: the Fillmore, Bill Graham Civic Auditorium (it was called the San Francisco Civic before Bill's death), the Oakland Coliseum, Oakland Auditorium, all the Days on the Green, and the list goes on.

Melvin then went on to work for Carlos Santana from 1989 to 1998 as his personal bodyguard traveling all around the world several times. He loved working with Carlos and traveling, but after nearly ten years on the road he was ready to come back home to San Francisco to stay.

Melvin then started working at Shoreline Amphitheatre as a stagehand for what was left of Bill Graham Presents. In January 2005 he began to work as a journeyman stagehand for IATSE Local 107 until his passing in 2014.

He loved music and was an encyclopedia of knowledge regarding music. He enjoyed all of the different and eclectic jobs he performed in the music industry across the decades. Although it is my opinion, I think he was most proud of being a Journeyman Stagehand. He cherished being part of a crew that put the stage/show together for all to enjoy, even though it's backbreaking work! I loved listening to all the stories of the music and people that Melvin met and worked with in his lifetime.

I believe that Melvin was truly loved and adored by all who worked with him for his no- nonsense attitude and loving kindness to the newbies that came up under him. He believed that he was one of the lucky few that worked with and knew Bill Graham personally, sometimes sharing birthdays as they were only a day apart. They had a genuine friendship and love for one another; one cannot ask for more.

MICHAEL CARABELLO

My Bill Graham Moments in Time

1967: This is the moment Bill Graham met Carlos Santana and me when we were climbing up a pipe to sneak into the Fillmore West aka The Carousel to see Cream and the Paul Butterfield Blues Band in San Francisco.

I talked Carlos into trying to sneak into the venue because neither of us had any money at the time. I, of course, talked Carlos into going first into the climbing venture.

I said it would be better for me to be behind him to keep him from falling to the ground. But the truth of the matter is that I wanted him to go first because if someone was going to get caught sneaking in, it wasn't going to be me.

Our goal was to get to the top of the roof so that we would be able to enter through the fire escape. Between the ground to the roof there was a large pipe that would somewhat be our ladder. While climbing this pipe we would have to pass a large window. As we came upon the window, we noticed it was open and then someone leaned out to help us in, or should I say dragged us in. This window just happened to be located in someone's office. That someone was Bill Graham. We got caught!

The next moment involves our band meeting regarding Woodstock, the Ed Sullivan Show, Fillmore East and the Schaefer Beer Festival in Central Park.

The Santana Band was beginning to be accepted as an up and coming group that had the goods in the music scene. Believe me, we did not see it that way. We were just kicking ass and having fun. Stan Marcum was our manager at the time, and the band was notified to meet at Stan's home in Mill Valley, California to discuss our first road trip to New York for gigs at the Ed Sullivan Show, Fillmore East and Woodstock.

We were sitting on the carpet in Stan's living room when all of a sudden the front door opened and in walked Bill Graham. We were all polite but amazed at his arrival.

We were about to be schooled in the BG Music School of Hard Ball. He coached us, trying to guide us in a whole new world that we were getting ready to enter. He could foresee what was ahead of us before we even realized just what that could be. Little did we know that he was our messiah.

He spoke to us about how New York audiences are so different than San Francisco's:

New York audiences tend to sit down and judge how you entertain them, whereas San Francisco audiences dance and are more interested in having a good time. Of course, the only person really paying attention to what Bill was saying was Carlos. Bill was now our coach on our quest, and we were his dream band. It was a perfect dream come true, especially with Bill's love of Puerto Rican and Latin music. It was a win/win situation for us all.

This moment recalls when Bill Graham called me into his office.

The Santana Band went to New York City to do a three-day run at the Fillmore East. When I arrived in town, I went to visit my friend Jimi Hendrix at his apartment for a time out. There he was with the clothing designer Harron, hair stylist Finney and the model Betty Davis.

Later, during our sound check, I was summoned to see Bill in his office. As I walked into his office, he asked me to sit down and said, "Michael, I don't know how to say this, but I got a call from Miles

Davis last night and he told me to tell you that you had better stay away from his wife, Betty. Tell that fuckin' Carabello kid to stay away from my wife."

I looked at Bill and said, "Really? You need to tell Miles to tell his wife to stay away from me. I'm not the Chaser. She's the Chasee. Is that it? I have to go back to soundcheck." I walked out of his office as confidently as I walked in. Miles showed up that night at our Fillmore East show. From that moment on we were friends. I'm now proud to say that I didn't back down from his threats or Bill's.

This moment takes place many years later and is about Mimi Sanchez.

Mimi was my wife at the time of this story. Mimi and her cousin Cuca loved Latin dance and would attend Latin dance shows in San Francisco at the Saint Francis Hotel, the San Francisco Civic Auditorium, and California Hall on Polk Street. These venues hosted artists such as Tito Puente, Eddie Palmieri, Larry Harlow, the Fania All-Stars, Celia Cruz, and Ray Barretto.

Bill loved Salsa music and also attended many of these shows, taking Mimi and Cuca as dance partners. He was a great Salsa dancer. I think that this had something to do with his growing up in the Bronx in a Puerto Rican and Black neighborhood of NYC.

If you ever have the pleasure of viewing the Francis Ford Coppola movie Bugsy, you will catch a glimpse of Bill as Lucky Luciano dancing with Cuca. It's priceless.

A moment in time at Studio 54

Many moons ago while living in New York I started hanging out at Studio 54, the Power Station recording studio, the Village Vanguard, 55 Grand Street, the Reggae Lounge, and other places where artists and musicians hung out.

One night I went to see my friend Eric Gale a guitar player. He was playing at a club on the Upper West Side called Mikells. Someone mentioned to me that Miles Davis was downstairs talking to the club manager. I hadn't seen Miles in years and heard that he wasn't doing that well. Of course, I went downstairs and said to him, "Hey Miles, we meet again." He gave me the Miles cold stare for about 40 seconds, then said, "Fucking Carabello." We hooked up again and ended up hanging out for a week and a half together at his pad.

Miles was just about to put together his new band with Marcus Miller, Bill Evans, Michael Stern and Al Foster. The word on the street was that Bill Graham and Carlos Santana were always sending invitations to Miles to come to a Santana show on the East Coast. It just so happened that the next Saturday night Carlos was playing at the Savoy. I had departed the Santana band, but I was always invited and welcomed at a Santana show no matter where or when.

So, I talked Miles into going with me to the Savoy to see Carlos. We took a cab to the venue. Just as we are getting out of the cab, who did I see looking at me but Ron Delsener and the one and only, Bill Graham. Bill gives me that Bill look of "how the fuck did you do this?" Carlos and Bill could not believe it. Carabello brings Miles to see Santana at the Savoy. Unbelievable.

A moment in time during New York summer sessions

I always went to New York in the summer for session work and auditions. I would stay until November when winter would appear. I would then return to Marin County in the Bay Area to spend the holidays with my family.

I started to get a lot of session work with artists such as Irene Cara, George Benson, Jim Carroll, Ron Dante and Ahmet Ertegun. This session with Ahmet turned out to be with Chris Kimsey at the Power Station recording studio with the Rolling Stones on Tattoo You. I was also rehearsing with the Stones every weeknight at Studio Instrument Rentals on 52nd Street in NYC.

At the same time, I was hanging out with Miles who was getting ready to play the Savoy. I asked Charlie Watts if he would like to go with me to see Miles at the Savoy on Friday night. Charlie was so excited. I figured out what night we would have off from rehearsal, which thank goodness was a Friday night. I contacted who I needed to and got us on the guest list.

Friday night rolled around and I was getting ready for the evening out when my phone rang and it's Charlie asking very politely if it would be possible for him to bring a guest. So, of course, I said yes to his politeness. I asked him what name do we need to add to the list? He says, "Mick Jagger."

Off we all went to the Savoy and to watch Miles' set. After the show, Mick, Charlie and I all went backstage to hang out with the backstage scene. It was particularly great seeing Charlie Watts and Al Foster talking. After that we were off to Studio 54 to party and meet up with Ronnie Woods. This ended up being an all-nighter. Next stop at 3:30 a.m. was the Reggae Lounge off Canal at 8th Avenue and Hudson.

Now we've been up all night partying and going to clubs and it was about 5:30 a.m. when Mick decided to let the party continue at his condo on the Upper West Side at Central Park West. Mick, Charlie, Ronnie and I jumped into a cab to Mick's place. We were hanging out having some drinks and before you know it, it's 9:30 a.m.

The building doorman called Mick to say, "You have a guest waiting for you here. Would you like me to send them up?" Two minutes later there was a knock at the door. When Mick opened the door, in walked Bill Graham and Jerry Pompili. Bill was not looking very happy.

I looked at Charlie and Ronnie, said goodbye, and I exited stage left.

Thank you, Bill and Jerry Pompili.

A moment with Rita Gentry – My Manager

If you are wondering about my connection with Rita, here it is: I used to live with Rita's first cousins, Brad and Leslie Sexton, whom I knew from Balboa High School in San Francisco's Excelsior District. Leslie used to call Rita and tell her how mad she was at this guy (me) for stealing her Dippity-Do for my hair. LOL! We go way back before Bill Graham and The Fillmore.

We are family and you can't take that away.

We are not only family, but she has been my manager for the past four years.

Hello…Hello…Hello

In sitting down to write these moments in time for Rita, I realized that if it wasn't for Bill being in my life, I would not have had the honor of playing with rock and roll royalty, being inducted into the Rock and Roll Hall of Fame, playing with and really knowing numerous top of the line musicians and having so many adventures. I'll never forget, my continuous friendship with Carlos Santana, and most of all, my love and loyal friendship with the incomparable Mr. Bill Graham. Thank you, Bill, for putting me into the game.

MICHAEL COATS

One of the joys of my life was getting a BGP check. It meant to me I had cracked the shell and gotten in. Getting in was everything. It was a tight family and not everyone gets in.

My experiences with Bill and BGP looked kinda like this.

My first personal encounter with Bill was at Winterland when I was a teenager and I learned firsthand about blocking doorways/fire exits. Let's just say Bill made it clear to me it was a no- no in that not-so-calm Bill way. But I learned a valuable lesson then that guided me as I was producing shows.

And I picked up his accent. There were a number of folks that did "Bill" well, Harry Duncan maybe the best. But I can hold my own, with my favorite Bill-ism being, "What about me?"

I was fortunate to have Zohn Artman as a pal. I remember him taking me for my first visit to Masada, Bill's home, in that Cranapple red VW of his. He also got me into shows which was great!

Eventually I started getting gigs with BGP or its assorted offshoots. I would do almost anything, though PR is what I do.

But I did a Stones runner gig at Candlestick and broke my hand. Bill paid the bill.

My first PR gig was Simon and Garfunkel at Oakland Coliseum. Then came the opening of Wolfgang's, Bill's nightclub in San Francisco, which was a day Bill and I spent driving around doing interviews in my 1962 Mercedes. I'm so glad it started after each stop.

In 1984 I went to work with Bruce Cohn and did many gigs with BGP with Night Ranger and, of course, the Doobies. I remember a particular day when Bill was taking a bunch of bands, including the Doobs, to Moscow and I made the mistake of answering the phone when Bill called and Bruce was out. This was before cell phones. Let's just say Bill wasn't happy that Bruce wasn't available!

Other gigs I cherished were the last Mountain Aire gig with the Doobies and Huey Lewis, working for Dell Furano at Winterland Productions for a number of years; doing some gigs with Bill Graham Special Events was fun too.

In closing, when Bruce and I started his charity concerts for his winery, the very first one we did was at the Sonoma High School football field with Graham Nash. I suggested to Bruce that we get Jerry Pompili to stage announce and do intros.

Bill would have loved it!

MICHAEL THOMPSON

I'm a former Bluecoat overnighter and founding drummer for the band Dog Beaver. I've got a couple of stories.

So, as an avid attendee at Winterland in the early 1970s I was familiar with who Bill Graham was. Had never met him. My buddy and I spent the night sleeping on the sidewalk at Winterland the evening of December 30, 1972. I woke up with typical aches associated with sidewalk sleeping and bourbon. I see Dead Heads walking down the sidewalk with steaming bowls of soup, chunks of French bread and coffee. I retrace their steps to find a small soup kitchen set up on the corner of Post and Steiner. I wait my turn in line and when it's my turn, Bill Graham serves me.

He is in the tent with a hippie chick and they are both working it, but it is Bill that serves me. Anybody who gets up before me to fix and serve me breakfast is AOK in my book. I've been a fan of his ever since.

When my high school buddy Steve Block said he could get me a job with BGP I jumped at the chance. I started the first season at Shoreline Amphitheatre. I worked my way up to overnight security with Mick Jones and Steve and Kenny Briggs. Best job ever! Still get to see the Dead and get paid to watch the gear and house while everyone else is gone.

So, we are doing the overnights at Autzen Stadium in Eugene, Oregon. The run is over and its load out time. I'm supervising the crew and not really much for me to do. Anne Scheer asks if I can give Bill and her a ride to the airport. I agree immediately. How cool is this. So,

I wait by the van and load the bags up. I've got Bill riding shotgun, his son Alex Graham, Steve Killer Kahn, Anne Scheer and I'm pretty sure Bob Barsotti also. Now, not being a runner, I have no idea that there are directions to the airport in the production office. As I pull out onto the surface street I ask, "Which way to the airport?" Bill bellows, "You wait until now to ask that question?" I replied that I figured since you guys had been there you would know the way. Needless to say, it was not a pleasant drive.

Bill wanted to leave Eugene early so they could fly over Crater Lake. I had to stop at a gas station, get gas and ask directions. Got lost. It was dark by the time I dropped them off at the airport. Alex attempted to be the peacemaker, leaning from the back seat between his dad and me for much of the trip. Not my best moment.

When U2 played Justin Herman Plaza in San Francisco I was giving breaks to Bluecoats. I come up to the entrance of the back-stage pass area which went out onto the Embarcadero. Steve Block and three other Bluecoats are working this spot. I tell Steve to take a break. Now people are tearing the caution tape down around the trucks and going where we don't want them to go. I step up to reset the caution tape. While I am doing this the two other Bluecoats working this area disappear. I hear from behind me, "I pay all of you and I've gotta do your job?" Bill is working the pass area now. So, I stand right next to him, he leaves, and I don't move an inch until Steve Block returns.

There was one time at Shoreline when I was working front of stage. All the Bluecoats had to pick up the trash on the lawn after the show. But my job, front of stage, had to stay in position until the house was cleared of patrons. Lucky me.

About eight rows back from front of stage was a group of about four or five frat boys and a couple of girls. Bill came to the edge of the stage looking out and surveying his domain and smiling. One of these young men yelled out to Bill, "Hey Bill! How come the beers cost eight bucks," obviously challenging Bill and looking to gain some credibility with his group. Bill stepped off the stage into the seats, like the giant that he was, and gave the entire group a lesson in economics: wholesale prices, vendor wages, sales, tax, employee salaries, profit, etc., etc. This went on for five minutes in Bill's booming voice. When he finished, he just turned and walked away, certain that he had educated them all. They then all left very quietly out of the venue. It was so fucking funny. A show after a show. Thanks Bill!

I really was a good Bluecoat. But these are my best Bill stories. I love him as a man and a boss. After SFX and Clear Channel took over, people asked me how I liked working for the new bosses. My response was always, "I work for Bill."

MICHAEL ZAGARIS

There are so many stories I could tell about Bill Graham. One especially memorable night was in April, 1970 when Miles Davis opened for the Grateful Dead at the Fillmore. I scored what I thought was LSD on Telegraph Avenue in Berkeley. The guy that sold it to me said, "This is strong stuff, only take half or I can't be responsible." Like he would anyway. I was having a bad week, it was raining that night, I was in line to go in, and the girl behind me told me how her boyfriend was shot across the street the week before. Wanting to escape the reality of the present I decided to take the whole thing.

I started feeling the effects shortly before Miles came on to play his Bitches Brew album. Halfway through the set I noticed that as tightly packed as the crowd was, suddenly it seemed as if there was a wide moat of space forming around me. I was trying to give my money away and people were anxiously looking away. I decided to leave, but when I got to the stairs the Hells Angels were coming up and I freaked. I turned around and fled into the kitchen where I ran into Bill. "Bill, you have to help me." Bill grabbed both of my shoulders and looked me in the eye and said, "Michael, you took LSD at Bill Graham's Fillmore West?" I said, "No, no, Bill I was dosed." He turned me around, "Come with me," pushing me inside his office.

"Stay here, don't leave," shutting the door. Bill's office was small, and every bit of wall and ceiling space was covered with psychedelic Fillmore posters. I felt they were all closing in on me, so I retreated under Bill's desk into a fetal position. The door opened a few minutes later and Bill walked in with Johnny Walker, his elderly door man.

Johnny was in his late sixties, a brother from the Fillmore who greeted the crowds nightly with banter like, "We're gonna cure the sick, we're gonna raise the dead, we're gonna grow some hair on a bald man's head! Have a lovely day!" Then he would hand you a poster for next week's show and an apple as you left.

Bill had brought him in to talk me down. Johnny knelt down in front of me, pulled out a half pint of old Mr. Boston gin that he had already been imbibing from and proceeded to regale me with stories of his days in Alaska as a fur trapper. It would have been quite an education straight, but on acid it was a whole other twisted reality. By the time the show ended I had begun to come down a bit and as I left Bill's office, he looked at me the way your father or uncle would look at you after you had disappointed them. He just shook his head and walked away.

MICHELLE FRINK

I first met Bill Graham at his house in Larkspur where he hosted and generously paid for my sister, Molly Frink's marriage to Steve Rigney. I had no idea then how he would affect my family. My son, Stephen was driving the guests up and down to Bill's house from an area where the guests were to park. Stephen had already been hired by Molly as a Bluecoat and he loved the work.

A year later my marriage was over and Molly suggested coming to BGP to work security. That decision changed my life. The following are a very few highlights of my work in rock and roll security.

At one of the earliest concerts at the Oakland Coliseum at about the halfway point, Steve Rigney, who was the head of Security, came and told me that Stephen had been pushed off a large equipment case on rollers backstage by a stagehand! He had fallen down on some upturned rollers. We went immediately to the hospital and after hours and many tests found out that there were no internal injuries. Bill was very upset by the trauma that Stephen had suffered because he felt that everyone should feel safe backstage. He advocated for Stephen so that he got what he deserved.

Backstage at a Laguna Seca concert weekend, I was able to thank Bill personally.

Then there was my first Bruce Springsteen stadium concert. I was in the payroll trailer with Molly, which was down the hill behind the stage. She got a radio call that a crowd was gathering behind the fence where you could see backstage and the show. They were blocking the path to the exit. So she sent me up to help clear the area. When I got up there Bill was pacing and yelling for people to move, then the police arrived. He yelled at them too.

Bruce's fans, many of which were Yuppies, resisted. The police were not used to dealing with this type of situation. Then as I started talking and moving people, seven or eight Bluecoats joined me. We cleared the area in 15 minutes.

My first time as a supervisor was Gate B at the Oakland Coliseum for the Rolling Stones Steel Wheels Tour, which happened shortly after the 1989 earthquake. B Gate was next to the BART train station so we got a major influx of persons every time a train unloaded. Bill was watching the gate for a time as he often did. My baptism of fire.

As the Day Supervisor for a Dave Matthews concert at AT&T Park in San Francisco, I was giving one of my Bluecoats at Dave's dressing room a break when Dave walked up and put out his hand and said, "Hi, my name is David Matthews." It was the only time that an entertainer formally introduced themselves to me while securing their dressing room. I was totally impressed!

Running the backstage for the Rolling Stones at the Oakland Stadium, I had to stop Jerry Garcia from going up the stairs into Mick Jagger's workout area. He was looking for the bathroom and not too pleased with me having stopped him! He said, "Well, where the fuck do I go?" I directed him to the nearest men's room.

Shortly later, backstage at the Greek Theatre in Berkeley, I looked into Jerry Garcia's dressing room and saw that he had fallen asleep with a burning cigarette between his fingers… the fingers he used to play his guitar! So, I tiptoed in and very carefully removed it. He was okay with it.

Miss Barbra Streisand was the only performer I saw who carpeted the entire concrete floor of the venue (in this case the San Jose Sharks stadium). I supervised backstage for her show. As I walked her back to go onstage, a Bluecoat called me over and pointed to a mouse that was scurrying across the floor. Luckily, Barbra did not see it.

My absolute best supervising experience was the day call at the Bill Graham Civic for the week of the visit of His Holiness the 14th Dalai Lama in 2007 with Tom Howard. It was challenging because security was extremely tight, as they feared His Holiness might be harmed. There were three times that people could enter during the day, which meant staffing the entrance three times for both entrance and exit through metal detectors. All bags were searched every time. I will never forget how the Dalai Lama interacted with people. He was loving, kind, but also playful. When asked what his favorite pastime was during one of the evening events, he laughed and said, "gossip." I just loved that answer.

I worked for 20 years in this business and now each time I hear a song or watch a band, it transports me back to the concert I worked and the people I loved. The imprint is on my heart.

P.S. My son, Stephen Feener, is now the President of Experiences at Superfly Productions.

MICHELLE ZARIN

How I met Bill: Bill loved all kinds of music (as I do) and loved putting different types together. I always thought that was unique and wonderful. Nobody else did that. He booked Tito Puente at Winterland. Don't remember the other act, but it was not Latin. I went to the gig with Tito and at sound check Bill was in a corner of the stage talking with his crew and dancing to himself. I saw he could dance and was on clave, essentially meaning on the beat of two. So, I asked him to dance. He gave me sort of a dirty look so I walked away.

Now it's show time. Unfortunately, Tito played a cha-cha, which was too slow for that crowd and room. I was on stage behind the big risers. Jimmy, his lead trumpet and main man, turned around and shouted down to me, "Michelle, get out there and dance!" I looked up at him shaking my head no. He shouted again, "Get out there and dance! We're dying out here!"

So I danced onto the stage in front of the band. Tito dropped his sticks and started to dance with me. He was a great dancer. The audience loved it and cheered. I went behind the risers again and Bill came over to me and asked me to dance, very sweetly. We danced. We danced great together. That was the beginning of my friendship with Bill Graham. We both loved all kinds of music, but our hearts and souls were with Latin music!

Another story: Bill and I shared a very deep love for Latin music and dance, today called Salsa. Back then it was just Latin music. He was a beautiful dancer and that compliment doesn't come easy from me. One day I decided to promote a Latin gig myself. I did Eddie Palmieri and Oscar de Leon at the Gift Center in San Francisco. I knew it would do well and it did. Sometime later I did it again with only Oscar de Leon at Cesar's Latin Club in the Mission District of San Francisco. My backer backed out.

I called Bill and asked him for $15,000 in case I needed help in paying the band. He yelled at me and then said that he would give me a week and if I couldn't get it anywhere by Friday, he'd give it to me.

I had never asked Bill for anything before. I called him on Thursday saying that I got the money from my father, but thank you anyway. I couldn't understand why he sounded so surprised.

The show was a sell out and somebody called the police because they said it was too crowded. Bill was there and prevented me from getting arrested. He worked the firemen and the police like crazy. He climbed the stairs in a sweat to see me and Colleen Kennedy sitting on the floor counting cash. He said that this was the toughest thing he ever had to do and then said, "If you want to start promoting Latin gigs, I will back you all the way." Instantly I said, "No way!" This incident had scared me.

Police, jail, not this Jewish girl from New York.

I hadn't thought about this for many years until now. We could have had a Latin Division at BGP and Bill would have loved it with all his heart. He told me one of the proudest moments of his life was winning the Wednesday night dance contest at the Palladium Latin Ballroom in New York City.

I understood, as did Tito Puente and Eddie Palmieri when I told them. They both respected and loved him very much.

I think of him every single day. I hate helicopters.

MICK BRIGDEN

Tour Manager, Stage Manager, Lighting Designer, Creative Director and Band Manager 1975–1991 Bill Graham Presents 1991–1998 Bill Graham Management

I've got many Bill Graham stories, but the one that comes to mind is: July 1981, New York City (always a great place to be with Bill, from the Carnegie Deli to the Garden, always a buzz).

Walking up Seventh Avenue with Bill and Jan Simmons at 2:00 a.m. while setting up the Stones 1981 U.S. Tour. A stoned hippie sees us and calls out Bill's name. "Hey Bill, good to see you man! Wish I could get some tickets for the Stones."

Bill walks over to the guy and stuffs a pair of Stones tickets in his shirt pocket, pats him on the back, and says, "Your lucky day!" The guy's eyes grow as big as baseballs and he does a complete backflip on the sidewalk landing on his feet. Absolutely priceless.

MICK JONES III aka Mick Flaire

I am listening to the Grateful Dead's concert from the Calaveras County Fairgrounds in Angel's Camp, California on August 23, 1987 as I write this story.

My name is Mick Jones and I have held a few job positions at FM Productions, Winterland Productions, Bill Graham Presents and SFX Entertainment/Clear Channel Entertainment/Live Nation since starting with the company on April 15, 1977.

When I started with the company back then it was named FM Productions and Bill Graham's personal business card read "Boss" under his name. I started out working at Bill Graham's Hayward, California poster and T-shirt store, which was also known as the Rock Shop, selling Fillmore posters, handbills, T-shirts and other memorabilia. We also sold tickets to local events, such as Bill Graham's Day on the Green concerts at the Oakland-Alameda County Stadium by way of the Bay Area Seating Service, referred to as BASS tickets.

The branch of FM Productions known as Winterland Productions was named after the Winterland Arena in San Francisco where Bill Graham had been producing shows that were too large for the

Fillmore from 1966 to 1978. He later opened up another poster and T-shirt store in San Francisco at 1333 Columbus Avenue in North Beach where I also worked.

On August 4, 1979 I began a 13-year run until 1992 as part of Bill's concert security staff known as the Bluecoats.

Also, during that time I was his Assistant Office Manager at the BGP office at 201 11th Street in San Francisco until a fire displaced us and we moved to 260 Fifth Street, San Francisco.

I also worked at Bill's first dance hall, the original Fillmore in two separate stints: the first time as the day office guy in 1988 and then again working security in 2011.

To say that I have a zillion Bill Graham stories that I could tell would be an understatement considering the 24 years that I worked with Bill, not to mention the numerous encounters with him just as a concert-goer for nine years before actually working for him.

And now for my favorite Bill Graham story. During the summer of 1987 Bill Graham and the Grateful Dead had taken some of the Bluecoats on tour with them to some select venues outside of Northern California to work security, including City Park in Telluride, Colorado, Autzen Stadium in Eugene, Oregon, and Angels Stadium in Anaheim, California.

At Angels Stadium where the California Angels major league baseball team played, the Bluecoats were brought down there to work alongside the house security staff for a tour date with the Grateful Dead and Bob Dylan. About an hour after the show was over the only people left on the field were the stadium staff, Grateful Dead crew-members, BGP production staff and all of us Bluecoats. Bill had been throwing a football around the field to various people and then all of a sudden Bill sees me just standing around watching the proceedings and hollers to me, "Mick Jones, go long!"

Now I'm thinking to myself at that moment, "Noooooo, are you kidding me?!!, oh please, don't do this to me!" You have to realize something about Bill Graham: he has one of the most competitive personalities that you'll ever see in a person. One of Bill's favorite metaphorical analogies was dropping the ball or baton, or whatever, which he would equate to once he turned it over to you he expected you to get the job done. Failure to do so was not an option. So, here I was about to live out that metaphor in real time, in a pass or fail situation. Bill then reared back and fired the football about 40 yards in my direction, as I'm running at a full sprint across the baseball outfield grass. It was like I was in a Hollywood movie, and not the "spill the wine" kind! That football seemed like it hung in the air for an eternity in slow motion. And then as the ball descended towards my outstretched hands, I reached out and caught it, pulled it into my chest and clutched that thing as if my life depended on it!

For all practical purposes, in my mind, it really did. After making (to me, anyhow) what I thought was a miraculous reception from "The Boss," I jogged back the 40 yards to Bill, totally out of breath, but trying hard not to show it and just handed the ball back to him, just like an NFL player would to a referee with all the reverence in which it was thrown to me. Bill then gave me a hearty handshake and said to me probably the most encouraging words I could have ever expected, "Nice catch, Mick. Good job!"

The bottom line is this: I didn't miss the catch or drop the ball. At that moment and still to this day, it means everything to me to make that play and to not let down "The Boss," my surrogate father and friend for life.

As of this writing I am still the longest tenured employee of the company that Bill Graham started in 1966 and about to finish my 42nd consecutive year and will begin my 16th concert season as a stagehand with the company on April 15, 2019.

This is my story and I'm sticking to it. Cheers!

MOLLY FRINK

Bluecoat/Security Administrator with Bill Graham Presents 1977 to 1989 His Power

I don't remember when I officially met Bill Graham, but I do remember the first time I saw him. Brian Auger asked me to volunteer for Bette Midler at Bimbo's 365 Club in San Francisco on November 29, 1977. This was my first show and I didn't know what to expect. Steve and I were standing in the lobby with Stan and Alberta Damas, when all of a sudden we heard shouting. Before I could see what was happening, Stan grabbed Alberta and me and pushed us into the bar area on the other side of the fish tank. We were quite put off, not because he felt the need to protect us women folk (although it was a factor), but because we didn't want to miss the fight that was brewing. Through our blurred fish tank view, we saw Bill and Ms. Midler's manager, Aaron Russo, facing off, rolling up sleeves, taking off expensive watches and yelling at each other. It was a sight to behold. The fight fizzled out and fortunately no one got hurt that night. It was the first time I witnessed the strength and power of my new boss.

His Humor

The Old Waldorf, Ricky Nelson 1980s Nan O'Shea

Many bigwigs were sitting at the big tables across from the bar, including Bill, some of the Barsottis and some management types. Bill invited my best friend Nan and me to join them. The lovely Old Waldorf waitresses were taking drink orders around the table. Bill was buying.

When it was my turn to order he asked, "What do you want?" I turned to him and said, "I don't drink! I'll have water." After a very shocked look on his face, as per usual when I say that (still have never been drunk), and much back and forth, doubting phrases, and gasps he jumped up from the table. He went over to the bar. I had no idea what he was doing, so I turned to join the conversation. Soon over my shoulder he presented me, waiter style, with a white napkin. On the napkin were a matchbook, an onion, a cherry, an olive, a slice of lime and a celery stick. "Here," he says, "Since you don't drink, I brought you everything free from the bar."

Later that same evening, after everyone had a great laugh at my expense, Bill set his sights on my friend Nan. She had never been around Bill before and she was a little bit shy (not her usual vivacious self.) We were all laughing and chatting, enjoying the festivities when once again Bill sprang up from his chair. This time Bill said, "I think Nan should meet Ricky Nelson!" As soon as the words were out of his mouth, he was off. We were all like, what? A few minutes later, sure enough, here comes Bill with Ricky Nelson in tow. He introduces him to the entire table and especially to Nan. Many hellos all around. Maybe Nan needed to meet Ricky Nelson. Ricky Nelson didn't need to meet Nan! I've never seen a singer so shy. He stayed only a few minutes and politely scurried back to his dressing room. Nan's face was beet red. Laughter ensued.

His Generosity

In October 1983, Bill opened his home to our family for Steve's and my wedding. It was a special day, mostly because it was the only day on the calendar when staff and Bluecoats could attend. Bill was returning from a movie shoot, and Steve and I were getting ready for the ceremony in Bill's bedroom (yes, we used the bathtub!) Steve went out to check on the set up which was perfectly prepared except for the rain. Fillmore Fingers was setting up the turkey feast, when Bill walks into his bedroom. I am alone at this point with my robe on. After a few hellos, how are you Bill asks if I am hungry. That is always a "yes."

Bill runs off to get what I assumed would be a cookie (not that kind) or something.

He brings back a red checkered picnic table cloth and spreads it on the bed, gets the silverware and cloth napkins, and then brings in a full roasted chicken with salad and bread. Of course, Tom and Gary, Bill's housekeepers, had prepared the food for Bill! To me, a nervous bride, it was generous and thoughtful.

We sat down and ate together like it wasn't any big deal! I was getting married in an hour. Or maybe because of that. He made our wedding special, along with the BGP family.

I asked him what he liked to do with his time off. He said, just this: Lying on the floor, newspaper in front of me, and the game on. Not sure what game was on, but later on all the men except Steve were huddled in his study to watch it.

Please Note: These stories are a very small sample of Bill's generosity and influence in my life. He was bigger- than-life, and also gentle and kind. He could be scary, but never raised his voice to me. He was my first spiritual teacher and a friend. He helped me in anonymous ways because of my disabilities and I will be forever in his debt.

Cheers, with water and everything free from the bar.

MONIQUE AGERTER-JOHNSON

I started working for Bill Graham Presents in 1989 at Shoreline Amphitheatre in the landscaping and irrigation department. In the same season, I started doing load out only for production and landscaping during the day. I ended up getting pulled out of the landscaping and irrigation department to go into the production department only, which became a wonderful move for me. That's where I found my family. There were many times that they could have gotten rid of me, but there was something they saw in me, but I just couldn't see it yet. Eventually, my Bill Graham family pulled it out of me and I saw that I was worth it.

There are so many great memories from doing shows at Shoreline, festivals and Days on the Green. We treated Shoreline as if it was our home. One thing that definitely stands out in my mind is that I felt very honored to be asked to do a task after Bill passed away, which was to go to his home with two other gentlemen to help in taking apart the props that were used for New Year's Eve shows with the Grateful Dead. We took the Grateful Dead skull apart, the Mushroom and the World and brought them all down to Shoreline backstage where they sit today. I felt very honored to be a part of that. I'm so very grateful to be a part of the Bill Graham Family.

MORTY WIGGINS

Office Schlep and Vice President of Bill Graham Management. I started in the mid-1980s to the late 1990s, and then again for a couple of years in 2000-plus.

My fondest connections with Bill were around our being Jewish. In the Eighties, Bill produced a series of high-profile benefit concerts and tours. The last significant one (after Live Aid and Amnesty) was a weekend of concerts titled Crackdown to combat the drug epidemic hitting New York City at the time. To rally the music industry around the cause, Bill hosted a kickoff breakfast at the Carnegie Deli. All the heavy hitters were there: Frank Barsalona, Walter Yetnikoff, Ron Delsener and about a dozen other music vets. After the meeting, Walter stayed behind and sat down with Bill at one of the restaurant tables in the back. I was a fly on the wall as they spoke warmly together in Yiddish while laughing, much to my delight.

Later that summer I was working with Bill in New York on this same Crackdown concert. It was a difficult time as the industry was "benefitted out" and didn't really want to hear about contributing or cooperating. Bill decided we would take the weekend off and go up to the Concord Resort in the Catskills. Michael Klenfner and his wife joined us. I rented a Chrysler convertible and we drove up from the city. When we got there Bill was treated like a favorite son returning home for a visit. It was right out of a Philip Roth novel.

When Bill decided to stage a rally in Union Square in San Francisco to protest then-President Reagan's visit to the Bitburg Cemetery, I volunteered to help. I could not have been prouder to work for him and the company. Shortly thereafter, the BGP office at 201 11th Street in San Francisco was destroyed by arson. Some things never change.

Bill and I conspired to have the Neville Brothers perform in Israel. I traveled with the band and Bill joined us there. Bill broke one of his cardinal rules by having his sister and her family sit on the side of the stage in folding chairs in view of the public.

Bill was not a religious person, but he was proud of being Jewish.

N

NANCY KERLIN SOLYAN

Like many of us that worked for Bill Graham, we have so many fond memories and stories of him, the staff and the sheer amazing camaraderie we had with each other. I am so honored and was so lucky to have been part of that team from 1986-1996, and continue to work for Another Planet Entertainment to this day at Outside Lands.

I had a few jobs at BGP. I was initially hired as a security guard because I had heard that Bill, Steve Wozniak and Anne Getty were going to open an amphitheater. I had to apply! I was 19. It was Depeche Mode, my first show, Shoreline's second show. I missed out on Julio Iglesias because it was my sister's birthday, June 29, 1986. But as fate had it, I met Chung Kuo my first day at Shoreline working the backstage fence line. He was pivotal in getting me many different projects and positions at BGP, essentially got me "in" to the BGP world. Getting my first official admin job as a receptionist at Shoreline, then box office attendant, then Terri Lynch's (Anderson) assistant.

I was at Shoreline for three full summer years. That is where I got a lot of my hands-on experience in production and operations, and I considered Terri one of my mentors. I soon got a promotion and went to the main office in 1989 as the payroll and personnel manager still working shows, but now with the Barsotti brothers as a production assistant. I worked countless Grateful Dead shows, Days on the Green, and every big show we did from 1989–1994. I worked with many of the production teams at BGP throughout the years too. There was Tom Howard, Ron Bergman, Nigel James, Dan Choi, etc.

I was not close to Bill, but he knew who I was! I paid his beloved staff! In those days we didn't have auto-deposit so I was tasked to walk to each person's desk or office and hand them their payroll check, never putting it in their inbox. That is how I know so many of the folks who worked in the office in those days. I viewed Bill in a light of admiration and a bit of a schoolgirl crush. He was handsome, intense, forthright and so inspiring to be around. What's that word? Infectious! He was a rockstar to me and to all of us!

It has taken me some time to process and figure out what I wanted say. It was a very hard year for me last year (2017) as I recovered from cancer. I wasn't sure what I had to say was important but then here I am writing. What I know is that experience was priceless, and I am happy to share my thoughts with you. I learned so much from so many people in that organization and beyond. I am in touch with a lot of them to this day. Rita Gentry is one of them, a rockstar!

In her 70s and kicking it like no other person. I love that woman! She, along with other Bitch Goddesses - they too were my mentors. I looked up to them. Gosh, there are so many stories there too! Sending out big love to you all, wherever you are!

I decided today I have two stories to tell. The first one is the first day I saw Bill Graham and the second story is the last day I saw Bill Graham.

I am 15, February 1982. I went to the Cow Palace in Daly City, California with a bunch of friends to see AC/DC. I think this was a multiple show run for the band. I think we went the first night and it was a school night, but we went anyway. My parents let me go with my girlfriends and some boys we hardly knew! Oh, the things we did! It was crowded and I was young and dumb and didn't really know that we should have picked a place to meet in case someone got lost! Well, that someone was me!

Soon after arriving at the venue I lost my friends, so I was by myself for about two hours. Thank goodness I found them. I at least had the forethought to go to the entrance and wait and one of my girlfriends showed up! But in that two hours, I was people watching, being observant to a fault! I wanted to find and be with my friends but something, someone kept my interest for the time being.

From drunken young kids barely able to walk to that fanboy buying merchandise and running back in to catch the song, to the friendly security guards willing to help me find my friends to…hmmm? This older, yet warm man speaking in this very low tone to kids with a gregarious attitude but super friendly. Who is that? He was at the entrance helping the guards using the verbiage to "open your bags and put your hands up in the air" so they could pat them down and check their bags.

I was drawn to this man. He went outside at one point as I watched from afar, how he dealt with a ticket problem. It looked and felt like a legitimate issue and he was there to make them happy and gave them two free tickets. "Miracles" in the Grateful Dead world. Back then you bought your tickets with cash at ticket outlets like Ticketmaster. He came back in and the BGP staffers all looked upon him with fondness and it was a pleasant and happy environment, sometimes intense at moments, but that person was Bill Graham. I remember telling myself that day that I am going to work for that man! Almost exactly four years later, I did! I was 19!

I am 24. As you know, there are many traditions in the world and some of us had our own personal ones, albeit not for BGP's Human Resources ears! But a handful of us had a ritual at the main office of BGP. Every Friday at 4:20 p.m., when KFOG plays The Toyes', "Smoke Two Joints", we would congregate on the rooftop of the offices or parking lots and greet each other with, "What time is it?" and smoke two joints!

On Friday, October 25, 1991 at around 4:20 p.m., three of us (I was with Maggie and Mick) went to the main parking lot. Done and talking, we were getting a little soaked as it was a misty early evening, not sure from rain or fog, but it was wet. My last image of Bill was Melissa Gold and him driving in his beautiful champagne colored convertible Mercedes Benz headed toward Market Street on Fifth Street with their hoodies on. We yelled something to them to get their attention, us waving. In return, both of their hands waving back at us as the top of his car pulled back into place to keep them dry. He had just come out of the building's only parking space. This would be the last time we would see him.

It's quite a nice way to remember him.

NANCY YOUNG

The Saga of Mouse

I got my dream job at Bill Graham Presents, a rock and roll office, working for a living legend and surrounded by an amazing family. I worked at BGP for 20-plus years and it was one of the greatest experiences of my life. My name is Nancy, but people used to call me Mouse. If you called and asked for Mouse, they'd put your call right through to me.

It was my extreme good fortune to get this job in 1985. I knew Elena Pena through her cousin. When Elena told me there was an opening, I interviewed and got hired.

In 1979, I'd volunteered with the San Francisco Mime Troupe. I learned that Bill got his start as a promoter of the Mime Troupe because they'd been denied a permit to perform in the park and that launched his career.

Bill was the master of promoters of rock and roll. Organization skills, drive, chutzpah and relationships with the musicians are how he got the job done. One time when I was backstage at Shoreline Amphitheatre, Bill asked me to make sure that Tracy Chapman got something to eat, which I did. People used to say that you were nobody until Bill yelled at you, but he never yelled at me, so I was in a class of my own.

Somehow a concept was created called the Bitch Goddesses of whom Rita Gentry is the once and future queen plus Jan, Sherill and Jackie. One day we took a limo to the Warfield Theatre where we had a photo-op with Spinal Tap. Thank you, Ms. Shelley Lazar for your part in making this happen for all of us BGP ladies.

There was so much love in the company. As far as events, the whole company once went to Santa Cruz Boardwalk where Bill rented the whole boardwalk for us for a day. Apart from that, we also had field trips to go bowling and a softball game. Once we went to his house that he called Masada, where we had his sister Ester's famous chopped chicken liver.

Every New Year's Eve there would be a parade at different venues, which were tribal events. Bill would dress as Father Time. We had another event called New Orleans by the Bay, which took place at Shoreline and at times Halloween spectaculars. Our office parties were, in and of themselves, amazing. It was there that Kevin Burns from BG Management called the 401k plan the 401ky plan. At the office I once heard Roger Clark say, "My memory is just a memory," and I've been quoting him ever since.

My memory is just a memory, but I hope these few memories of mine bring some joy to your heart.

NARADA MICHAEL WALDEN

Bill was kind to me and liked my music. We first met when the Mahavishnu Orchestra played Winterland for the first time. We played there about three different times, once also with Jeff Beck.

He once asked me to produce The Neville Brothers. It didn't quite work out at that time. We also met in his office a few times to share ideas about a solo career.

The below shot was at his home with his new remote in hand. He was very proud of his painting that he had hiding his TV. The picture/painting would rise up, showing the big screen hidden TV. He got a crack-up showing me this after we performed outside on his lawns for Barbara Boxer. It was Clarence Clemons and my band together. Big fun!! I also met and hung out with his son at this occasion.

Bill was my friend!

He was always up front, honest, and liked life to be uplifting. I enjoyed that he shared his heart with me and he dug my spirit too!

Long live Bill Graham! Our mentor and brother! Bringing it all together! Lovingly, Narada Michael Walden

NEIL MARQUIS

The first time I saw Bill Graham was when my sister, Bea Oliver, got me a job as a Bluecoat for the Rolling Stones event. I started work at 6:00 a.m. on the day of the show and was assigned to line duty in the parking lot and I got tear-gassed.

After being sent to Rock Med I was sent inside to work one of the wings that went out into the audience. I was in heaven! I was on a springy piece of wood between the scaffolding and just before the show started, who climbs up beside me…Bill! He introduced himself and shook my hand and thanked me for being there.

A few minutes later a guy in the crowd in front of us called Bill an asshole. What does he do? He jumps over the wall into the audience to confront the guy. I didn't know what to do, so I jumped over too. By the time I pushed my way through the crowd, Bill had already made a friend with the guy and was shaking his hand. He then talked to several different people and then made his way over to the wall. I gave him a boost back to the top of the wall. He climbed back over and I walked out to the end of the wing to the pass gate and spent the rest of the night on the wall listening to the Rolling Stones.

NICK NICORA

How Fillmore Fingers Began

For my birthday, July 14 in 1974, my then-girlfriend (and now my loving wife of 39 years) Joanmarie, treated me to a backstage show at the Day on the Green. I asked how she got the tickets as very few people were backstage — we were looking out at 55,000 people from the bleachers. Crazy! She mentioned that Dave Furano, the President of Bill Graham Presents was her father's godson. Who knew?

Well, a few years later after moving on from Bellarmine High School to the University of Chico State, I asked Joanmarie if I could get a meeting with Dave to discuss acquiring a band for a party at my fraternity house Phi Kappa Tau at 611 West Fifth Street in Chico. I had spent most of my high school and the beginning of college throwing large parties. So, of course, I decided to pick it up a bit and get a major live band. Not just your local cover band, but the real deal. To my amazement she set it up the meeting at 11th and Howard in San Francisco — the BGP home office.

I arrived at the office and was quickly put in front of Dave Furano, where I asked if I could acquire a band for a party. After the laughter subsided, I was asked if I would like to work for BGP. Dave said someone who had enough guts to ask for something like that might be a good employee. Later, actually a few years ago, Dave informed me that my soon-to-be father-in-law asked him to give me a job as he believed

I was going to ask his daughter to marry me. He then explained to me the that promoters have local rights to different regions like Chico.

Dave expressed that I would have to deal with a promoter named Roy Dubrow. I was also informed of the potential cost of such an endeavor. Well, long story short, I accepted the offer to work at an event of Dave's choosing.

A few weeks later, I received a call from someone who I assumed was Dave's assistant, and was asked if I would like to work the Day on the Green concert set for April 26, 1976. Of course, I was scheduled to rush my fraternity that week as I was a pledge and had to tell my friends that I would not be able to participate. Luckily, my friends, being the great friends they were, moved the pledge date so I could work the show. When I showed up at the concert at seven in the morning, I was brought into the production trailer where Dave was set up. He told me my job was to clean the backstage. So off I went, picking up every piece of garbage I could find for the next 10 hours. I knew I had cleaned as much as I could, so I asked Dave if there was anything else I could do. We then walked around to check my work. Dave said it looked like Disneyland. Being a big Disney person, I was happy with his analogy.

I was then given the job of making sure all the beverage stations around the backstage area were full and ready to go. I made a few changes, working with the local beer company—putting refrigerated water coolers around, as well as placing jockey boxes with keg beer in select locations. Most people at that time had never seen the easy-flow beer dispensers, as they were new portable technology and not known, so it became quite the conversation to not have to pump the keg. Well, that led into making the breakfast table in the tunnel of the Coliseum: I started by putting out fresh Danish pastries and dough-nuts from my favorite locations in Oakland, and of course, that led to toasters and electric grills for bacon and pancakes, which was a major hit with the riggers who were first on the job.

My big break came when a semi-truck was blocking the ramp going down to the stage and the driver was nowhere to be found with the keys. I remember Dave and Bill Graham yelling, "Does anyone have the keys? Can you start this semi?" I walked over to Dave and said, "I think I can start it."

He looked at me with a confused face and told me to go for it. I went back to the breakfast area and looked in a road case and grabbed a few pieces of small wire. I made my way back and went under the dashboard and pulled off the back of the key socket. I then used my wires to jump the ignition and the truck fired right up. As I was coming out of the truck, I finally came face-to-face with Bill as he had seen me. I'm sure Dave had told him who I was, but we never connected.

"How did you learn how to do that?" he asked.

I looked at him. "I grew up in Oakland." Then I walked away.

I saw him laugh, but little did I know that moment would allow me the opportunity to start working with security, front of house, back of house, stage work, all of it. Bill once introduced me to the tour manager of the Who as his "yellow pages," and the name stuck. He would put me on task, and I would find out how to fix the situation.

Sooner rather than later, I was creating large-scale backstage environments and managing the beverages in the dressing rooms. We would construct these massive backstage party spots. When the band showed up, they we in full action, but when they left the stage after the show it was gone. One night, I was sitting with Bill in one of the environments and he asked me, "Now that you've been around the company and all aspects of the business, what would you like to do with your life?"

"You know what we do here for the bands," I said. "I'd like to do this for the crowds that pay to come see the bands. Food and beverage with a bit more flare than just hot dogs and popcorn." No disrespect to the late Bill Fritz, of course.

Well, a few days later, Bill called me into his office and asked how much money I thought it would take to start such an endeavor. We figured it would take $85,000 and we'd need an office. "What should we call it?" I remember him asking as I looked up at the many framed pictures in his office.

My eyes landed on the picture of Bill in a Fillmore Fingers basketball jersey flipping the bird "How about Fillmore Fingers, because we will fill more fingers with food."

The rest is history.

NIGEL JAMES

In 1982 I was working for International Talent Booking Agency in London as a runner/driver for both Barry Dickens and Rod McSween. In September of that year Neil Young played three nights at Wembley Arena (the 26th, 27th, 28th). Montrose (Ronnie Montrose) was the opening act.

Barry called us together and explained that we had to clean up the dressing rooms for them and we needed to get a sofa, carpet, chairs, lighting and paint the walls as they were absolutely filthy. (In those days in England one did not titivate a dressing room like the ambience that went on in the US; support bands just got a room with a couple of plastic chairs and a mirror and some small refreshments.) Barry explained to us that the manager for Montrose was a guy called Bill Graham and that he, Barry, did not wish to get a phone call from San Francisco in regard to why we did not "respect" Montrose. I remember thinking, who is Bill Graham?

Nine years later I joined Bill Graham's company BGP in San Francisco. Unfortunately, he died not long after I began my job there. However, I do remember that he used to park his car on the ground floor of our office building and would take a rickety old elevator to the first floor where Rita Gentry, Steve Paine and I had our desks that were located just outside the elevator. Each day we would hear the rickety elevator at about 10:30 to 11:00 a.m. rising up to our floor, and we knew Bill was on his way. I think we all used to look at the door as it opened to judge just what type of mood Bill was going to be in that day.

I remember when Bill bought a page of protest in the New York Times when President Ronald Reagan visited Bitburg, Germany. If he was alive today, I wonder how many ads he would have taken out in the New York Times about the Orange Blob President of today.

Others, I'm sure, have told their stories of working very close to Bill. I will just add that Bill always told you exactly what was going down in a very straightforward fashion, not mincing any words. These days, I truly miss this.

P

PATTIE O'NEAL SPAZIANI

In 1975, I was living with Steve Kahn and working with a catering company. I flew to Colorado with Bill and Steven in Steven's plane to work as production assistant on a Rolling Stones show in Fort Collins.

When the local caterer did not show up the morning of the show and did not answer her phone, someone went to her home and found that she had had a mental breakdown (or something like that) due to a breakup with her boyfriend. Bill went crazy as not only did he have the Stones coming, but Elton John was showing up as well. As Bill was pacing with his head in his hands and cursing. I told him if he gave me a bunch of cash, a van and five people I would get if covered. Barry Fey (his partner in this production) wanted to call a catering company from the Yellow Pages, but Bill told him, "She's a smart girl. She will figure it out."

I got a closed party equipment and costume rental place to open its doors and raced around to grocery stores. The son of the party supply people went to college there and rounded up some beautiful girls to act as servers. By the time The Stones arrived, I had the local college girls in French maid's outfits, serving high tea and finger sandwiches with a silver tea service and served a full-on roast dinner with Yorkshire pudding and trifle after the show.

Bill was so impressed that he asked me right then take over the catering at some of the larger shows and Day on the Green shows, since Narsai David was winding down that part of his business.

So I came home after that weekend with a new business.

Then years later, after many years of catering with BGP as my main client, I found myself spending more and more time in the production offices assisting the booking of hotel rooms for the groups. In those days, you picked up the phone and called a Holiday Inn and asked if they could accommodate 50 rooms in two days and then you gave them the names on the phone and sent a courier with a cash deposit or wire transferred funds. It was a lot of methodical work, not so much suited to most of the volatile road managers, so Bill would come in the kitchen from time to time and ask me to make some calls and put out fires with disgruntled hotel managers.

I also owned two restaurants in San Francisco at the time and was getting very burned out from working. So I decided to take a break, sold the restaurants and catering business and moved to London for a few months in the mid-80s to see if my current long-distance relationship could withstand the rigors of a normal life and landed a job as a consultant in opening a few clubs and restaurants in London.

Bill heard through the grapevine that I was not really happy in London and called and asked if I would consider becoming a travel agent for the bands he was managing. I called a friend of mine that was a corporate travel agent who wanted to learn more about production travel and convinced her that we could work together, each of us teaching the other a different aspect of the business. I was to start working with this agent on a Monday and on Sunday, the owner of the agency called me and said that Jocelyn had slipped on her steps and hit her head and was in an induced coma at Marin General but they expected her to make a full recovery soon, so if I would come in on Monday they would help me until Jocelyn got back to the office, maybe in a few weeks.

When I arrived on Monday, everyone in the office was hysterical as they had just found out that Jocelyn had died. I figured that there was no way I could pull off this business and called Bill to tell him so. His very words to me were, "You are a very smart girl. You will figure it out. I have faith in you. So, get to work, I am sending you over six tours".

So, I figured it out and owe Bill my two great careers.

PAUL LOBSTER WELLS

KSJO's 10th Anniversary Show at Winterland on May 19, 1978 and Why Bill Yelled at Me Backstage

He had to have someone to yell at. It wasn't my fault that he was the only one at Bill Graham Presents NOT in on the fact that the old Ice Follies rink had been booked as KSJO's 10th Anniversary Show. Bill knew me, but no one else at the catered party backstage with 200 people in attendance. It was the staff, management, family and advertising clients of the radio station. We also had an enormous cake!

I was a Bronx kid, so I could take the volume level, thrusting my hands in my pockets and looking down at my shoes as he "gave a Gerschrei." He had to put a fire out and was none too happy about it. At the time, Bill and BGP booker, Danny Scher, would call me on a fairly regular basis when booking shows in San Jose and even questions on artists for Days on the Green. KSAN at the time was eclectic and punk, but KSJO was the station that ROCKED.

We broke artists like AC/DC before their record company released them stateside and were often on the leading edge. We had a great signal that competed heavily for listeners in Alameda and San Mateo County in 1977; we owned 18-34 year old men and adults in Santa Clara County.

Danny Scher and I originally met when he was the student concert promoter at Stanford University and I was the music director of the campus radio station, KZSU Stanford. We simultaneously found the same jobs on a professional level. KSAN became the Jive 95 as a freeform FM rock radio station in April of 1968 when Tom Donahue got there after leaving KMPX. Little known fact is that KSJO flipped to that format as well in May of 1968. So, when it was announced that KSJO would hold its 10th Anniversary Show at Winterland, KSAN had a cow. Usurping the 10th Anniversary party from them was a coup.

At the time, Sammy Hagar was just getting his solo career going, having left Montrose and had just released his second album, Red. No one played it more than KSJO. At the time, Sammy was touring as a support act for Alvin Lee and Ten Years Later. We added Hoodoo

Rhythm Devils to open, but flipped Sammy as the headliner. When Alvin Lee arrived at Winterland and looked up at the marquee on the corner of Post and Steiner, he flipped out. His name was BELOW Sammy Hagar's! Old Alvin threatened not to play.

That's when Bill was called in. I later learned that Bill gave Alvin Lee another gig at the Henry J. Kaiser Auditorium at the tail end of the tour. Of course, KSJO had to promote it...heavily!

So Bill came roaring into the party and confronted me.

Bill: "Who are all these people back here? Do YOU know what I had to do to get Alvin Lee to play tonight? What the fuck do YOU know about booking shows?"

There was more, but I calmly and humbly explained that it was KSJO's 10th Anniversary Show and apologized that he wasn't made aware of it. That was the reason the ticket price was $3.92 because our dial position was 92.3. It was a catered party, the backstage food and drink was on the station. Also, I had arranged for Neal Schon to fly in from the Journey Infinity Tour and jam with Sammy, his band, Eddie Money and his guitarist Jimmy Lyons at the end. Alvin Lee disappeared during Sammy's set, but I later found out from The Red Rocker that Alvin angrily kicked in the monitor speakers before his opening act on much of the tour...Sammy Hagar hit the stage. The irony was the jam I put together was in honor of Bill.

From my teenage years going to The Fillmore East to my moving west when it closed and all the BGP shows I had seen to that point, mostly at Winterland, I wanted to create a "Great Live Moment" for Bill. Those one-time-only jams at the end of a show, a surprising combination of musicians blows the roof off a venue with an already ignited crowd.

By the end of that night with country music legend Bobby Bare in tow (as a possible Bill Graham Management client), Bill was happy.

PETER COYOTE

As you know, Bill was the manager of the San Francisco Mime Troupe while I was an actor/director there. A mad time, before the music scene had taken off. The first three rock and roll light shows at the Fillmore were actually benefits for the Mime Troupe, and while the Troupe was discussing whether or not we should lease the Fillmore and run these dances ourselves, Bill had a Saul-on-the-road-to-Damascus conversion and took it out in his own name. The rest is history!

Some in the Troupe resented him for this, but I didn't. I knew that he was born to do this, and stayed close to him.

One day he called me up rather desperate, telling me that he needed an acting teacher. Barry Levinson was casting him as Lucky Luciano in the movie Bugsy and he hadn't acted in years. I put him in touch with a great teacher in New York.

About a year later, I was about to go to Paris to film Bitter Moon with Roman Polanski. I attended a benefit for the Holocaust Oral History project, which was run by my late cousin, Lani Silver. I introduced Bill to her and he'd become her angel and major benefactor. Bill and I and his girlfriend sat together and we had a wonderful time.

He was very excited about the film. Barry had helped him locate his salsa-dancing partner, a Puerto Rican girl (now woman) he hadn't seen since he was 18. They flew her out and she was in the movie dancing with Bill. We were like two old veterans talking over the years and a very long friendship.

I left about a week later and was working in Paris when I turned 50. My assistant then had put together a packet of cards and letters and sent them to my apartment and they arrived on my birthday. It was end of day, a foggy autumn, and as I was reading through the cards, a piece of paper slipped out. I picked it up and it was a newspaper clipping chronicling Bill's death in a helicopter accident. I burst into tears, something quite uncharacteristic for me. Maybe it was turning 50; maybe it was realizing that I probably would not have the time to have a friend for as long as Bill and I were friends. Maybe it was sorrow that just when things were breaking just right for him, he got snatched away.

I still think of him with great tenderness many years later.

Q

QUEENIE TAYLOR

Production Secretary; Bill's Secretary; Advertiser; Ticketing; Nightclub Co-Manager; Special Events Booking

June 24, 1972-July 1987; November 1989-June 1991 (18 years)

When Rita first asked for a Bill Graham story, I wrote a few, and then realized they were really all about me. That's how Bill was: he helped you to learn about yourself and what you could achieve. His inspiration might at times have been radical, but it worked, and I am a completely different person as a result of my relationship with him.

I first heard of Bill Graham when I went to UC Santa Cruz in fall of 1966. Friends and I journeyed to the Fillmore and Winterland for concerts almost every weekend.

I first met Bill when my friend Georgiana and I asked for his autograph in the lobby of the Berkeley Community Theater around 1971. He was pretty surprised but accommodating. I came to learn that he didn't avoid the spotlight, but he preferred promoting artists to promoting himself. That autograph was burned in the 201-11th St fire (along with my fabulous Wolfy Wolfgang's fuzzy hat I got at the Telluride Music Festival BGP produced). He spelled my name "Queeny."

In 1974 the publishing company I worked with in Sausalito (coincidentally next door to the Record Plant) decided to relocate to the country, which held no interest for me. I started reaching out to everyone I knew to try to find a job in the music business (a decision I have intermittently regretted, but that's another story.) I met writer Ed Ward, who knew writer John Morthland, who somehow knew Barry Imhoff, who was VP at BGP at the time. I sent in my little resume and

343

got a job as production secretary for Patrick Stansfield for the CSNY tour at
$600/month.

I didn't see Bill for a few weeks, and then he wondered how I had gotten hired without an interview with him. I asked what he wanted to know about me and he said, "Where do you want to be in five years?" He might as well have said, "Where do you want to be in five days." I was so uninterested in the future, but apparently my answer was proficient enough for me to stay employed. Within six months I was his personal secretary (as we were called at that time). My crowning achievement was finally getting Bill to communicate himself on the phone with his ex- wife Bonnie. Their acrimonious divorce and her move with Bill's son David back east had resulted in a stalemate, which I finally insisted irritably had to end, kind of a "man up" moment which I like to think paved the way for slightly more cordial relations between Bill and Bonnie through the years.

From 1976 to 1979 I worked in press, advertising, marketing and ticketing with Zohn Artman. In 1980, Bill decided to eliminate some competition from Jeffrey Pollack by buying the Old Waldorf nightclub. He told me that "the agents will eat you alive but I don't have anyone else to book the place," and so began my 20- year nightclub adventure. I lived at the Golden Gateway Center, so conveniently got to walk to work, but which also meant I had no life outside work (yet another story for another time).

Luckily, Bill's prediction didn't completely come true; I just had a different kind of relationship with agents than some men did (and I mean that in a completely platonic way, mostly).

Time passed. We booked The Kabuki and other clubs and the Old Waldorf moved and became Wolfgang's. Our club gang was David Mayeri, Jan Wexner, Steve Pate, Toni Isabella, and other luminaries like Kevin Chisholm, Candace Jacobus, Clarice Lacau, Louie Beeson, Thane Thomas and for a while, Bill's sister Esther Chichinsky provided food. In 1987 I had a baby, and shortly after that Wolfgang's burned down. While I was waiting for my new marching orders, Bill gave Michael Bailey all my agents, and I joined forced with Bob Brown, Boz Scaggs, Dawn Holliday, Bonnie Simmons, Harry Duncan and a few others to start Slim's Nightclub. That wasn't a very popular move with Bill, and three years later he wooed me back to BGP, where I didn't have the most substantial job ever, but felt that I was home.

Then Bill died, and Toni Isabella hatched a plan to get Disney to buy BGP. (Since I got most of the blame for this, Toni remains the irritated unsung antagonist.) This story is quite complicated and interesting, and ended with my being fired. It wasn't exactly the "best thing that ever happened to me," but it wasn't the worst. One unexpected event I remember is that on the Wednesday before Bill died, he called me into the conference room and told me how much he valued my work and asked my opinion about others in the company. He never did that before (or, obviously, after); I don't know why he did it, but it's a precious memory.

Some always-fond memories include being a New Year's Baby at the Cow Palace with Father Time Danny Scher, Blue Oyster Cult and their manager Steve Schenck and his wife Seena Amsell. I also served as Baby at the nightclubs with Toni Isabella, with Bob Johnson or Harry Duncan as Father Time.

One of the lasting effects of all that time in music and at BGP is that I absolutely can't listen to music while I work. Bill never allowed it, and after a while, every song I heard anywhere became attached to some personal story circling around the BGP universe in some way. Some of those stories and memories were pleasant, some were not, but all were distracting and pulled me into the past.

"River Deep, Mountain High"—Tina Turner at the Old Waldorf

The Cure — playing at the I-Beam

"When Doves Cry" — Prince at the Stone

"Stairway to Heaven" — Peter Grant and Jim Matzorkis at the Day on the Green

Red Hot Chili Peppers — Old Waldorf with socks over their junk (or would that be "junks"?) "Girls Just Wanna Have Fun" — Cyndi Lauper at the Waldorf the night John Lennon died Bob Seger — Bill yelling at me because my ad had left out "and the Silver Bullet Band"

Elvis Costello — settling with Jake Riviera at the Berkeley Community Theater

Bob Dylan — eating dinner next to Cameron Crowe and Mary Beth Medley in a North Beach restaurant after the final date on the 1974 Dylan tour

Obviously, the list goes on forever, and the music never ends. I just haven't added enough new content to my repertoire (excepting the Dandy Warhols).

I treasure what I learned, and everyone I met and worked with, and still know, or don't know, living and not. I sometimes can't even imagine how the person I am now was ever the person I was then, but I can't deny that everything actually happened. If Bill was still alive, I am quite sure I would still be in his orbit. That remains a bittersweet dream with apples around the edges.

R

RACHEL MATTHEWS

The year was 1990 or maybe 1991. I was working as Vice President of A&R at Hollywood Records, a pop music label I had started at Disney. Toni Isabella was trying to get Bill interested to working with Latin groups, one of whom was Chayanne a pop singer out of Puerto Rico, and a former member of Los Chicos.

The three of us went to Puerto Rico to see what Chayanne was all about: me as an A&R person seeking to sign a new artist to Hollywood Records, and Bill and Toni seeking to discuss managing up-and-coming Latin artists as a new avenue of income.

The show was held at the soccer stadium in San Juan. It was sold out. We sat in the front row on folding chairs next to the Governor of Puerto Rico. There was a full orchestra on stage with Chayanne. It started to rain halfway through his performance, and this is when Bill came to life.

Chayanne decided to leave the stadium as all of the musicians left the stage to protect their instruments. Bill ran backstage and grabbed (literally GRABBED) Chayanne off the helicopter he was attempting to enter and told him in no uncertain terms that this was his moment! "Get back out there on that stage and finish your show IN THE RAIN! Your fans will love you for it – it will be unforgettable."

Chayanne at this point had NO idea who Bill was. Their manager explained rather quickly as Bill was getting very animated. Needless to say, Chayanne went back on stage and finished the show. He was on the front cover of the big Puerto Rico newspaper the next day lauding the amazing show in the rain!

Humorous side note: I had bright fuchsia-colored hair at the time of the concert…in the rain and I was wearing a white blouse. Toni and I could do nothing but laugh - at me, at Bill…at the rain.

RACHEL MORALES WARNE

I started working in the parking lot of Shoreline Amphitheatre in 1987. I ended up in the payroll/finance office departing in 1996.

My favorite Bill Graham story and the one that my kids ask to hear is the following: I was on break for the night at Shoreline Amphitheatre. I was coming down the stairs from the bowl to the plaza. Bill came up next to me, taking a walk of the bowl.

I smiled and said hello. In front of us were a group of very young and new traveling Deadheads.

They were carrying on, very loudly saying how Bill Graham just doesn't understand, how he was just about the money and doesn't care about the music or the Deadheads.

I was shocked and angry at the same time and I was just about to defend him, which is weird because he was right there. As I was about to speak up, he touched my shoulder and shook his head to me "no." He really didn't want to cause a scene or embarrass them. He let them have their night. He just wanted to blend in.

I loved seeing him always walking the bowl and walking with a certain anonymity. I was always bugged that people thought he didn't care about the music experience because, clearly, he did.

"A fellow who does things that count doesn't usually stop to count them." - Albert Einstein

RAY ETZLER

When I approached Bill Graham's office at the Fillmore West to ask for a raise from $15 to $25 per night for cooking at the grill six nights a week, the dialogue was typical Bill with his statements about "you kids" (he was nine years older than me) who wanted to work for nothing to be at the center of the music scene. I reminded him that he had called me through his manager, Paul Barretta, at the Fillmore, I didn't call him. Long story made short, he said, "Stay where you are and if you need anything else, it's yours," with an emphasis of hand clapping together to punctuate his statement. I smiled and left the office to return that night to the grill and hamburgers.

About two months later I was in need of $200 and went to Bill's office during the day to ask him for a loan, which could be deducted from my pay. He went into an impassioned commentary about his overhead and expenses. I interrupted him to state, "I'm not here to make an offer to buy the business. Bill, your response can be the word 'no' to a loan." He said, "No!" As I left the office I uttered his words to me two months before: "Anything you need, it's yours!"

For the next month following that day Bill Graham was a ghost to me and didn't come near the grill or behind the counter. One night his doppelganger, Barry Imhoff, came to the grill and said, "Ray, I got you a raise to $25 per night." My response to Barry was, "You got me nothing and it's not enough!"

Bill Graham reappeared back of the grill smiling and cooked himself a hamburger the next night. He and I had an understanding after that which lasted for the years to follow.

I spent 30 years of my life with Bill Graham and Bill Graham Management.

RICHARD (RICK) BELLAMY

I knew Jeff Davis' sister (Jeff worked the box office at BGP). We were neighbors in Fremont, California and after Jeff died I ended up working with BGP in the box office, and parking lots and traffic. I was a fan who spent about $100 a year on four or five shows at Shoreline, Henry J. Kaiser or Oakland Arena.

The first few days I started working for BGP I was singled out by someone whose sole job was to come around and watch the people that were working and doing more than having fun while doing so. I was working the one-way ramp at Shoreline for the pedestrians making sure they crossed in a safe manner and some lady came out of the blue and gave me a Chevy's Restaurant gift certificate for $10 with which I could actually buy a lunch back then in the mid-90s, and a T-shirt (which I still have) that has many different pictures of Bill scattered in blue print. These were the first freebies I ever got from BGP.

I worked for BGP from 1995 to 2007 at Shoreline receiving many memorable things such as posters, T-shirts, etc. for my service doing everything from stagehand to dressing room coordinator to traffic director. All of these jobs have afforded me countless wonderful memories. Thanks to Jeff Davis (the loss of his life was a tragedy) - I thank him for the career that I now know, love and hold dear.

RICHARD LOREN

The Yin and Yang of Bill Graham

Bill Graham was a complex guy, and my relationship with him was equally complex.

Much of Bill's tenacity and aggressiveness stemmed from an incredibly difficult childhood. He had lost his mother in the Holocaust and barely escaped to the United States. He was a survivor who grew up tough and smart on the streets of New York and eventually found his way to San Francisco, where he made a name for himself both as a music promoter and as a force to be reckoned with.

When I was the agent for Jefferson Airplane, during my early days in New York at APA (Agency for the Performing Arts), Bill was the Airplane's manager. He gave me possible booking time slots and then rejected or accepted my proposed offers based on the venue and the promoter's guarantee to the artist.

Booking the Airplane was the big break that helped me segue into representing other big-time rock bands, and I appreciated his help. By the time I was appointed the Grateful Dead's agent and general manager eight years later, Bill had become the golden boy of entrepreneurial rock 'n' roll emulated by promoters nationwide. He had also earned a reputation for unscrupulously exploiting bands financially.

As manager of one of those bands, I had to keep a close eye on him, as much as I hated to do so. True to what I'd heard, I found he was padding expenses, under-counting the gate, and trying to pull off a bunch of other unethical practices. Bill knew how to charm the artists and was their backstage buddy. He impressed them with his creative pairing of musical acts and the promotion of worthy benefit concerts.

My relationship with him was different. I was hired by the Dead to manage their financial affairs and couldn't ignore what he was doing. The band knew about his practices through me, but we could do little short of refusing to work with him.

Bill and I fought tooth and nail for years until I was finally worn down and at my wit's end. In April 1979, just before a show in San Jose, his cheating finally sent me over the edge, and I was hellbent to get out from under any dealings with him.

I called John Scher. "I'm fuckin' fed up! I can't deal with Graham any longer. He's jerking me around with the expenses, trying to pull things over on me right and left, and driving me fuckin' nuts! I'll give you my agent's fee if you strike the deal! I've had it with the fucking crook!"

"God! I'd like to help you out, but there's no way I can get involved without Bill's consent," John responded.

"Do whatever you have to do. I've had it!"

At first Bill was thrilled to have me out of the picture; he welcomed John's involvement, but he underestimated him. The tickets had gone on sale, but Bill still hadn't submitted the expenses. John called him to ask why he hadn't received them. Bill unloaded on him in no uncertain terms.

In Dennis McNally's book, Long Strange Trip, the Dead biographer quotes Scher recounting his experience: "It was my first experience with a Bill roar. He went berserk, 'I have to deal with a fuckin' Jersey asshole to book my band? You motherfuckin' ingrate scumbag.' It was a nonstop lunatic binge for twenty minutes, and then a hang-up. I called Loren, and said I quit. The Dead did the gig, but from then on my relationship with Bill was acrimonious."

Speaking truth to power hurt me in the long run. Two years down the line, after I had resigned from the Dead, I offered Bill a major share in a moneymaking movie-music venture that he refused not from a business point of view but from lingering resentment.

It was an unfortunate situation.

Bill died in a helicopter crash in 1991 at the young age of sixty. He was a larger-than-life personality who defied categorization, contrasting his shady business practices with great personal generosity, his combativeness and compassion, and his vulgarity with sensitivity. I will always have mixed feelings about Bill and will never forget him.

God bless.

Do I contradict myself?
Very well then I contradict myself,
I am large,
I contain multitudes.
Walt Whitman, *Song of Myself*

Please Note: This story was taken from a book called *High Notes-A Rock Memoir…*Richard Loren and Stephen Abney © 2014

RICHARD MERCOURIS

I had the fun of knowing Peter Barsotti from another life, having mutual friends. My first gig with Bill Graham Presents was in 1976 working as a part-time stagehand for Jefferson Starship at the Greek Theatre in Berkeley, California.

That led to other calls and eleven months later, due to some startling personnel changes immediately following The Last Waltz, I was offered a full-time position as stage manager working directly under Peter Barsotti and Danny Scher.

I was a little older than some of the other guys and I had experience working at the Avalon Ballroom every other weekend during my days in the Army at Fort Ord. These things probably helped move me along, as well as my emotional maturity. Ha!

My most vivid personal memory of working with Bill Graham is the last Sex Pistols concert at Winterland, January of 1977. After the two warm-up acts (one was a band called The Avengers and I forgot the other) and before the Sex Pistols came on stage, Bill decided that he and I would split the stage in half. Anything that was thrown on his side, he would keep; conversely, I got to keep all of the silly stuff on my side of the stage. Jim Matzorkis was doing stage security in the rear to keep the flank secure.

It actually was a great and fun show even at the end when Johnny Rotten was chanting, "This is no fun, This is no fun!" As well as, "Have you ever felt that you've been cheated?"

Crazy fun times and wouldn't have missed it for the world.

RICHARD SEGOVIA

In 1985, Puro Bandido was looking for a singer for the band. I got a call from a friend and he said he got a call from a guy named Johnny Gunn who was looking for a percussionist. At the same time, Puro Bandido was looking for a lead singer.

I auditioned in Hayward, California and that's when I met Johnny Gunn who looked like a bandido. Johnny was very good friends with Eddie Money. Eddie at that time was being managed by Bill Graham. From what I've heard, Eddie Money and Carlos Santana were like his godchildren. Johnny also co-wrote the song "No Control" with Eddie on his album No Control.

Eddie did a few shows with Johnny Gunn's band, but then decided to put his own band together. He took me, Johnny Gunn, Chris Solberg and the horn section from Johnny's band. We then did some shows for Bill Graham: New Year's Eve at the Cow Palace in 1985—Eric Martin Band, Eddie Money and Night Ranger. Now I was finally working for Bill Graham. I would pick up my checks at the Bill Graham office on Union Street in San Francisco, which was also the management office for Eddie and Carlos. Bill Graham didn't know anything about our Latin rock band Puro Bandido.

Puro Bandido was playing at Union Square in San Francisco in 1986. Chris Solberg was helping the sound guy for the sound mix for the band. Bill jumped over a police barricade to say hi to Chris and checked us out. He asked Chris, "Who are these guys?" He looked at Chris, looked at Johnny and looked at me and asked, "What are you guys doing here?" It was right after our New Year's Eve gig with Eddie Money.

On May 7, 1988 Bill Graham had us open for Pancho Sanchez, Eddie Palmieri and Santana for the Cinco de Mayo concert for the Blues for Salvador Tour at the Greek Theater in Berkeley. I had an opportunity to speak to Bill Graham backstage. He shared with me the love he had for Latin music. He even had me sit in with Carlos Santana, which was one of my biggest dreams, as a timbales player, and being born and raised in the San Francisco Mission District where Latin Rock was created.

He loved us so much that on May 29, 1988 we were asked to perform at the benefit for AIDS concert with Linda Ronstadt and Pete Escovedo. I couldn't believe that he put us on primetime television with them. After the show he told us to keep practicing. Bill had us opening up for Tower of Power, Sheila E., Willie Colon and Hector Lavo getting the band tight.

In May of 1991 we did a photo shoot for him. We were getting ready to sign a management deal with him. On October 25, 1991 I was home watching television and I heard that Bill Graham was killed in a helicopter accident while leaving the Concord Pavilion. May he rest in peace.

RICK SWIG

The first time I ventured forth into the Fillmore Auditorium was September 11, 1966.

I believe that Bill Graham assisted the Both/And Jazz Club in producing the show, which featured the Jefferson Airplane and the Great Society, along with jazz and Blues greats Jon Hendricks, Big Mama Thornton, and Joe Henderson.

It didn't matter to me because it was just cool being in the hall with the music and the Bill Ham light show, and besides I had just celebrated my 15th birthday!

The big introduction was nine months later in June, when Jimi Hendrix opened for the Airplane and Gabor Szabo. What a mismatch and what a legendary show!

The show began with sneaking up the stairs past the proprietor Bill Graham because I was absolutely sure that this fifteen-year-old was going to be stopped and tossed out for being underage. Success!

I managed to get in and began a now-going-on-56-year love affair with the venerable Fillmore Auditorium. Later I also developed a personal relationship with the man at the top of the stairs, Bill Graham.

My first actual meeting with Bill Graham came in, I believe, in 1969 at the old Bill Graham Presents offices on Golden Gate Street in San Francisco. I think I was just delivering some records or promo material related to some band that was about to perform at the Fillmore.

At the time I was working for a record distributor, H.R. Bashford Co., in San Francisco. The big excitement was meeting the man who had his name on the posters and sometimes introduced the bands at the Fillmore.

A couple of years later, I was more formally introduced to Bill at the 11th and Howard location of BGP, where I came to visit dearest wizard, Zohn Artman, along with Mary Roach and Dilly Dally, who worked in the office.

It was there that I experienced a closer view of Bill Graham. As I sat with Zohn, Mary, or Dilly at one end of the building, there came a giant screaming noise from the other end, which was accompanied by what sounded like the slamming down of a telephone.

I wondered who could have been the source of that cacophony, and it soon became apparent, as Bill Graham came storming into our area. When he saw me, he quickly stopped, while calmly and politely introducing himself to me. He could not have been more warm and pleasant.

It was the beginning of a long, cherished, and dear relationship. And a few minutes later, I heard more shouting and some more slamming onto a poor, unsuspecting telephone.

RICK TURNER

Wikipedia says of me: American builder of guitars and basses.

At an appropriate moment say, guitar techs say, "Hey, I have an instrument that I think you guys might like to see." Usually that was it; that was my "in." One unofficial duty of guitar techs is to spot interesting stuff on the road and bring it to the attention of their bosses. And generally I would be invited to stay, be given a backstage pass, etc.

But, I also knew that if Bill Graham ever figured out that I was hustling instruments in his venue, on his stage, I would get permanently banned from any BGP venue. So I stayed pretty under the radar. I knew that Bill had seen me working shows as part of Alembic's sound and recording crew so there was a slight familiarity, and I probably registered as part of the virtual woodwork; he'd also seen my face at shows to which I'd been invited by clients, but I also knew that I was on thin ice being there and doing what I was doing.

In 1974 George Harrison's bassist, Willie Weeks, invited me to the show at the Cow Palace, and I had full backstage access and all that. I was back talking to David Crosby and maybe Graham Nash, both of whom I'd done extensive guitars for and Bill Graham spotted me, came over and said, "Who the fuck are you? Get out!" David immediately said, "He's with us." End of problem.

Years later I was at Bill's house, Masada, in Mill Valley with my friend, Mimi Farina. Bill looked at me, looked again, and said, "I know you, don't I?" I just said, "I've been around the music biz here for a long time and yeah, you've seen my face." After that he couldn't have been nicer.

RITA BARELA

In the mid 1970s I moved to San Francisco from Los Angeles on a whim because I wanted to explore my interest in psychic healing, which was more apt to happen in San Francisco than in Los Angeles. I had met a man in Sausalito during my first SF visit that did gardening as a hobby and once I'd moved here he took me to something called The World of Plants at a venue called the Cow Palace.

I was somewhat interested in plants, but what blew my mind was the egotistical promoter of the plant show whose name was plastered everywhere and in every direction. At that time I was irritated by someone who would so shamelessly and blatantly promote himself instead of the product. What did I know?

I had never heard of the man before, although he was very famous in the Bay Area and throughout the music industry – I had worked in the film industry prior to this.

Little did I know that shortly thereafter I would be working for this man who became a mentor, inasmuch as he taught me what to do. I also learned from him what not to do. Not sure he'd like what I've said above, but I think he would be proud of me for speaking my truth. We would live to have few altercations, but to also honor a very strong bond.

That man was BILL GRAHAM.

RITA GENTRY

My first day at Bill Graham Presents was on February 26, 1979 and my last day, 20 years later, was February 26, 1999.

I had tried many years previously to get a job at BGP, but it never panned out. I believe the stars were aligned when I decided that was where I wanted to work after many years working with bands and booking agencies in the San Francisco area. I was also in the midst of a divorce with a four-year-old son.

I interviewed to be Danny Scher's personal assistant who at the time had the office directly across from Bill Graham's office at 201 11th Street, San Francisco. He was the main booker in direct association with Bill. Bill was out of the office when I interviewed, so I had to come back to speak with Bill directly, which I did. When I walked into his office it was like meeting with the Pope. That man had more charisma and machismo at the same time. I know he asked me questions at that time which would not be allowed today, but I won't get into that. I feel that I was streetwise enough to maneuver my way through the questions. At the end of the interview on my departure from his office, I asked him if I should kiss his BG ring like the Pope or the Godfather and he smiled.

I nervously awaited to hear back from BGP whether or not I got the job, but the phone never rang so I thought I didn't get the it. The following Monday, I received a phone call from Danny Scher asking me why I hadn't reported for work. I told him that I had never received the phone call that I got the job (he forgot to call me…LOL!) So, the next day I started my new job at Bill Graham Presents and the journey began. Little did I know that I would fall in love with my job, Bill, and all the beautiful people that I worked with over the years.

Working at BGP was like going to college and getting a degree in the public assemblage business. Remember, Bill started the following: great catering for artists and workers (employees), the selling of swag (T-shirts, key chains, stickers, etc.), making it safe for show attendees going into a venue, while attending the event, and leaving the event. He was definitely my master and guru at the same time.

Even many years after his passing, it seems that almost a day doesn't go by that I don't think of him, make reference to him in one way or another or see something that reminds me of him. Now that's pretty incredible.

My jobs at BGP consisted of personal assistant, contracts for all shows booked, production assistant, special events coordinator, and the best of all jobs that I did at BGP: being Bill's secretary. Favorite shows that I worked on: Days on the Green, Barbra Streisand's comeback at the MGM Grand in Las Vegas, Earthquake Benefit, Nelson Mandela event, Ben & Jerry's events in Golden Gate Park, Lollapalooza, A Gathering of the Tribes, Prince, Grateful Dead shows, the Warfield shows, The Fillmore shows, Las Vegas shows, etc.

I was so fortunate to be able to work, learn and experience so much in an industry that was an adventure every day.

My drug of choice has always been music and I was able to get a fix every single day. So, with that being said, thank you so much from the bottom of my heart, Bill, for letting me experience the best of the best and for being my angel in human form; now you are just my angel!

ROBERT ALTMAN

I had known of Bill Graham since he opened the Fillmore East in March, 1968. I mean, I lived a few hundred yards away with Annie, my old lady, in a second floor, cold water flat in the Lower East Side, aka the East Village. We lived above our Tribe's psychedelic shop, the Electric Lotus.

In fact, I took my first ever rock photograph at the Fillmore East... of Jim Morrison.

It turns out that Bill Graham and I had a few things in common:

We both grew up in the Bronx, NYC - Bill after he immigrated to the U.S. at 10 years old;

We both attended DeWitt Clinton High School; We both attended City University Colleges of New York - Bill at City College and me at Hunter College;

We both worked as waiters in the Borscht Belt (summer resorts and escapes from the City to the Catskill Mountains; We both left

New York and Jim Morrison, Fillmore East. March 1968 moved to San Francisco and finally, we both somehow got involved with the Sixties Generation and particularly the music business. He - the great impresario, rock concert promoter, manager, record producer, et al.

Now, I will be the first to admit that I never knew Bill well. In fact, it was kind of the opposite. Do you remember the Jack Lemmon character Ensign Pulver from the movie "Mr. Roberts"? Pulver was on the same ship as his ornery Captain Morton, played by Jimmy Cagney. Pulver spends most of his time idling in his bunk and avoids the captain at all costs, so much so that Morton is actually unaware Pulver is part of the crew.

I think two incidents set me up for my wariness and restraint. The first time was after a concert or political gathering. We were in an auditorium. The lights went up and there was Bill Graham and his former "boss" R.G. Davis, founder of the San Francisco Mime Troupe (where Bill got his first job promoting entertainment.) Whatever it was about, words were exchanged. And words flew. They became sharper, louder. It was actually entertaining and neither Bill nor Davis would back down. I'm sure it only it lasted a few short minutes but it seemed like forever. You could tell that the two, besides disagreeing, also had love and respect for each other. The things you remember....

The second red flag (for me): I was at the Rolling Stone office and my older brother-in-arms, photographer Jim Marshall, was on the phone arguing a point about his supposed parking place at a Bill Graham venue. Jim wasn't yelling, as he was known to do, but his phone correspondent sure was. It was Bill on the other end. You could hear Bill, over the phone, over the Rolling Stone hallways. And Jim wasn't trying to get off the phone, as I surely would have. He kept trying to make his point and Bill kept yelling louder and longer. Well, that was the second lesson for me - I would never piss Bill off. I might have gotten a bit further in life if I did, but dare I? No.

So, that's how I was with Bill, a well-mannered, low- visibility Ensign Pulver. He knew I was alive; he knew who I was - a young rock photographer, a photojournalist from early Rolling Stone.

I did everything I knew to just not piss him off.

Bill always allowed me great stage advantage, as well as back stage access. I'm sure he saw the promotional results in the magazine, so it was good business for him. Plus, I think he actually liked me. I was always his great admirer. I'm sure that rubbed off too.

Once, maybe 12 years on or so, in 1980, I had the gumption to ask to be photographed with him. I was up visiting the BGP office for one reason or another and I asked my old friend Queenie Taylor, Bill's then-secretary, if she could make it happen. I had known Queenie since she was 19 when she knocked on my door wanting a photo of Keith Richards - she got one.

So, Queenie kind of pushes me into Bill's office, gently, her hand on my back, but a push I get. Bill looks up, sees this and says, "Robert, we bark, but we don't bite." Snap. I've always loved him for that.

I remember Bill pulling up to the Golden Gate Park Bandshell in a motorcycle attached to an extra side seat. Well, this biker crew, who I don't think recognized him, started making what you might call "remarks." Bill carefully removed his helmet and other gear and then gave these guys the look. And then he opened his mouth, as only Bill could, and the gauntlet fell. This motley crew fell away quietly and quickly. I have to say, I was impressed. That was pure power at work.

Occasionally, I covered the Day on the Green concerts and one time I caught Bill side stage reading the riot act to the Beach Boys' then-organist, Carlos Muñoz. "Your band best be onstage in five minutes or they won't be there at all." It made for an interesting Day in the Life photograph.

A few years later in 1970, after she indeed became a star, Laura played the Berkeley Community Theatre under the care and promotion of Bill. I'll never forget this: all she cared about among the roomful of friends congratulating her afterwards was Bill Graham.

"Bill! Did you hear me dedicate 'Wedding Bell Blues' to you? Didja?

Bill and Laura Nyro

"Bill, I love you so, I always will but kisses and love won't carry me 'til you marry me Billlllll."

My former wife Holly, aka Anaja, had opened a modeling agency in San Francisco in 1975. A few years into that, she approached Bill to co-produce an evening called the Artists and Models Ball. It was very successful and I was quite proud of her. Bill gave her a lot of rein and, even with a lot of other concerts going on that night for him to tend to, he was kind enough to stop by, encourage all and then slip away.

A few years later in 1980, John Lennon was astonishingly gunned down and taken from us. My wife Holly thought San Francisco should put a memorial together for him, as New York was doing, and once again turned to Bill for support. Without hesitation, he whipped up a stage and sound system in front of City Hall and we all had a place to be with each other, to talk, hug and grieve.

Eleven years later I heard the tragic news that there had been a fatal helicopter crash west of Vallejo, California, and that very possibly Bill Graham might have been lost in it. I immediately phoned my dear friend, composer and vocalist Barbara Mauritz. Barbara had been very close with Bill for years and he loved her as a person and for her enormous talent, so much so that he became the manager for her band, Lamb. She was sure he wasn't on that chopper. If only.

Gone from here Bill, but never, ever forgotten. You are one in a million and I will always look up to you.

ROBERT WILLIAMSON

There are so many wonderful and magical experiences through the years that I was blessed to know as a Bill Graham Presents employee. I feel I was also lucky to have had the opportunity to work with Bill occasionally one-on-one. The Holiday Festival had me booking live entertainment, and as an assistant stage manager for gigs Bill would let me know specific tasks he wanted done. Over the years I was so proud to know and work with him. When I received my union card I was concerned he might not like that fact. So, I told him about my decision to go union and I said, "I know you don't like unions." He responded that he just did not like some union individuals. He never treated me any different after that. I truly miss him.

One of the most memorable gigs over the span of 40-plus years as a stagehand was the ARMS concerts at the Cow Palace in San Francisco, December 1, 2, and 3, 1983.

Almost seven years after I did my first show with BGP, the Dead and Santana at the Cow Palace, the home of the Grand Nationals, became the scene of one of the greatest shows ever promoted by Bill Graham. By this time, I not only did load ins and outs, I was a Bluecoat doing security as well.

For this show, I was placed at the entrance of the main backstage dressing room. I was blessed with getting to interact with every performer as they arrived and hung out for the three days of shows, a dream gig with the likes of Clapton, Beck, Wyman, Watts and the list goes on. But the most amazing part was on the second night as the show was nearing the end. Scott Ferry, who was doing stage security, said Bill himself had invited us to his home in Marin for an after-show party. I was skeptical and asked Scott if he was sure I was invited. He said, "Yep!" I had never been to Masada and knew this would be a night to remember. By the time we got to Bill's house it was quite late, but the party was in full swing. Many of the show's performers were there as were many of Bill's employees. I was in awe of the beauty of the estate and proceeded to enjoy myself with everyone else.

At one point I was approached by a couple of Bluecoats who asked if I could help them. It seemed one of the shuttle vans used to transport people from the City to Bill's house was stuck in the mud (at the Friday night show we knew there was a massive storm was brewing in the Bay). The driver of the shuttle, in an attempt to free the van, got it stuck near a fence in the mud as the rain began to really come down. I managed to clear it from the mud and I was asked to drive it to the top of the hill to Bill's house.

By 2:00 a.m. the party was starting to break up, but the storm was getting worse. The wind was howling as people began to load back into the vans to be driven back to San Francisco. One of the vans was loaded and ready to go and I was asked to drive it down the hill. The wind was now blowing with such force that tree branches were falling in the road and trees were swinging wildly. Charlie Watts and Jan Hammer were in that first shuttle and I noticed how wide their eyes were as we headed down the road. After I got the van to a safe part of the road someone else took over the driving. I went back up the hill to see if there was anything else I could do. As I was getting ready to leave to head back to the City, I saw Bill standing at the front door of his home and I asked him, "What do you think of this storm?" Bill looked at me and said, "Isn't it amazing," as he looked out at the chaos the storm had created. I heard later that morning that a test vehicle was blown over as it drove across the Golden Gate Bridge, so the bridge was closed due to 160 mile per hour winds.

After all was said and done the Saturday night show went on as planned and I will never forget the night I got to visit Bill's home in Marin.

ROGER P. CLARK

Growing up, or more precisely being born and raised in Berkeley in the 1960s and 1970s, was a party at ground zero and little did we know – a pretty good place to be from.

The Berkeley Hills Kids already had done everything way before folks around the country were still trying to decide whether to grow their hair out. We were game for anything new and ca-ray- zee, cherry picking the best indulgent pastimes from the hippies, the cold-water surf scene, the casual delinquent community, the Black Panthers... oh yes, and musicians! Drugs were still unadulterated for the most part, and there was an evangelical spirit to getting high and sharing. Uncomplicated sexual interaction was the coin of realm and there it is again – sharing.

If there was such a thing as the San Andreas Fault of social and artistic change, it was shaking continuously, and we were sitting right on it, riding it. Junior and senior high school were spent cutting school to surf. Went to college for a few insincere years, nine months in India, then home to discover the social power of being in a band. That worked out for a while, in part thanks to the mystery of otherwise intelligent females that had a weakness for musicians despite their wildly fluctuating financial state.

After a couple of years of faking it as "work" after my brush with smalltime rock stardom ran dry, I crossed to the dark side – the business side of the music circus. Thanks to the fact that I knew most of the music business press from my small-time rock star charade, I was lucky enough to have transitioned into a job as the Minister of

Propaganda for Bill Graham Presents. I had met Bill more than a few times at shows, though usually I was the plus-one of one of the least favorite, and widely read local music writer.

My pals in the press were as amused as I was that I had landed in that spot. My job largely amounted to saying "no," lying transparently, and accumulating favors in exchange for tickets and access. The schism in the cult- like company's relationship with the press – the tough guys and gals mostly thought the press worked for them – and the continual struggle to disabuse them of this notion – that perhaps the quaint idea of give and take was worth considering - made the job a little like being the ping pong ball. My loyalties were regularly questioned. Little did they know....

Four years into my sentence I received a phone call in the wee hours of the morning from Bill Graham, calling from somewhere in a far distant time zone, announcing briskly that I would be leaving for Jakarta to advance the promotion of one of the first-ever big rock show to take place there – that would be a "yes, Mr. Graham." I had just a few days to pass off the work I'd been dodging at the office to other unsuspecting folks, no one having a clue how long I'd be gone.

The year was 1988 and Mick Jagger and Keith Richards were huffing and the Stones were not rolling anytime soon. Mick Jagger decided to indulge himself with a solo album to be called Primitive Cool, and committed to a companion tour of Asia and Australia, backed by a crack band – Joe Satriani as Mick Taylor, Jimmy Ripp as Keith Richards, rock star dreamboat Suzi Davis on keyboards (road veteran with acts like Sheila E. and Billy Idol and a hippie pedigree as daughter of FM radio legend Norman Davis), Simon Phillips on drums, Bill Wimbish (Living Color) on bass.

Bill Graham knew that while the Stones were on hiatus, (temporarily, everyone hoped) they were actively being courted by other well-financed promoters, like Michael Cohl's Canadian organization (he's the heir to the Molson Brewing empire.) And far be it for Mister Jagger to not use this to leverage his advantage.

Feeling that his long-term alliance with the Stones as tour promoter was getting shakier, Mr. Graham saw this solo tour as a way to continue a close relationship, at least with Mick Jagger. Meanwhile, his organization, Bill Graham Presents, was stretched pretty thin by the usual busy late summer/fall concert season. Complicated by the massive second Amnesty International tour, it was chock-a-block with high maintenance superstars and traveling to some very unlikely and remote global concert locations, like Zimbabwe.

The Primitive Cool Jakarta show was being bankrolled and promoted by an inexperienced wealthy local family who had been bugging Mr. Graham to bring shows there for quite awhile. Of course, A Year of Living Dangerously, clove cigarettes and Krakatoa, East of Java were the sum total of my knowledge of Indonesia – all of which appeared in my nervous dreams on the 14-hour flight to Indonesia.

We stopped first in Hawaii for an hour, then nothing again until a refueling stop on Biak, one of the first islands at the top eastern part of the Indonesian archipelago. Just across the turquoise strait was the "primitive" remote island that westerners know as New Guinea, split between the Indonesian province of Irian Jaya and New Guinea, much in the way as Dominican Republic and Haiti, and was home to "lost" bone-in-the-nose shrunken head tribes. Cool. At the early morning refueling stop at the "airport" in Biak, I bought some highly decorated, long skinny gourds used as penis sheaths by the underdressed locals. (On my return I actually had the honor of explaining to a U.S. Customs agent exactly the function and fashion of these items.)

Leaving Biak in the middle of the daily dawn-of-man sunrise, the airstrip and a modest terminal carved out of the jungle faded as we headed to next stop, Bali. There, all passengers were obligated to deplane and were escorted by uniformed soldiers with machine guns to the terminal, which was immediately shut down for three or four hours while the dignitaries from an all-Asia economic summit took their sweet time making their way to their airplanes to their home countries. Our arrival in Jakarta was very late at night.

In the morning we set off in a vain attempt to get any clue as to the promotional efforts by the local promoter and their effectiveness, riding around the funky suburbs in their armored Mercedes looking at various kiosks and newsstands where tickets were to be sold. The local promoter communicated to all that there was some lack of credibility amongst the residents of Jakarta and neighboring Asian countries that Mick Jagger was actually going to perform in Jakarta. The local promoter used their moneyed crowd connections and set up a week of feverish promotional activities to froth up some measurable excitement. Jagger's publicist, Tony King, and his two former Royal Marines bodyguards traveled in a posse and tightly managed each appearance. I handled, after a fashion, the international press, the unruly photographers and camera crews. The large group of Asian newspaper photographers I was in charge of credentialing were not schooled in the niceties of that process and upon first meeting them as a group with my handful of passes, they immediately mobbed me and tore them all from my hands.

Okay, that went well!!!

The first event planned for that feverish week was a photo op at the airport when Mick Jagger arrived from Singapore. The following day we made our way to the airport where we were met by the same group of hungry photographers from all over Asia with passes and without passes. While we were negotiating with the security at the airport to gain access to the tarmac where the helicopter was waiting to whisk Jagger off to the hotel, the group of photographers independently had already found their way onto the tarmac and were running in every direction to elude the military security, who did not appear to be amused at this nonsense. The press contingent found out before we did that, in addition to Mick Jagger being on the plane from Singapore, the body of the Indonesian Ambassador to Finland, a casualty of a presumably alcohol-related traffic accident, was also being delivered home and was to be received in a solemn ceremony at an adjoining hangar. The photographers were running back and forth between these two events causing a diplomatic kerfuffle.

Suddenly there he was, strolling across the tarmac to the aged military helicopter, turning around with a big lippy smile, doing the slow-mo Queen's wave, then gingerly hopping into the chopper with the rest of the gang, and off to land on the roof of the fancy hotel five miles way. In short, they ditched me with a crowd of worked-up press and military police. I finally commandeered a cab and arrived back at the hotel a good three hours of chaotic traffic later. There was a small reception for the assembled production staff, and I was greeted with enthusiastic slaps on the back for a job well done. Huh?

Next day was weirder – at the Presidential Palace, governmental headquarter, in a conference room with a couple of dozen dignitaries, some in uniform, some in the latest Armani double breasted gangster drag. I was not among the seated, but against the wall at the door, along with Tony King, Jagger's personal publicist, and the two burly bodyguards. There was only one photographer, not counting office staff shutterbugs, and as the event was wrapping up, the gentleman in the orange camouflage shirt, beaucoup medals and greased back hair sidled up to me. He introduced himself as the head of state security forces (not so secret policy) by whispering, "Ah, those were your people who caused such a scene at the airport yesterday." "That's me," I smiled. He segued smoothly and asked if I could get him an autograph for his wife. I said sure I could try to get Mr. Jagger to comply, and he said, "No, Tom Jones." I stifled a laugh and said next time Mr. Jones comes to San Francisco that I would do my darnest – but, in return I jokingly said, I wanted an orange camouflage death squad uniform shirt. He barked at an assistant, who returned minutes later with a still-in-its-package shirt.

I was going to make a joke about mine missing the medals, but experienced a rare episode of discretion considering his job description.

We broke the happy huddle and walked to the indoor balcony, where the President and his lampreys stopped for a quick photo with Little Lord Jagger for my hoard of shutterbugs who were all clustered behind a barricade at the bottom of a grand staircase. In a blink of an eye, the object of their desire and his posse disappeared. As I ran down the grand stairs hoping to catch up, I caught sight of the gigantic crowd choking the entranceway, spilling out onto the major boulevard leading up to the Palace. As I exited, some of the press spotted me and started pushing their way towards me. Meanwhile, Mick Jagger, his publicist and his two bodyguards were nowhere in sight, me, still not getting it that they were halfway back to the hotel by some security slight of hand. It took a good hour for me to extricate myself from the mob with the help of some uniformed fellows and made my way back to the hotel by cab, the long way apparently.

Again, back slaps and kudos upon my return and it dawned on me that this was my role - lightening rod/decoy to help the star crowd slip the scene.

By now these events had generated many repetitive articles, front page picture spreads, and the excitement could now be felt. On the last day of the PR blitz we were scheduled to visit the Disabled Persons Home out in the suburbs of Jakarta, this program being a pet charity of the wife of the Prime Minister. This visit was viewed by most in the crew and press to be anticlimactic and redundant, considering the massive avalanche of Mick Jagger press coverage the previous riotous appearances had generated.

When the caravan of vans reached the lovely manicured compound, we were down to a couple of photographers and one camera crew, all of whom peeled off after just a bit into the tour.

The Prime Minister's wife and her posse of society matrons, who took up one van, climbed out carefully, all 12 of them, as to not soil their pink and black silk uniforms. After having visited a few bungalows housing rehabilitation programs such as basket weaving and radio repair (I kid you not), it became clear that the institutional view of people with handicaps, deformities, and serious life-compromising conditions, as well as blind and deaf people, were all the same – all lumped together and treated like they were retarded in yet to be woke Indonesia.

After our little tour, the school officials led us to a small auditorium with old-fashioned movie theatre seating and a low stage. Mick and his peeps in front, the sponsors in the second row with the school poobahs, and the all the staff and the chaff behind them. I stood by the edge of the stage and watched the festivities, and after some national anthems and a short speech from the Prime Minister's wife, a raggedy group of four blind kids were busy setting up some cheap musical equipment. The setup complete, and after an awkward five minutes of relative silence, they launched into a Creedence Clearwater song (of course) with great enthusiasm and not a bad sound, especially considering the available equipment. Of course, next came the inevitable invitation for Mr. Mick and his guitar player (who brought an acoustic) to grace them with a number. Mind you, there were no members of press on hand nor did I even have a camera in my possession. Mick and guitar player Jimmy Ripp popped out their seats and bounded up onto the stage. After about a minute of conferring with the blind boys' band leader, the unmistakable guitar riff opened of "Honky Tonk Women," and damn if the funky little band, all shit-eating grins, hit the groove and held it for dear life. Instantly, the stage was filled with members of the school student body, dancing wildly and screaming along. A legless man who danced on his hands proceeded to repeatedly swing his trunk against Mick Jagger's legs, who promptly picked the half man up and danced around with him. I was laughing and crying at this soulful spectacle, doomed to be undocumented as far as I can determine.

Needless to say, my perception of Mr. Jagger evolved quickly from that of seeing him as a charming, but stuck up perfumed hanky rock royalty ponce, to this make it all free loose guy dancing gleefully with a half man in the midst of a crowd of crazy worked up handicapped kids. In the suburbs of Jakarta. No press.

At a reception for the crew later that night, I took a weak stab at being cool and asked M'Lord Mick if that was his first half a man, and he replied, "Oh, no, I danced with one in Spain one time back in the '70s." Been there, done that, more than once.

Well, the big show itself was another story.

ROGER HAMMAR

I started working for Bill Graham Presents as an usher in 1984.

The first showed I worked was the Grateful Dead at Berkeley High. I had the pleasure of meeting Bill at several shows through the years and he was always smiling and had a kind word to say…a real mensch.

Still ushering 35 years on…

Thank you, Bill, for the opportunity and all the great music.

RON BERGMAN

Production manager until replacing Peter Barsotti in 1986 as production director (which is a whole other story as there was a price to pay).

Began working at Bill Graham Presents in 1978 and still working there today (Live Nation).

I began working with Bill Graham Presents in 1978. Prior to that I was working with a small promoter company doing shows in the Santa Cruz/Monterey area. We were doing shows that caught Bill's attention as he hired the person booking our shows and that was my introduction to BGP. I worked as a stagehand for a few years and finally was given an opportunity by Peter Barsotti to stage-manage a few shows. I was hired temporary full-time in 1981 when Bill was producing the Stones tour and much of our staff was out with the tour. I had two six-month deals and was hired permanently in February 1982 (still listed as my hire date with Live Nation).

As to my favorite Bill story, I have several but will share two with you.

First was some sometime in the mid-1980s and I was production manager for a benefit concert at the Greek Theatre for a Mexican-American organization. I cannot recall who was the headliner, but this was how Bill operated in assisting organization produce events at cost if they arranged their own talent. I recall it was probably an afternoon Sunday show at the Greek Theatre and we had an early load in, probably around 6:00 a.m. The weather was calling for rain, and in the morning, it did not look promising. At the Greek, if inclement weather was a possibility it was always a tough call either go ahead and load in or would we have to move the date to another venue or postpone the show. If it was a BGP show I knew I could gamble and load in and hope for the best.

Since this was benefit and essentially not BGP money I was torn to figure which way to go. I figured it would be best to call Bill (even at that hour) to seek some input from him. I called Masada, Bill's home. He did answer and I started to explain the dilemma...until I heard snoring on the other end of the phone. I tried to get a response to no avail and ended up hanging up.

Now this was during Bill's Halcion period, which I assume is okay to mention since he talked about it with Robert Greenfield in Bill Graham Presents. I decided to go ahead and load in. I ended up lucky as the weather improved and the show went on.

Bill came to the show and when I saw him, we were talking and I said to him, "You know we talked this morning on the phone." Of course, his reply was, "We did?" I got a sheepish laugh and an apology.

My other Bill story is more a Bill moment and something to this day I recall vividly and proudly. It was for the Nelson Mandela Rally at Oakland Stadium in 1989 organized by Bill and BGP. My responsibility for this event was as the liaison between our production and the U.S. State Department Security force that was protecting Nelson Mandela. State Department Security was like the Secret Service, but protected foreign dignitaries that were not heads of state. It was very interesting working with the State Department Security thru the planning stages, as it was very different from our normal event environment. My moment with Bill was when he was introduced to Nelson Mandela. Being with him I was able to shake Mr. Mandela's hand. Just an incredible moment and something I was able to share with Bill.

RON SCHAEFFER

Bill and Bill Lite

During my high school and university years, heading to the Fillmore(s)or playing there, was the peak experience for me, my musician friends, and anyone into the breaking San Francisco psychedelic, blues, and rock music scene. Of course, the concerts and dances that took place there are legendary. Going to the Fillmore was like trekking to Mecca. I went there with friends and dates whenever my meager funds allowed.

After one particularly amazing night with the Who at the Fillmore, Pete and Steve Barsotti, band mates, and a few friends gathered in their Berkeley flat until the early morning hours, blissfully coming down from the experience. We played and sang along with every Who record, while debriefing and analyzing the magic we had just witnessed. We loved the Who, how they took the audience flying through peaks and valleys on a full trip.

But there was something else…something uniquely special about the venue and the production elements that intertwined with the music, and the scene. Particularly fascinating was how we watched Bill Graham and crew work in sync with the band to build on the musical energy, with lighting, and sound; orchestrating a peak musical crescendo, and dazzling visual experience for all in attendance.

We were all blown away by how Bill did what Bill did. We all agreed he was tuned in to the musical moment and the crowd's musical experience. It's easy to see how he was later referred to as THE Impresario. More than a master of ceremonies, he was innovative and a presentation artist in his own right. Call it experiential, mind-blowing, and a transcendental experience, whatever you think. But the vibe at the Fillmore resulted in some of the best musical performances of the day. I was especially into British Invasion and Blues bands, and saw all the greats. The street word was all the best performances of any band happen at the Fillmore. I echo that sentiment.

Some of the recordings that instantly still come to mind from the Fillmore are live records of Chuck Berry, Cream, and Aretha Franklin.

Clearly, we all loved music and performance.

That night all agreed if we followed our passion into the business, we should focus on being with the trailblazer, innovator, and dynamic producer of the moment. Obviously, the place to be was Bill Graham Presents and the Fillmore. In future years, all of us enjoyed the privilege and challenges of working with each other, in some capacity, at Bill Graham Presents.

I was hired part-time by Bob Barsotti, about ten years after that fabulous Who show. The opportunity to work in Bill's company was a ten-year goal. When Bob asked, I was ready and jumped at the offer. I became the Director of Video Operations for live concerts and concessions television. An instant challenge, he needed a new TV director with musical production and engineering experience. I had to wear all hats, and maybe even dance as well. One of my first productions was a week-long run with The Grateful Dead at the Oakland Auditorium. Baptism by the Dead or by fire, take your pick.

I found the Bill Graham Presents of my era a high-energy company, and full of thoughtful, visionary critical thinkers. It was fast-moving like most of today's dynamic dot-com powerhouses.

The daily make-it-happen dynamic was not unlike the network broadcast news world I was working in. I already knew the language. In your face, salty communication filled with creativity, hyper drama, and pressure you tried to keep just under a boil. Bottom line, in both businesses the show must go on, go on on time, no excuses.

I got a front row seat on the roller coaster, experiencing Bill's management style, process, and obsessions in real time.

Bill's Style

First off, he cut to the chase in any negotiation or confrontation. As Bob Barsotti once described, "Bill always goes for the jugular, no fucking around." I witnessed this first hand. Sometimes he used in-your-face confrontation or sometimes just two or three pointed quiet questions. His style could be confrontational or abrupt, but when everyone wants something from you at every moment how do you filter the noise and move forward?

In-your-face confrontation is a technique he employed to eliminate obstacles and keep a razor-sharp focus on a l point or action, usually resulting in a single move to resolve a critical issue. Bill employed it as a means to navigate swiftly through a pit of snakes. Later when I worked for Steve Jobs, who also employed this style, he too always had the last word in critical situations, and tagged Bill's style with, "do it, or I will fire you and get someone who will."

Obsession and Process

His energy was astounding, no brakes, and full speed ahead! Through sheer personal force of will and personal charm, he became a vortex that cut all layers of bullshit to make magic happen. One phrase of the time captures the essence: "totally balls to the wall." His expectation of anyone working for him in any capacity was: "THINK." Do the maximum best possible job at whatever you're doing, think of the production process as creating art. If you did that, kept the focus on the show, you were gold.

The annual highlight for me and my small TV and sound crew (Steve Paine, Susan Campbell, Jim Terrell and George Hubbard) was Bill's entrance and midnight count down as Father Time at the Grateful Dead New Year's Eve shows.

Midnight was Bill's moment to shine. The question everyone at the show voiced was, "Did you see last year's float? How will Bill top that this year?" The video record displays the pageantry of a true showman.

From today's perspective, Bill was an innovator and set the standards for a new industry, identified the pieces of the puzzle before him and realized how they integrated in the big picture. The results were global innovations in booking, staging, sound, lighting, graphical presentation both on stage, in video clips and psychedelic street posters.

Shortly after Bill died, I was working on a documentary piece about Bill Noyce, the founder of Intel.

In the process, I had time for several close discussions with members of his former executive team. It was obvious they missed their Bill, as I did the recent loss of Bill Graham. I asked why they missed their Bill, why they loved working for him, and how had they found a similar dynamic in new work situations going forward. The universal comment was, "I looked for a new boss that creates a collaborative, interactive, demanding but open work environment like Bill (Noyce) did." I could relate, I was also looking for a new Bill.

In 1991, I needed a new passion and to identify a future career path related to television, music, and theatre.

To me the path was obvious; the buzzword at time was "multimedia," which I suspected would be the inevitable convergence of music, television, and internet, morphing under the umbrella of the high-tech computer industry.

I focused on positioning myself where I thought this convergence would happen. One of my primary targets was Apple Computer. Eventually I joined as full-time staff, in charge of the Broadcast, and Events Production group.

Steve Jobs returned to the company not long after I was hired, a real breath of fresh air to a struggling company. Here was my "new" Bill.

Steve's similarities in style to Bill Graham were pronounced: Steve was also a showman with a laser focus on detail, fully in command of the emotional and technical details that would carry an event.

The corporate culture, interaction, collaborative elements, and the ability to present, justify, and heatedly argue the merits of an idea or task were front and foremost. The salty language, pointed confrontation, and crisis navigation paralleled the concert business and were reminiscent of my time at BGP.

Steve chose Grateful Dead and Beatles music as the introduction to his events. Like Bill, his love of music was paramount. If he hadn't had such a personal passion for music there may have been no iPod.

My crew and I worked on and/or produced countless meetings and events in the Apple Town Hall Theatre with Mr. Jobs.

Early on, those of us that had a background in concert production began noting how doing things the Bill Graham Presents way for Apple events was what worked. We also realized Steve and Bill shared similar attitudes and ways of interacting with all the players.

After a time, we began privately referring to Steve as "Bill Lite," joking at first, but as time passed the name stuck, and came to be a term of respect for two impactful powerful personalities.

For over 16 years, I had the pleasure of working with Bill Graham Presents. Then continued another fast moving 25 years for five CEOs at Apple Inc.

ROSANN DAVI KAHN

I met Steven Kahn in 1984 while working at the Oakland airfield. I was the divisional assistant to the operations manager of a fixed base aviation service. I also assisted in selling "air time" or "jet time" for the owners of private aircraft who were on a lease back program with our company. I was instructed to call Steven Kahn because Bill Graham told my manager that Steven was in charge of all matters relating to aviation and his jet, and that Steven would be signing the contract (if it met with Steven's approval).

I would, from time to time, see Steven as he came and went through the terminal with the Santana Band members; he would (when he was home in the U.S.) fly the band from venue to venue. On this day, he came in to see me with a signed lease back contract, that is how I met him. It was aviation and rock and roll for the next eight years.

Steven played a tremendous role in Bill Graham Presents; he wore many hats. His official titles were Production Manager for Carlos Santana, Personal International Production Manager for Bill Graham, and corporate pilot. During an international concert production event for Bill Graham, a cost of production sheet would be given to Steven, and he would always strive to meet the cost estimate, ensuring BGP made money and/or the concert met the bottom line. Bill highly rewarded him for his efforts and professionalism.

Steven met Bill Graham at Woodstock. Steven said that he was on tour with Spanky and Our Gang. At some point during the concert it began to rain and the stage lost power. Steven said that he figured out how to power the stage; when Bill Graham asked who powered up the stage, Steven was pointed out. Bill came up to Steven and offered him a job touring with Santana on the spot. Steven began working for Bill Graham at Woodstock (on tour with Carlos Santana where he remained for 20 years or more).

As Steven's career grew in worldwide concert production, so did his responsibilities. Steven was production manager for the first Soviet American concert on July 4, 1987 in Moscow. I believe the Nitty Gritty Dirt Band performed years prior - after that, Russia refused American concerts because they did not want their youth influenced by Western rock and roll. Steven was production manager for Amnesty International in Costa Rica with Bruce Springsteen, and Amnesty International in India with Sting, to mention a few. The tour I was most fascinated with was Mick Jagger in Jakarta, Indonesia. It became a concert with issues because of a riot that ensued. Bill said that President Suharto's people were to provide military support for crowd control and safety, but the military failed to do so. I still have the newspaper articles.

A moment to remember on the Jakarta tour for me personally was when I saw Bill standing backstage alone behind one of the winged side ramps. I went to him to see how he was doing because so much was happening around us. He asked me if I had ever seen Jagger perform and I told him, "No." Bill then wrapped his arms around me (my back to him) and said, "Watch." Bill and I stood watching Jagger singing, twirling, and strutting - he was coming down the ramp toward us. Bill said to me, "Watch him. Look at the way he moves!" The next thing I knew, Jagger spun around and sang a few words of Brown Sugar to us; I almost fainted. Bill roared with laughter at me. That was it. I will always be a Jagger faithful. He is a wonderful performer and was very nice to me after the concert at the crew party.

As for my relationship with Bill, it was solid. Bill and I became very close; we traveled worldwide together constantly. At my marriage to Steven at Masada, Bill took me by my elbows and told me that he felt as if I was marrying his eldest son, and that Steven's job was international (it took him away from home at least six to eight months a year). Bill said his gifts to me were first class air tickets anywhere in the world to meet up with my husband anytime I wished. Bill was true to his words.

Looking into Bill's personal life from my point of view, he was very much like my dad (he traveled and spent lots of time away from home). I think his business life and employees came before all else. But setting aside his hectic business schedule above all - he loved his sons, David and Alex, more than anything on earth. Steven often commented that, "Bill lived for those boys." Submitted in memory and with respect to all.

ROSIE McGEE

The very first time I saw Bill Graham he made a singular impression on me. Even then, at the first Mime Troupe Benefit he'd organized (at the Calliope Warehouse, November 5, 1965), he had this certain intense, focused energy that was in stark contrast to the very stoned folks swirling all around him. Little did I know he'd become a pivotal figure in our budding music scene, but I did notice him.

As our scene developed through the late Sixties and Bill opened the Fillmore and went on to manage and book various bands, I was always at least three degrees of separation away from him, although we knew each other well enough to say hello. At the time, a Phil Lesh's girlfriend, that girl who danced onstage with the Dead, and that girl with the camera, my interactions with Bill were of little substance. But every time he and I were in the same room, even at the other end of a large 'room' like the Fillmore, I was aware of his presence. It wasn't just that he was loud - he was; nor that he invited attention - he did, always; but even just standing there, his presence had, well, an indefinable weight.

As I watched him through the years, I came to see him as an actor who'd created a larger-than-life public persona he really enjoyed manifesting, whether to intimidate, cajole, or invite admiration from his "audience," or just for the sheer pleasure of how it felt to play that part. I suspected that the private Bill Graham was as intense and quick-witted as his public counterpart, but far more interesting. But although Bill and I had a number of decent conversations as our cultural scene matured, I never really got as close to him as I wished I could have.

In the late 1980s, as Jerilyn Brandelius was compiling what would become her wonderful book, The Grateful Dead Family Album, she asked me if I would write up some of my early- days Grateful Dead stories for her book. I was thrilled to be asked, hoping it would lead to my being published for the first time.

Around the same time, she asked Bill Graham to provide the foreword for her book, an assignment he declined at first, but took on with dedication once he'd agreed.

Bill and I never discussed our writing assignments with each other, and yet, we were in synch from the first strokes of our pens. Out of all the possible ways we could describe the meaning of the Grateful Dead Family, we both chose to describe a tree - a family tree.

Bill's foreword, a brilliant piece of writing, includes this phrase: "The family tree of the Grateful Dead would resemble a cypress, twisted by the winds of time and hanging on by its roots."

And my essay includes this: "If you tried to delineate a Grateful Dead family tree, it would not be effective to use the traditional bloodline progression of the 'begats'...(the tree) would have to be felled, its great trunk sliced open and the concentric rings examined to define the widening circles that shaped it."

Several months after the publication of Jerilyn's book, Bill spied me standing in the wings of the Greek Theater during the Dead's set break, and he got my attention by pointing at me as he walked toward me, a big smile on his face. I smiled and pointed back, and when we got within earshot of each other, we both started to say, "I read your piece in Jerilyn's book!"

This kicked off a whirlwind conversation between Bill and me, amplified by the wild flailing of two Europeans who couldn't really express themselves without using their hands.

Standing in the sun with the backstage buzz humming all around us, we had a forehead-to- forehead, fairly long (for Bill), intense talk about the content of our essays, and our feelings about the Dead and the Family. It was a rare moment of deep connection between us, and when we'd said all we needed to say, we each went our own way.

Rosie McGee, photographer and author of Dancing with the Dead — A Photographic Memoir.

ROSE SULLIVAN

I have many stories about Bill, but this one in particular is about my going to Bill and admitting I had a problem with drugs. I asked him for health insurance so I could get treatment. He said no. He couldn't do that and I started to get up and he barked, "Sit down, we're not done." LOL! I was shaking in my tennis shoes. But then he proceeded to find out where I wanted to go and he paid the $10,000 plus out of his pocket for me to attend a 40-day rehab in Arizona. He called me every week too. He was a wonderful, caring human being as well as a strong, willful man, but I loved him then and to this day.

I regret to this day that that wasn't the actual date of my long-term recovery, but since I now have over 25 years of sobriety, I like to think he forgives me and knows that he gave me my road to sobriety.

As I write this, I am moved by tears remembering his caring nature and generosity.

S

SALLY MANN ROMANO

Excerpted from The Band's With Me by Sally Mann Romano (all rights reservéd)

Toward the end of that year, in December 1973, when both Bobby Weir and Spencer Dryden were on the road, Bill Graham conceived an extravagant, once-in-a-lifetime Christmas present for a few of his minions, molls, and pet monkeys, graciously inviting me, Frankie Weir, the unparalleled rock photographer, Herbie Greene and his wife Maruska, who was Bill's sanctified secretary, Zohn Artman (Resident Wizard at Bill Graham Presents, as irrefutably evidenced by his business card), Jerry Pompili and several other carefully selected self-grooming folks Bill deemed capable of wearing properly pressed evening clothes with the requisite grace and élan, or at least without drooling into their dickeys, to the Venetian Room at the Fairmont Hotel to see Marlene Dietrich. (Please indulge me while I repeat the featured attraction: MARLENE. FREAKING. DIETRICH.) Rest assured, no one has ever had to ask me twice to an event of such colossal cultural import, and in any case, turning down Bill Graham's magnanimity on any occasion - colossally cultural, culturally colossal, or otherwise abusively alternative - was never on my frequently edited list of lofty aspirational goals. Thus, with characteristic laser-like foresight and planning acumen, I immediately secured the services of my over-forebearing babysitter and then - about 45 days out - began getting dressed for the Really Big Show, which if memory serves, involved reverse-engineering a near-exact replication of Jerry Hall's last best look—if Jerry Hall were two feet shorter, ten pounds heavier, and constitutionally incapable of ever ever ever considering

Rupert Murdoch attractive. (His wallet? Well, that's a different matter altogether.)

Finally, on the appointed evening, at the appointed hour, Bill called Frankie and me - his spiffed- up, spit-shined, Trixie and Dixie Doublemint dates - at the appointed place, ascending the steep driveway to Frankie and Bobby's glass house in a black limousine the approximate length of the QEII, its running lights glowing and floating in the December dark like falling-down- drunk gold stars. With a degree of panache he seldom, if ever, displayed when reading the riot act to Blue Cheer and other repeat decibel-level offenders at the Fillmore, Bill disembarked from the rear of his super-sleek showboat, a vintage bottle of Rémy Martin 1738 Royal Accord Cognac casually tucked under one arm and other essential party favors at the ready in an easy-to- access breast pocket. After a few rounds of refreshments to stoke the bonhomie and re-tune our prevailing rock-and-roll frequencies to rarely accessed cabaret mode, we leaned back into the rich Corinthian-leather seats of Bill's stretched-out limousine, rolled down the driveway in the highest of high styles, and sailed over the rust-red Golden Gate Bridge into an alternate entertainment universe and the most incongruous night of our thought-we-had-seen-everything lives.

At the Fairmont, for the Dead among us, accustomed as we were to febrile fans speaking in tongues and removing their clothes onstage while roadies swarmed like shutdown cornerbacks to prevent them from toppling the skyscraper-high speaker towers onto the band's unsuspecting heads, Marlene Dietrich's sublimely lit, impeccably micromanaged stage show was a revelation. Her 473-page contract rider called for every table in the Venetian Room to be cleared of all dishes, cutlery, ashtrays, even the water glasses, once dinner had been served to the audience, and then - and only then - when absolute silence and stillness prevailed throughout the expectant room, would La Dietrich deign to appear.

After a few anticipatory numbers by her pianist (sitting in for Burt Bacharach), Dietrich, a mere 72 years of age at the time, stutter-stepped onto the stage wearing a floor-length swan's-down coat, The Dress, a sheer confection of soufflé chiffon encrusted from bodice to hemline with crystals that shimmered in the overhead spots like Ethiopian opals, designed by Hollywood costume designer, Jean Louis, especially for Dietrich with a gravity- and age-defying nude understructure - a NASA-worthy feat of engineering that succeeded utterly in creating the illusion Marlene Dietrich still had the body of a 19-year old nymphet and that she had covered its youthful magnificence, just barely, with several thousand strategically placed Taylor-Burton- megawatt jewels. Mesmerized into incoherence, our entire table gaped like gap-toothed rubes at the prismatic, cinematic apparition that was Marlene Dietrich, who understandably remained somewhat stationary once she had been escorted and anchored to her mark in front of the microphone stand by a matched set of drop-dead gorgeous stagehands. (True, they had nothing on the Grateful Dead/New Riders crew, but still, one couldn't help noticing.)

Once the show got underway, with Bill Graham singing along with unabashed gusto to "See What the Boys in the Back Room Will Have," "I Get a Kick Out of You," and every other song on the menu, the rest of us fell into the throes of a collective, set- long, out-of-body experience which threatened to go full-tilt catatonic during Dietrich's husky finale: an inexorably louche, languid, and world-weary rendition of "Where Have All the Flowers Gone." Pete Seeger, Peter, Paul and Mary, the Kingston Trio, and all the rest of those comparatively weak sisters were forever erased from the soundtrack of our minds, and, for once - for obvious mental health reasons - we were grateful beyond our ability to express that the evening's apéritifs had not included the usual frothy punch bowl of lysergic acid diethylamide. Some visions are disorienting enough on the natch, and a nearly nude septuagenarian Blue Angel is definitely one of them.

SCOTT WALL

Bill had promised his son that he could have the car of his choice on his sixteenth birthday. Well, his son picked out a Jag just like his Dad's. Bill objected! It was his first car, it would get wrecked, he meant a simple car!

This evolved into a bet. Football - the office versus the stagehands. Bill's team was, of course, the office. I was on the stagehands team and our captain was Bill's son. I played center and Bill played nose tackle.

After the first couple of plays, Bill looked at me and asked, "Are you giving it all you've got?" I answered, "Bill you're fifty-something."

I boosted my game up a little, but after a couple more plays Bill goes, "If you don't give me everything you've got, you're fired!" So, I did, and on the next play I broke his middle finger. I have to tell you he got his finger splinted and finished the game.

The next time I saw him, he had one of those metal cages on it and told me it was broken, but that all was cool. He had told me to do it after all.

SHELDON SHULTZ

I have many, some funny, some just awful, and some run of the mill stories. Dealing with Bill as an agent was never a fun chore. I ran the New York Music Department at International Creative Management from about 1973 until 1998. I took over from dear Herb Spar who passed away much too early in his life. Tom Ross was co-head and was in Los Angeles.

Tom always told me that he had a great relationship with Bill, but Bill always told me differently. I assumed early on that this was Bill's way of keeping ICM off balance.

I'm sure he told Tom I was an asshole, but he always told me Tom was an asshole. Bill was a master manipulator and very clever in many ways.

Now to my story of one of Bill's crazy exploits: It was the US Festival in San Bernardino, California. A huge three-day event. I had Ray Davies on the Saturday show. I received a call from Bill at about 5:00 p.m. New York time. He was livid and screaming at the top of his lungs.

His problem was that Ray would not go on stage at his appointed time, but insisted on going on AFTER the sun went down. This was an old rock and roll trick used by musicians back then. The contract read differently, of course, but that was Ray being Ray.

I asked Bill if Elliot Abbot was there with Ray. Elliot was Ray's manager at that time. He said he was, but he was unable to get him to the phone at that moment. Bill, unbeknownst to me, had Elliot's very valuable vintage Mercedes Benz convertible hoisted up ON A FORKLIFT and was hauling it off to the backstage area to some place, God only knows where. Of course, Elliot was beyond crazy with fury and anger at the time and feared his car would be damaged! So, he could not have a "discussion" about Ray.

So now, Bill is screaming at me and I mean really screaming! It quickly occurred to me that I was on a speaker phone in his trailer and he had a bunch of his staff there to listen and watch him perform. I heard laughing and giggling, but Bill continued his rant at 1000 decibels. This was not unusual for Bill. He was a performer, as we all know. This was his "Fuck with the Agents Act!" I then told him to go fuck himself and hung up. He called back and was now really boiling.

I said that when he returned Elliot's car safely he should talk to him as there was no reason for me to talk to Ray about this. I was at 1000 decibels as well. I know one could not outshout Bill, but in those days, it was fun to try to do so. We hung up and I assumed he was happy with his performance and that the staff was entertained as well. As I recall, Ray did not go on 'til the sun went down.

I was pissed and did not speak to Bill for several months. He called and I would not take his call. Then one day I received a BGP show poster of the Grateful Dead with an autograph signature from Bill to me. A week or so after that Bill arrived in NYC and came to my office unannounced. We sat and chatted and never mentioned the Ray Davies matter, then I took him out to lunch. That was how rock and roll worked in those days: Unwritten Rules...Try not to stay pissed off with each other, we all need each other, and...well...it's only rock and roll!

I often talk about Bill to my dear friend Danny Scher always ending in a laugh. Bill was a trip!

SHERILL CONLEY (formerly Rohde)

I started working at BGP in 1982. At that time, everything was paper – paper show sheets and show folders in filing cabinets, paper tickets sold by actual people at record stores, a telex machine for international messages; I kept a spiral bound calendar on my desk to write down newly booked shows. No computers, no email, no fax machines, no cellphones. In terms of technology it was a long time ago. In terms of my life, it seems like it was just a little while back.

I was actually hired as Bill's secretary. Unbelievable, right? I'd graduated from college, landed a job at a small record company, the profits of which went up someone's nose (so '80s), and I kept sending my resume to Bill Graham Presents. I wanted to be near the music and in San Francisco, BGP was the music. I wanted to work there. Period. Bless you, Steve Welkom, for hiring me way back then. It was the beginning of an 11-year rollercoaster ride filled with excitement (I think we were all adrenaline junkies), hard work, lots of fun, and a dose of pain (is there anyone who can say they didn't cry at that job)? Not surprisingly, I didn't work out as Bill's secretary – very few could fill those shoes for reasons the BGP family knows well - but I was fortunate because Gregg Perloff needed an assistant, and I made the move to what would become a ten- year gig with Gregg and Sherry Wasserman. Right place, right time, and I count myself very lucky.

We used to say BGP was a family, and it was true: a crazy mash-up, a kaleidoscopically dysfunctional family full of characters and personalities, black hats and white hats, and some of the best people I've ever known, led by the master, Bill. With Bill, you never knew who was walking through the door on any given day. It might be the Bill who was funny, generous, magnanimous, driven and wildly creative. Or…it could be the Bill who would verbally remove your head from your neck if you looked at him the wrong way. A real crapshoot, and you learned to live with it. And while Bill was the overarching force, the leader, the light, my coworkers…my coworkers. What an incredible group of people. The cast changed over the years, but I can safely say that each of them made an impression on me, were part of my education and the intricate fabric that was my time at Bill Graham Presents. There is a connection there that is unbreakable.

Which brings me to one of my earliest recollections, though oddly it's not about Bill. One day early on while I was still Bill's assistant, Bill asked to see an old show folder and told me to have Rita help me find it. At the time, Rita Gentry was Danny Scher's assistant (and Rita, can I tell everyone that was a love/hate relationship?!) I dutifully left my desk and told Rita that Bill had sent me to her for help. Rita got up to help me, but as she did so, she looked at me with a gimlet eye and said in her gunslinger drawl, "You know, sometimes you have to help yourself." Was I intimidated? Oh my god, yes! I'd never met such a tough woman before; I was really cowed by her. Did I take it to heart? You bet I did. I've never forgotten the import of those words – practically and spiritually. I couldn't have imagined it at the time, but Rita became a mentor and eventually one of my dearest heart sisters. She is a constant and an inextricable part of nearly every BGP story I could tell.

Which makes me think about the women of Bill Graham Presents. We were an unusual bunch, equal parts toughness and vulnerability, trying to be strong and enduring in a decidedly male- dominated, often brutalizing environment. We watched out for each other, had each other's backs, were the shields in the storms that inevitably swept through the production department. I can remember some women coming to work there who didn't approach it that way, and they just didn't last long. Who knows what they saw that made them want to leave? All I know is that it was a challenging environment, and if you couldn't count on your girl to have your back, then it just wasn't going to work. It's safe to say the show, literally, could not have gone on without us.

And I have to say that while most of us worked in supporting roles, there was one woman who had transcended that: Sherry Wasserman. By the time we'd moved to Fifth Street, Sherry was throwing down with agents and managers, and booking shows right alongside the men. In those days, there were a few well-known female agents, even fewer influential female managers, but in the promoter world there was Sherry. I don't think I realized it at the time, but she was a trail-blazer who opened doors that needed opening.

At the Fifth Street office, there were five of us who sat at desks arrayed in a line facing the executives in the window offices who, in turn, faced us – we called those offices the wall of cheese. Offices pour les grands fromages of the company. Those five desks were hot seats, a direct line of communication to the heartbeat of the company, booking shows. To say it was fast and furious doesn't begin to describe how it was. For example, the phone would ring incessantly – I think I had four incoming lines on my phone – and we had to place outgoing calls for our bosses. So, often two lines would be ringing while I was on eternal hold for someone to come on the line for Gregg or Sherry. Stress! To this day, the sound of a ringing phone makes me flinch, and I bless the day smartphones and texting were invented.

But it was so much fun. We laughed a lot, talked a lot, did crazy things together and were so excited about the music because we got to know about it first. We loved our bands, and each us had "our" artist; I fondly remember Toni Isabella, at the height of punk, alt, rap and hip hop, having a thing for Jon Bon Jovi and she was so relentlessly cute about it you had to love him too.

So, yes, "the women of BGP" were unique, resilient, strong, outspoken and charismatic, and Bill liked to take the women out on the town from time to time. There was the luncheon in the private dining room at Vanessi's on Broadway that lasted into the night with more wine and food than I think I'd ever seen at that point in my life. The men of the office really couldn't stand being left out and crashed the party, bringing bourbon balls as an offering.

And there was the night Bill took us to the Fairmont to see Tito Puente. We all tried to look decent at salsa dancing (Bill was a pro), and at dinner, Bill asked a question that would bring a lawsuit these days: other than your significant other, who would you most like to sleep with? And yes, like a parishioner in the confessional, we all answered!

But as women we banded together. We were close socially as much as professionally. The long- gone Fuji-ya restaurant in the Embarcadero Center was a favorite gathering place (kamikazes!), and all of this eventually led to the birth of something so amazing it lives on in legend (if only in our own minds): The Bitch Goddesses. Prime time soap operas were a big thing in the '80s and '90s, most notably Dallas, with Charlene Tilton epitomizing the evil beauty that became known as the bitch goddess. Given that we were all equally beautiful and could be pretty bitchy if required, someone once referred to us by that epithet, and it took on a life of its own.

Our first performance was at one of BGP's incredibly fun, over-the-top Christmas parties, this one at Wolfgang's. Jan Simmons, Rita Gentry, Jackie Kalkanian Miller and I performed a song I no longer remember with some of our Dog Beaver office-mates in the back up band. It was ridiculous, audacious and salacious. And we became a "band", performing again at the next Christmas party with whips and chains provided by Bill's house men, Gary and Jay, and even participating in Bruce Cohn's celebrity golf tournament (although none of us had ever played golf...as if that mattered!) The Bitch Goddesses eventually left performing and went into management; Bill and Gregg were our first band. It was more fun than anyone had a right to have, and led to many more BGP women entering the Bitch Goddess world.

So, while this remembrance could easily have been about epic shows, or incredible music moments, or meeting artists (to whom we were forbidden to speak), what lives on for me are the enduring friendships. We shared a unique moment that was a confluence of time, culture, place (because San Francisco rocks), and creativity. We were part of the ongoing creation of Bill's legacy. You can't reproduce that or relive it, and the people I shared it with are forever part of my history. It was truly a once in a lifetime experience and I feel so, so lucky.

Epilog: One day, Bill called me into his office saying he had two tickets to see Marvin Gaye at the Circle Star Theater but couldn't attend; would I like to go? Yes, with so many exclamation points! At the show, I bought a large Marvin Gaye pin for Bill as a token of my thanks and gave it to him the next day. A few weeks later, some agent or manager was awful to me on the phone, and I sat at my desk, which was just outside Bill's office, crying. As I said, all that fun at BGP came with some pain. I went to the bathroom to freshen up, and when I returned to my desk, there was the Marvin Gaye pin with a large yellow sticky note affixed to it, and in Bill's handwriting: Dry the tears.

Forever grateful.

SONYA COX

Unfortunately, my first Bill Graham Presents security job was in 1991 at the beautiful memorial of Bill Graham's death that was held in

Golden Gate Park in San Francisco. I never got to meet him, but in my 12 years of working security I never heard a bad word spoken about him. I only heard of what an amazing and original person he was.

Over the years I've been lucky enough to hear many stories told to me by BGP employees of their experiences with him. I only wish that I could have met him because I could have then thanked him for everything that he has done for music and concerts. I know that this may sound crazy, but I've always felt his presence at every show. Lastly, working this job has educated me so much regarding people that you can't learn in school.

STEPHANIE SCOTT TELLES

I have never worked for Bill Graham, but I had an experience that showed his caring side.

I have been friends with Rita Gentry since high school. We hung out and did teenage things like cruising and flirting with the boys.

Rita kept me informed over the years of upcoming concerts and events. We were so excited when Bill Graham opened the Shoreline Amphitheatre. Shortly after it opened, I bought my 16-year-old daughter, Nina, tickets to attend a concert there.

Nina and her friend went to the concert together and I waited outside of the venue to pick them up after the show was over and bring them back home. I was shocked to learn upon their arrival home that Nina had been injured.

Their seats were located about 20 rows up from the front of the stage. Nina told me that she had been struck in the back of her head by a whiskey bottle that had been thrown from a row somewhere behind her.

Nina and her friend had been standing up dancing at the time and it knocked Nina to the ground. She felt very dizzy, so her friend helped her to the medical station at the venue.

The medical team wanted to take her to the hospital for X-rays, but Nina declined the offer since she was 16 and wanted me to be there. When we got home, I immediately took her to the ER that night and they discovered that the bottle caused a crack at the base of her skull.

The next day I called Rita and told her what had happened, and she immediately passed this information on to Bill.

To my surprise, he called me and wanted to know how Nina was feeling and wanted to pay any medical bills she had or may have. I told him that she was double-insured and no money had to come-out-of-pocket.

He wanted to know if Nina felt that they were thoroughly searched upon coming through the security check. Nina said "No." She did not feel the security at the entrance gates were doing their jobs.

Bill said that the safety and security of the concert goers were very important to him.

He was going to have more training for those employees immediately.

Bill called us again a few days later to check on Nina.

Then he called us a third time and said he was sending us VIP Parking Passes along with food and drink vouchers for our next concert. At no time did we ask Bill for anything, but he offered these items on his own to try and make up for the bad experience Nina had.

Since then we have since then enjoyed many more concerts at Shoreline Amphitheatre over the years and never had a problem again.

STEVE ROZZI

I'm 71 years old and I used to attend shows at Winterland in San Francisco where Bill was the promoter. I don't remember the year, but it had to be the early '70s and the Grateful Dead were headlining.

The Dead are playing on stage and they are really into one of their drag-on songs and it was getting towards the end of their show. All of a sudden, the band starts staring towards the rafters up above them so it seemed like the audience started looking up too.

There's a guy who has somehow climbed up in the rafters and everyone could see that this guy was thinking about jumping. Slowly, Jerry Garcia and the band members started backing up and they all stopped playing, making the venue become very quiet.

Now the stage is empty and someone in the audience yelled out, "Give him a drum roll." Bill Graham came running out onto the stage and told the crowd, "This is not funny. We're talking about a man's life."

Then it became really quiet again and Bill ended up talking the guy into climbing back down. Bill Graham saved that person's life! I will never forget that night.

STEVEN GREENBERG

Rita's note: Steven Greenberg told this story to Kitsaun King and Kathy Suhy before he passed away on February 18, 2012. At the time of his death, Stephen owned and operated 230 Fifth Rooftop Bar in New York City.

Kitsaun King and Kathy Suhy were in New York City to see a couple of Santana shows. Whenever they were there, their dear friend Steven Greenberg would take them out for dinner, and they always got a great story about Bill with it.

This particular time, Steven told us about how Bill had always wanted them to partner up on some venture, so when Steven opened the Roxy Disco Roller Skating Rink in 1979, Bill really wanted to be involved. Steven decided he would have Bill provide security, and Steven couldn't have been happier with the result. He knew he didn't have to give security a second thought, as Bill had taken it to a "whole 'nother level!"

During that time in New York, the drug scene was getting pretty bad, and one of those drug problems was manifesting itself right across the street from the Roxy. A gang was always selling drugs there, and Bill was really fed up with it, so he told Steven he was marching across the street and getting rid of them. Off Bill went with his "one man army" approach, returning a short time later looking pale.

Steven knew something was very wrong.

Bill relayed how he had confronted the gang when one of the pushers sucker-punched him hard in the side of the head.

Bill suffered a very serious injury from the assault, as he lost his hearing in that ear for some time. Steve said he had never seen Bill so beaten down.

That night Bill told Steven he didn't want to be partners anymore in the Roxy, so Steven gave back all the money Bill had originally invested, and Bill left.

He told Kitsaun and Kathy that he never really saw Bill recover from that assault.

STEVEN MARCUS

Seeing an ad in the paper today for the sale of the Bill Graham Estate for $27,500,000, it is nothing like the home I visited twice back in the day. The original had two bedrooms, den, a large living room and a HUGE chef's kitchen. I loved driving up the driveway that had sensors that activated the various New Year's Eve floats that Bill road in on. They are now located at Shoreline Amphitheatre.

He was such a wonderful host. He took me to his den and said, "You'll like this!" He showed me a bookshelf that had a ton of video tapes of Winterland concerts. He let me stay in there to just look around and check them out.

I loved the rows of dried flower wreaths in frames that were hanging in the dining room from all of the New Year's Eve shows. I think he remembered the NYE when his wreath fell off his head into the crowd. I saw exactly where it fell and who had it. I ran and got it from the stoned Deadhead who caught it. I got his name, phone number and address and told him that Bill will be forever grateful. I ran backstage and gave the wreath to Bill… he smiled.

SUE FINN

Never really knew what my title was and I always tell people that I came with the club (the Old Waldorf) where I started with the original owner, Jeffrey Pollack, who owned it in 1978 before Bill purchased it. Worked for Bill from 1980 until 1983 assisting Queenie Taylor.

The Old Waldorf

Tina Turner played the Old Waldorf in 1983 before "What's Love Got to Do with It." She came for a soundcheck and was appalled as to how grimy the backstage dressing room area was, definitely not up to her standards. She insisted on seeing Bill. I don't remember the rest, but he must have come since she played that night.

Merle Haggard was playing the Old Waldorf and Bill wanted to get him a gift. I was chosen for the task. I remember picking two things, but I don't remember what the other one was. The gift was a suede vest. I had to go to his bus to give it to him. I remember it being a not so pleasant encounter. I don't think he was very appreciative.

The Kabuki Theater

Tom Petty was booked to play the Kabuki Theater in 1983 and Bill wanted it announced by radio stations, not in newspapers. I was elected to call all the stations in the area that played Petty. There may have been between six to eight at the time. I had to do it from my home at 10:00 p.m. on a specific night. In those days we had no cellphones, so I made the calls from my home one after another as quickly as possible.

Working for Bill was definitely not a nine to five job.

SUGAR SIMS

My first encounter with the Bill Graham company was when I was hired by Bruce Jennings who was the owner of Event Security. Bruce was a good friend of Bill Graham and helped in the making of a great security company. We got things done.

My first show was The Last Waltz. In the city of San Francisco at the closing of the venue Winterland I worked my first Grateful Dead show. I had never seen anything like it before. All the people were crammed into the building and on the outside of it too. There were so many people looking for that "miracle" ticket. Working outside of the building, it my job was to check bags and bodies as they entered the venue. I would say, "Have your tickets out and ready. No cans or bottles. Everyone is subject to a search." Part of my job was to search the women and the men for any of these items. It was a job that is not for everybody to do. I found out that you need a special gift to be able to pat down hundreds of people before the show starts. It is quite a feat. From the very start I knew that this was the job for me. I got to finally tell people what to do.

I became part of a family that took me on wonderful journeys. Coming from a little town called Oakland (the eastern part of Brookfield Village) I was one of six children (five girls and one boy). Being the oldest, I left home at the age of 16 thinking that I knew everything and I knew nothing at all. If I could rewrite anything, it would have been to continue with my art classes in school and staying in school. But as life goes on, I chose to venture out on my own. In my day, you were seen and not heard; you stayed in a child's place never letting one's thoughts to be heard.

I went through a lot and learned a lot about being on my own. After a very bad relationship, I moved to San Francisco to get away from the abuse. My friend, Jackie Robinson, lived on Divisadero Street where I met Ms. Freddy Hinkle who worked for Event Security, a company that worked for Bill Graham Presents. There weren't very many Black women on the staff at the time. You worked just as hard as the men and you definitely had to hold your ground.

Through them (Event Security) I got a chance to travel and work with The Grateful Dead and many other groups.

I got a chance to work at the Fillmore, the Warfield Theatre, the Paramount Theater in Oakland, the San Francisco Civic Auditorium, Concord Pavilion and Shoreline Amphitheatre.

If I had not come into contact with Bill Graham Presents I would not have been able to experience the following: A promoter job with Sugar Sims Comedy and Music Review, which was held at the Last Day Saloon in San Francisco.

The chance to see what it was like to fly first class to Telluride, Colorado being the only Black woman on the staff of the Telluride Music Festival. After the show, I ended up at the only radio station in Telluride and spun them some soul music, especially "California Dreamer" by Frankie Beverly with the group Maze. What a treat that was at three in the morning.

The chance to work at the following shows: Working at the Rolling Stones concert at the Oakland Coliseum while also being able to babysit my granddaughter; meeting Tom Petty and the Heartbreakers for 27 days and also being able to sing and dance with Tom and the band at The Fillmore and Sting at the Greek Theater in Berkeley, etc.

I give thanks to being part of the Bill Graham Presents family making it possible for me to meet all of the different people involved behind the scenes in the production of a concert/show which makes it all happen, such as stagehands, caterers, front of stage, behind stage staff, security and even the cleanup crews.

I want to thank Bill Graham, Bill's immediate family and the Bill Graham Presents family for their friendship. If I hadn't had Bill and Bill Graham Presents for about 30 years of my life, it would have definitely been very boring.

If I could rewrite my life I would not change a thing….

SUSAN BARSOTTI

Today would have been Bill's 89th birthday. We muse about what Bill would be doing if he were alive now. Faced with current calamities, we often ask ourselves, "What would Bill do," because his moral compass was worth following. Soon we'll gather at the Fillmore in San Francisco to celebrate him - a fundraiser, of course. Upon entering that hallowed music hall, we'll be offered a shiny, red apple from a tin bucket at the top of the stairs.

My Bill story is about the apples and meeting Ralph Moratz. Early in 2012, Bonnie Simmons, who is the Executive Director of the Bill Graham Foundation, took a call from a gentleman named Ralph Moratz. As a Jewish child in Berlin during the Second World War, Ralph had survived a brutal journey across Europe with a group of other refugee children. As an adult, he had reached out to other survivors through a Shoah webpage, and had been collecting people's fragmented memories of escape from the Nazis. A picture he'd posted caught the eye of the director of the Jimi Hendrix Museum, who recognized a youthful Bill Graham, aka Wolfgang Grajonca, and he sent a message to Ralph. Now Ralph was posthumously reconnecting with his childhood friend and fellow survivor, Wolf.

My husband Bob worked with Bill and is the president of BGF. When we heard about Ralph, we immediately made plans to meet with him the following April. Bob and I arrived early at our meeting place, and were soon joined by Ralph, who was silhouetted as he approached our table. It was immediately striking to observe his bearing, body posture and long stride - even down to the bowed legs and flat feet, he appeared so similar to Bill's physicality. It was stunning, and very moving. He began to share memories of his great childhood friendship with Wolfgang, and the many hardships they'd endured during their exodus from Nazi Germany to the U.S.

The group of children had spent a very difficult period at Chateau d'Quincy outside of Paris during German occupation. They were surrounded by enemy soldiers, and were often very hungry. The group of about 40 boys had divided themselves by age into groups called the Army, Air Force, and Navy. As members of the Air Force, Bill and Ralph were sent on missions by the older kids' Army. One such mission was to sneak out at night to find food for the group, which included raiding nearby orchards. Ralph recalled how he and Bill would gather huge armfuls of apples, as many as they could carry. It was very dangerous as there were enemy forces all around, yet the boys were caught up in the adventure and did as they were told. Ralph said many times the apples were all they had to eat for days at a time.

Bob and I had been silent, so rapt were we hearing Ralph's recollections, but with the apple story, I felt a jolt. "Were they red apples?" I asked him. Yes, he confirmed, always red apples.

Bill was a great storyteller, and generous with his memories, yet we'd never heard a mention of this amazing part of the story from their time at the Chateau. Was it possible he had no actual memory of risking his life to gather life-giving apples for their group? Ralph told us that many of the survivors' recollections were indeed fragmented, so it's entirely likely Bill had forgotten or repressed this detail. Regardless, it seems that red apples represented to Bill a feeling of fellowship and hospitality, even life.

SUSAN NICHOLS

I started at Bill Graham Presents in 1984 working on a concert site and working sometimes in the BGP office up until 1988. I then changed to be an on-site person working at the concerts. I was picked up by the Grateful Dead during 1988, but still told Berna (who booked the employees for shows) that I would always work if it were possible to do so with Tom Howard, Ron Bergman, Steve Paine or Steve Macfadyen.

During 1988 was the Amnesty International tour and Bill was mostly out of the office during my office time working there, which means I didn't get to see or interact with Bill much. Bill did wonderful things for his staff and especially the great Christmas party that happened each year for employees. When I did attend these parties, I always made sure to seek him out and to personally thank him (not sure if many did), as that was the way I was raised.

Bill would put on appreciation parties during a Grateful Dead show/run would usually be held in the rooftop suite of a hotel that we would be staying at. On this occasion in Las Vegas we were in the Frank Sinatra suite, which Frank had stayed in at one time. During this party about six of us women who had worked the show were having fun and all laying down on the bed that Frank Sinatra slept in. Bill heard us all laughing and carrying on and walked to the door of the bedroom stopped and then suddenly did a running jump to land in the middle of the harem. At this point someone grabbed a camera and took a picture of him and us six women on the bed. What I do remember about him was that I thought he had been given a terrible haircut due to his role in Bugsy.

I can only think of one other confrontation with him. He did know that I worked for him, but thank goodness he did not yell at me but he was yelling at the guests at a show. It was during a Lollapalooza show and the guests of the Butthole Surfers showed up on the wrong day, but I knew they were friends of the band and I knew they were on the list for the correct day. I gave two stick-on backstage passes to two of the four of them. So, the security person escorted them into the venue (two with passes and two without). The two that did not get passes yet were River Phoenix and his girlfriend Susan. Susan ran off to pee and River tried to find her, which made it difficult to find them to give them their passes. I ran off to the Lollapalooza production office to get River and Susan their credentials. While I'm in the production office I look out and see that Bill was in River's face so much that they were almost touching noses. I did not dare walk out between those two men to hand them the passes; that would seem very uncool for me to do to Bill. So then I ran into the Shoreline production office screaming to Rita, "Bill's kicking out River Phoenix!" Rita, as cool as she could be, looked out the window and told me, "Everything's okay Sus." When I left the Shoreline production office I then saw Bill and River arm in arm and our house photographer was taking pictures of them. Once the photo shoot ended I gave River and Susan their proper credentials.

Thanks to music that I love and BGP it led me to working with Robbie Taylor and the Grateful Dead.

T

TARA MANN

Bill Graham was a modern-day prophet. Like all those who came before him who were deemed "prophets," it was most certainly unbeknownst to him in the midst of the wizardry he was conducting. Bill had no idea the legacy he would leave to the fans and performers of live music events all over the world: that people could gather in a safe and peaceful environment was unprecedented prior to his creation/manifestation of the live music experience and it was magic!

I remember telling people I worked for Bill Graham and was received with raised eyebrows, "Oh the evangelist?" Okay, let's step it back here a little, "No, the rock and roll impresario." Responses ranged from, "Oh cool," to cocked heads with a confused expression on their face. I was always shocked that there were people a similar age to myself from the Bay Area who did not know the legendary Bill Graham. Obviously, those people who were not in the know were also not live music fans.

I don't remember the first time I saw Bill in the office, but I do remember the first all-staff meeting in our "corporate" HQ. All the department heads: booking, production, AKG (the nightclub division), accounting and finance, etc. and every single one of us gathered together to listen to Bill. When Bill spoke, everyone was silent. What I felt then and can articulate now that was so mesmerizing at that first meeting: the energy I felt from Bill. I had not witnessed that type of power so up- close and I felt the electric current that Bill carried. Bill was so respected and such a force that he could not only hold the creative tension amongst his direct reports, he could cast out energetic flames or spirals of turbulence and pull energy in a way to keep all the departments cohesive with creative output extraordinaire.

When music programs in public schools were on the chopping block to be defunded, Bill held a brainstorming/focus group at his home, Masada, to address this travesty. He hired a professional facilitator to manage the event. Attendees included Jerry Garcia, the California superintendent of public schools, Paul Kantner, Angela Alioto, Art Agnos, Governor Jerry Brown, and others who were a list of who's who in the San Francisco Bay Area. Bill also extended the invitation to everyone in our office to participate. I had never met anyone who could command respect across multiple circles and be the creative force behind new programs that served the greater community. That was the magic and power of Bill Graham. Many years later, the Bill Graham Memorial Foundation was formed to support music programs, the arts and education.

Bill Graham changed the course of my life and livelihood. I learned from Bill that I could do/be anything if I set my mind to it, was creative and was willing to work hard.

After Bill died in the tragic helicopter crash and before the memorial at the Polo Field in San Francisco, the Grateful Dead had a four night run of shows at the Oakland Coliseum: October 27, 28 and 30, 31. On the day of the Halloween show, I was working at the office in the nightclub division. We were all just trying to put one foot in front of the other and grief was the dominant unspoken feeling for all of us. I received a call that day from a dear friend of mine. She asked if, on her behalf, I would bring in hundreds (more like thousands) of candles that people would be instructed to light in honor of Bill Graham at the show that evening. I so desperately wanted to help my friend out and I just couldn't do it. I told her I was sorry, and she was very understanding. I spoke not a word about her request. Here is the story told by Poppy Davis who defied the "rules" that evening because she had a vision. With love she threw caution to the wind so that all the Deadheads could honor and respect Bill Graham that evening. Here is her recounting.

"There was a four-night run at Oakland before the memorial at the Polo Field, so no public memorial had yet happened at that time.

During the first three nights we took up donations for candles to share with everyone on the last night of the run, Halloween. My friend Kate Bengford was a good former Catholic and she worked the Yellow Pages and charmed the church supply stores and got us four big boxes of votives. I don't know how many were in each box, but the boxes were a good 36 x 48 and the votives were the really short ones.

On Halloween, Ethan Benjamini had a pass, and he was a big dude who could carry two of those boxes, so he walked two in through backstage and no one questioned him. Kate came in through the front with the third box. The Red Coats (security officials who worked for the Oakland Coliseum) asked her what was in the box and she smiled and said, "Candles!" which they chose to hear as "candies" and waved her in. I had the fourth box. The Red Coats asked me what was in the box, and I said "candles" and you know my diction leaves no room for interpretation, so they said, "Those can't come in." I said they were for the Bill Graham memorial and I needed to talk to a Bluecoat (BGP staff). I had to repeat that I needed to talk to a Bluecoat for a while, but then they flagged one down for me. I just said, "These are for Bill. I need to talk to Peter or Pilar."

Of course, in retrospect I should have just found Pilar sooner and arranged for all the candles to go in through the back, but really the whole point was that it was from the Deadheads and it was for Bill and all of BGP so we didn't really want to do it through them. The Bluecoat took me back to production and there was Pilar. I told her what was up, and she went and got Peter.

As soon as I saw him, I blurted out that they were "safety candles and they go out if they fall over," which was total bullshit I had just made up. I also told him three boxes were already in - which I did not actually know to be true. He just nodded and said okay, and I walked into the show from backstage and found my people who had already handed out the first three boxes and got to work on distributing the fourth box. We had also printed up instructions that said everyone should light the candles at the end of the first set before the lights came up.

They closed the first set with "Let It Grow," and during the last jam little candles started to flicker all around the Coliseum. It was an honor to play a small role in honoring such a great man who brought SO MUCH JOY AND LIGHT into the world.

His presence is still a gaping hole in our community.

So, here is the beauty and magic of this amazing tribute to Bill Graham and BGP. The year was 1991, we weren't using smart phones, there was no, "let's find candles for cheap on the internet," there was no "flash mob" light your candles now. It was that grassroots, word of mouth passing of information that we so rarely see today as we are all inundated with immediacy and reliance on our smartphones and social media. When "Let It Grow" came to an end and those candles started to flicker, I knew who was at the center of this tribute. While I couldn't help my dear friend that day, I certainly wasn't going to stop her.

Every single person who held a candle did so in reverence. There were no fires started in the Coliseum by careless fans. This was the legacy of Bill Graham: He created a safe space for people to gather, listen to music and in doing so allowed for the collective conscious to rise and ascend into the light.

Rest in Power, forever and always, gratitude and awe.

TERENCE McCULLOUGH

I love music. Frankly, I don't understand someone who doesn't. Growing up in a musical family (mom sang opera, and dad is a big band jazz drummer - a legitimate, working one, for a long time). It was just part of our everyday existence. My entire world, from birth, has been richly filled with beautiful music. Preferably live.

Naturally, from a very young age I was obsessed with live shows. Living in the Phoenix/Glendale area of Arizona from 1976-1980, I was glued to my FM radio. KDKB and KUPD were "the" stations for rock and roll (my preference, although I love most types of music). I was living there with my mom. On November 10, 1979 Kiss had a date booked on their Dynasty tour at the Veterans Memorial Coliseum in Phoenix. I convinced my mom to let me go. Alone. I was 12. My first live show. Imagine that now. It was definitely another time.

We moved back to California in 1980. I split my time between mom and dad in the Los Angeles area. Two very different households.

During this time, mom took me to two big-ass rock shows at the Fabulous Forum in Inglewood. In July 1980 (there were four shows, I don't remember the exact date) it was my all-time favorite band – Queen, on The Game tour. The other? The Who on June 20, 1980, on their first tour after Keith Moon died. That was my 13th birthday present. Thanks mom! You ruled.

Mom and I moved to Santa Monica together right after that. My older brother, Ron, had relocated to San Francisco a few years prior. I periodically flew up to see him on PSA Airlines at 19 bucks out of LAX…of course, discovering partying, girls and more live music. This was the legitimate beginning of my Bill Graham experience.

In 1982 over Christmas and New Year's I flew up to see Ron who was a biker badass and huge Grateful Dead fan. On New Year's Eve (his birthday by the way), Ron looked at me and told me to put on my most intimidating biker getup (I actually did have some legit gear, but that's a different story for another time) because we were gonna jump on his Triumph Bonneville 500 and blast across the Bay Bridge to the Oakland Auditorium. I asked him what was going on over there. He said we were going to see the Grateful Dead. I said we didn't have tickets and this show was probably the hardest show to get tickets for on the planet. He looked at me like he was gonna beat my ass and told me to shut up, mount up and hang on. Now THOSE were prophetic words.

We got to Oakland Auditorium and parked the bike. This was when camping was still allowed across from the main entrance on the lawn. This was also my first Dead show so I was taking it all in. It was unbelievable. Those who know, know. Those who don't know absolutely missed out. I asked him just exactly how he was going to get us tickets. He laughed and told me to follow him. We walked right up to the backstage door on the side of the building just as it opened. He walked right at the security dude, menacingly, and said, "We got business." The guy took one look at us in our HA wannabe gear with our hard looks on our faces and stepped aside. We walked right in. Walked through the backstage area (me doing my best to keep it together) and into the crowd. True story, as I live and breathe.

At midnight Bill rang in the new year as Father Time. That show literally took me to another place. That night I knew. I just knew. I was moving to San Francisco and was gonna do this show thing for a living.

This wordy setup I hope you now understand was necessary. It sets the stage for the rest of my musical career and that Bill Graham would be the most formative employer and acquaintance in this business that I ever had the joy to know.

Fast forward a few years. I had made good on my promise and in 1985, mom and I had relocated to the Bay Area. I began my local club and arena gig odyssey. It was amazing and joyful. How much better it was in Northern California! I went to as many live shows as I possibly could.

Eventually, I began inquiring of the ever present - and respectful, cool and quirky - security folk that wore these curious blue vests as to whether they liked their gig.

They all said they loved working shows. I asked who they were working for. They said Bill Graham.

Now, as I said, I had this really rowdy and crazy big brother that I hung with intermittently. He was firm in his opinions for sure. One of those opinions was that Bill Graham had singlehandedly formed and blossomed the live music scene in the Bay Area, making it the best world. And I took my brother seriously.

So, naturally I was super intrigued when these folks told me who their employer was. So I asked how I could get in. I was told to send my resume to BGP's office on 5th Street in San Francisco and I did.

Wouldn't you know it, a little while down the line there I was sitting in that very office being interviewed by Bernadine Ferguson for a part time job as a Bluecoat (the blue vested folk). Bernadine (Berna from now on - she was firm on this) hired me on the spot. I don't know if it was my brawny good looks, musky cologne or pure desperation, but I jumped at the chance to join the team. And so it began.

A bit or irony: My first Bluecoat booking was a run of Dead shows at Frost Amphitheatre at Stanford University, May 1988. It was three shows. I couldn't believe I was actually now part of the event. First day - parking lot. Ah, the glamor. Second day - search and stuff. A bit more glamor. But the third day! Backstage pass gate. On the day that the gig and all involved celebrated Billy Kreutzmann's birthday. There I was after the show at his birthday party backstage. The first time I ever met Bill Graham. Wow - what a first booking.

My experience working for Bill Graham Presents will never be equaled. What I refer to is the unique approach that Bill and his managers and supervisors used to train and teach us. They were staunch in the principles of being NICE as much as possible. Having gone to shows a bit in other areas and venue systems, I had always felt that security was typically rude and unnecessarily aggressive and bossy. Bill's staff hated that approach and trained us to treat the fan as the person who was paying YOU with their hard-earned money, to respect the ticket holder and to treat them as you would want to be treated. So simple, yet so rare. I took this to heart and I still behave this way.

As a result of a lot of the skills, training and relationships attained through BGP and its operations, I was blessed to be hired for my first tour as a guitar technician in 1990. This was for the Bay Area band Vicious Rumors.

As time and shows went on, I like to think that I had progressed to the point of being accepted by the production folk at BGP. I had made friends with so many amazing people and wanted to do more advanced stuff. So, I applied for and secured a position as a regular venue employee with the focus of stage technician at Shoreline Amphitheatre and this was 1991.

Now I was working in a very different environment, around different people and learning so much more about the overall scope of event management. It was awesome. Bill, Rita Gentry, Mary Conde, Steve Macfadyen, Sherry Wasserman, Peter and Bob Barsotti and on and on. The same approach was ever-present in their tutelage as well. Be nice. Be firm. Be smart. Be gentle. Be a FAN!

I was asked to provide a bit of my BGP history and maybe a story or two. Here's another good one and then I'll shut up.

On May 9, 1991 Guns 'n Roses booked a warm-up show for their Use Your Illusions Tour at The Warfield Theater in San Francisco. The show was announced on local radio stations the day of the show and tickets sold out in an hour. Naturally, I wanted to go, but couldn't get tickets. I went down there any way with the "I Need a Miracle" mentality. It was a zoo. Lots of barricades going down Market Street for crowd control. Naturally, The Warfield staff had it totally sorted, but it was definitely not looking good for this guy getting in. I got frustrated and leaned up against the wall outside the gig. The doors were open and the line was moving in. I was really bummed now, but I figured I would hang and wait a little longer.

I looked up and Bill was standing out in front observing the line moving in as he liked to do. We made eye contact and he clearly recognized me. I immediately thought I was in trouble as BGP frowned upon employees using influence of any kind for personal advantage and I didn't want Bill to think I was trying to slide in using my employee status.

"Ah, shit. He's coming over to me. I'm doomed." I thought to myself. Bill walked over to me, quickly and with purpose. He looked me square in the eye. "Here it comes. He's gonna ream me good." He put his hand out and stuffed a red Globe paper ticket into my hand. "You go in and have a good time."

I had no words other than thank you. He was having none of it. He just grinned and went back to watching the line move. That sums up Bill.

Did I go in? What do YOU think? Of COURSE I did. And the show was absolutely crushing. They packed more gear into that place than I had ever seen, including multiple boom cameras for an obvious video shoot. I swear that The Warfield show is part of the "You Could Be Mine" video that came out the next month. This is just an incredible example of Bill wanting a fan to be able to enjoy the show.

Eventually, my path took me to full-time touring. I began as a backline technician, did my time the right way and graduated to tour manager. I have been all over the world and inevitably I'm asked how I started in this nutty business. When I say Bill Graham Presents, it is always received with huge respect, worldwide and still to this day. It is the first and most important entry on my touring resume.

The mark this man left on the music business will never fade. Thank you for changing my life for the better, Mr. Graham.

TERRI LYNCH ANDERSEN

I had moved from my hometown of Yreka to Concord, California in 1978 to go to school at Diablo Valley College. While taking a bowling class (you heard that right), I met Brian Auger, a dynamic, fun-loving guy who was just as serious about his college career as I was at the time. We became pretty much inseparable at that point, a great friendship that has lasted to this day.

Among his many duties with BGP back then, Brian was the head of the volunteer usher team. I started ushering for Brian and pretty soon I was supervising and then running the usher program with Brian, mainly at the Greek Theater, Berkeley Community Theater and the fabulous Warfield Theater. These years account for, hands down, some of the best memories of my life.

When the office on 11th Street was destroyed by arson in 1985, I helped establish the new offices on Fifth Street and then stayed on for a couple of years as the office gofer. In 1988, I took the job as House Manager at Shoreline Amphitheatre in Mountain View, California, the 25,000- seat "jewel in the crown" of Bay Area venues that BGP had built and opened in 1987. I went on to become the assistant manager at Shoreline and worked there for nine years. (I could write a separate book on the amazing family and incredible times we had at that magical place.)

I met my future husband Tom on the "other side of the fence" at Shoreline when he was the Mountain View Police liaison for us, helping me with security, sound complaints (ugh!), and the endless traffic headaches. Our twin boys were born in 1996 and in 1997, we retired from Shoreline and moved to Nevada City, California. We continued working for a few more years as traffic consultants for BGP (shout out to Danny Scher!) in their efforts to develop amphitheaters throughout the northwest.

When the kids started school, I started driving a school bus so I could be on the same schedule with them. It was so much fun I stayed at it for another 15 years and I'm retired completely now. A few years back I sat for a four-year term on the city council here and was

Mayor of Nevada City for a year in 2014. Great experience - everybody should try it if they can!

Our boys are 24 now; Ryan is an Army medic in Texas and Chris is going to school here in the area. Tom and I spend our time in our cabin in Nevada or in our motorhome on the Oregon Coast. Life is good. When I look back on my 19 years with BGP, I know I'm one of the luckiest people in the world to have been involved with that family of people at that time doing what we did. We weren't the best at what we did. We were the only ones who did what we did.

Here are a couple of Bill stories.

When I was working in the office sometime in the early '80s, I was tasked with spending a couple of days in the "listening room" compiling what I think was the equivalent of a mix tape for Bill. I had lists of individual songs off of albums that had to be recorded onto a master tape. I can't remember the format, just that it couldn't be rushed with high-speed dubbing or anything because the sound quality was crucial. It must have been vinyl to tape. Anyway, because each song had to be played through in real time and properly sequenced, I remember spending hours in earphones listening to a lot of amazing music - all of Bill's favorite stuff: Blues, jazz, classical, flamenco, a little bit of rock - just an amazing, rich variety. I remember being surprised at the range of music Bill listened to personally when I suppose I'd always associated him with the rock and pop that we promoted and managed. I mean, no offense Bourgeois Tagg, but this was a real, layered tapestry of interesting, quality music.

Bill came in a couple of times to check on my progress. I don't think he was in a hurry; it just seemed like he wanted to talk about the music and see what I thought about it. We talked a lot about jazz and he asked me who my favorite singers were. I told him I thought Sarah Vaughan was the best female jazz singer of all time. He said, "Oh no. There's no question it's Lena Horne. Listen closely to that soulful, sexy voice and you'll see what I mean." I asked him what was his favorite album of all time and he said it was Miles Davis Kind of Blue. (I'm 90 percent sure it was that album.) He asked me if I knew it and I was embarrassed to say I hadn't given it a serious listen. He was adamant that I do so and made me promise that I would. He said it was at the top of the list for anyone wanting a serious understanding of music.

We talked more about other pieces and he explained how some things reached him on a cerebral level, some things on a gut level. It was fascinating listening to him talk about that side of himself. I felt so fortunate to have had that brief, intimate time with him outside of our usual stress and chaos. I listened to Miles Davis. I didn't get it!

That was a lifetime ago. Maybe now is the time to give it another try.

The next one, if brief: few of us used to stop into a bar called the Chieftain, near the office on Fifth and Howard, after work on nights we didn't have a show to work. (Brian remembers it as the home of the Cadillac Slammer. It's still there.) It was next to the Chronicle building and was always full of newspaper folk. One evening, three or four of us were heading over there when Bill saw us from the parking lot and asked where we were going. We told him and he asked if he could join us. A few minutes later he parked his car right in front of the bar on Howard Street. Was it a yellow zone or a red zone? Who can remember? We hung out for an hour or more and swapped stories with Bill.

Quite a few beers and Slammers later, someone must have alerted us to the fact that the police were ticketing Bill's Jaguar. All I remember after that was all of us hanging out the front door with Bill yelling, "What the hell do you think you're doing? You can't touch my car! THIS IS MY TOWN!!!" I remember thinking, "He's got a point."

TERRI McKEOWN

I remember Huey Lewis and the News were doing a couple of shows at Cal Expo Amphitheater in Sacramento. Fillmore Fingers was doing the catering. We had a screened-in, make-shift kitchen that we used. It served its purpose in those early days, with everything jimmy-rigged, long extension cords and often blowing fuses. We were lucky we were able to feed the crews and artists with minimal glitches.

We loaded in on Friday, got prepared and day one catering went off without a hitch. At the end of the first show, Bill comes into the kitchen calling my name. "Oh Jesus, what did I do?" was my first thought. He tells me he's invited the whole 49ers football team to the show on Sunday and wants to feed them. I just stared at him. He's telling me the menu and where we are going to set up extra seating and my thought is: I don't have food to feed these people. This is before 24- hour grocery stores, the Internet and food delivery service.

Panic sets in. I can't tell him no. This is the man who can make anything happen and expects his employees to do the same. Okay, okay, I say. He leaves thinking all is good. I immediately left the venue with a fellow worker and went to the only grocery store (Pak-n-Save) that was open until midnight. We got there five minutes before it was closing. I asked to speak to the manager and explained who I was and whom I was shopping for and thankfully they let me shop past closing. I packed my little red Honda Si to the brim with groceries and back to the venue we headed. Didn't get much sleep that night.

The 49ers arrived at the show, and we fed them along with everyone else and all had a good time. Bill thanked me and the staff for our efforts. He knew what he had asked of us. I knew this man loved to feed people and was proud of what we did. That day defined me as a Rock and Roll Caterer.

This was just the beginning of Bill calling out my name wanting to talk food.

TERRY POTT

My memories of Bill Graham started in Vietnam. I was a river rat in the Navy running Swift boats. When we weren't getting our butts shot off, we would listen to an underground rock station that we could pick up through the Armed Forces Radio Network. One night we were sitting around listening to music and telling which groups were the best. When my turn came after hearing about the Stones, the Dead, Moody Blues, etc., I said: "It's not the bands for me, it's Bill Graham I most admire because he knows and hangs out with all of them."

When I got out of the Navy, I went to Ohio State, got married and then in 1975 moved to San Francisco from Cleveland. Kate, my wife, got a job at a law firm in San Francisco and met Jan Simmons, her BFF for the last 40-plus years. Jan quit the law firm after a year and went to work for Bill Graham Presents.

Not long after she became Bill's Number One. Jan, Kate and I played a lot of racquetball. Bill was complaining he was getting fat, and Jan suggested he play racquetball with me. So, here I am, playing with my idol, the man I most admired! I promptly kicked his ass every week, but he kept playing every week because Bill doesn't give up! Time went on and we became good friends.

One weekend, Bill, Jan, Killer (Steve Kahn), Kate and I flew in Bill's plane to Canyonland, Utah for the weekend. We had a ball hiking all day. At night we watched an old movie (plugged into a generator) in a tent. Killer's friends met us at the campground and set it all up. Roughing it!

When Bill was on tour with Bob Dylan in Europe in 1984, he sent tickets to Jan, Kate and me for the last two stops on the tour in London and Dublin. When you read my wife's story she will tell you that story.

My heart was broken the day Bill died as I had lost a friend who always had a million stories to tell and a smile on his face.

Bill was truly a generous, kind and thoughtful person. To this day I still always think of him.

THOMAS HARVEY

I often marvel at the many amazing people that I met along the way, both within Bill Graham Presents as well as the Tower Records organization. I think about how much my life has benefited positively by virtue of association with both entities.

I only worked at Tower Records for about six months after high school before I took off on a six- month trip around Europe right before I entered college, but the friendships I made were indelible, as much so as the ones that I made during my ten year tenure at Bill Graham Presents.

As you can probably imagine, I'm pretty busy these days, juggling time between corporate events and big rock shows, not to mention my own projects, family, kids, etc., but at some point in the near future, I look forward to sitting down and doing some serious writing myself.

TOM SMARE

I started working for Bill Graham Presents in 1986 and am still working at the same facilities today. My jobs consist of Guest Services Director at Shoreline Amphitheatre, usher, Bluecoat, operations and box office staffer.

Not necessarily a shining Bill moment, but this encounter between Bill and me affected me and does to this day: In 1982 I was a young Deadhead who was also a huge Bill Graham and BGP admirer who thought Bill and BGP were the best in the business and could do no wrong.

On December 26, 1982 my friends and I arrived around 10:00 a.m. at the Oakland Auditorium for the Grateful Dead show that night. Our tickets were being held at will call so we got a spot in that line and waited all day so we could get the coveted front row balcony seats we loved.

When the doors finally opened at 6:00 p.m. the ticket holders' line began to move inside immediately, but the ticket sales/will call line did not move, which was unusual. Five minutes, ten minutes, fifteen minutes went by and no movement in our line and I became more and more upset as I watched hundreds of people file in from the other line, knowing the best and now even decent balcony seats were gone.

At that point I saw Bill Graham walking by the stalled line with a serious scowl on his face. I meekly called out, "Hey Bill, the line's moving kind of slow." He glared at me and kept walking. A moment later someone behind me yelled, "This system sucks!"

The next thing I know someone is yanking on my pants leg from the street below me and screaming at me. I turn and see it's THE MAN himself, Bill Graham and he's bellowing at me and yanking on me like I've never been bellowed at before. He eviscerated me, called me every name in the book, cursed me up and down. "Who the fuck do you think you fucking are? You have something to say to me, say it to my fucking face you fucking asshole! You criticize me to my back! You're a fucking coward! You think my system sucks try running one yourself, you piece of shit!

412

This went on for a minute or two and the sheer power of his verbal attack left me speechless. No one had ever spoken to me that way before, and certainly not the main man, Bill Graham himself. His tirade got the attention of the hundreds of people hanging out in the park, they saying, "Hey man, Bill's reaming somebody. Check it out!" and I was suddenly the unwanted center of attention on the receiving end of one of Bill Graham's infamous verbal beat downs.

I was certain he was going to throw me out of the line and maybe crack my skull and I couldn't get a word in. When he finished his first tirade with, "And shut your fucking hole." I felt like I had been slapped in the face and I was finally able to try to defend myself.

Even after I convinced him that it wasn't me who spoke behind his back, he continued to rip me for being an ungrateful fan who didn't appreciate that there was obviously a problem in the box office and I should be "fucking patient" while they worked it out.

I didn't see it that way and tried to tell him what I thought, but that went nowhere fast and finally a few Bluecoats came over and walked him away. The situation left me shaking and muttering the remainder of the evening while I sat in the rafters of the sweaty old building.

I was so upset by what had happened that a few days later I wrote Bill a letter reminding him of the situation and telling him that I didn't think he treated me fairly and that I didn't think his organization had handled the problem correctly. Surprisingly, he wrote back to me saying that he remembered the incident and agreed with me, apologizing for his behavior. I appreciated that, but mainly I was left with the feeling that I had been wrong about Bill and his company always being the best at everything and it got me thinking about how, in my opinion, the situation should have been handled.

Ultimately, the whole thing actually inspired me to want to work for his company, feeling for the first time that I had something valuable to add to it. When the opportunity arose a few years later for me to get involved with Bill Graham Presents, I held onto that feeling and all through the many years that I've worked in the various areas of public assemblage for BGP and its remnants. I've always remembered that night on the steps of the Oakland Auditorium and how I felt as a helpless patron, and have always used that feeling to inspire me to look past my viewpoint as a staffer and try to see and understand the needs and feelings of the patrons, and try to help them as best as I could at all times.

I believe that I've done a decent job of that and I believe that the interaction I had with Bill that night so long ago has helped me and continues to help me be a better staff person. I'm a teacher by profession, and I've always believed that Bill Graham was a teacher and that he had an innate ability to inspire people even when he was at his worst; that bummer of a night actually inspired me to develop what has been a long and successful association with the company I've always admired.

TOM STACK

Telluride, August 15, 1987

The Grateful Dead were nearing the end of their first show during the much-hyped Harmonic Convergence weekend in Telluride. Fearing the large crowds soon to be descending on Colorado Boulevard's restaurants, Anne, my girlfriend at the time, and I took off before the encore and got an upstairs table at an almost-empty Mexican restaurant. From our perch, we could watch and hear the goings-on outside, not feeling crowded, which was perfect for our still simmering mushroom buzz.

We ordered fast and were served almost immediately. The crowds below grew and grew; the lines at the restaurants extended outside and down the street, a street misnamed a boulevard. In its day, Colorado Boulevard was merely a wide dirt path, horses tied in front of saloons, banks, flop houses, shoot-outs at sunset, bank robbers, maybe even Butch and Sundance.

In the distance, the sound of approaching drums, pulsing and swirling, whistles, chanting - what could it be? With our bill paid, we jetted from our table, down the stairs and out into the street, where we encountered African men and women dressed the part, drums and dancing, and in the middle of it all, Bill Graham. Bill was leading the couple dozen some odd folks in this ever- growing mass, Baba Olatunji and the Drums of Passion the energetic core, and Mickey Hart sweeping up the rear, herding the new adventurers into the adoring flock.

Bill would then use his basketball coach whistle to stop the procession, like a creek jammed by a boulder, people spilling up into the restaurant lines, store porches; the drums were pounding as loud as I've ever heard drums. I found myself centered near Bill and one-on-one with one of the stunning dancers in the group, Anne over there in her own one-on-one with a drummer. The energy at this point was spiraling higher and higher; Baba had us chanting, howling, wailing for more. Then, with one long whistle, Bill began the march anew and down the boulevard we'd go for another 50 yards or so, 'til he did it all over again: the halting whistle, more people joining, Mickey and Baba raising the level of excitement with each beat of the drums, the utter irony of these African natives marching down a street populated by the cowboys and settlers of the American Wild West; the dichotomy was undeniable and more than pronounced in our current state.

And there was Bill, sweat pouring off his forehead in the late day dusk, grinning ear to ear, right in the middle of something you just knew he thought up a couple of hours ago. We marched up the hill to the gym and the sold-out show with Baba Olatunji and the Drums of Passion, packing that room and throbbing for another couple of hours, an encore of unprecedented proportions.

Universal Amphitheatre Los Angeles, August 24, 1989 Part One

The Who performed Tommy in its entirety on August 22, 1989 at the Universal Amphitheatre in Los Angeles. It was a benefit concert, $250 face value, which was a ton of money in 1989. Jan graciously invited me to join her on this trip, along with Maggie, David Graham and his current girlfriend, and Bill. We took off from Novato in Bill's plane, with Steve Kahn serving as the pilot. I was offered the shotgun seat and I jumped at the chance.

It was a beautiful summer day as we flew down the middle of the state. I had to pinch myself as I looked over my shoulder and saw Bill Graham shuffling paperwork and handling his business behind me in his own plane! "I can see for miles, and miles...."

This night was a pleasure cruise for Bill. He did not have a hand in producing the show, meaning he was not wearing a laminate or any credentials. At a certain point in the evening as we were all watching the show together, Bill excused himself and exited the row. A few minutes later, he came back, but before he could enter the row and come back to his seat, he was stopped by the usher, who asked for his ticket. This could have gone either way. It was clear the usher had no idea who Bill was.

Bill either didn't have his ticket or couldn't locate it, and the usher wouldn't budge. But when was the last time Bill Graham needed to produce a ticket at a concert? I watched as the two of them carried on a short conversation. In the meantime, I borrowed an extra stub and walked it down to Bill to give it to the usher.

When I got there, Bill was telling the young usher what a great job he was doing, how important his job was, and how his boss was lucky to have him. He did not play the Bill Graham card, or make a scene, yell at the usher, any of that. Bill acted like a complete gentleman. He toiled, for once, in anonymity, and he appeared to enjoy it.

Part Two

Later on that evening at the huge celebrity benefit backstage gathering (Bill eventually scored some laminates for us), Jan and I were brought into an exclusive area: Sylvester Stallone, Timothy Leary, Cheech and Chong, Tom Cruise, a wild mix. To say that David Graham and his girlfriend were acting affectionately would be an understatement. Bill was talking with Pete Townsend and to his right and my left was Roger Daltrey. Bill tapped the sitting David on his shoulder and said, "David, you remember Uncle Roger, don't you?" David looked up from his lip lock, and replied, "Sure, hey Rog," and got right back to work with his girlfriend, pretty much blowing off Roger Daltrey!

Daltrey looked at me, with the most amazing blue eyes I've EVER seen on anyone, and he was speechless. Bill's jaw dropped too. I laughed and said, "I'll talk to you, Roger," and introduced myself. We chatted for a bit about the show, the upcoming gig in Oakland next week, whatever. He turned his full attention to me, 'cause young David was way too busy...rock and roll. What a night!

Last Story: It was a late July, 1989 afternoon when I pulled into the parking lot at 5th and Mission. Jan and I were going to a Giants game that night, and I was swinging by the BGP offices to pick her up. As I climbed the stairs and walked towards Bill's office area and Jan's desk, I could hear yelling. Bill was letting some poor guy really have it on the other end of the phone. Jan gave me the eye to sit down, which I did, and sat quietly. Bill had that half window to his office, so he could see me come in while he was on the phone. He finished this poor soul off with a couple of expletives, slammed the phone down, and made his way to the waiting area. I did not have any idea what to expect when he approached me. He extended his hand, and said, "Hey Tom, who's pitching for the Giants tonight?"

What?

It was an absolute 180-degree attitudinal swing. Was he acting on the phone, positioning, negotiating? It was hard to tell, but the moment became immediately ingrained in my mind. He literally flipped a switch and came back to the present. Amazing....

TONY BIANCALANA

My name is Tony Biancalana and I was born in Bernal Heights in San Francisco, two months before the first BGP shows at the Fillmore.

I went to Day on the Green shows, Winterland and the Old Waldorf. I started working for Bill Graham Presents doing security when I was 18 in 1984 at the Kabuki Theater, the Fillmore and as a show janitor at the Warfield in 1985.

The first time I met Bill was at Wolfgang's and he was going through a door from a closed off area with his back towards me. I said, "Excuse me sir, that's an off-limits area." He turned around and I saw it was Bill. I then quickly apologized and he just looked at me and nodded.

At the Beastie Boys show at Wolfgang's he spent the whole night pretty much doing security with us. The show was way sold out and there were hundreds of people on the street with no tickets. At the end of the show I was at the front door with Bill and shots rang out and there were pieces of the marquee from above falling down on us.

When Wolfgang's burned down he was there the night of the fire to check things out. Same with the Neville Brothers show at the Fillmore in 1988 when the Duquette Pavilion burned down next to the Fillmore staying there until the fire went out.

In 1990, Kenny Briggs' job was to do security at the front desk at 260 Fifth Street, the BGP main office. He had tons of vacation time and Karen Magnuson, the office manager, told him he had to take at least two weeks off. My wife and I had recently had our first son who was a couple of months old so I was more than happy to pickup the extra hours when Kenny asked if I could fill in for him. Kenny trained me how to lock up and told me that sometimes Bill would stay late. You would have to make sure everything was locked up and ask Bill if you could leave.

So, of course, my first day I started at 10:00 a.m. Now, it's 7:30 p.m. and I go upstairs to check things out and Bill is at the copy machine in his office dancing to some Latin music with his back to me. I said, "Excuse me Bill, I'm filling in for Kenny. Everything is locked up. Is it okay if I go?"

I could tell that I'd startled him and then I saw his eyes relax and he says, "You're that kid who works for David." (Mayeri). I said, "That's right. I'm Tony Biancalana. Is it okay if I leave?" He just looked at me and said, "Go ahead," and went back to his desk.

I will never forget him, his work ethics, and tenacity.

Bill would check every area of the club, pour drinks behind the bar, pick up trash, and was always interacting with the paying customers, whether they were complaining or praising him. He was not afraid to get his hands dirty.

It was like working for your father. In some ways I think Bill had his own family taken away from him by the Nazis in Germany and created his own with BGP.

I'm honored to have been a part of that family.

To this day, I am trying my hardest to keep his legacy and work ethic alive at The Fillmore. I was born into that family in 1965 and hope to leave it with my children who also work at The Fillmore.

I wrote this poem about Bill this morning (7/28/2020)
Family taken away
You escaped the pack
Raised by wolves
Persecuted by the horror of men
You fought them back with laughter, love and music
Feeding them apples as they bit your fingers

You won their trust by trusting them
Teaching them to trust one another
Never forgetting where you had come from
Or where you had been
You created a new Wolfgang

TONY KILBERT

Bill Graham…a larger than life spirit, a formidable presence of straight ahead power. If you escaped the Nazis as a young child with one of your sisters, you might have those attributes too.

As a promoter in the business of rock and roll, Bill drove a hard bargain and he worked with the biggest names in the industry: legendary tours with the Stones, the Grateful Dead, Santana and so many more, to say nothing of running seminal venues like the Fillmore West and Fillmore East.

The variety of shows he initiated are still talked about today, from over-the-top worldwide tours to fundraisers and special social and political events. Bill Graham remains an implacable music business and pop culture legend.

His tough-edged stance and forceful voice made people quiver. Even standing still, you could feel his inner gears, primed and ready to pounce or just raise holy hell. Nobody has ever done it bigger or better than Bill and they never will. But on occasion, Bill might pull back the curtain and unexpectedly reveal a more fun-loving persona - but just for a bit. Let me share my glimpse of that rarity with you.

I first met Bill Graham in October, 1972. I had landed a weekend slot at KSAN-FM in San Francisco in September of that year. I was 23, fresh from college in Illinois and thanking the gods that the country's premier underground rock radio station took a chance on this kid from Chicago. I owe my entire career in the music business to the door being opened by Tom Donahue, the station's vice president and general manager, and a very good friend of Bill Graham.

Tom Donahue was a heavy hitter in American radio. He was a contemporary of Dick Clark in Philadelphia rock radio in the '50s, and a 'boss jock' in the early '60s in San Francisco who brought The Beatles to the Cow Palace on their first tour of the states. Tom owned racehorses and even a record company called Autumn Records that recorded soul singer Bobby Freeman's, "The Swim." Autumn Records also hit the charts with the Beau Brummels tune, "Laugh Laugh," and Tom recorded the Golliwogs before they changed their name to Creedence Clearwater. The engineer for Tom's record company was Bay Area DJ and future hit maker, Sly Stone.

Some people know Tom Donahue as the man who inaugurated the format of freeform radio with San Francisco's KMPS-FM in 1968. The San Francisco music scene was exploding with great, soon to be iconic, bands like Jefferson Airplane, Quicksilver Messenger Service, the Grateful Dead and more.

They played heady shows with multi-tiered bills presented by people like Chet Helms at the Family Dog and, of course, Bill Graham's Fillmore West. Tom's station KMPX was at the nexus of this social and musical explosion - all the musicians, all the promoters and all the record companies came through the station 24/7. The hipness factor was palpable and all the attendant products, from jewelry and clothes to restaurants and music stores, got in on the action with their advertisements on KMPX.

Bill Graham and Tom Donahue were major players in the country's hottest music scene. It goes without saying there was mutual admiration between these two heavyweights. Each admired the other's savvy and effectiveness. They were titans in their respective mediums and they each had massive effect beyond their home base of San Francisco.

Every wannabe promoter or radio station bigwig across the country wanted to be them, a smashing success in their market; that imitation was the most sincere form of flattery. Tom and Bill set the templates up and everyone wanted "some of that," even if you didn't understand that timing is everything and the duplicates are never as strong as the originals.

By the time I got to San Francisco in September, 1972, Tom Donahue had taken his radio juggernaut to Metromedia's KSAN-FM and Bill Graham was worldwide with Bill Graham Presents or simply, BGP.

Within the first month of my dream job at KSAN, a programming announcement was made that would stop every Bay Area music fan in their tracks: The Fillmore Special.

Bill Graham would come to the KSAN studios and he would broadcast live on the air from Friday night, October 27th at 6:00 p.m. until Monday morning at 6:00 a.m. October 30th. This would be a one-time only marathon of music and memories. Bill would go one-on-one with each KSAN disc jockey and share his personal recollections of his many shows and his reflections of the many artists he worked with. Each hour would be programmed with Bill's deep tape collection of live shows and KSAN's enormous record library. KSAN's Milan Melvin and yours truly were tasked with gathering and cataloging all the materials for each hour and assembling the packages for easy access. I knew our record library but the Bill Graham archives were like going to the Temple of Thebes, daunting and sacred.

The Fillmore Special was a total success; people stayed home and listened to the radio to hear some real-time magic. Imagine Bill Graham and his memories and that incredible music for an entire weekend in your home or maybe your car. The intimacy of radio took over the nine Bay Area counties and put every one under a spell. Even David Bowie's first San Francisco shows, ironically presented by Bill, and bombed. Bowie and the Spiders from Mars two-night weekend stand at Winterland, October 27th and 28th, only drew a few hundred people to each show.

For me, at two months on the job, I was living a dream that I'm still not believing happened. Bill Graham on a first name basis, entrusted with his personal tape collection and working in very close quarters for a marathon weekend??

The cherry on top was the combined Bill Graham Presents and KSAN-FM celebration dinner at Fleur De Lis French restaurant one month after the broadcast. I told my boss, Tom Donahue, when he walked in the place, "I'm still fucked up Big Daddy." Tom just laughed out loud, smiled and looked over at Bill grinning.

Fast forward to September, 1991, just one month before Bill's tragic helicopter ride after a Huey Lewis and the News concert at Concord Pavilion. A German TV show had contacted me about a historic San

Francisco music feature they were producing. They wanted a short interview with Bill to give the piece some color and authentic gravity. I called Bill's secretary with the request. "We just need 30 minutes, a quick in and out, no muss no fuss interview in Bill's office." I got the okay the next day.

The day of the interview, Bill was in a great mood and the two-man TV crew had their German efficiency "on lock." We plugged in, had a great conversation about the past, present and future of the San Francisco music scene and we all shook hands when it wrapped in just 20 minutes!

Then, as if on cue, the phone rang and Bill's secretary alerted him that it was someone he'd been wanting to talk to. Bill excuses himself and takes the call, it's obviously important. Grabbing the phone, Bill rips into the caller and unleashes a classic salvo of epithets - the fury, the passion and that powerful distinctive voice going through the phone line like a tsunami. There was a momentary pause and you could sense the caller on the other end gather himself. In that brief millisecond, Bill looks up at us all and smiles like a Cheshire cat. He nods his head up and down with confidence and then jumps back in for round two.

We all saw it; a duality was revealed, the fearsome music promoter and the mischievous child existing at the same time. The actor stepped out of the frame; he broke the fourth wall and then went right back to work. The ninja was on his toes, enjoying the craft he created and excelled in, but the original kid was still there too and having big fun. I'll never forget it.

TONY LINDSAY

One of the great things that I remember about Bill Graham is how he was always so hands-on with all Santana shows. He would watch, listen and then pass on his notes to us after the show.

There are not many promoters or even managers that I know of that would add that special touch like he did.

TRACI HOWARD

I was a Bluecoat from 1987 until 1997. I have a ton of stories, but I'll keep it simple.

I've always heard people say if Bill didn't yell at you, he didn't notice you. I'm glad to say that Bill never yelled at me. I did have the experience of him stopping by many times to check in at different shows.

I enjoyed working the paddock area with David Graham and his buddies when they were home from college at the last official Grateful Dead show, which was Laguna Seca Daze in Monterey, California. Good kids - crazy job! They used the paddock area for Deadhead backup camping. Big mistake! It's where they work on the race cars. This area had just been resurfaced too. The campers pounded their tent stakes into the pavement. Not a good idea. I think it's why it was the last Laguna Seca Daze!

But I'll share a great little story. I was working Paul McCartney at UC Berkeley. I was giving breaks after taking tickets. One of the areas was the backstage parking lot. A guy called me over to ask me to play a joke on someone. He pointed out a type of green sportscar and told me, "It's my friend's and I'll pay you $100 to just let the air out of the tires. What could it hurt?" I knew whose car it was and laughed my ass off at that guy. It was Bill's car. He tried to assure me that Bill would think it was funny. I told him that might be true, but I enjoy my job way too much to risk it.

TRISH BOULB

My first show was Paul McCartney at Berkeley Stadium on April 1, 1990. I was willing to go as high as $80.00 for two tickets to see an icon. My boyfriend at the time worked at Stanford Hospital, with usher extraordinaire, Patricia Webb. She informed him how to call and get the information about ushering, as a volunteer, for the Berkeley show. The package of info I received from BGP stated something to the effect of "Ushers should wear black pants and white shirt/blouse or nice casual suit/sport jacket, comfortable shoes, flashlight," and so on.

I had a killer three-piece beige suit and a long-sleeved white blouse. What the hell did I know???

Brian Auger was the first person I met from BGP, as he gave instructions at the Greek. When we got to the stadium, before we got to listen to the awesome soundcheck, we were handed maps of our positions. First 26 rows, CENTER STAGE. I had no idea what that meant. A lot of chairs still needed numbering and I was all too happy to assist Barbara Super. I remember her telling me that black and white would have been more appropriate, but that I looked very nice. I was then asked to go to stage right (whatever the hell that meant) and double check that all seating stickers were on securely. Of course, you probably know where I went. I asked one man if this was stage right and Bill asked me, "Do you know your left from your right? It's over there. You look okay., but you'll learn," and pointed. I didn't know who he was, but I wanted to die.

And when an experienced person told me what was what, I still wanted to die.

Being center stage and running my ass off, much of the patrons in my sections thought I was some kind of person in charge (three-piece beige suit). A lot of parenting skills, being creative, a lot of sugarcoating, and pure BS got me through the night. And what a most wonderful night it was! So much, that Barbara Super asked me to come to Shoreline Amphitheatre and volunteer. Three shows there and I was on the payroll. I just finished my 28th season now with security. But I would volunteer anytime needed in a heartbeat.

I know this one was a long-winded paragraph, but I want people to know how much of an effect Bill had on so many of us in his teachings, his caring of details, and his absurd way of letting you know he cared for the family that made magic happen.

Sometime in the 1991 season, Bill was setting up a ball toss for two free lawn tickets, which was held at the Center Stage Bar, now Lucky's Place - Velcro balls and a large round target. I happened to be walking through the plaza when I heard, "Hey you! Stand right about here and throw three balls at the bullseye." I said, "Bill, I can't hit the broad side of a barn." "Just do it!" he said. "I want to see if the throw line is too close." Ball one went in the bar. Ball two hit Bill in the shoulder, and as I went to throw ball three, Bill screamed, "Fuck this! Go find somebody that can throw a fuckin' ball…by the way, have you eaten today? Here's a meal ticket."

That's when I knew Bill…..

In 1993, I was asked to be a part of the security team for the Grateful Dead's summer of 1993 tour. We got to the hotel in Eugene, Oregon and checked in. We then went to Sugar Sims' room. Anyway, there was Sug, Julianna Soumarocoff, Colleen Kennedy, Chris Allan and other BGP veterans I had never met before. We were indulging in party favors and alcohol when Chris said, "Has anybody told Trish?" I was pretty buzzed and wasn't caring who I was confronting (I was still considered a newbie), and I screamed, "Told Trish what?" Chris replied, "You're going to be doing overnights with Steve Block, Mike Wentworth and Mike Nelson." My confused reply: "What the fuck Is an overnight? Is it some type of initiation?" I mean, come on. Three men and a baby! The crowd in the room roared and I made the most remarkable, lifetime friends. RIP Steve and Mike.

Lollapalooza 1992, I was ushering the wheelchair lift at Shoreline. Three six-foot-plus men came and sat in Row C of Section 201 right behind the wheelchair platform. I went and asked them if I could see their tickets please. "We don't need to show you no fuckin tickets!" I said, "I let you sit here for two songs and with your reply, my guess is that you probably don't belong in this row." "We're sittin' HERE!" they yelled in unison. I said, "Look, I can get someone that is bigger and badder than me to help out, but I'd like for you to enjoy the show you came to see, so you can go back to your seats or show me your tickets that you belong here. It really doesn't matter to me if I have to call upon my team."

The guy in the middle stood up and drew his fist back (yes! I was scared as hell) and said, "Fuck you!" I looked at my watch and told him that I would be much obliged, but I didn't get a break for another 20 minutes. All three laughed and stated that was one of the best responses to that remark they had ever heard. They told me I was "all right" and left to go back to their real seats in Row S. Humor gets me out of a lot of situations, plus the fact that my Brain Button says, "I'm a keeper."

I hope whoever reads my stories finds joy in doing so. I've enjoyed reliving them. I'm not sure if Bill really knew how much he taught us how to get the job done. We all handle things in different manners and we continue to learn and teach. Each situation is as different as our personalities.

We are a true team.

We have each other's backs, whether we are friends or not. We are family AND we are a force to be reckoned with!

We are the best at what we do!

Thank you Bill, for all that you did and for all we still do and love in your honor.

V

VIVIANA LATRIMURTI

The year was 1979, December, post-Christmas and my first backstage catering event for the Grateful Dead at the Oakland Auditorium. Apron Strings was the name of our catering crew: Bettike Barsotti at the helm, Trisha Holmes, Shane Barsotti and me, Viv, the "gourmet chef."

As we unloaded the groceries into the kitchen (the first of five consecutive show daze), I opened the oven door to light the pilot and screamed as a mouse lay dead before the unlit gas flame. Everyone stopped and ran over to see what was happening. An engineer rescued the stiff rodent from its greasy recess.

Okay. We were set back an hour or so, but we had plenty of prep to do before serving baked whole stuffed salmon for the band, crew and backstage guests the first night. Roundabout 3:00 p.m. Jerry Garcia, Phil Lesh, Mickey Hart and Brent Mydland arrived backstage, sitting at a long table and asking for wine which had been chilling in the walk-in refrigerator. I obliged, grabbing four bottles and the trusty wine opener. As I exited the walk-in refrigerator, I felt myself go off balance sliding on the holly berries which decked the floor. I sailed across the wet tiles ending up underneath the band's table. I broke a finger, but was still clutching the four bottles of wine which stayed intact! Jerry looked down at my tearful eyes and smiling face and said, "Good job, Viv!"

W

WALLY J. HAAS

Let me share the first time I met Bill. It was shortly after I had taken over managing The Sons (The Sons of Champlin). As I recall, when the band asked me to do this, they failed to share with me that they had an interim manager who was away mourning the death of her father.

That person being, of course, Julie, who would later become my wife.

It was not love at first sight. In fact, it was anything but that. So, we co-existed as the management team with me being the manager and she overseeing the finances. One of the first weekends of this new arrangement had the band playing a gig at Humboldt State on a Saturday night and then opening a show at Winterland on Sunday night. I should have known things weren't so great between us when Julie gave me something like $50 for expenses for the gig at the college (be sure and bring back receipts, etc. she said). How do you take a band to a gig overnight on $50 bucks? But I digress.

So, fast-forward to Sunday night. The band is at my apartment in San Francisco and it's around 6:00 p.m. when we get a frantic call from Charlie Kelly who is at Winterland asking me, "Where the fuck are you guys?

We are supposed to be on stage in 15 minutes." Julie had given me the wrong start time. To this day, we aren't sure if that was an intentional act, but with that in the background, I get to meet Bill Graham for the first time.

Oh, was that special.

I think you can picture how that went. "Who the fuck do you think you are showing up late to one of my gigs." Then he really got mad. Anyway, to top it off, the band decided to play a 25- minute encore at the end of their set, which set off Bill one more time.

Fortunately, we became good friends. Over the years, besides the usual Bill stuff, he showed me many acts of kindness. In fact, we were scheduled to have lunch the Monday after his helicopter crash.

WAVY GRAVY

There I was backstage at a show with the Grateful Dead in the Jerry area.

Steve Parish and I were getting delightfully altered when suddenly Bill appears and swoops in and hands me a piece of paper... which I then, scrutinize and discover that it was a check for $10,000 for SEVA.

I said, "Bill, why are you doing this?"

He said, "Because you did not hit on me my friend."

WILLIE JOHN CASHMAN

Winterland

I'm no historian, but these are a few things that I picked up along the way. Winterland was built as a boxing arena. If you've ever been in the parking garage in the basement you may have seen the large cinder block "room" in the middle of the parking area. It housed the boxing ring, which was on hydraulics and came up thru the floor of the arena. When it became an icehouse, it became a permanent ice floor and refrigeration plant. In the basement there were two 100 hp compressors pumping anhydrous ammonia through the coils under the floor to freeze the ice floor.

An older fellow named Otis ran the plant, which, by the way, looked like what you might see on a German U-boat. Mostly, I'd hear Otto complain about "those fucking hippies." Finally, he retired. Then came a much younger, much more hip man named Randy. We got along pretty well, so I spent what time I could (when doing shows) hanging with him in the plant learning what I could. Like, even up to the final show there were tons of that ammonia under the sidewalk on Post Street.

Once, I was working security for Patrick Stansfield for a band (I don't remember the name of the band). The band was playing on stage. Patrick came out from behind a curtain and told me, "No one else on stage!" A few minutes later, up walks this photographer and tries to walk on stage. I stopped her. Then she erupted. She called me more dirty names than I had ever heard in my many times of working the front door as security. Eventually, Patrick reappeared and let her on the stage. By the time the evening's performances were concluded, I received a very insincere and forced apology. And life goes on. By the way, the photographer is the now infamous Ms. Annie Lebowitz.

My Story

Back in my old neighborhood in Chicago, somewhere around 1966, a friend of mine, Bill Knecht, was working at the Motorola TV plant where he met the road manager for HP Lovecraft, Patrick Hanks. Shortly after, my friend Bill K. was hired on as a roadie for the band. The band's equipment van was a constant source of problems and breakdowns until Bill K. suggested that they bring the van to the auto shop that I worked at. After doing so, they began to enjoy many miles of trouble-free travel.

Sometime later, Patrick decided to leave the band and Bill K. took over his position. He then talked me into quitting my job and to start going out on the road with them as a roadie - done deal. I was a hot rod, greaser punk type of a guy. All I knew about rock and roll is what I heard on the radio. I didn't even own a pair of bellbottom jeans, but I got my first taste of rock and roll.

My first taste of rock and roll... well, that lasted something less than a year. They got a tour booked on the East Coast but their budget couldn't afford the extra roadie. Early 1968, back to wrenching on cars. In June of 1969, I turned 21 and time to do something. So, Bill K. and I take a vacation to San Francisco. Now comes the good part. I'm in S.F. for three days and I discover that Patrick Hanks is managing The Fillmore West for Bill Graham. Suddenly, I have a new job and address. What's the first thing I do? Take a week off and go cruising California.

Bill

Shortly after getting his Jaguar XKE, Bill pulled into the 201 11th Street office looking for Jay Drevers or me, explaining that there was a yellow paint scuff down portions of the left side of his car. No body damage. The paint came right off with a little rubbing compound. Done...ha! The next few weeks he came in with the same stripe. It was driving him crazy and we were kind of enjoying it.

Someone had finally recognized the color. Figured it out yet? It was from the rubber lane dividers used on the Golden Gate Bridge.

IN MEMORIAM

If I have forgotten someone or if I've misspelled someone's name I apologize. RIP

Al Auger
Ann Brown
Art Abuse-Mike Hazelett
Bill "Hippie Bill" Garbe
Bob Johnson
Brian Dwyer
Cameron Hester
Chris Cabaluna
Clyde Taft
Dave Hill
Dell Furano
Don Weber
Drew Holmes
Eduardo Fabio
Fernando Castanaedo
Gary Moncayo
George Heatharington
Graham Stevens
Henry Sullivan
James Augustus
Jeff Stein
Jim Matzorkis
Joe Jose Bordis
John McGinnis
John Wolbert
Kerry Reick
Larry Winterbottom
Mark Muna
Melissa Gold
Michael Ahern

Andy Rice
Ann Krcik
Bea Oliver
Bill Graham
Bob Moreno
Bruce Jenney
Charlie Diamond
Chris Cahill
Clyde Williams
Dave Murphy
Dokie Brian Milne
Dr. Skip Gay
Dwion Gates
Ernie Gallegos
Frank Rockwell
Gary Orndorf
George Turrini
Gregg Scooter Totten
Israel Moyston
James Battle, Jr.
Jim Downey
Jimmy Lobell
Joe Peppars
John Mulshenock
Johnny Walker
Kevin Dunn
Lynn Chisholm
Marshall Holman
Melvin McGarr
Michael White

Angelo Barbaria
Arnold Pustilnik
Bettike Barsotti
Bill Sawyer
Brenda Hederman
Brooke Botticelli
Cheryl Blevins
Chris Charucki
Danny Ferriera
David Steidel
Don Cheeseman
Dr. Terry Carr
Edan Hughes
Ester Chichinsky
Frank Talavera
Gene Lewis
Glen Rinzler
Hector Lizardi
Jack LaFever
Jeff Davis
Jim King
Joanne Cauteruccio
Joe Trips
John JT Toomey
Keith Homb
Larry Catlin
Marge Robiedo
Matt White
Michael Klenfner
Michael Baldwin

Michelle Castro
Mike Christie
Mike Wittnor
Patricia Holmes Lobell
Peter Barsotti
Resa Warren
Richie Wights
Samuel Begler
Shelley Lazar
Smokey Potis
Steven Killer Kahn
Tom Jay
Vincent Ramrod
Zohn Artman

Mick Brigden
Mike Nelson
Nate Flye
Patrick Stansfield
Presley Pedilla
Richard Cicchetto
Ricky Remington
Scott Ferry
Shorty
Stan Damas
Susan Seymour
Victor Morita
Warren Pilcher
Kevin Burns

Mike Bradford
Mike Santos
Neil Sorensen
Paul Majeski
Randy Bachman
Richard Murphy
Rudy House
Sheila Rene
Lawrence DeLouvre
Steve Block
Tom Howard
Vince Burgess
William Garby

Made in United States
Orlando, FL
11 December 2022